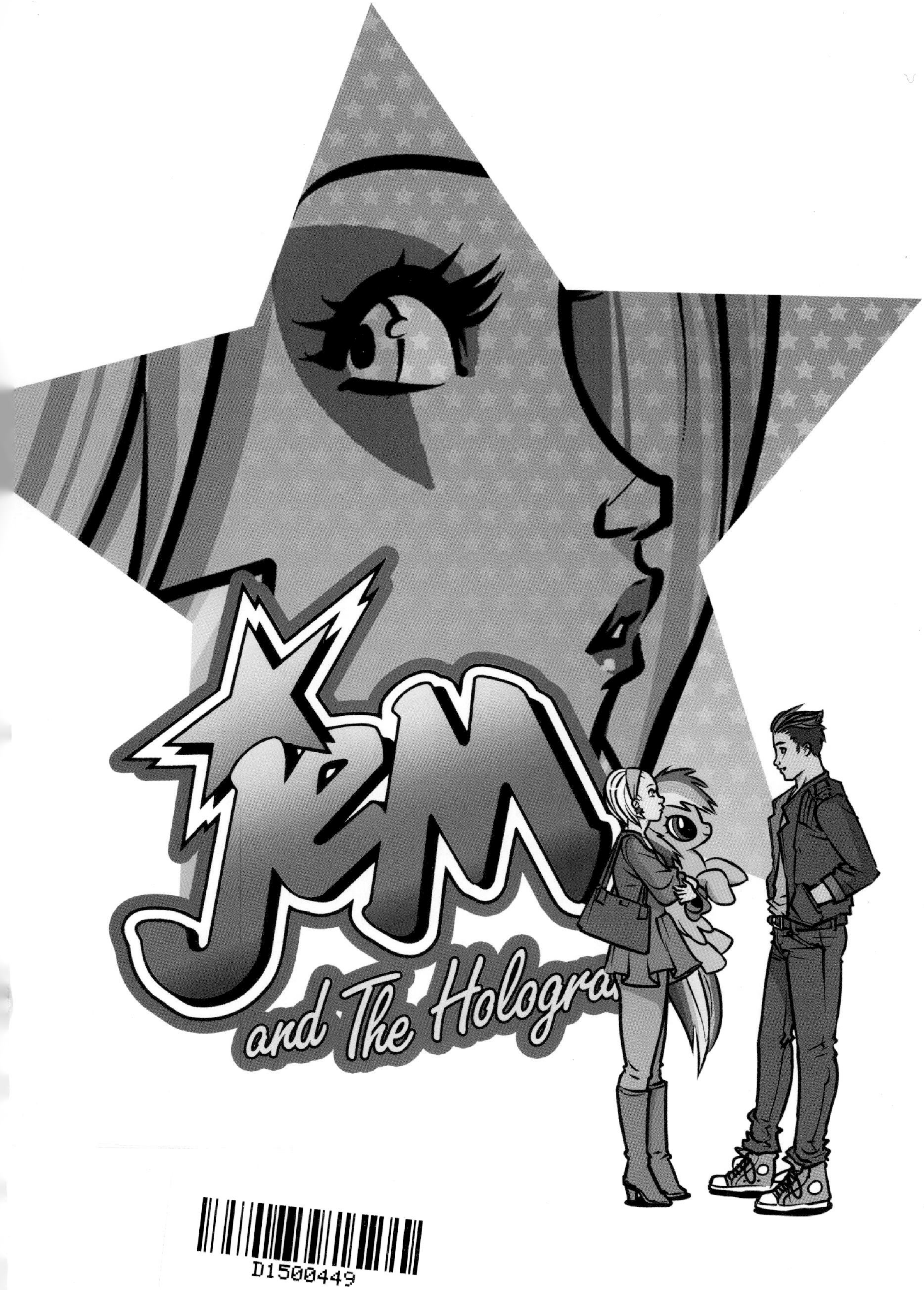
Jem
and The Hologra

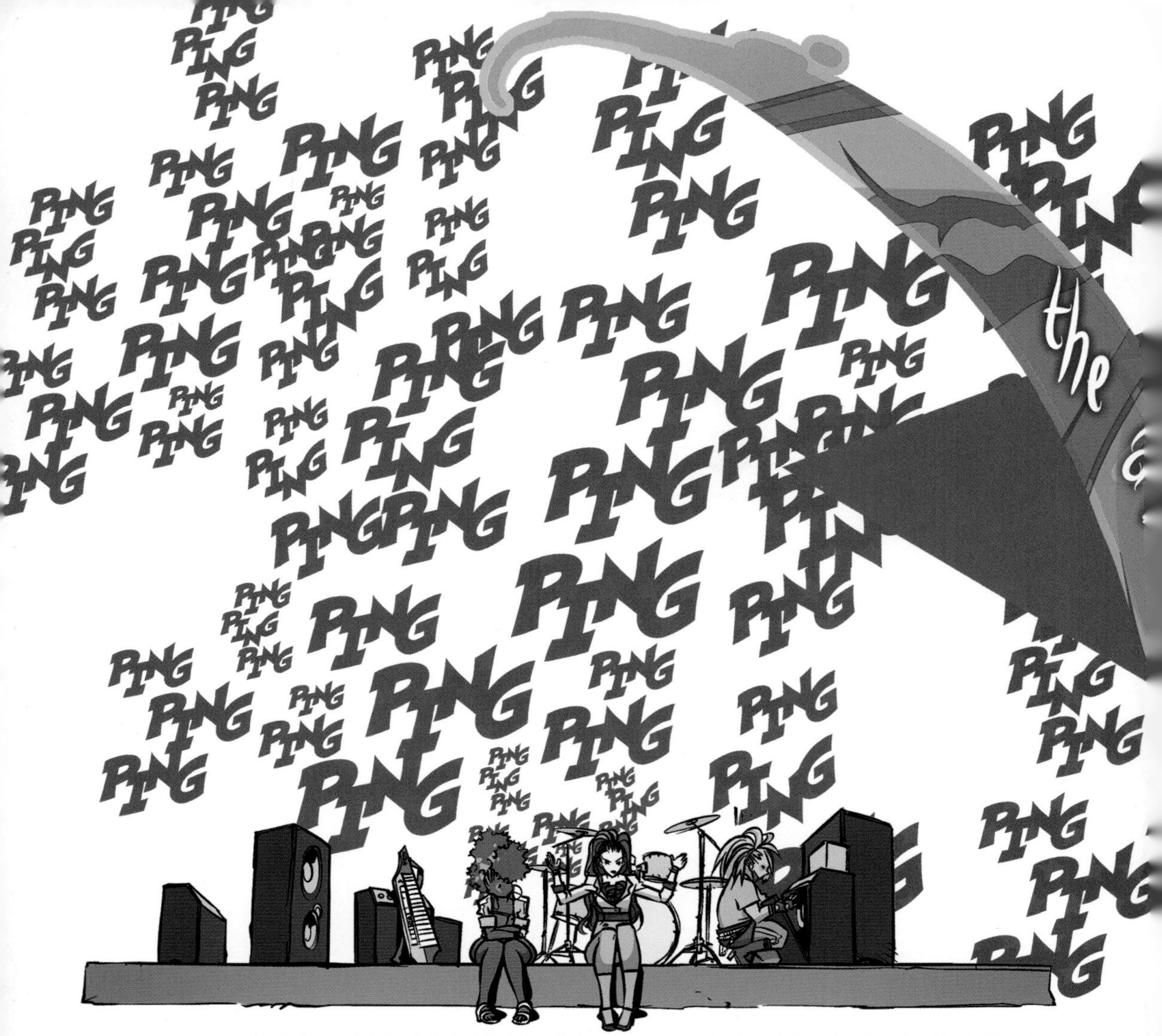
PING PING PING
the

WRITTEN BY **KELLY THOMPSON** • ART BY **SOPHIE CAMPBELL**

STORY BY **THOMPSON** AND **CAMPBELL** • COLORS BY **M. VICTORIA ROBADO**
LETTERS BY **SHAWN LEE**, **TOM LONG**, AND **ROBBIE ROBBINS**
SERIES EDITS BY **JOHN BARBER**

COVER BY **SOPHIE CAMPBELL**
COLLECTION EDITS BY **JUSTIN EISINGER** AND **ALONZO SIMON**
COLLECTION DESIGN BY **SHAWN LEE**

Special thanks to Hasbro's Heather Hopkins, Ed Lane, and Michael Kelly for their invaluable assistance.

ISBN: 978-1-63140-395-8

18 17 16 15 1 2 3 4

IDW® Licensed By: Hasbro

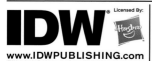

www.IDWPUBLISHING.com
IDW founded by Ted Adams, Alex Garner, Kris Oprisko, and Robbie Robbins

Ted Adams, CEO & Publisher
Greg Goldstein, President & COO
Robbie Robbins, EVP/Sr. Graphic Artist
Chris Ryall, Chief Creative Officer/Editor-in-Chief
Matthew Ruzicka, CPA, Chief Financial Officer
Alan Payne, VP of Sales
Dirk Wood, VP of Marketing
Lorelei Bunjes, VP of Digital Services
Jeff Webber, VP of Digital Publishing & Business Development

Facebook: **facebook.com/idwpublishing**
Twitter: **@idwpublishing**
YouTube: **youtube.com/idwpublishing**
Tumblr: **tumblr.idwpublishing.com**
Instagram: **instagram.com/idwpublishing**

Originally published as JEM AND THE HOLOGRAMS issues #1–6.

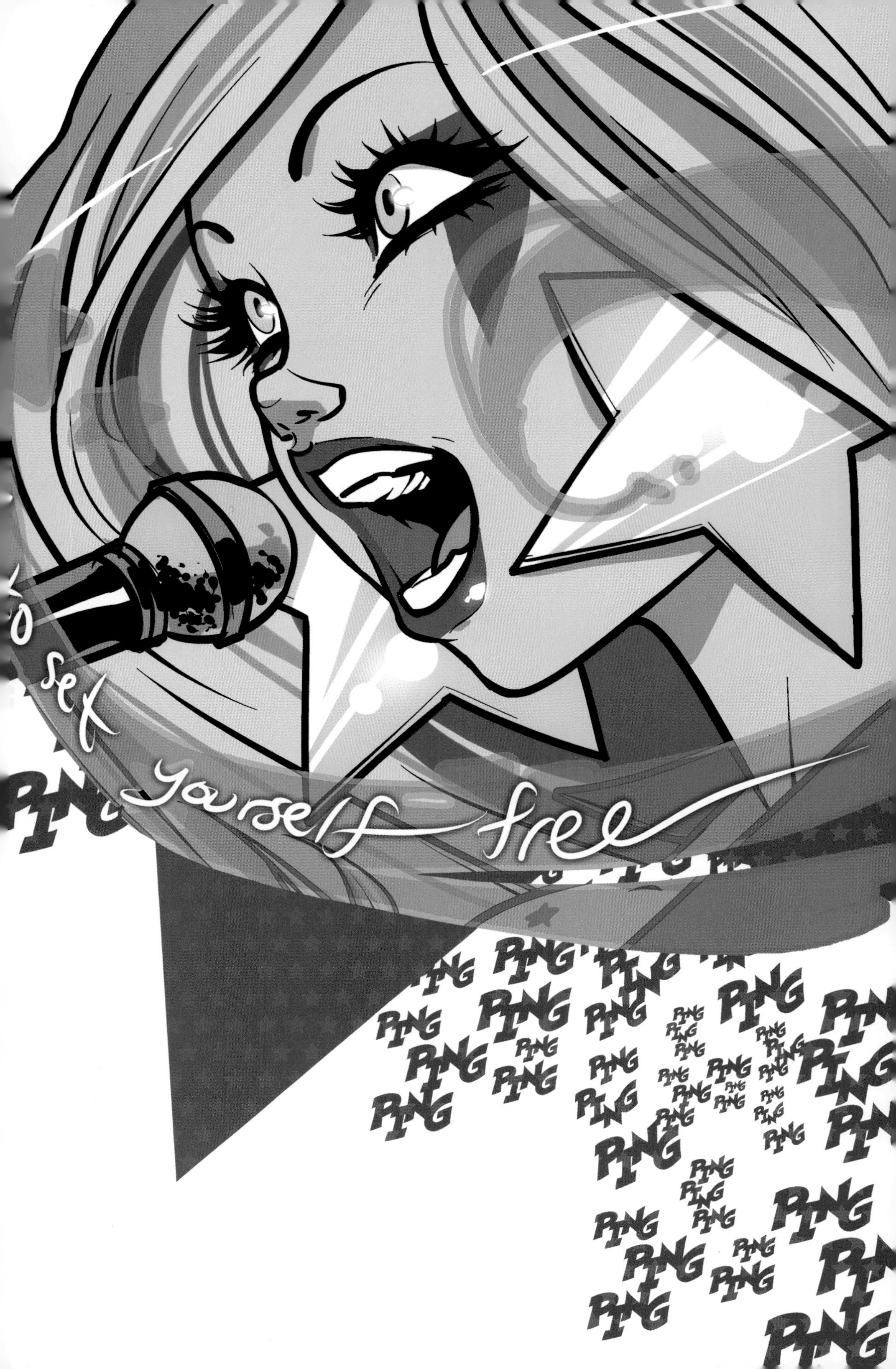
o set yourself free
PING
PING
PING
PING
PING
PING

ART BY **AMY MEBBERSON**

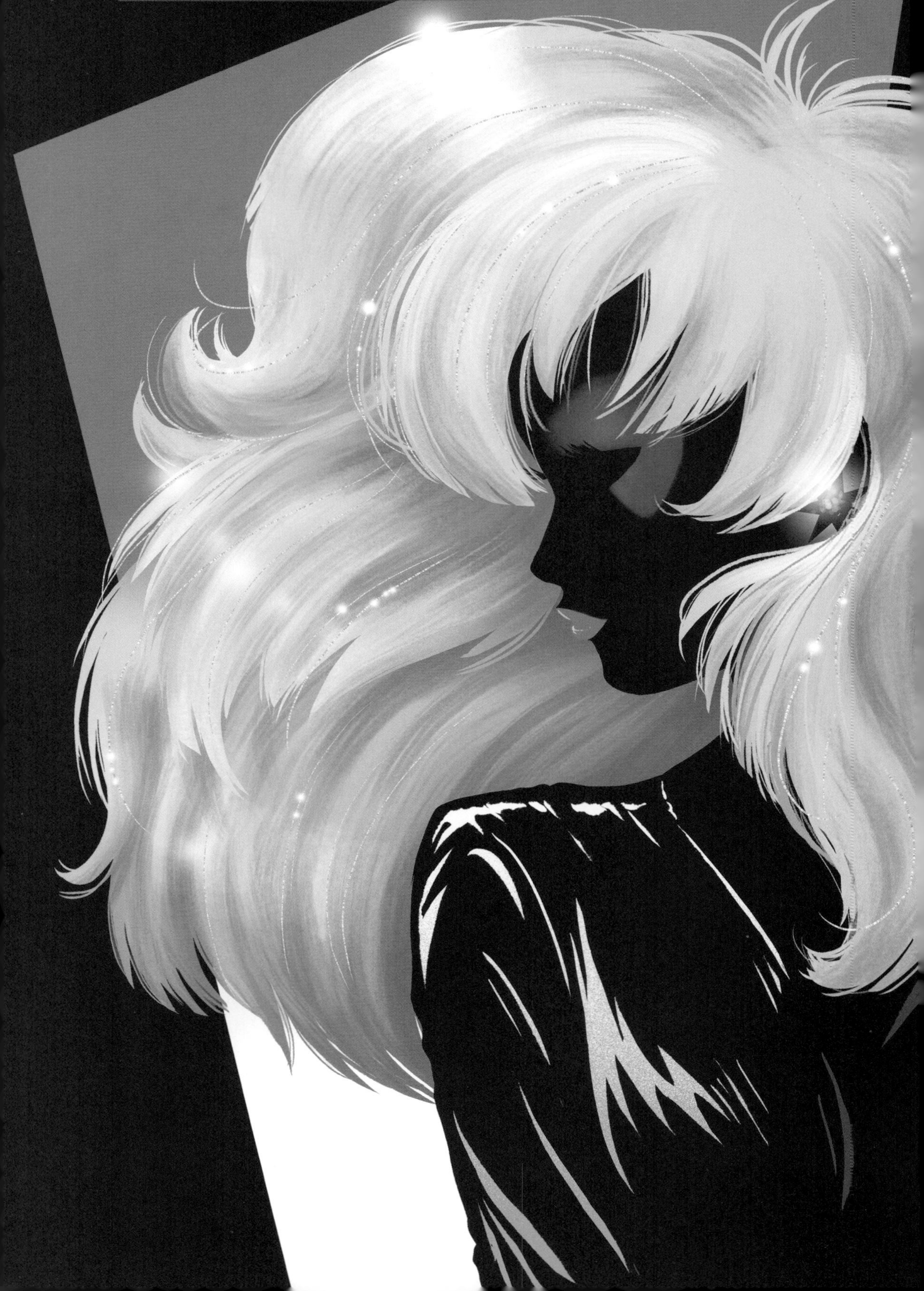

INTRODUCTION

Welcome one and all to Jem and The Holograms' debut volume! A comic that we boldly (and perhaps naively) hope will be a place for new fans, old fans, cynics, and optimists alike to discover something that they can fall in love with—and who doesn't want to fall in love? Falling in love feels so good.

There's no way to pretend that this Jem and The Holograms is the same as what came before. Nearly 30 years have passed and we've shifted mediums. Moving from cartoons to comics means you have different story demands. Writing a full season of half-hour cartoons for television is an entirely different beast than creating one story arc that plays out over six issues (and six months). Understanding from go that the medium would (and should) demand different things of us as creators helped to shape what we wanted to do with these remarkable women, how we wanted to approach their story, and how we thought we could best contextualize them to the modern age. Above everything else we wanted to do these ladies justice. Part of that meant introducing them to a whole new generation of readers as well as reviving them for old fans with some fresh changes that might help them discover these characters they loved all over again in a slightly different light.

When thinking about what *Jem* was really about—more than just their outrageous '80s fashion, music, and general sensibility—I realized that they were about representing the epitome of the modern woman.

Smart, driven, capable, ambitious, and fascinating fashion-forward career women. For all the '80s awesome hair and fierce clothes, that's what they were REALLY about.

Being the "epitome of a modern woman" in 1986 of course meant they were magnificently 1980s. For *Jem* to be relatable and accessible to a new generation and to also hold true to being that "epitome of a modern woman," they had to evolve to become magnificently *2015*.

So that is where we began as we re-imagined these incredible women for the modern age. How had music changed in three decades? How had celebrity changed? What did the landscape look like now for a woman trying to carve a place for herself in the world? And how would our characters respond to those changes? What would the same stories and ideas re-interpreted through a modern lens look like? These are the questions that I found myself fascinated by, the ones I wanted to explore for these women.

Early on in the process of bringing these women back to life I realized that nostalgia was both our greatest strength and greatest weakness. Nostalgia is a wonderful thing and part of what makes us all so excited to see Jem again, but nostalgia is also a liar. Nostalgia can hold us back in that it's an emotional, even sentimental attachment to something personal and important to us,

but not necessarily the reality. What *Jem* meant to each of us individually changed how we viewed it, and sometimes even changed us, and that's impossible to compete with. You can't ever live up to, let alone outshine, something so powerfully personal… something so nostalgic. So that became part of taking on *Jem*, too—learning to let that go, to let *Jem* be drawn from its rich history, but also allowing it to become its own beautiful butterfly, breaking free from a 30-year cocoon that naturally changed it into something else.

I hope you will all give that new butterfly a chance.

I believe our *Jem* butterfly is smart and funny and emotional and—it goes without saying—filled with amazing makeup, clothes, hair, and music, and I think it deserves a chance to see if it's got what it takes to make you fall in love. As a sidebar: Kimber is hilarious. Well, they're all hilarious sometimes, but Kimber definitely takes home the shiny crown and sash of hilarity.

Now for the gushy stuff. I cannot thank IDW and Hasbro enough for allowing Sophie and I to re-imagine these women in this new context. It's a huge responsibility (such a responsibility I can't really think about it sometimes or it feels like looking directly into the sun). I'm so honored and grateful that IDW and Hasbro trusted me with this task and I will do my level best not to let anyone down. That said, I am basically nothing without Sophie Campbell, whose talent, enthusiasm, rabid love of *Jem*, and unwavering friendship made all of this possible. I couldn't have even begun to take this on without her. And without editor John Barber's guiding hand Sophie and I should surely have been in the weeds immediately and eventually would have walked ourselves right off a cliff, so thank you, John, for keeping us grounded in all the right ways and still letting us get weird.

However, mostly I owe thanks to Christy Marx who originally brought these astonishing women to life nearly 30 years ago. She gave us all such vibrant and captivating women that three decades later we are all still enthralled by them. And for me, they feel so real that it was almost easy to breathe new modern life into them once again for this new medium. I hope we do them all justice. We certainly tried our absolute best to keep the soul, the very lifeblood that Marx breathed into them, alive and well. Everything has been done with the utmost love and respect for what came before and I hope you guys can feel that in the book.

To all the fans that *Jem* has meant so much to over the years, I hope we have given you a book you can dig into and fall in love with, even if it's not exactly what came before.

Kelly Thompson
Writer

1

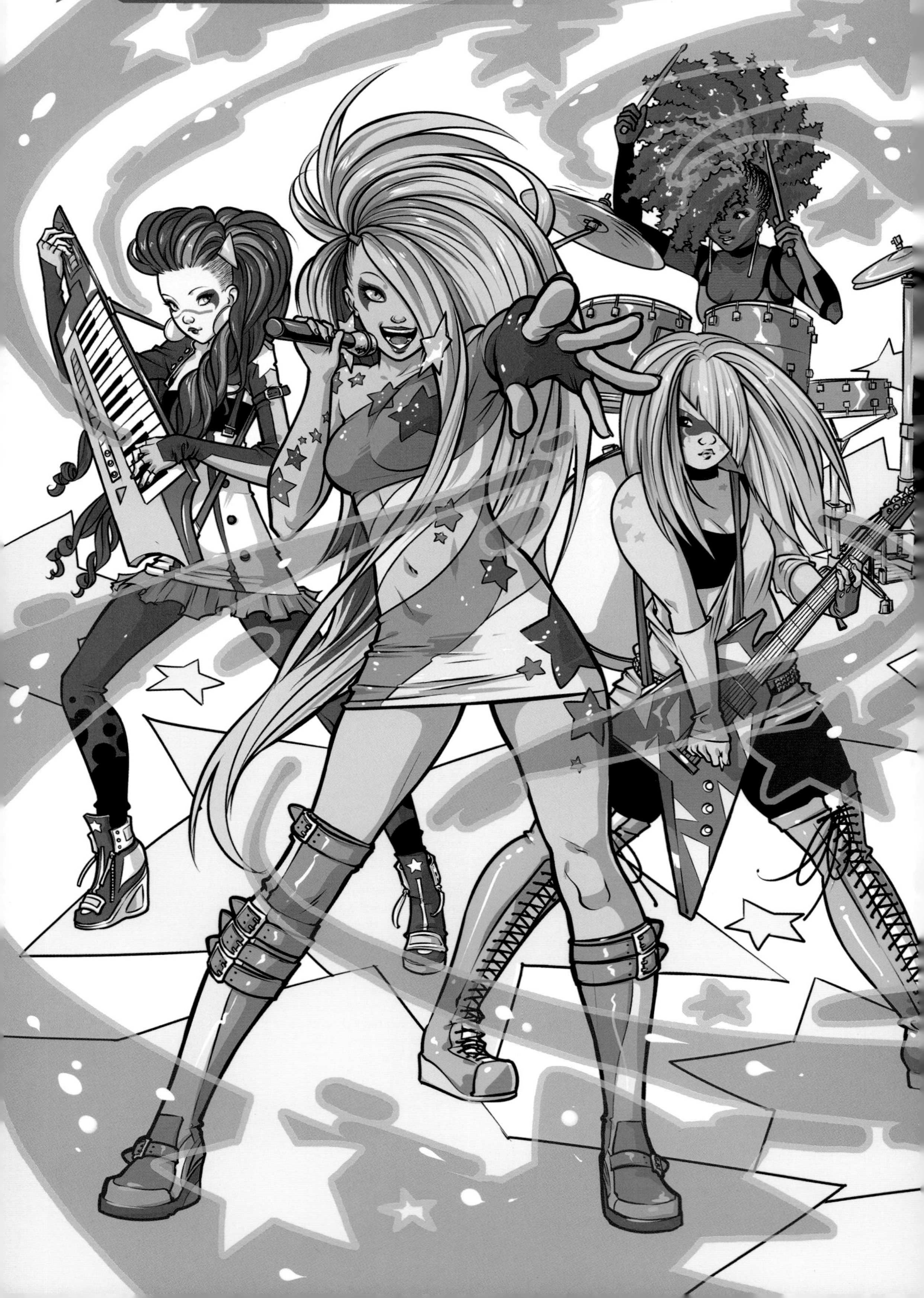

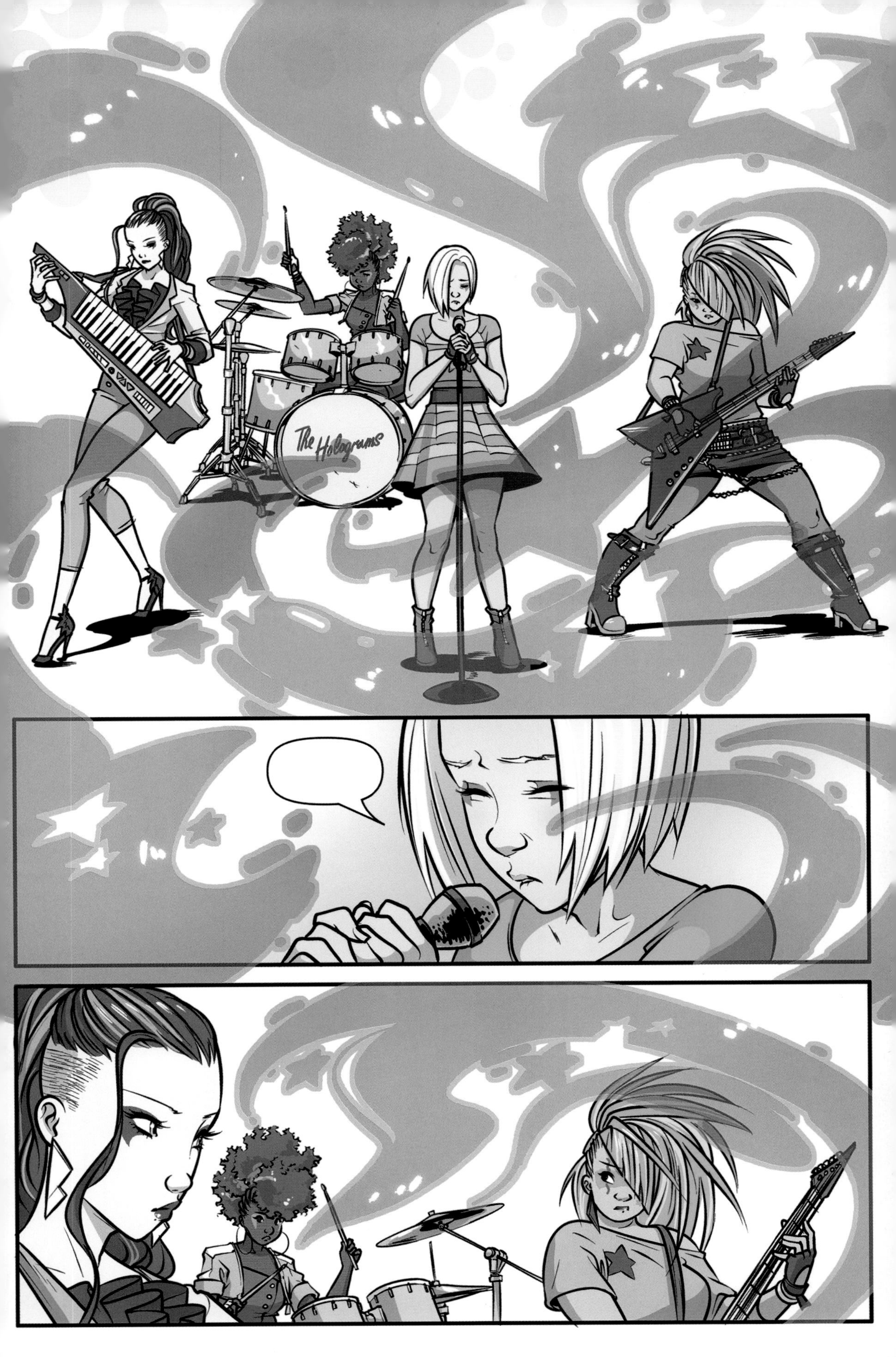
The Holograms

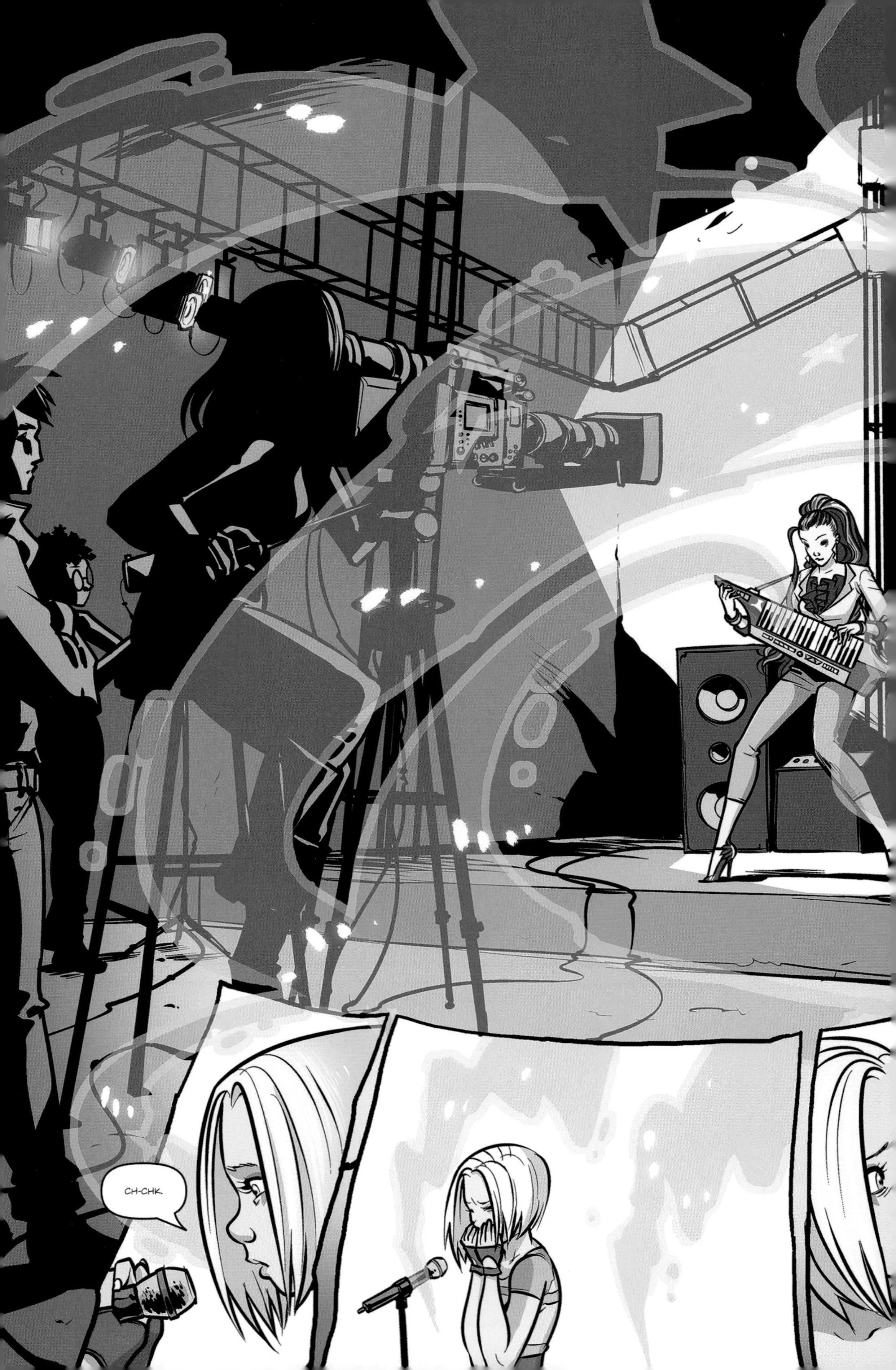
CH-CHK.

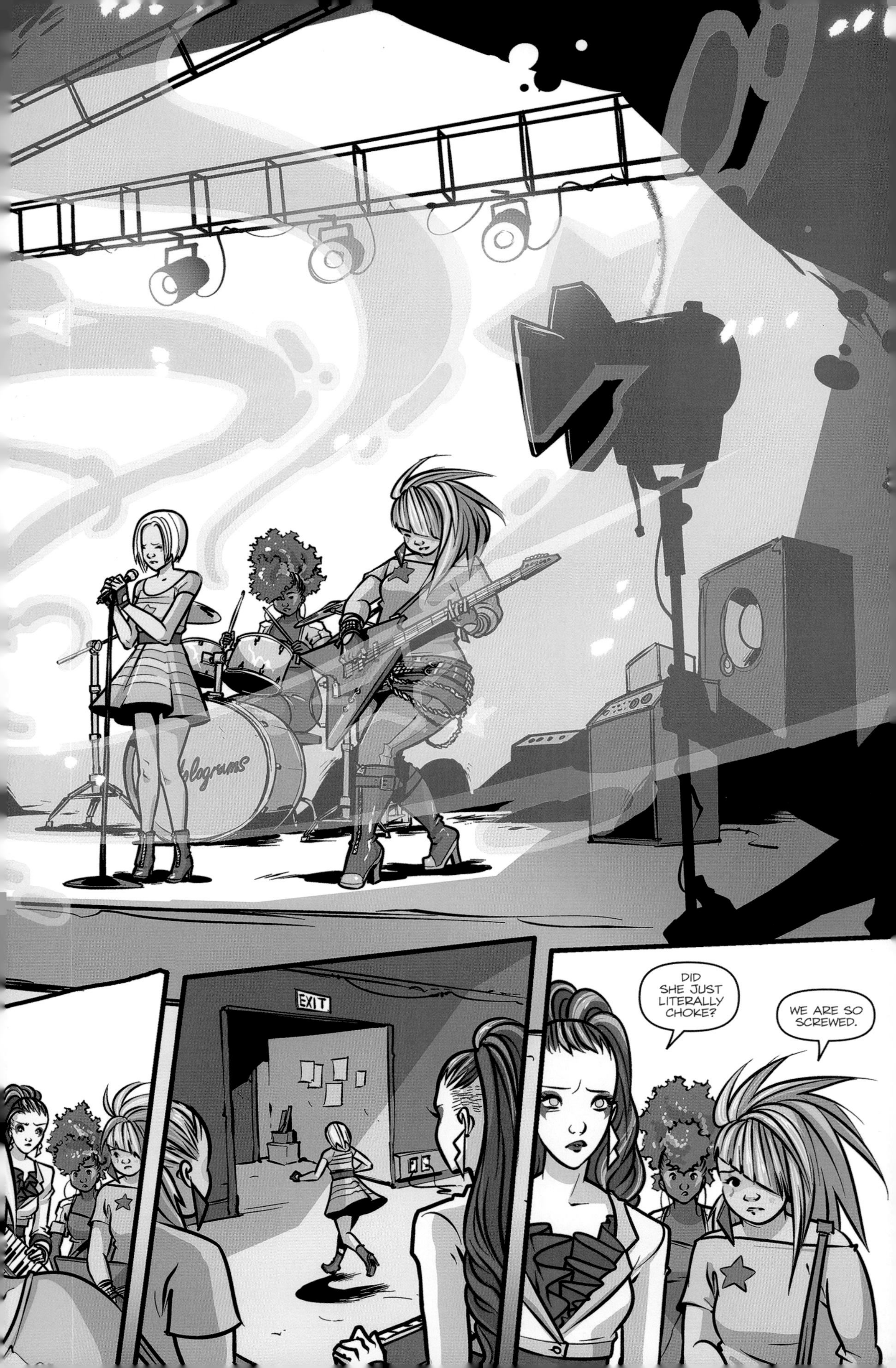
EXIT
DID SHE JUST LITERALLY CHOKE?
WE ARE SO SCREWED.

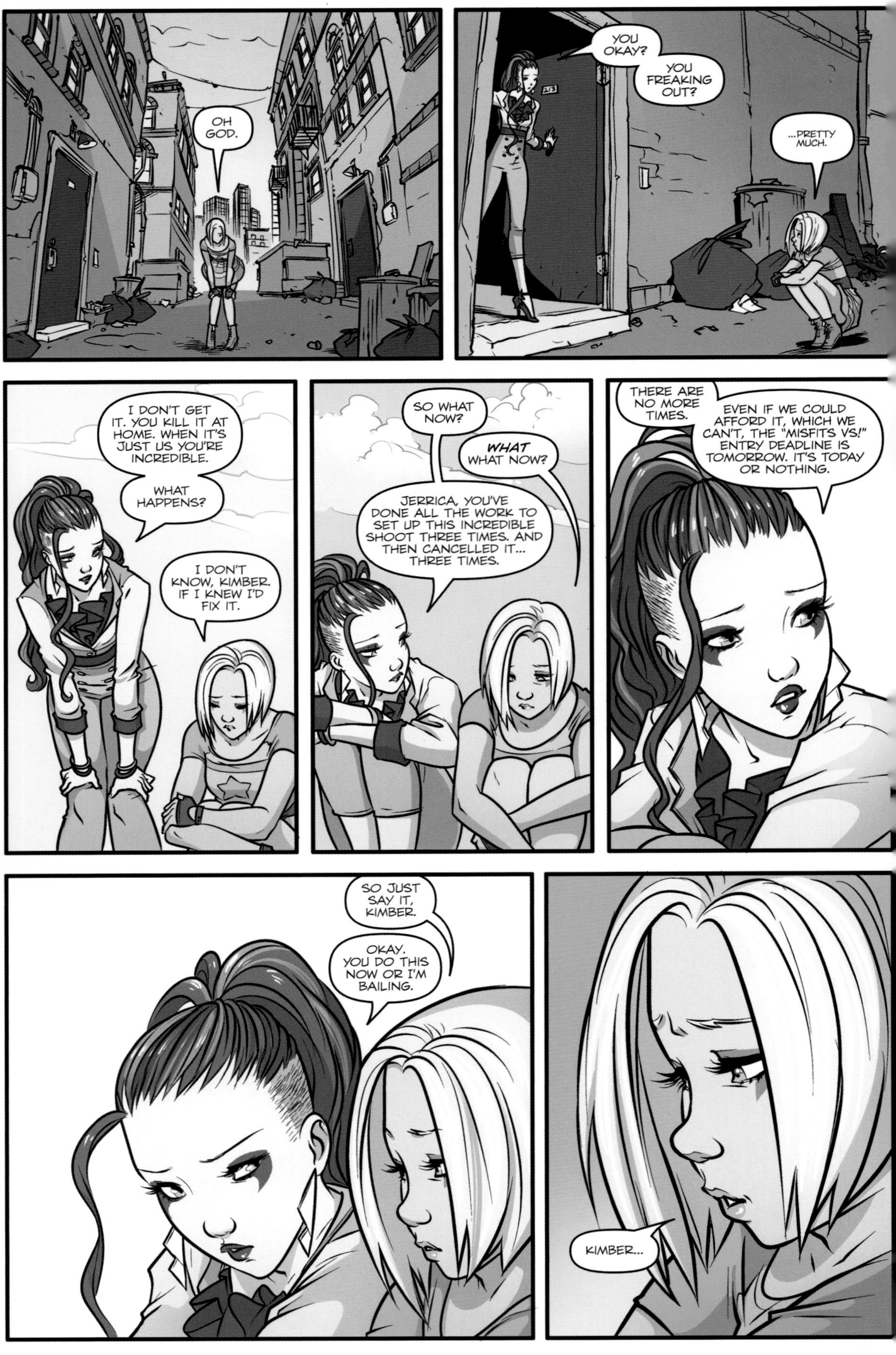
OH GOD.
YOU OKAY?
YOU FREAKING OUT?
...PRETTY MUCH.
I DON'T GET IT. YOU KILL IT AT HOME. WHEN IT'S JUST US YOU'RE INCREDIBLE.
WHAT HAPPENS?
I DON'T KNOW, KIMBER. IF I KNEW I'D FIX IT.
SO WHAT NOW?
WHAT WHAT NOW?
JERRICA, YOU'VE DONE ALL THE WORK TO SET UP THIS INCREDIBLE SHOOT THREE TIMES. AND THEN CANCELLED IT... THREE TIMES.
THERE ARE NO MORE TIMES.
EVEN IF WE COULD AFFORD IT, WHICH WE CAN'T, THE "MISFITS VS!" ENTRY DEADLINE IS TOMORROW. IT'S TODAY OR NOTHING.
SO JUST SAY IT, KIMBER.
OKAY. YOU DO THIS NOW OR I'M BAILING.
KIMBER...

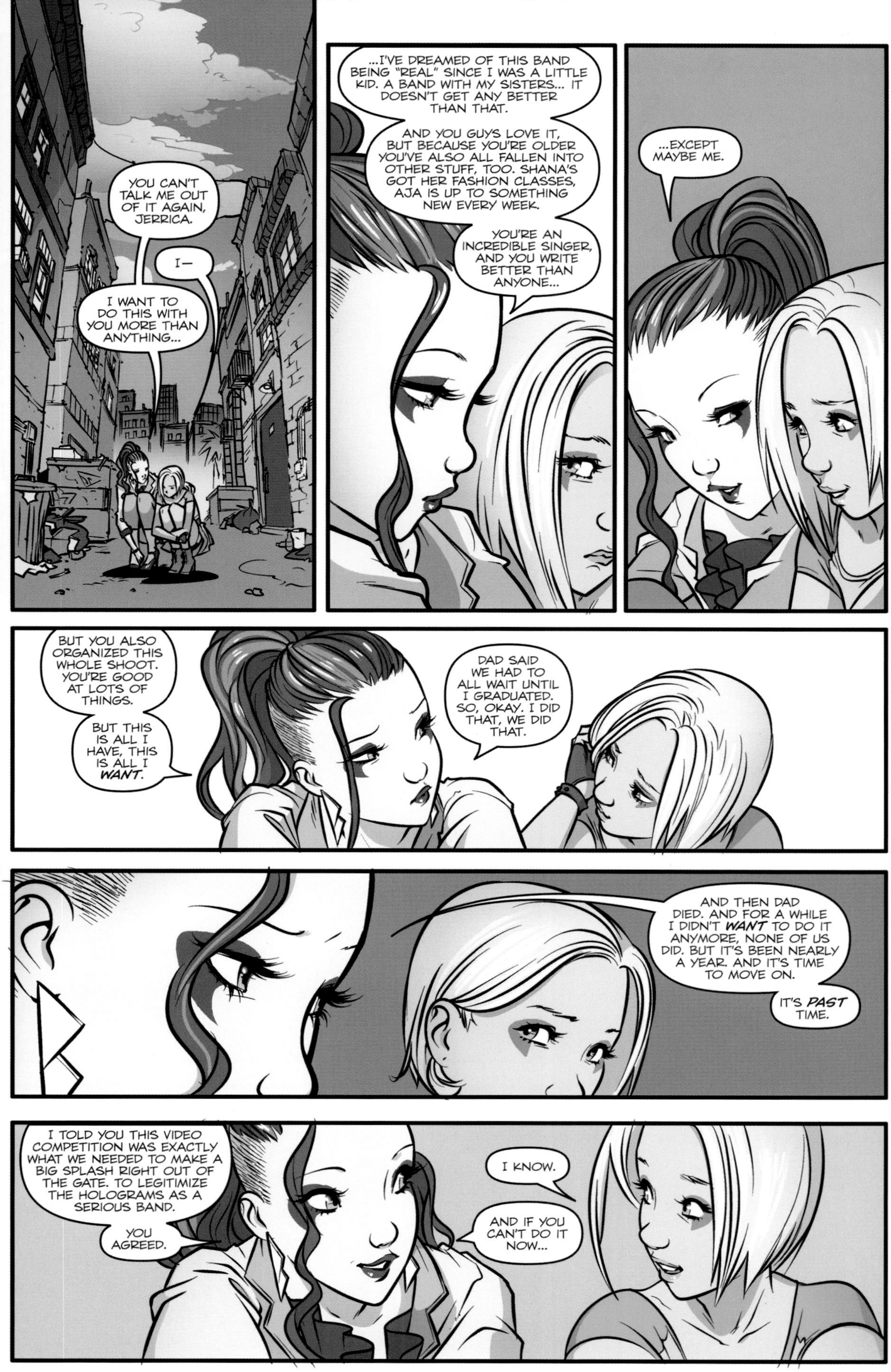
YOU CAN'T TALK ME OUT OF IT AGAIN, JERRICA.
I—
I WANT TO DO THIS WITH YOU MORE THAN ANYTHING...
...I'VE DREAMED OF THIS BAND BEING "REAL" SINCE I WAS A LITTLE KID. A BAND WITH MY SISTERS... IT DOESN'T GET ANY BETTER THAN THAT.
AND YOU GUYS LOVE IT, BUT BECAUSE YOU'RE OLDER YOU'VE ALSO ALL FALLEN INTO OTHER STUFF, TOO. SHANA'S GOT HER FASHION CLASSES, AJA IS UP TO SOMETHING NEW EVERY WEEK.
YOU'RE AN INCREDIBLE SINGER, AND YOU WRITE BETTER THAN ANYONE...
...EXCEPT MAYBE ME.
BUT YOU ALSO ORGANIZED THIS WHOLE SHOOT. YOU'RE GOOD AT LOTS OF THINGS.
BUT THIS IS ALL I HAVE, THIS IS ALL I *WANT*.
DAD SAID WE HAD TO ALL WAIT UNTIL I GRADUATED. SO, OKAY. I DID THAT, WE DID THAT.
AND THEN DAD DIED. AND FOR A WHILE I DIDN'T *WANT* TO DO IT ANYMORE, NONE OF US DID. BUT IT'S BEEN NEARLY A YEAR. AND IT'S TIME TO MOVE ON.
IT'S *PAST* TIME.
I TOLD YOU THIS VIDEO COMPETITION WAS EXACTLY WHAT WE NEEDED TO MAKE A BIG SPLASH RIGHT OUT OF THE GATE. TO LEGITIMIZE THE HOLOGRAMS AS A SERIOUS BAND.
YOU AGREED.
I KNOW.
AND IF YOU CAN'T DO IT NOW...

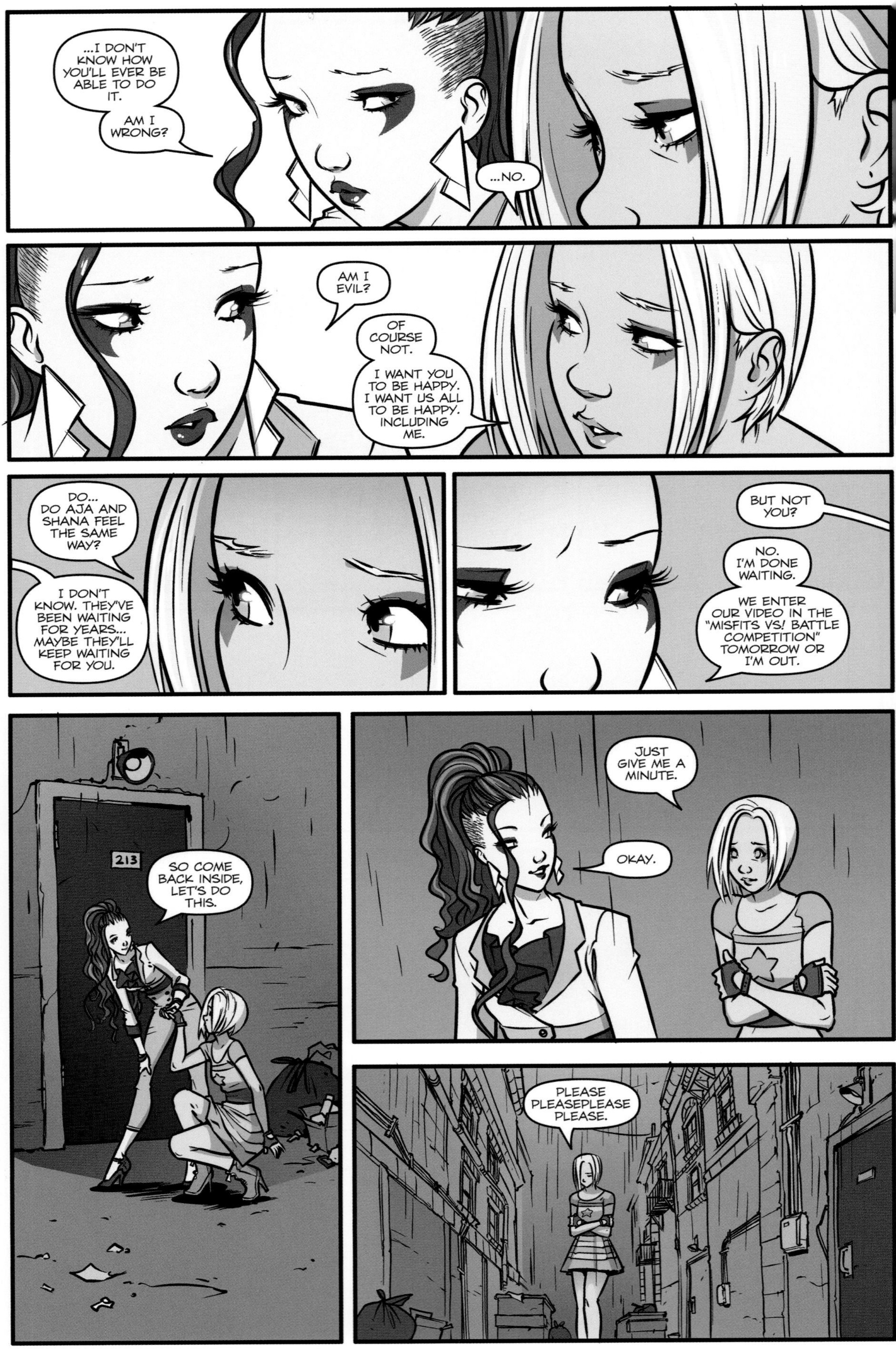
...I DON'T KNOW HOW YOU'LL EVER BE ABLE TO DO IT.
AM I WRONG?
...NO.
AM I EVIL?
OF COURSE NOT.
I WANT YOU TO BE HAPPY. I WANT US ALL TO BE HAPPY. INCLUDING ME.
DO... DO AJA AND SHANA FEEL THE SAME WAY?
I DON'T KNOW. THEY'VE BEEN WAITING FOR YEARS... MAYBE THEY'LL KEEP WAITING FOR YOU.
BUT NOT YOU?
NO. I'M DONE WAITING.
WE ENTER OUR VIDEO IN THE "MISFITS VS! BATTLE COMPETITION" TOMORROW OR I'M OUT.
213
SO COME BACK INSIDE, LET'S DO THIS.
JUST GIVE ME A MINUTE.
OKAY.
PLEASE PLEASEPLEASE PLEASE.

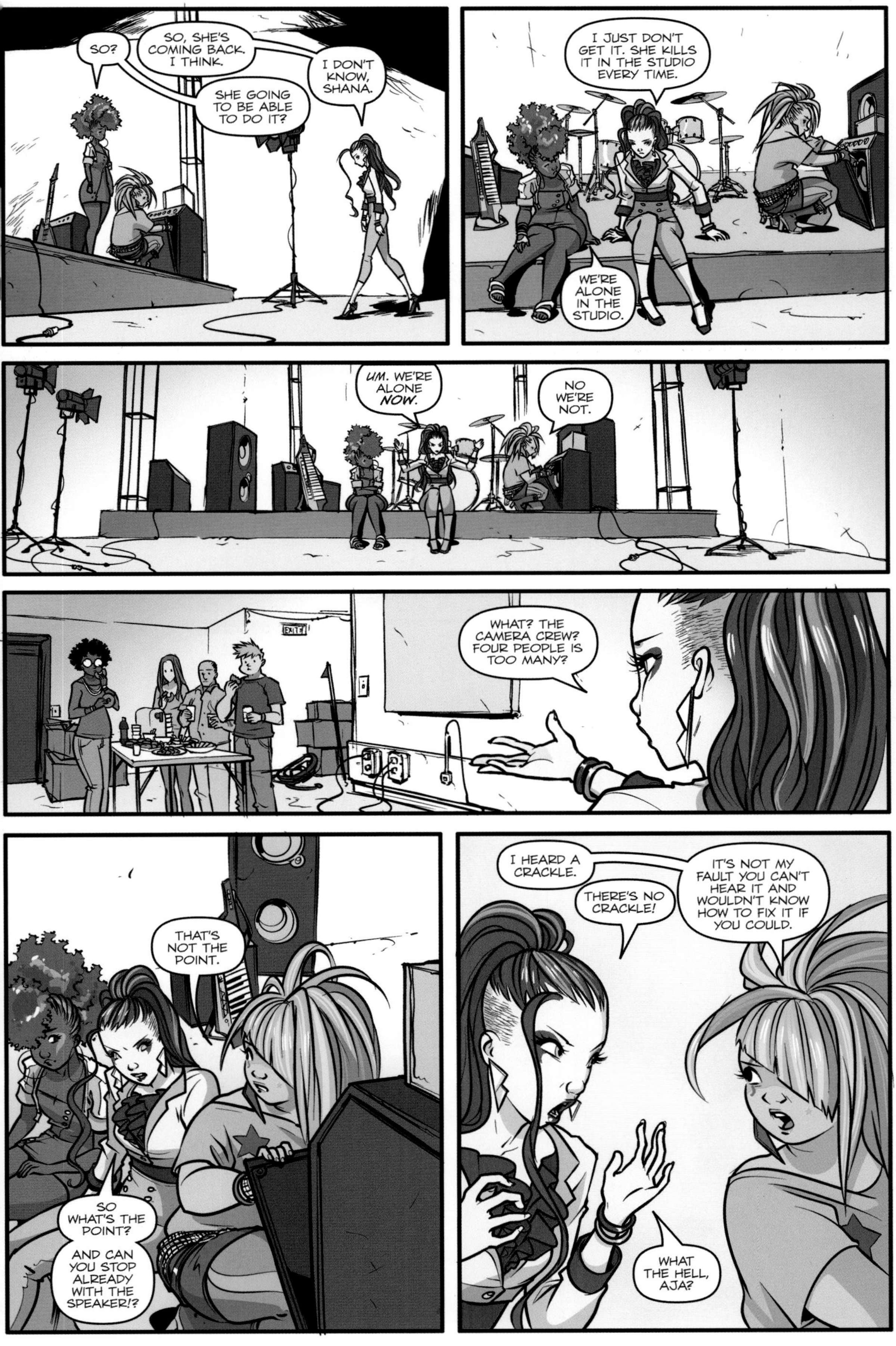
SO, SHE'S COMING BACK. I THINK.
SO?
SHE GOING TO BE ABLE TO DO IT?
I DON'T KNOW, SHANA.
I JUST DON'T GET IT. SHE KILLS IT IN THE STUDIO EVERY TIME.
WE'RE ALONE IN THE STUDIO.
UM. WE'RE ALONE NOW.
NO WE'RE NOT.
EXIT
WHAT? THE CAMERA CREW? FOUR PEOPLE IS TOO MANY?
THAT'S NOT THE POINT.
SO WHAT'S THE POINT?
AND CAN YOU STOP ALREADY WITH THE SPEAKER!?
I HEARD A CRACKLE.
THERE'S NO CRACKLE!
IT'S NOT MY FAULT YOU CAN'T HEAR IT AND WOULDN'T KNOW HOW TO FIX IT IF YOU COULD.
WHAT THE HELL, AJA?

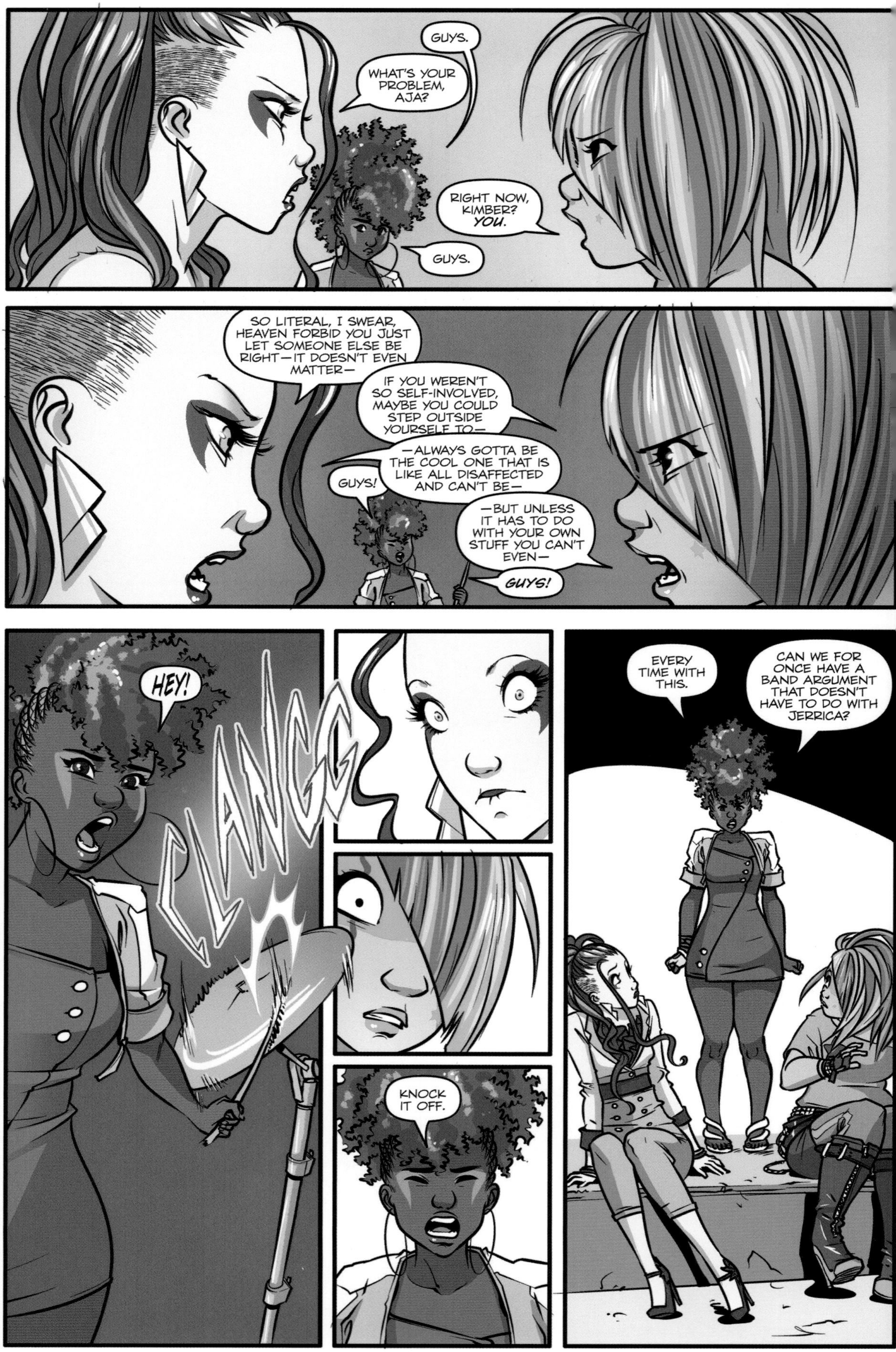
GUYS.
WHAT'S YOUR PROBLEM, AJA?
RIGHT NOW, KIMBER? YOU.
GUYS.
SO LITERAL, I SWEAR, HEAVEN FORBID YOU JUST LET SOMEONE ELSE BE RIGHT—IT DOESN'T EVEN MATTER—
IF YOU WEREN'T SO SELF-INVOLVED, MAYBE YOU COULD STEP OUTSIDE YOURSELF TO—
—ALWAYS GOTTA BE THE COOL ONE THAT IS LIKE ALL DISAFFECTED AND CAN'T BE—
GUYS!
—BUT UNLESS IT HAS TO DO WITH YOUR OWN STUFF YOU CAN'T EVEN—
GUYS!
HEY!
CLANGG
KNOCK IT OFF.
EVERY TIME WITH THIS.
CAN WE FOR ONCE HAVE A BAND ARGUMENT THAT DOESN'T HAVE TO DO WITH JERRICA?

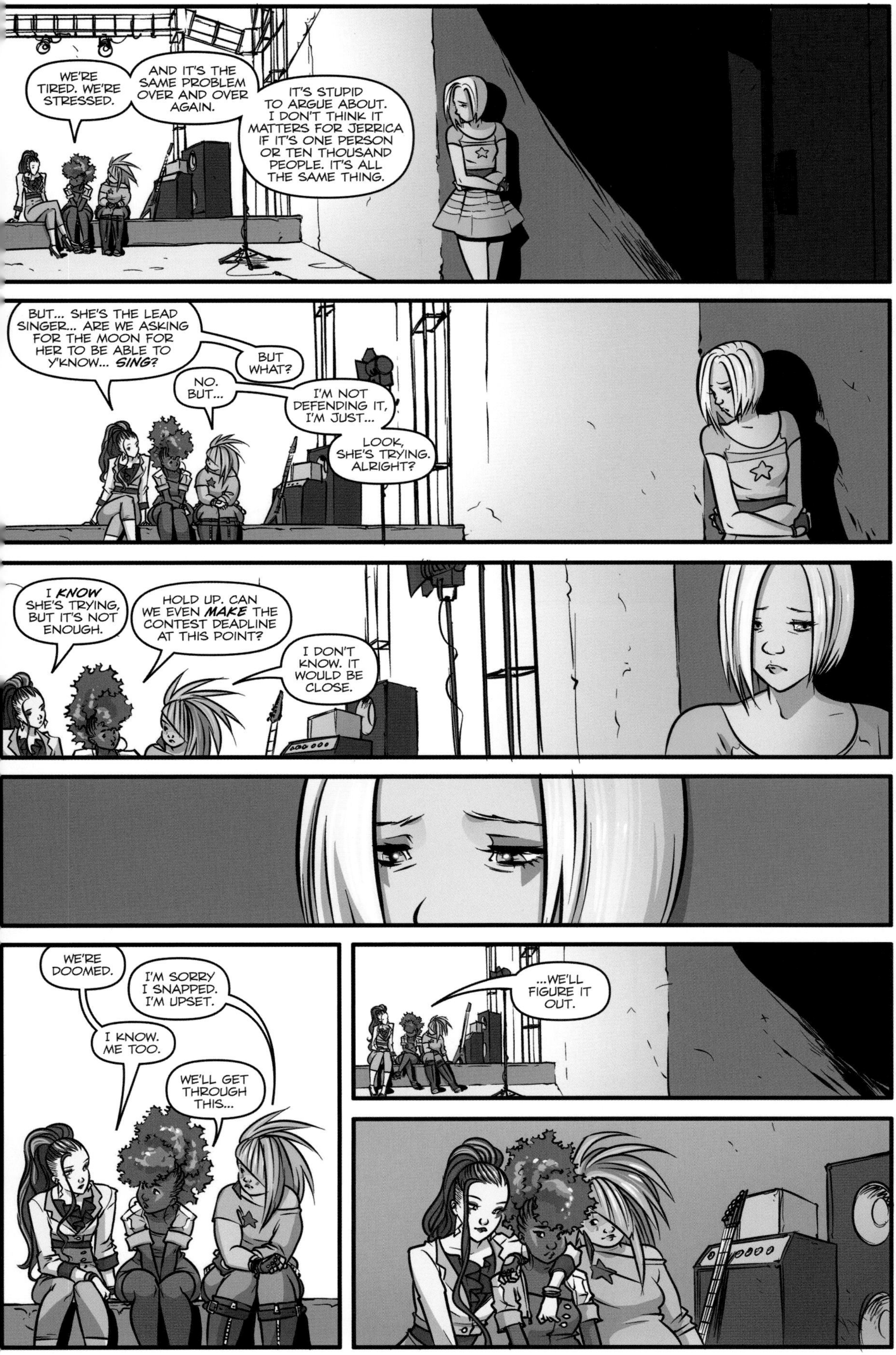
WE'RE TIRED. WE'RE STRESSED.
AND IT'S THE SAME PROBLEM OVER AND OVER AGAIN.
IT'S STUPID TO ARGUE ABOUT. I DON'T THINK IT MATTERS FOR JERRICA IF IT'S ONE PERSON OR TEN THOUSAND PEOPLE. IT'S ALL THE SAME THING.
BUT... SHE'S THE LEAD SINGER... ARE WE ASKING FOR THE MOON FOR HER TO BE ABLE TO Y'KNOW... SING?
BUT WHAT?
NO. BUT...
I'M NOT DEFENDING IT, I'M JUST...
LOOK, SHE'S TRYING. ALRIGHT?
I KNOW SHE'S TRYING, BUT IT'S NOT ENOUGH.
HOLD UP. CAN WE EVEN MAKE THE CONTEST DEADLINE AT THIS POINT?
I DON'T KNOW. IT WOULD BE CLOSE.
WE'RE DOOMED.
I'M SORRY I SNAPPED. I'M UPSET.
I KNOW. ME TOO.
WE'LL GET THROUGH THIS...
...WE'LL FIGURE IT OUT.

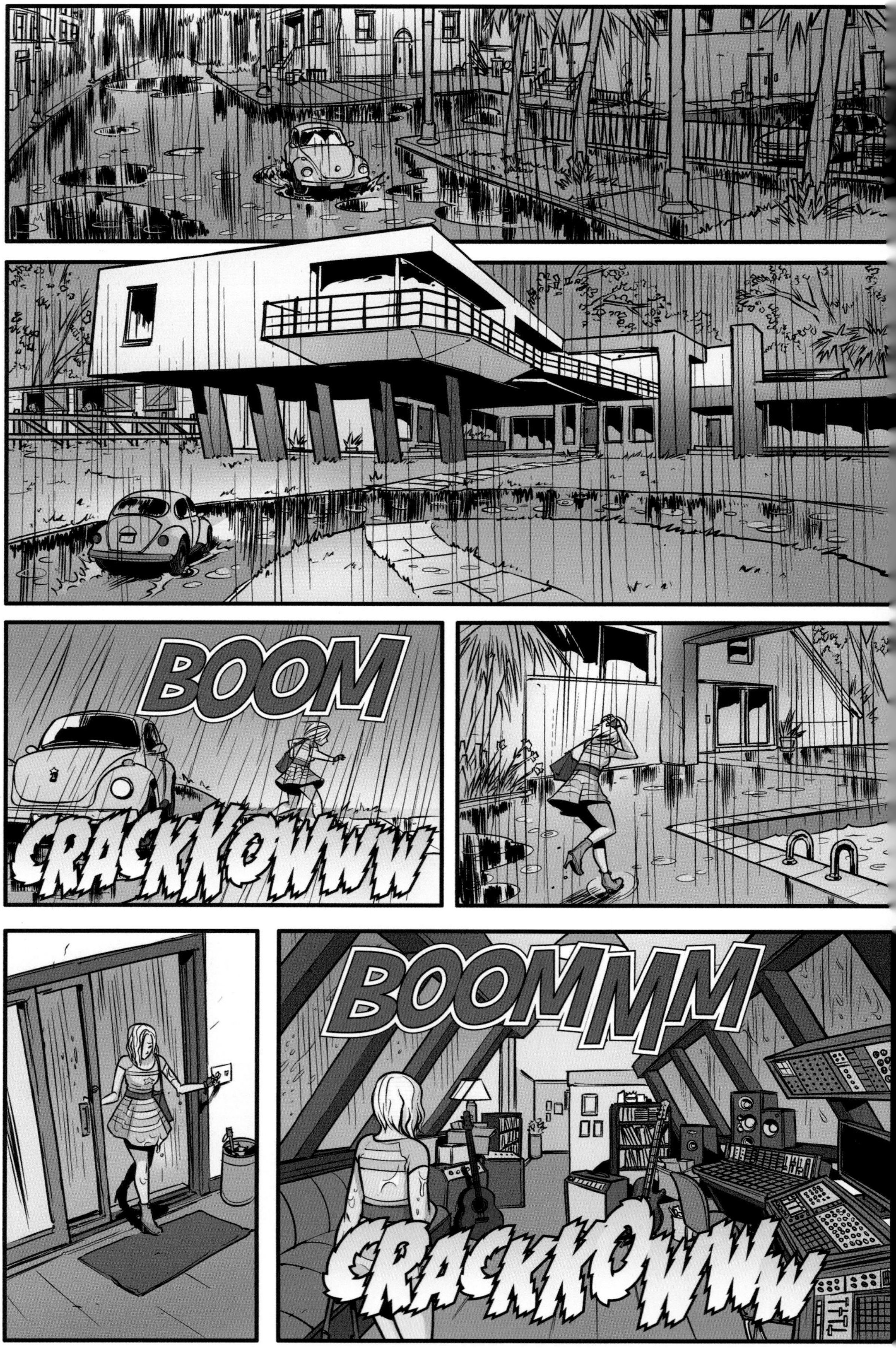
BOOM
CRACKKOWWW
BOOMMM
CRACKKOWWW

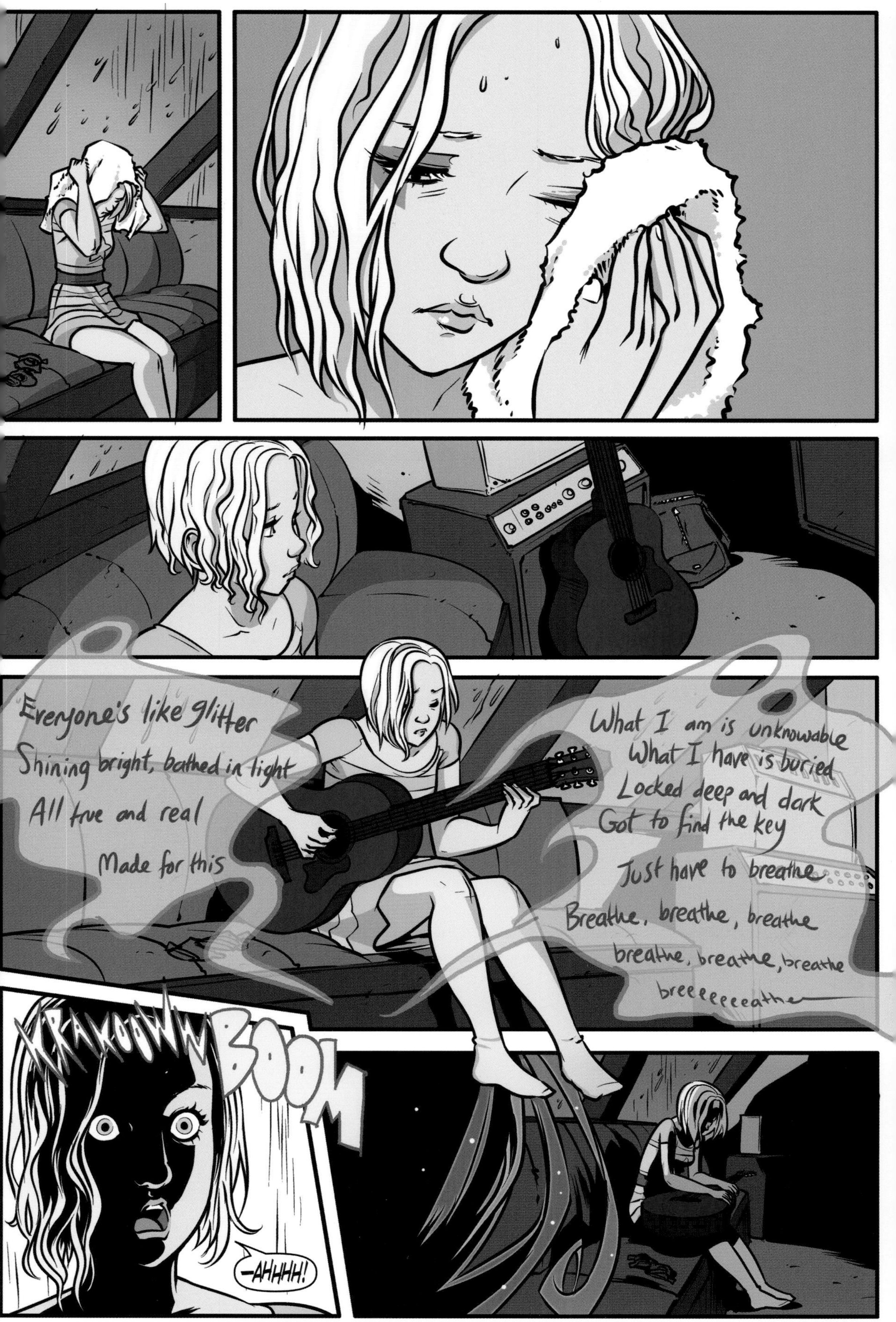
Everyone's like glitter
Shining bright, bathed in light
All true and real
Made for this
What I am is unknowable
What I have is buried
Locked deep and dark
Got to find the key
Just have to breathe
Breathe, breathe, breathe
breathe, breathe, breathe
breeeeeeeathe—
KRAKOOWN BOOM
—AHHHH!

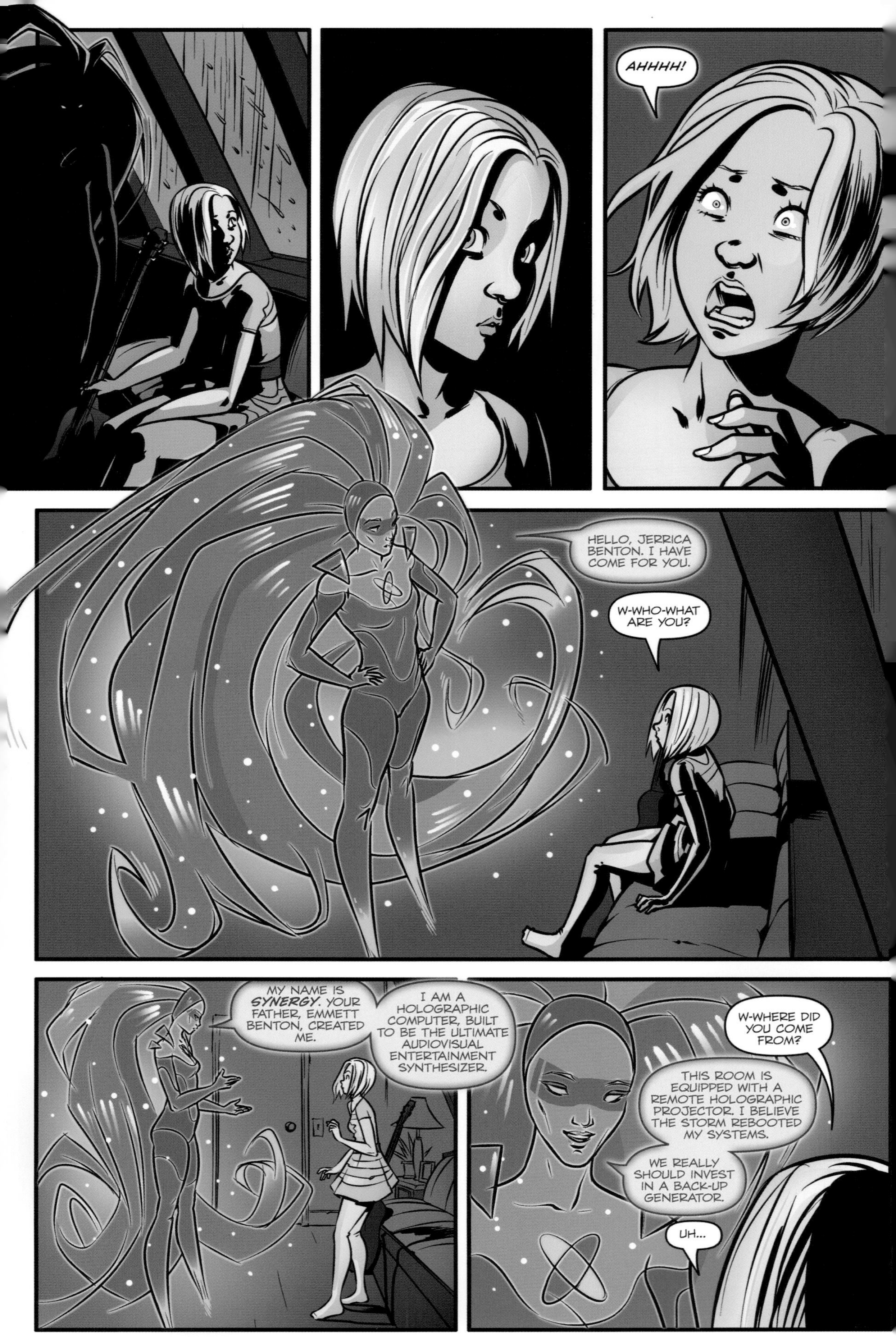
AHHHH!
HELLO, JERRICA BENTON. I HAVE COME FOR YOU.
W-WHO-WHAT ARE YOU?
MY NAME IS SYNERGY. YOUR FATHER, EMMETT BENTON, CREATED ME.
I AM A HOLOGRAPHIC COMPUTER, BUILT TO BE THE ULTIMATE AUDIOVISUAL ENTERTAINMENT SYNTHESIZER.
W-WHERE DID YOU COME FROM?
THIS ROOM IS EQUIPPED WITH A REMOTE HOLOGRAPHIC PROJECTOR. I BELIEVE THE STORM REBOOTED MY SYSTEMS.
WE REALLY SHOULD INVEST IN A BACK-UP GENERATOR.
UH...

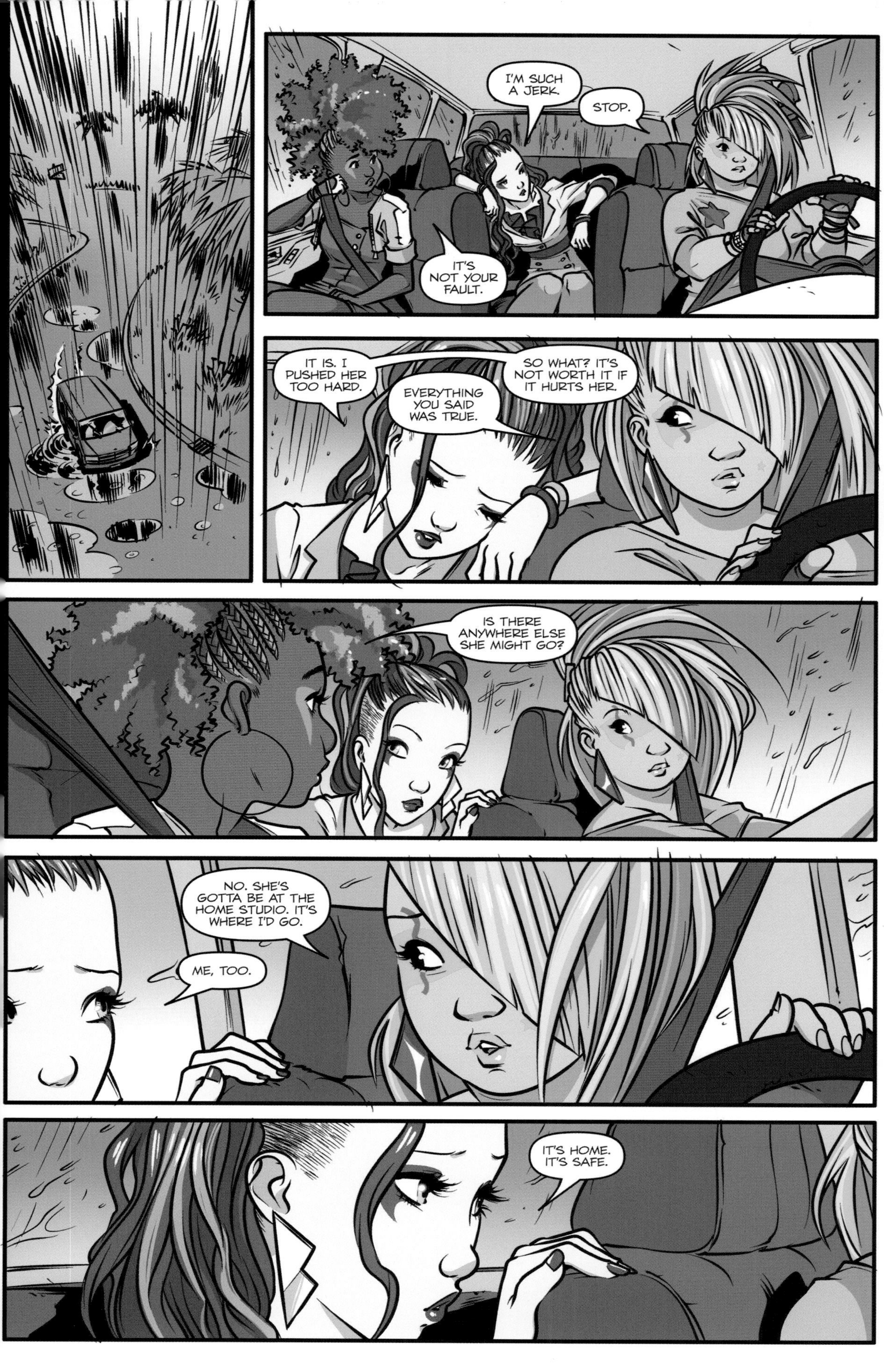
I'M SUCH A JERK.
STOP.
IT'S NOT YOUR FAULT.
IT IS. I PUSHED HER TOO HARD.
EVERYTHING YOU SAID WAS TRUE.
SO WHAT? IT'S NOT WORTH IT IF IT HURTS HER.
IS THERE ANYWHERE ELSE SHE MIGHT GO?
NO. SHE'S GOTTA BE AT THE HOME STUDIO. IT'S WHERE I'D GO.
ME, TOO.
IT'S HOME. IT'S SAFE.

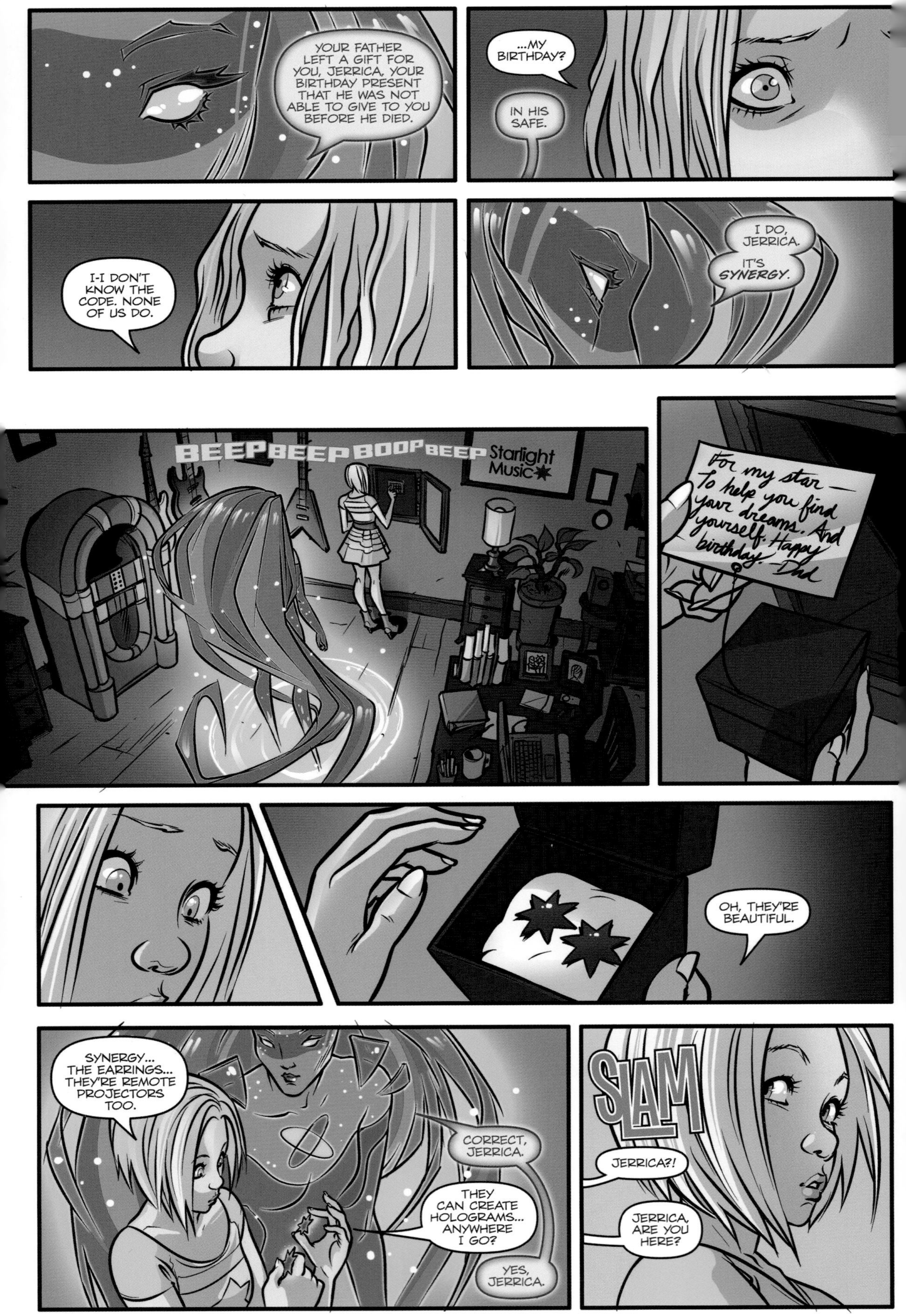
YOUR FATHER LEFT A GIFT FOR YOU, JERRICA, YOUR BIRTHDAY PRESENT THAT HE WAS NOT ABLE TO GIVE TO YOU BEFORE HE DIED.
...MY BIRTHDAY?
IN HIS SAFE.
I-I DON'T KNOW THE CODE. NONE OF US DO.
I DO, JERRICA.
IT'S SYNERGY.
BEEP BEEP BOOP BEEP
Starlight Music
For my star — To help you find your dreams. And yourself. Happy birthday. —Dad
OH, THEY'RE BEAUTIFUL.
SYNERGY... THE EARRINGS... THEY'RE REMOTE PROJECTORS TOO.
CORRECT, JERRICA.
THEY CAN CREATE HOLOGRAMS... ANYWHERE I GO?
YES, JERRICA.
SLAM
JERRICA?!
JERRICA, ARE YOU HERE?

JERRICA?
IS YOUR FRIEND... GLOWING?
WHAAAAT IS HAPPENING?
HELLO KIMBER, AJA, SHANA. SO NICE TO MEET YOU ALL. I AM *SYNERGY*.
UH. HELLO?
JERRICA? WHY IS YOUR REALLY VERY STRANGE FRIEND GLOWING?
HER NAME IS SYNERGY, SHE'S A HOLOGRAM... OR... SHE'S A COMPUTER, I GUESS. DAD BUILT HER.
AND NOW I BELONG TO ALL OF YOU.
DAD LEFT ME THESE EARRINGS... THEY'RE REMOTE PROJECTORS. I THINK... I THINK I KNOW WHAT HE HAD IN MIND.
HAHA. FUNNY. TALKING HOLOGRAMS. MAGIC EARRINGS. VERY FUNNY, JERRICA.
AM I HAVING A STROKE? WHAT IS HAPPENING.
?

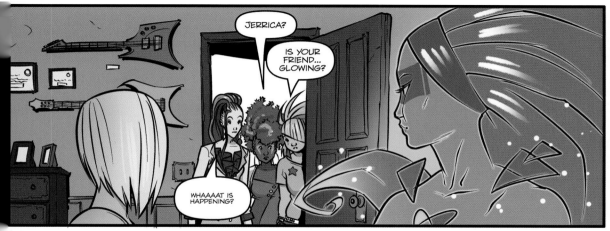

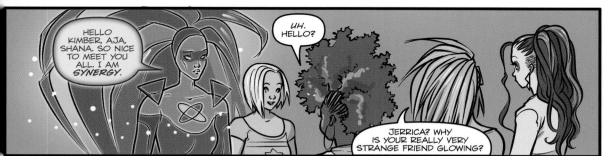

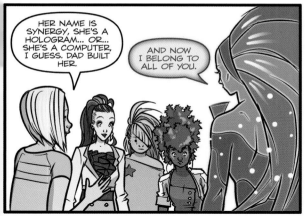

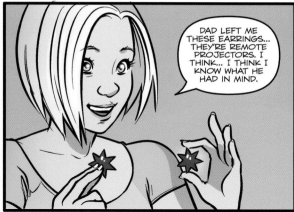

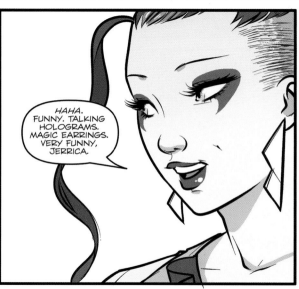

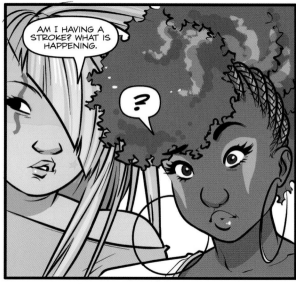

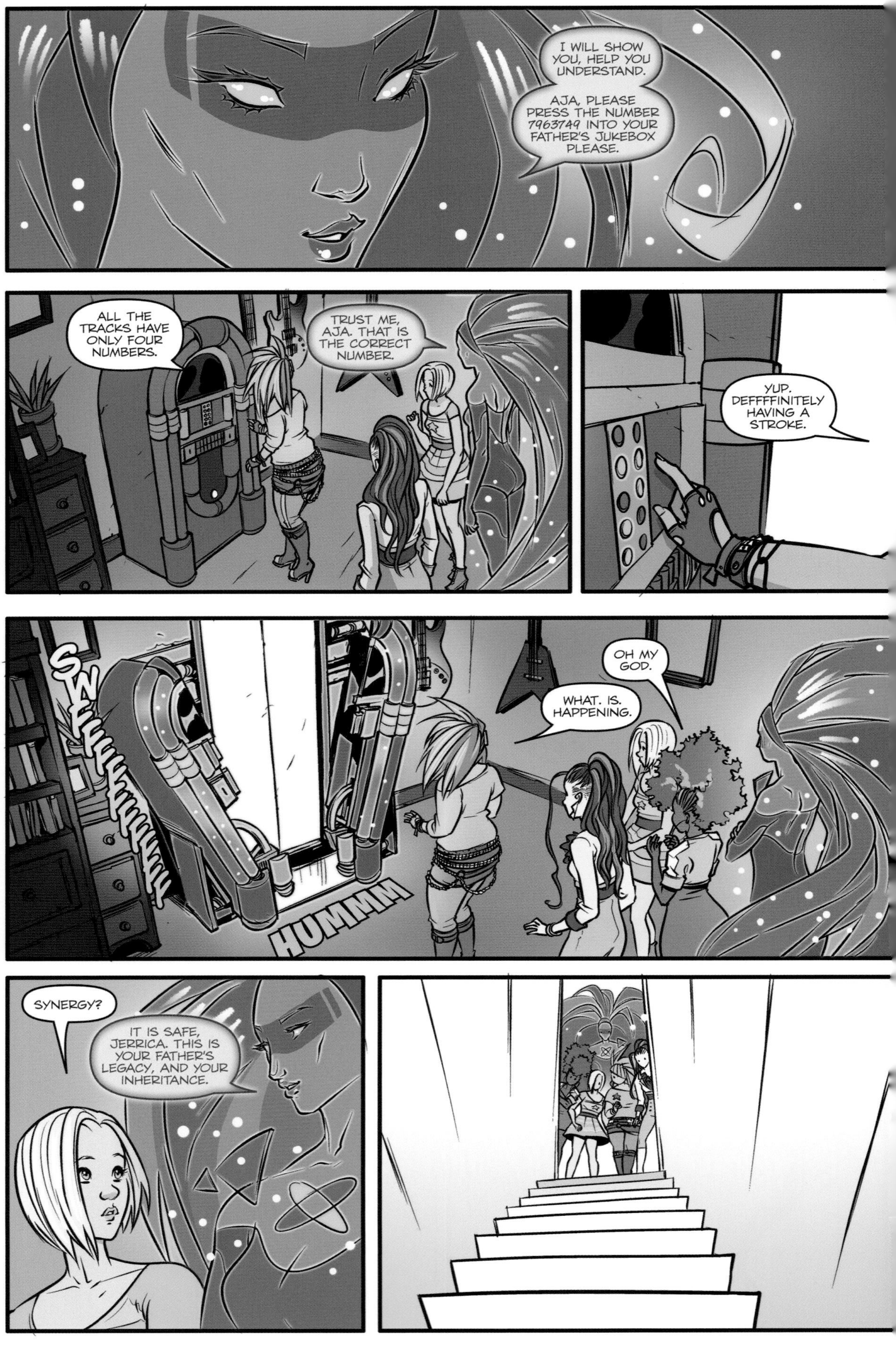
I WILL SHOW YOU, HELP YOU UNDERSTAND.
AJA, PLEASE PRESS THE NUMBER 7963749 INTO YOUR FATHER'S JUKEBOX PLEASE.
ALL THE TRACKS HAVE ONLY FOUR NUMBERS.
TRUST ME, AJA. THAT IS THE CORRECT NUMBER.
YUP. DEFFFFINITELY HAVING A STROKE.
SWEEEEEEEEE
OH MY GOD.
WHAT. IS. HAPPENING.
HUMMM
SYNERGY?
IT IS SAFE, JERRICA. THIS IS YOUR FATHER'S LEGACY, AND YOUR INHERITANCE.

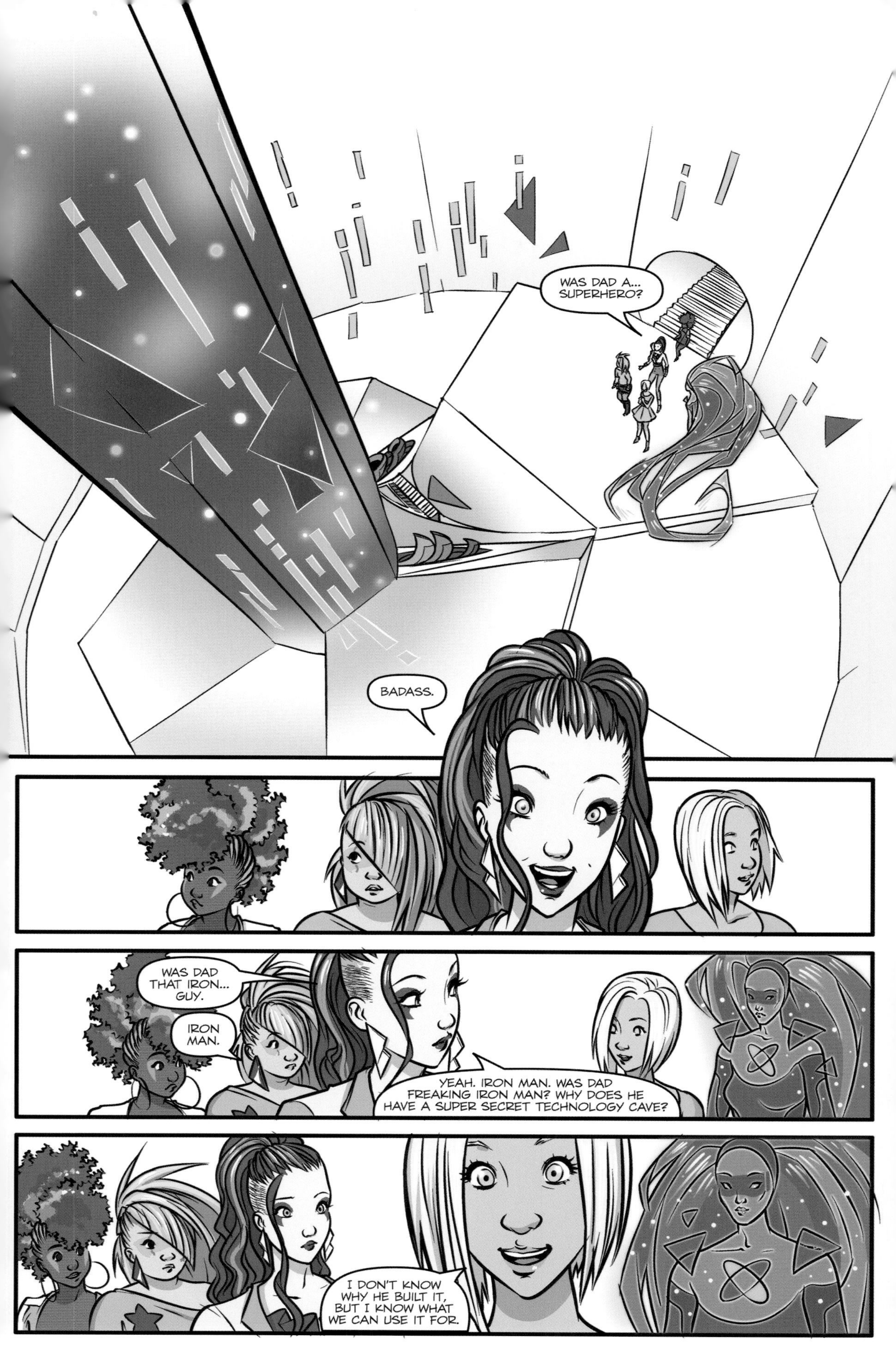
WAS DAD A... SUPERHERO?
BADASS.
WAS DAD THAT IRON... GUY.
IRON MAN.
YEAH. IRON MAN. WAS DAD FREAKING IRON MAN? WHY DOES HE HAVE A SUPER SECRET TECHNOLOGY CAVE?
I DON'T KNOW WHY HE BUILT IT, BUT I KNOW WHAT WE CAN USE IT FOR.

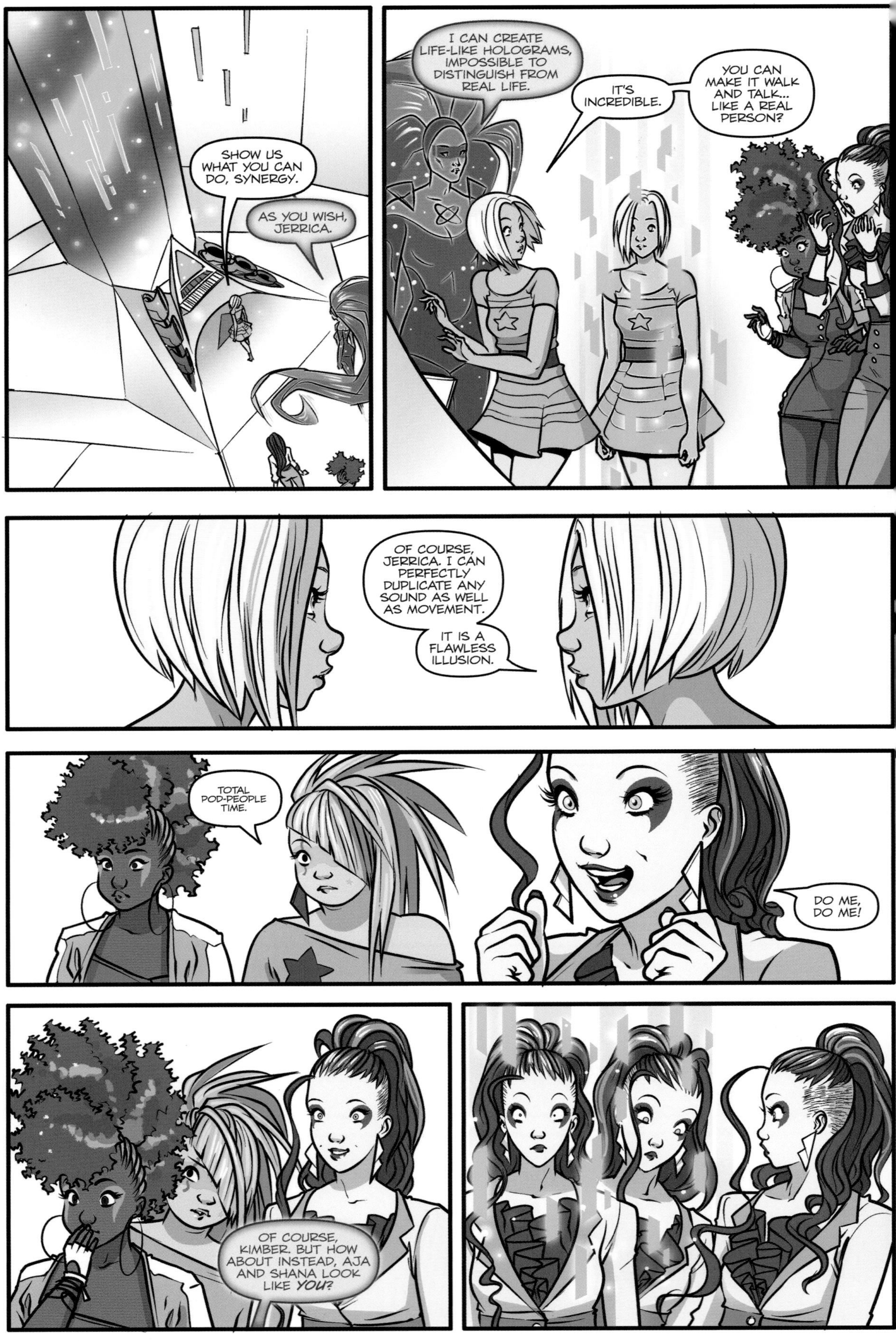
SHOW US WHAT YOU CAN DO, SYNERGY.
AS YOU WISH, JERRICA.
I CAN CREATE LIFE-LIKE HOLOGRAMS, IMPOSSIBLE TO DISTINGUISH FROM REAL LIFE.
IT'S INCREDIBLE.
YOU CAN MAKE IT WALK AND TALK... LIKE A REAL PERSON?
OF COURSE, JERRICA. I CAN PERFECTLY DUPLICATE ANY SOUND AS WELL AS MOVEMENT.
IT IS A FLAWLESS ILLUSION.
TOTAL POD-PEOPLE TIME.
DO ME, DO ME!
OF COURSE, KIMBER. BUT HOW ABOUT INSTEAD, AJA AND SHANA LOOK LIKE *YOU*?

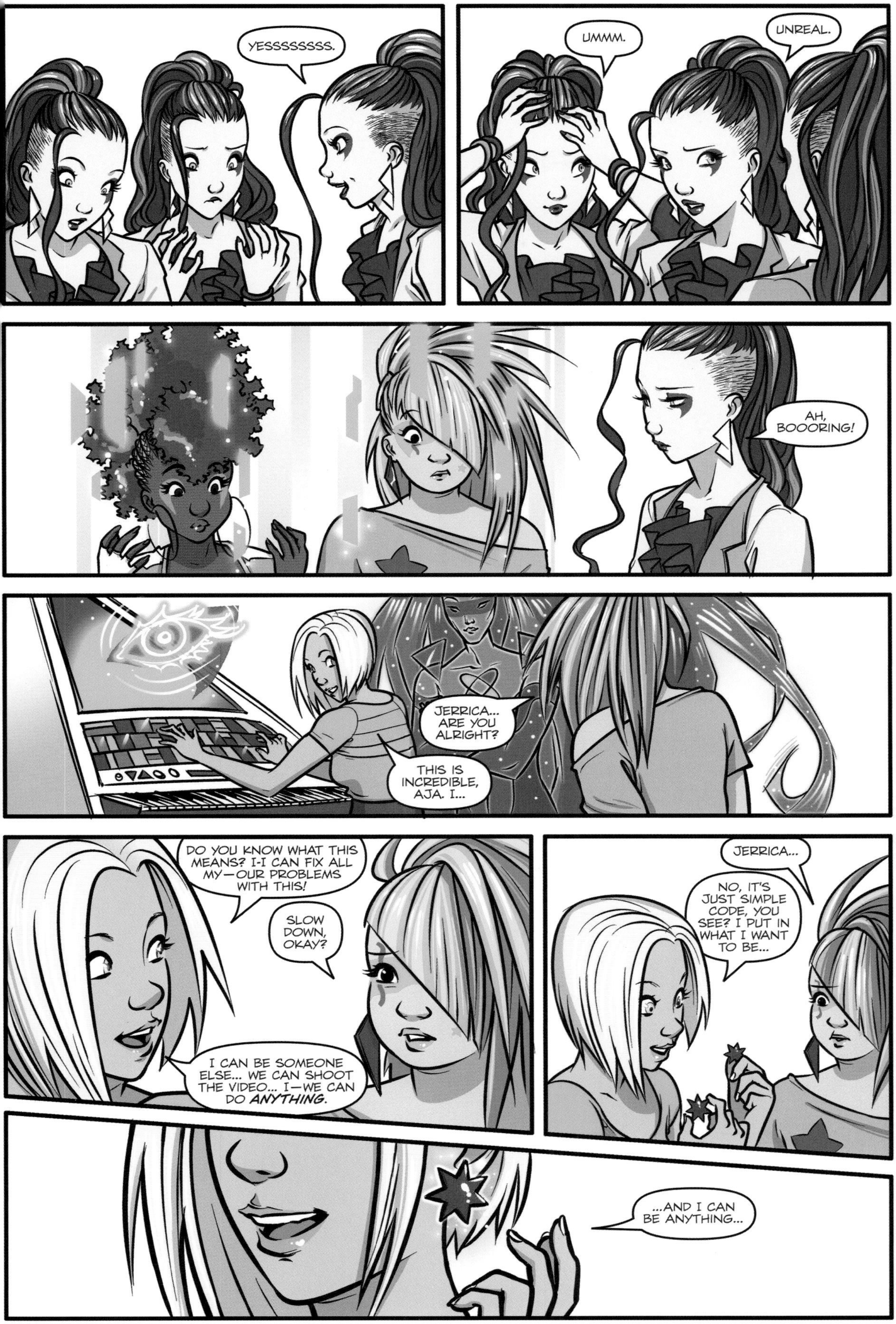
YESSSSSSSS.
UMMM.
UNREAL.
AH, BOOORING!
JERRICA... ARE YOU ALRIGHT?
THIS IS INCREDIBLE, AJA. I...
DO YOU KNOW WHAT THIS MEANS? I-I CAN FIX ALL MY—OUR PROBLEMS WITH THIS!
SLOW DOWN, OKAY?
I CAN BE SOMEONE ELSE... WE CAN SHOOT THE VIDEO... I—WE CAN DO ANYTHING.
JERRICA...
NO, IT'S JUST SIMPLE CODE, YOU SEE? I PUT IN WHAT I WANT TO BE...
...AND I CAN BE ANYTHING...

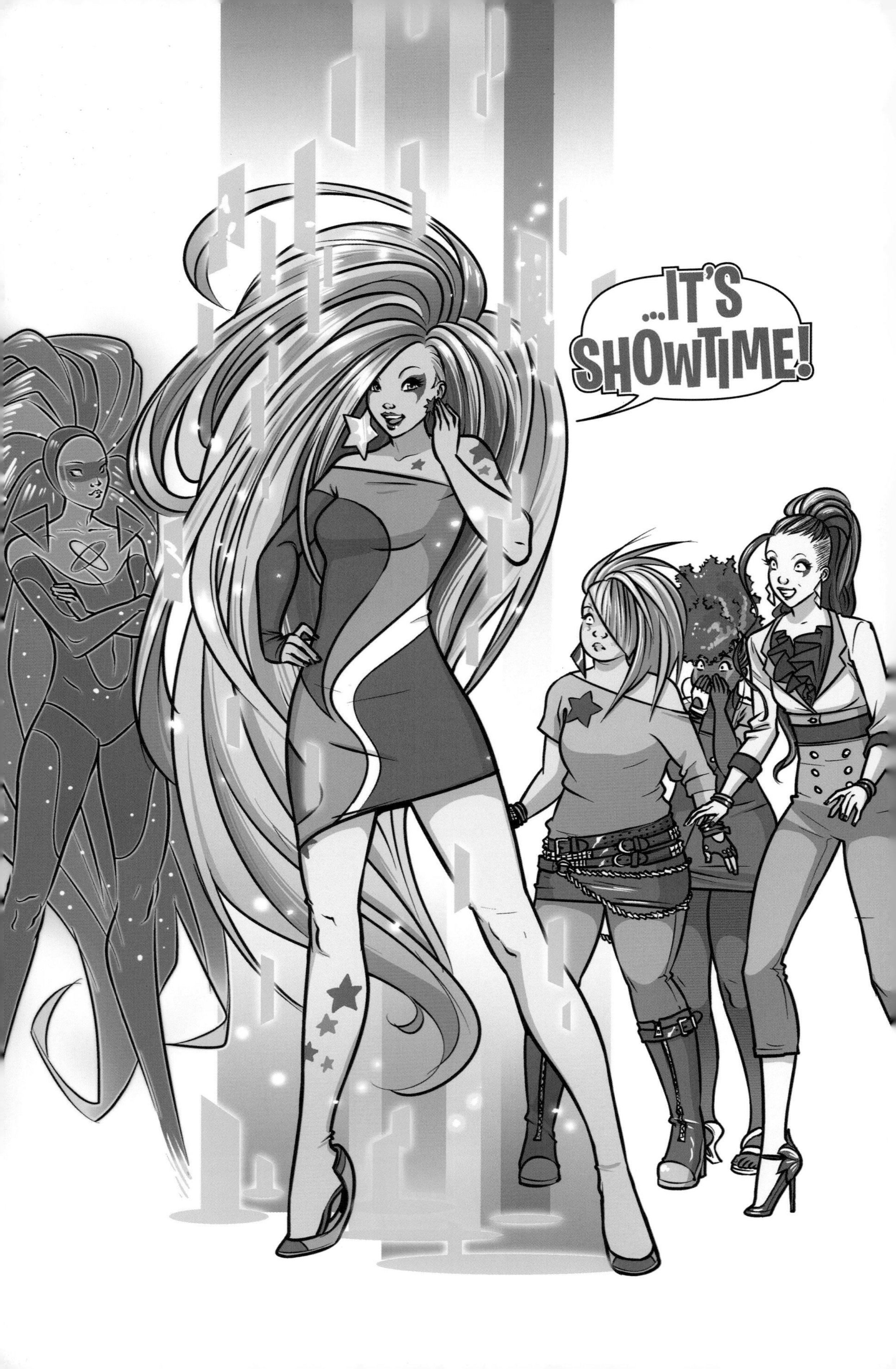
...IT'S SHOWTIME!

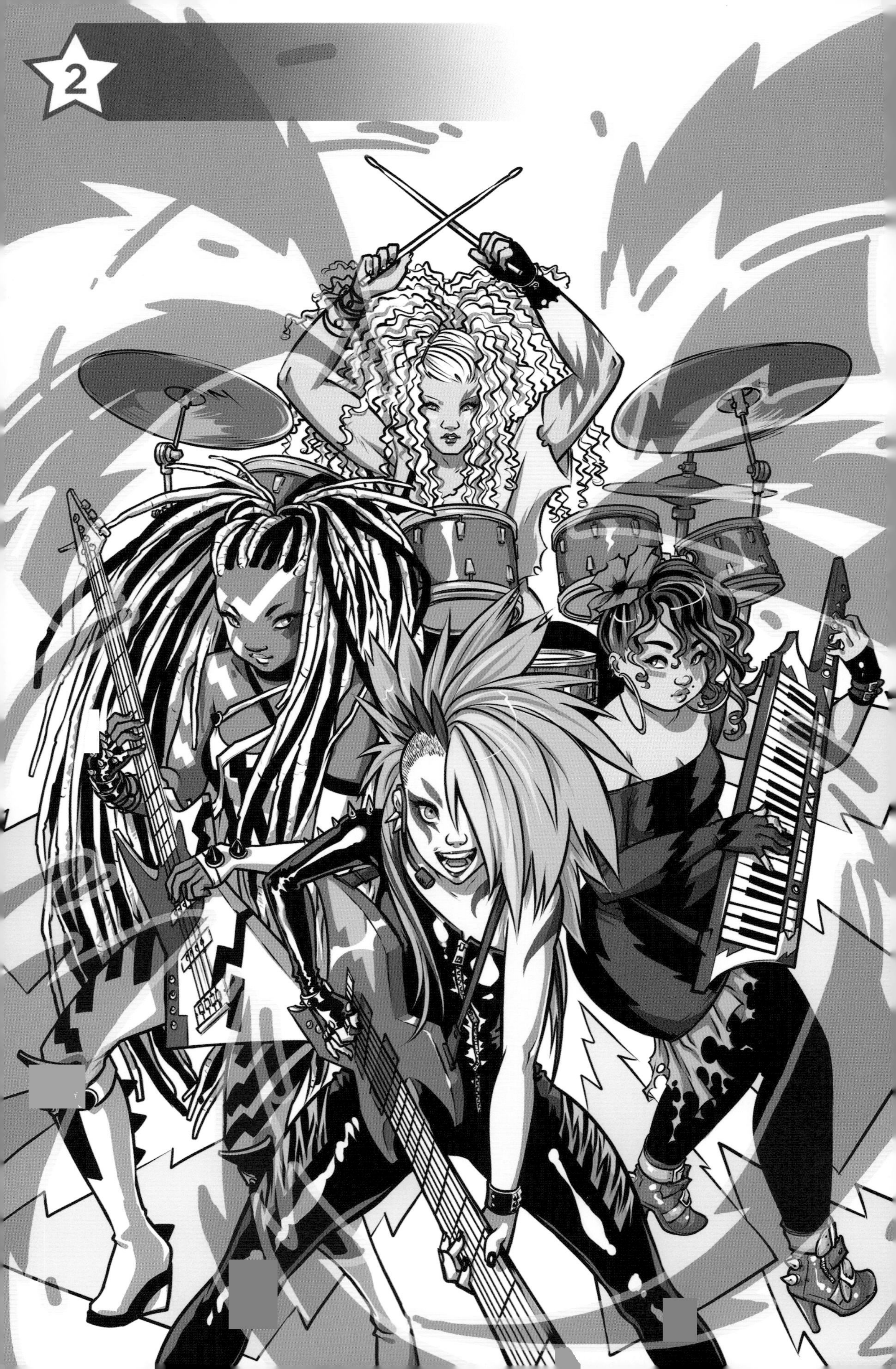
2

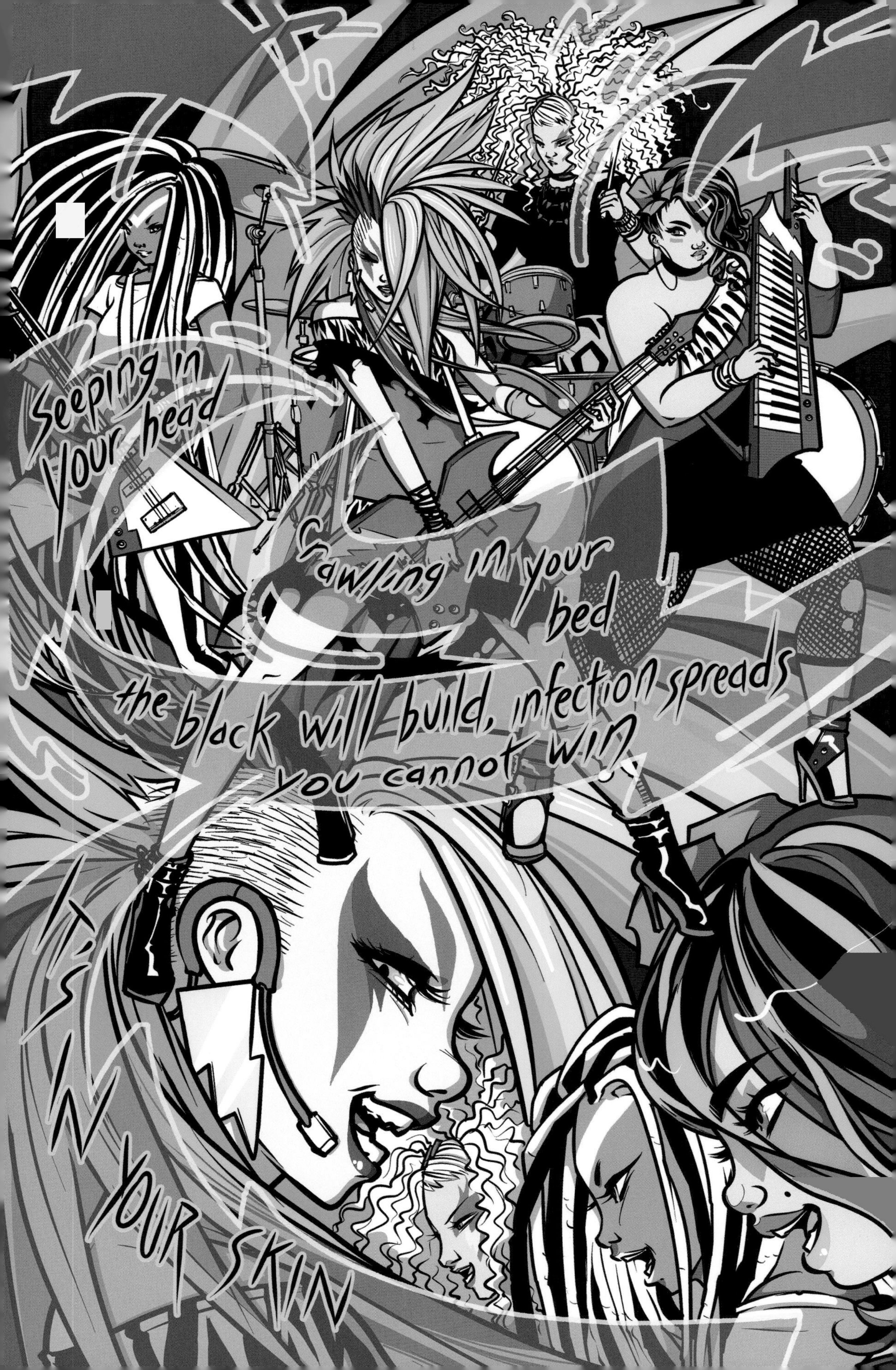
Seeping in your head
Crawling in your bed
the black will build, infection spreads
you cannot win
IT'S IN YOUR SKIN

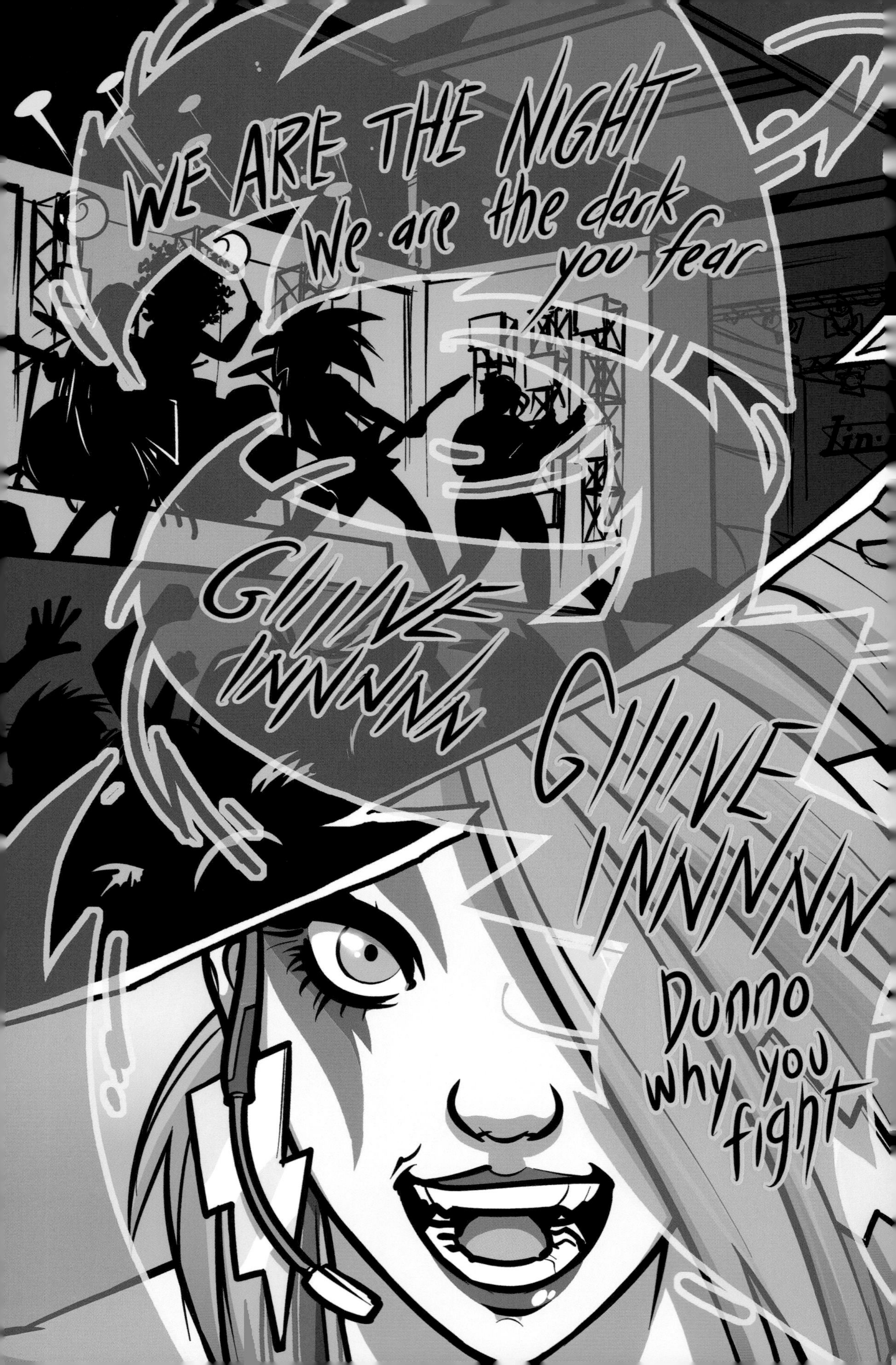
WE ARE THE NIGHT
We are the dark you fear
GIIIVE INNNNN
GIIIVE INNNNNN
Dunno why you fight

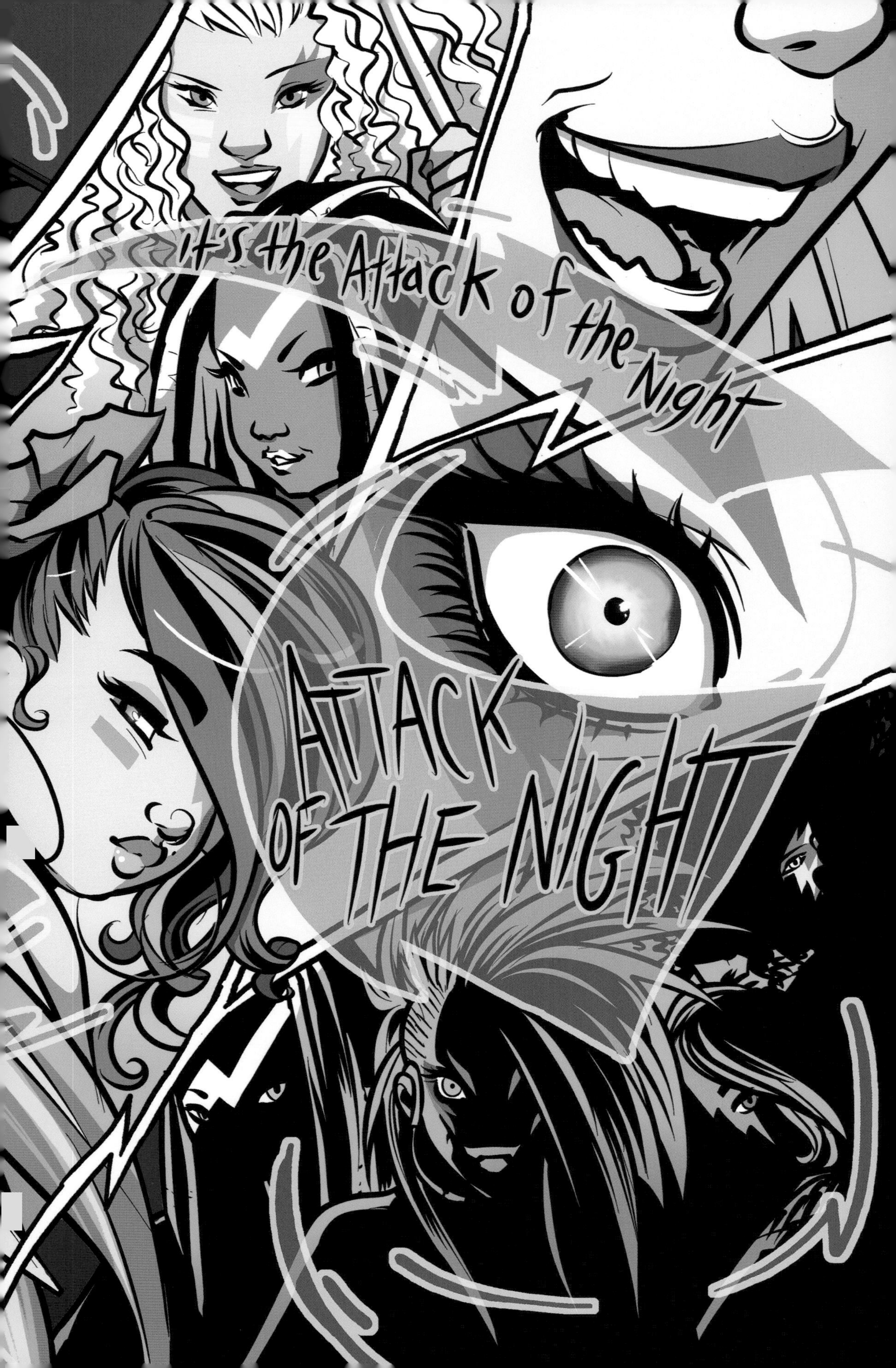

it's the Attack of the Night
ATTACK OF THE NIGHT

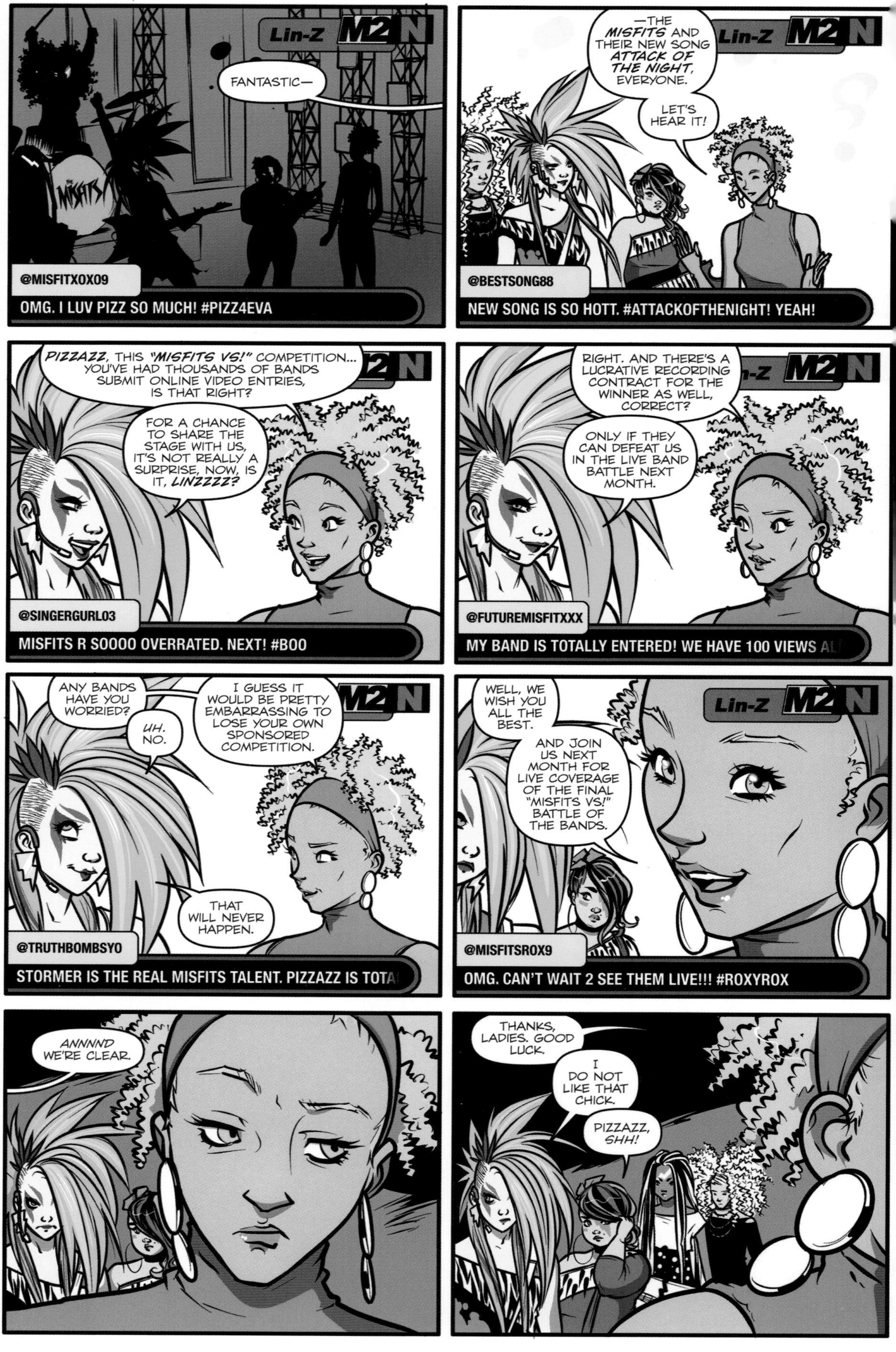
Lin-Z M2N
FANTASTIC—
@MISFITXOX09
OMG. I LUV PIZZ SO MUCH! #PIZZ4EVA
—THE MISFITS AND THEIR NEW SONG ATTACK OF THE NIGHT, EVERYONE.
LET'S HEAR IT!
Lin-Z M2N
@BESTSONG88
NEW SONG IS SO HOTT. #ATTACKOFTHENIGHT! YEAH!
PIZZAZZ, THIS "MISFITS VS!" COMPETITION... YOU'VE HAD THOUSANDS OF BANDS SUBMIT ONLINE VIDEO ENTRIES, IS THAT RIGHT?
FOR A CHANCE TO SHARE THE STAGE WITH US, IT'S NOT REALLY A SURPRISE, NOW, IS IT, LINZZZZ?
@SINGERGURL03
MISFITS R SOOOO OVERRATED. NEXT! #BOO
RIGHT. AND THERE'S A LUCRATIVE RECORDING CONTRACT FOR THE WINNER AS WELL, CORRECT?
ONLY IF THEY CAN DEFEAT US IN THE LIVE BAND BATTLE NEXT MONTH.
@FUTUREMISFITXXX
MY BAND IS TOTALLY ENTERED! WE HAVE 100 VIEWS A
ANY BANDS HAVE YOU WORRIED?
UH. NO.
I GUESS IT WOULD BE PRETTY EMBARRASSING TO LOSE YOUR OWN SPONSORED COMPETITION.
THAT WILL NEVER HAPPEN.
@TRUTHBOMBSYO
STORMER IS THE REAL MISFITS TALENT. PIZZAZZ IS TOTA
WELL, WE WISH YOU ALL THE BEST.
AND JOIN US NEXT MONTH FOR LIVE COVERAGE OF THE FINAL "MISFITS VS!" BATTLE OF THE BANDS.
Lin-Z M2N
@MISFITSROX9
OMG. CAN'T WAIT 2 SEE THEM LIVE!!! #ROXYROX
ANNNND WE'RE CLEAR.
THANKS, LADIES. GOOD LUCK.
I DO NOT LIKE THAT CHICK.
PIZZAZZ, SHH!

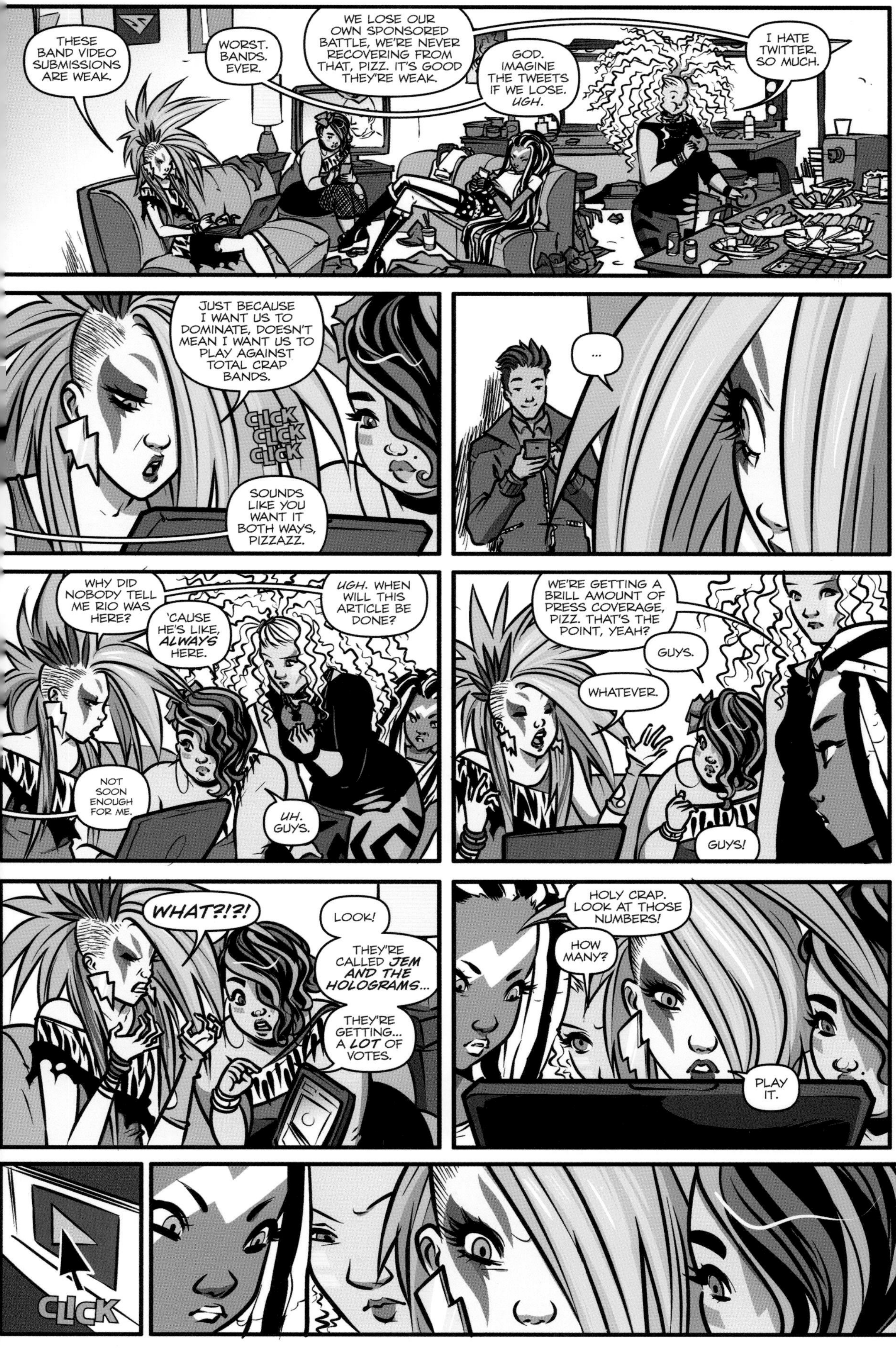
THESE BAND VIDEO SUBMISSIONS ARE WEAK.
WORST. BANDS. EVER.
WE LOSE OUR OWN SPONSORED BATTLE, WE'RE NEVER RECOVERING FROM THAT, PIZZ. IT'S GOOD THEY'RE WEAK.
GOD. IMAGINE THE TWEETS IF WE LOSE. UGH.
I HATE TWITTER. SO MUCH.
JUST BECAUSE I WANT US TO DOMINATE, DOESN'T MEAN I WANT US TO PLAY AGAINST TOTAL CRAP BANDS.
CLICK CLICK CLICK
SOUNDS LIKE YOU WANT IT BOTH WAYS, PIZZAZZ.
...
WHY DID NOBODY TELL ME RIO WAS HERE?
'CAUSE HE'S LIKE, ALWAYS HERE.
UGH. WHEN WILL THIS ARTICLE BE DONE?
NOT SOON ENOUGH FOR ME.
UH. GUYS.
WE'RE GETTING A BRILL AMOUNT OF PRESS COVERAGE, PIZZ. THAT'S THE POINT, YEAH?
GUYS.
WHATEVER.
GUYS!
WHAT?!?!
LOOK!
THEY'RE CALLED JEM AND THE HOLOGRAMS...
THEY'RE GETTING... A LOT OF VOTES.
HOLY CRAP. LOOK AT THOSE NUMBERS!
HOW MANY?
PLAY IT.
CLICK

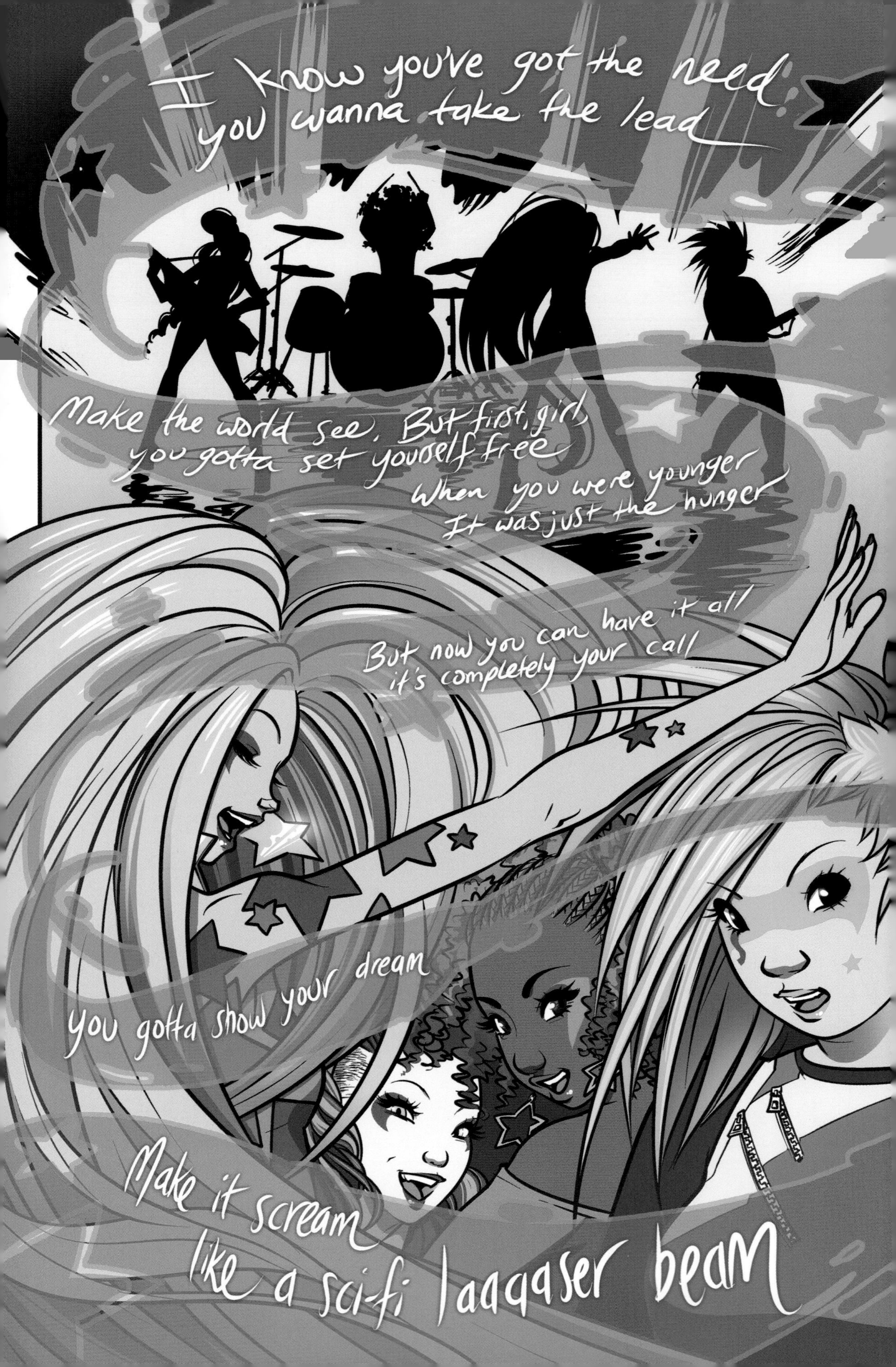
I know you've got the need
you wanna take the lead
Make the world see, But first, girl,
you gotta set yourself free
When you were younger
It was just the hunger
But now you can have it all
it's completely your call
you gotta show your dream
Make it scream
like a sci-fi laaaaser beam

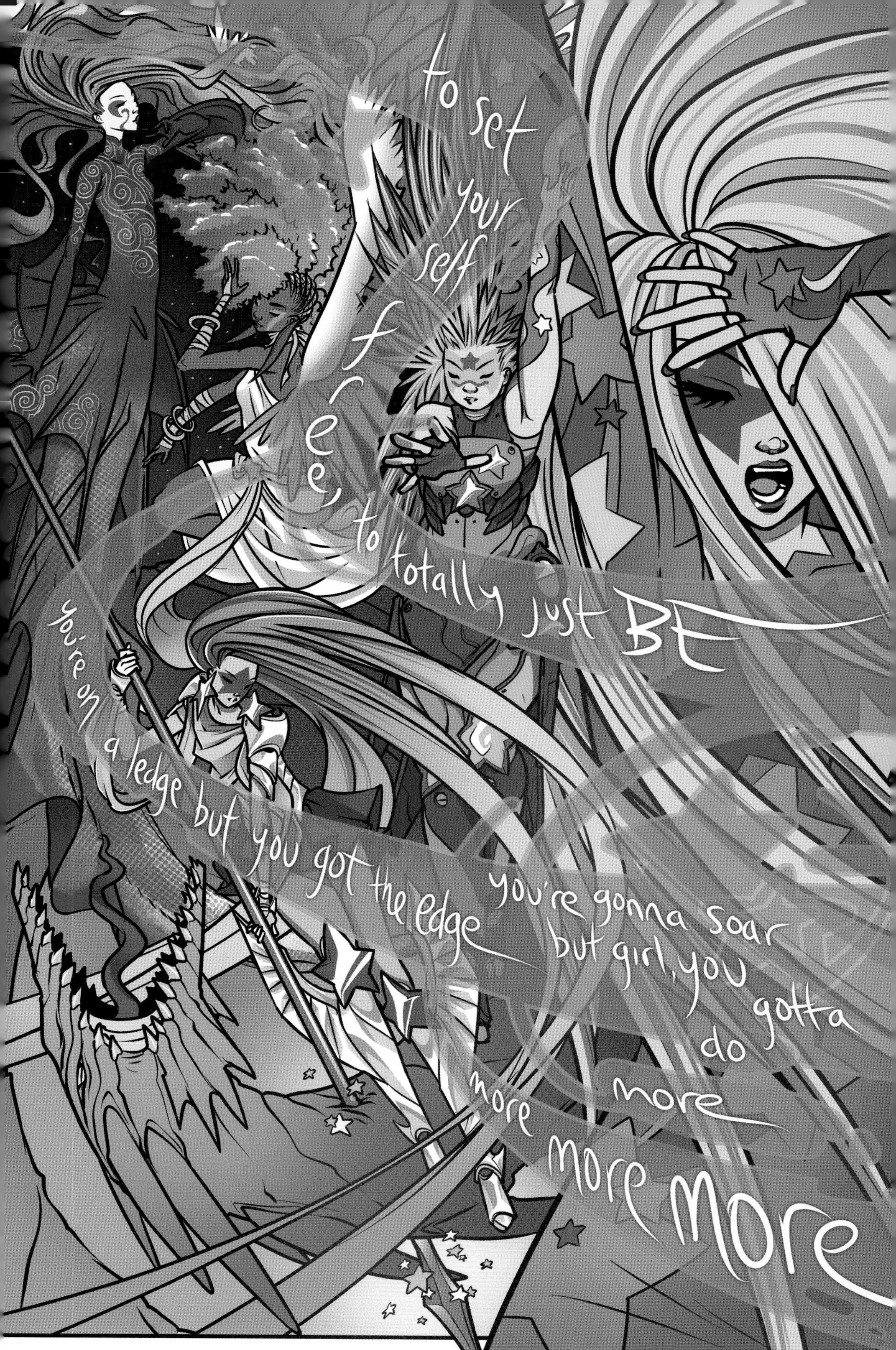
to set your self free, to totally just BE
you're on a ledge but you got the edge
you're gonna soar but girl, you gotta do more
more more MORE

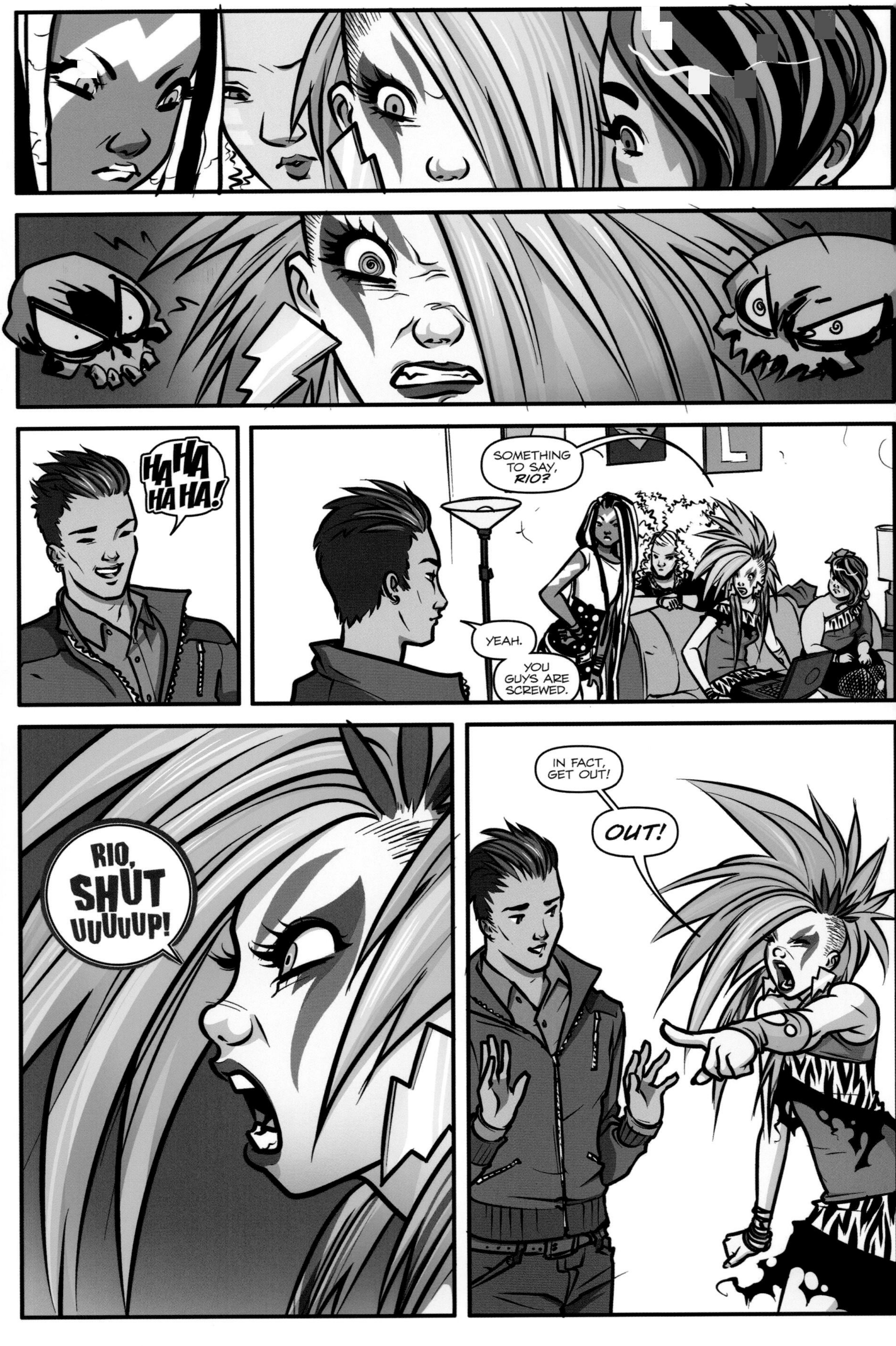
HA HA HA HA!
SOMETHING TO SAY, RIO?
YEAH.
YOU GUYS ARE SCREWED.
RIO, SHUT UUUUUP!
IN FACT, GET OUT!
OUT!

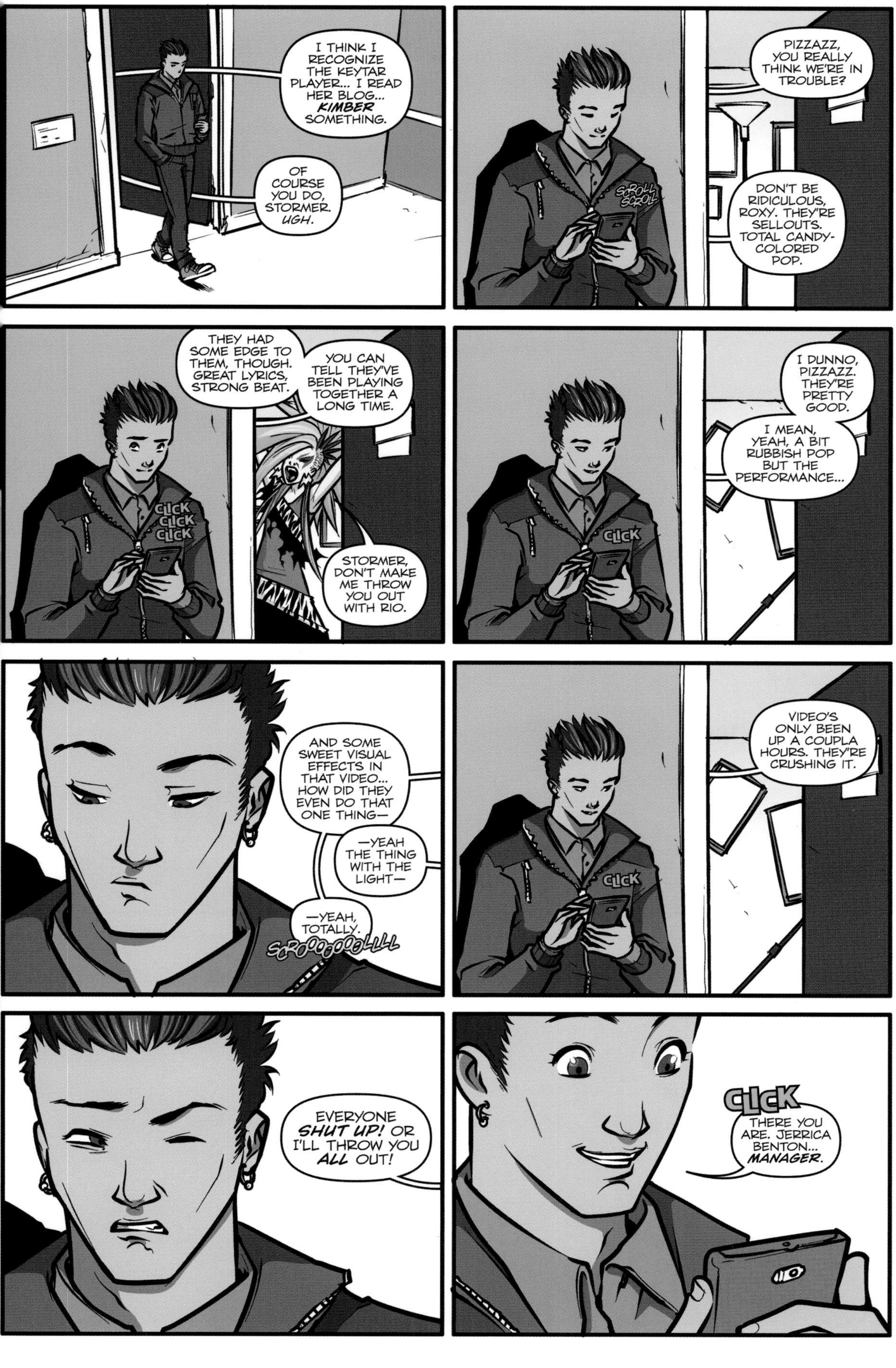
I THINK I RECOGNIZE THE KEYTAR PLAYER... I READ HER BLOG... *KIMBER* SOMETHING.
OF COURSE YOU DO, STORMER. *UGH.*
PIZZAZZ, YOU REALLY THINK WE'RE IN TROUBLE?
SCROLL SCROLL
DON'T BE RIDICULOUS, ROXY. THEY'RE SELLOUTS. TOTAL CANDY-COLORED POP.
THEY HAD SOME EDGE TO THEM, THOUGH. GREAT LYRICS, STRONG BEAT.
YOU CAN TELL THEY'VE BEEN PLAYING TOGETHER A LONG TIME.
CLICK CLICK CLICK
STORMER, DON'T MAKE ME THROW YOU OUT WITH RIO.
I DUNNO, PIZZAZZ. THEY'RE PRETTY GOOD.
I MEAN, YEAH, A BIT RUBBISH POP BUT THE PERFORMANCE...
CLICK
AND SOME SWEET VISUAL EFFECTS IN THAT VIDEO... HOW DID THEY EVEN DO THAT ONE THING—
—YEAH THE THING WITH THE LIGHT—
—YEAH, TOTALLY.
SCROOOOOOOLLLL
VIDEO'S ONLY BEEN UP A COUPLA HOURS. THEY'RE CRUSHING IT.
CLICK
EVERYONE *SHUT UP!* OR I'LL THROW YOU *ALL* OUT!
CLICK
THERE YOU ARE. JERRICA BENTON... *MANAGER*.

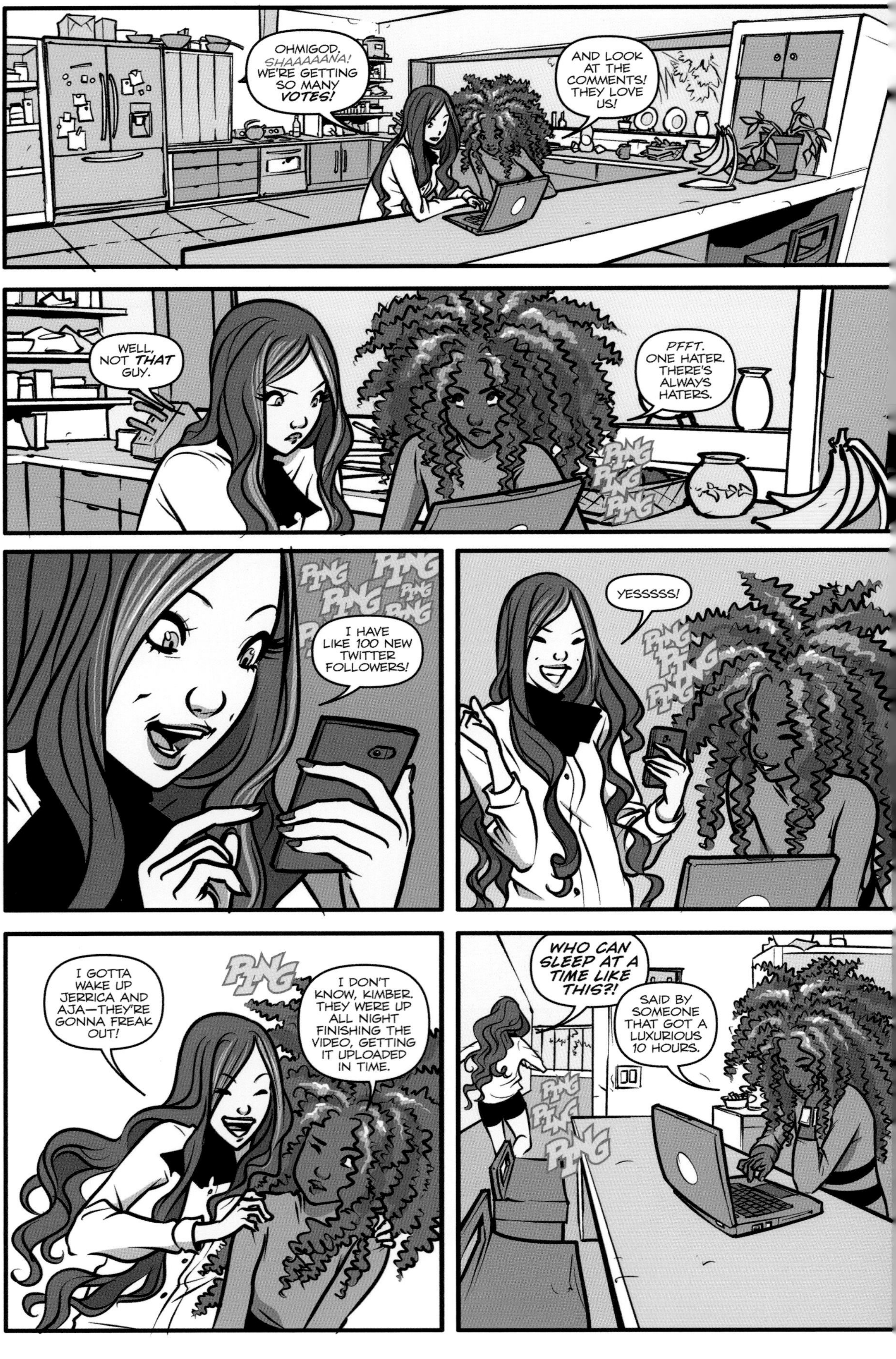
OHMIGOD, SHAAAAAANA! WE'RE GETTING SO MANY VOTES!
AND LOOK AT THE COMMENTS! THEY LOVE US!
WELL, NOT THAT GUY.
PFFT. ONE HATER. THERE'S ALWAYS HATERS.
PING PING PING
PING PING PING PING PING
I HAVE LIKE 100 NEW TWITTER FOLLOWERS!
YESSSSS!
PING PING PING
I GOTTA WAKE UP JERRICA AND AJA—THEY'RE GONNA FREAK OUT!
PING
I DON'T KNOW, KIMBER. THEY WERE UP ALL NIGHT FINISHING THE VIDEO, GETTING IT UPLOADED IN TIME.
WHO CAN SLEEP AT A TIME LIKE THIS?!
SAID BY SOMEONE THAT GOT A LUXURIOUS 10 HOURS.
PING PING PING

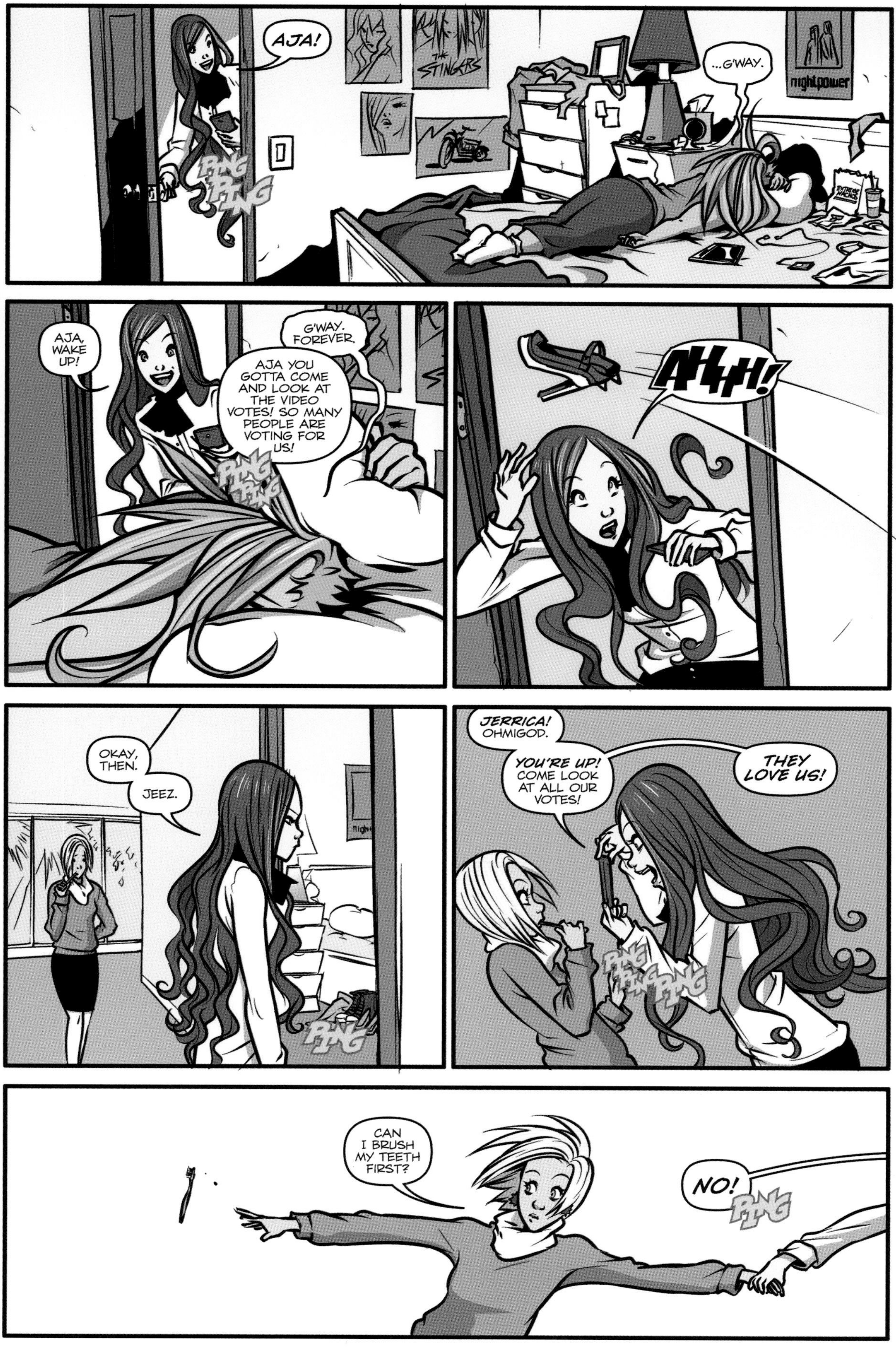
AJA!
THE STINGERS
nightpower
...G'WAY.
PING PING
AJA, WAKE UP!
G'WAY. FOREVER.
AJA YOU GOTTA COME AND LOOK AT THE VIDEO VOTES! SO MANY PEOPLE ARE VOTING FOR US!
PING PING
AHHH!
OKAY, THEN.
JEEZ.
PING
JERRICA! OHMIGOD.
YOU'RE UP! COME LOOK AT ALL OUR VOTES!
THEY LOVE US!
PING PING PING
CAN I BRUSH MY TEETH FIRST?
NO!
PING

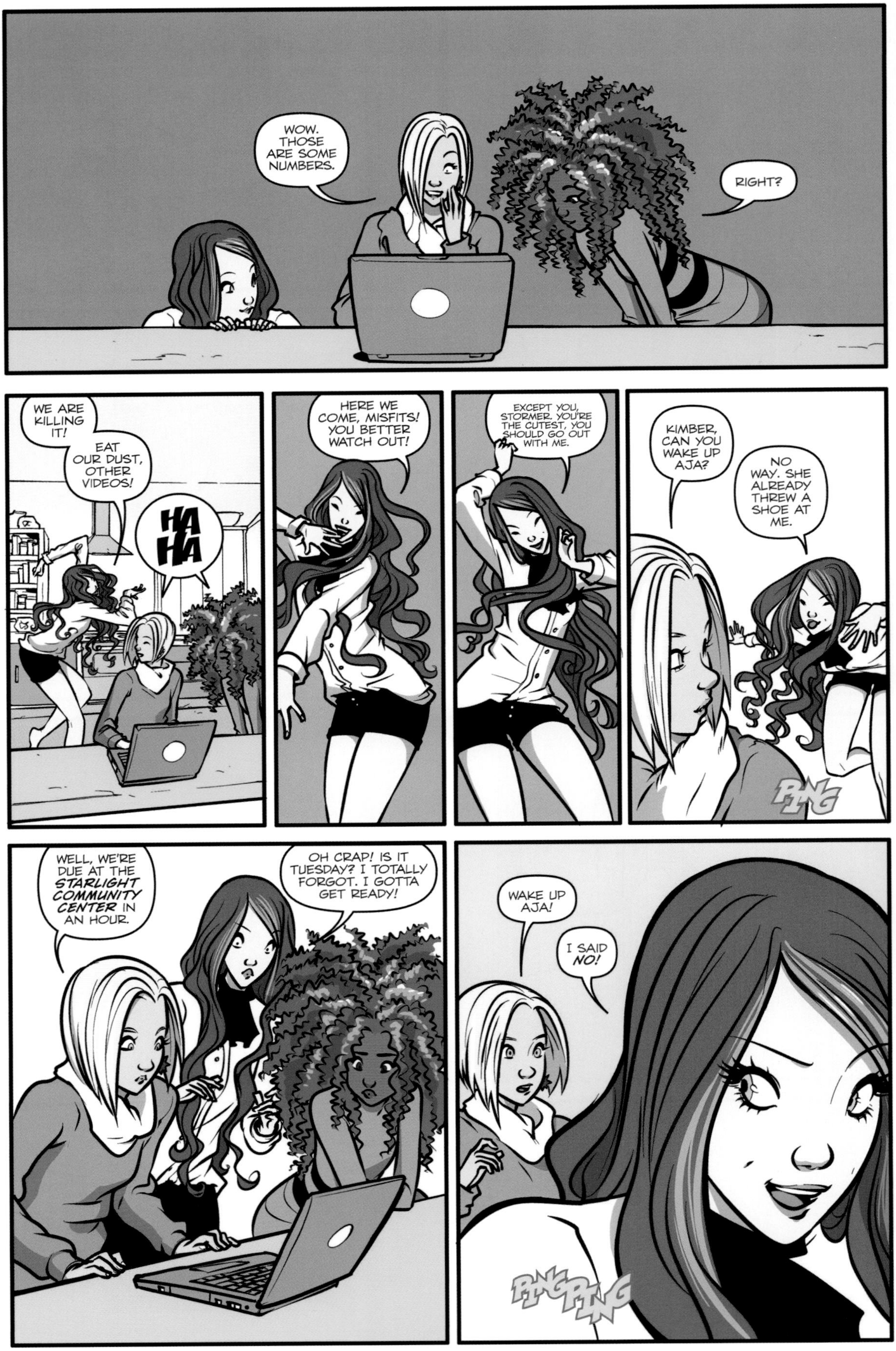
WOW. THOSE ARE SOME NUMBERS.
RIGHT?
WE ARE KILLING IT!
EAT OUR DUST, OTHER VIDEOS!
HA HA
HERE WE COME, MISFITS! YOU BETTER WATCH OUT!
EXCEPT YOU, STORMER. YOU'RE THE CUTEST, YOU SHOULD GO OUT WITH ME.
KIMBER, CAN YOU WAKE UP AJA?
NO WAY. SHE ALREADY THREW A SHOE AT ME.
PING
WELL, WE'RE DUE AT THE STARLIGHT COMMUNITY CENTER IN AN HOUR.
OH CRAP! IS IT TUESDAY? I TOTALLY FORGOT. I GOTTA GET READY!
WAKE UP AJA!
I SAID NO!
PING PING

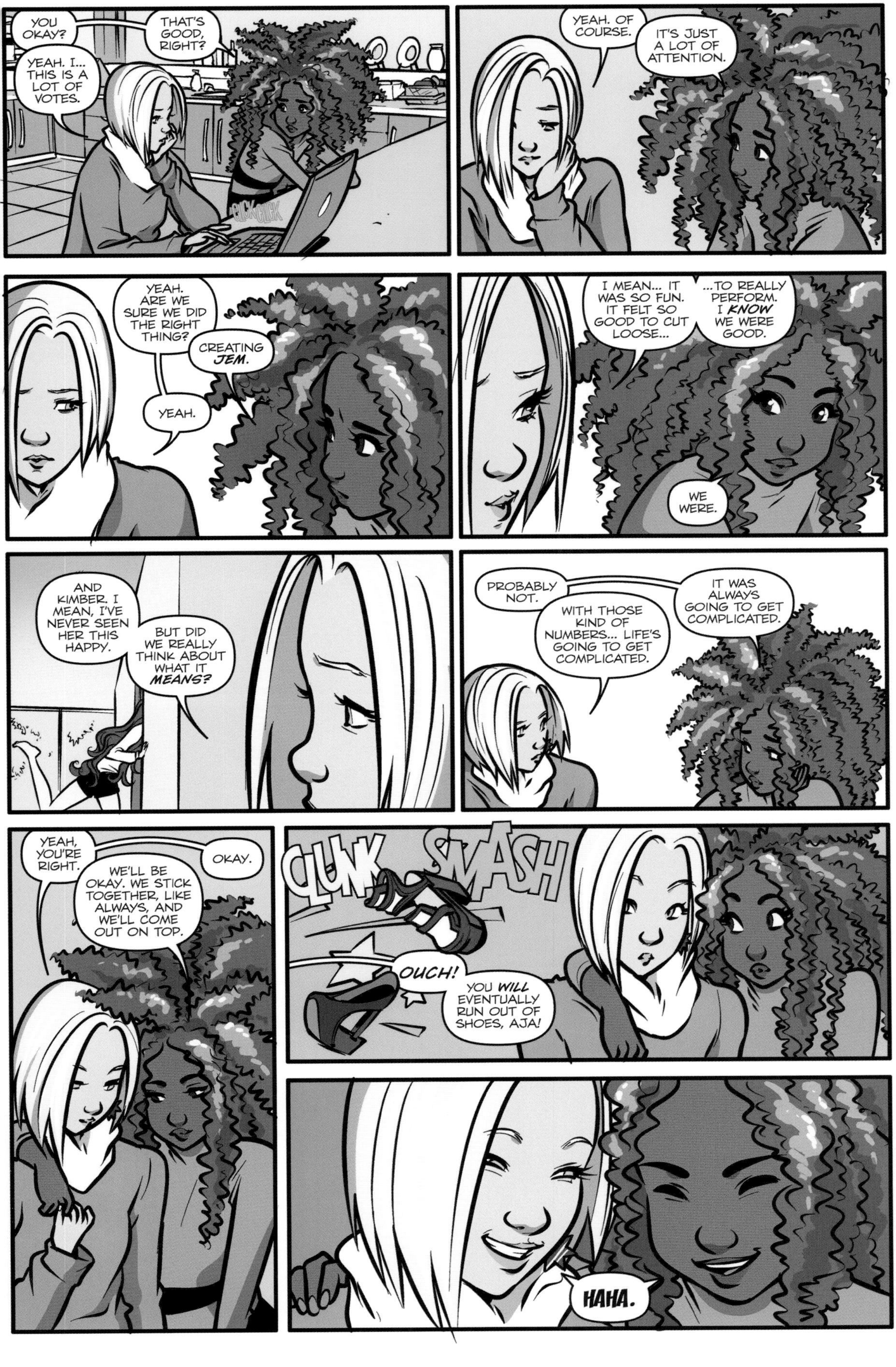
YOU OKAY?
THAT'S GOOD, RIGHT?
YEAH. I... THIS IS A LOT OF VOTES.
CLICK CLICK
YEAH. OF COURSE.
IT'S JUST A LOT OF ATTENTION.
YEAH. ARE WE SURE WE DID THE RIGHT THING?
CREATING *JEM*.
YEAH.
I MEAN... IT WAS SO FUN. IT FELT SO GOOD TO CUT LOOSE...
...TO REALLY PERFORM. I *KNOW* WE WERE GOOD.
WE WERE.
AND KIMBER. I MEAN, I'VE NEVER SEEN HER THIS HAPPY.
BUT DID WE REALLY THINK ABOUT WHAT IT *MEANS?*
PROBABLY NOT.
IT WAS ALWAYS GOING TO GET COMPLICATED.
WITH THOSE KIND OF NUMBERS... LIFE'S GOING TO GET COMPLICATED.
YEAH, YOU'RE RIGHT.
OKAY.
WE'LL BE OKAY. WE STICK TOGETHER, LIKE ALWAYS, AND WE'LL COME OUT ON TOP.
CLUNK
SMASH
OUCH!
YOU *WILL* EVENTUALLY RUN OUT OF SHOES, AJA!
HAHA.

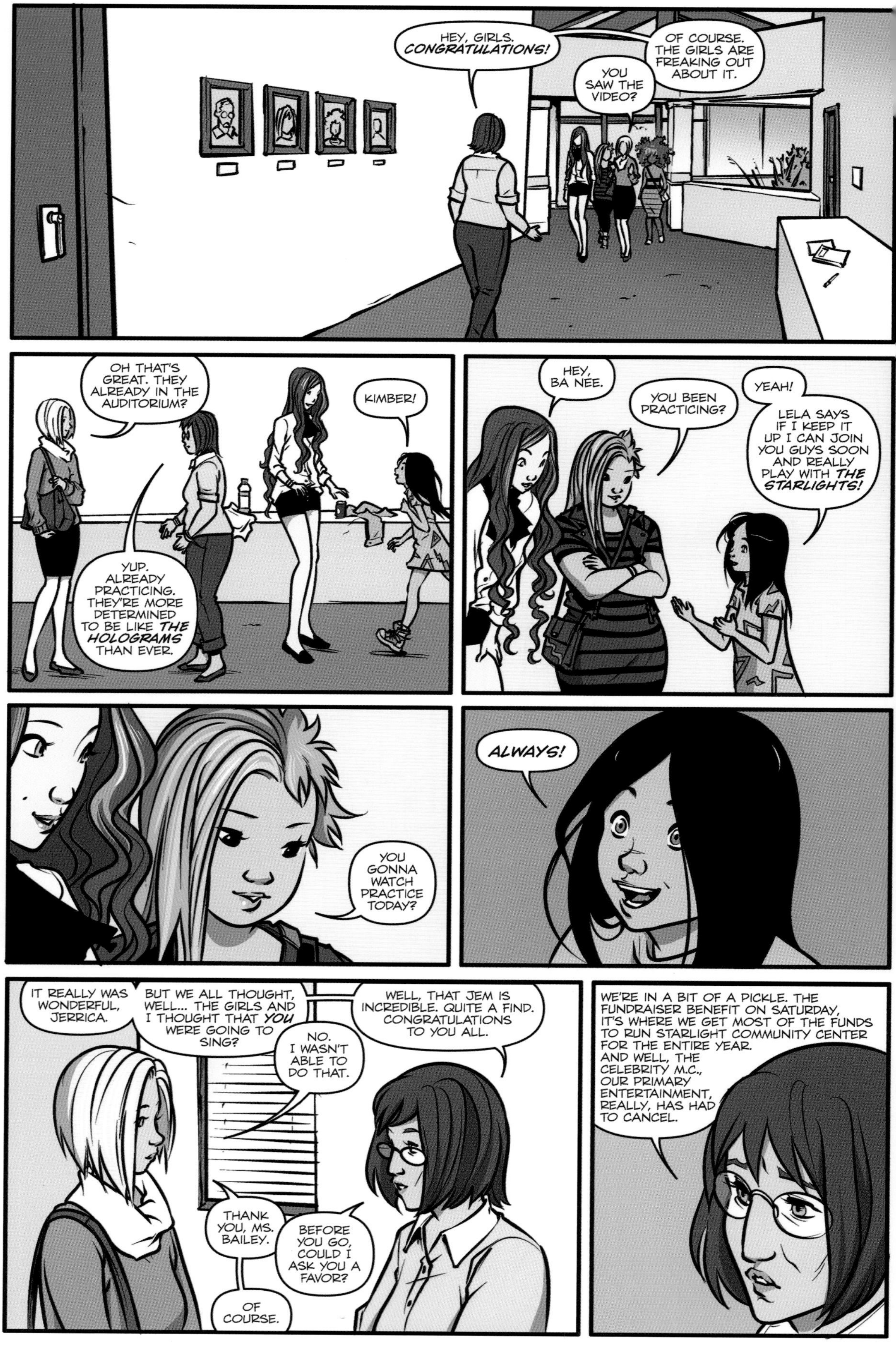
HEY, GIRLS. CONGRATULATIONS!
YOU SAW THE VIDEO?
OF COURSE. THE GIRLS ARE FREAKING OUT ABOUT IT.
OH THAT'S GREAT. THEY ALREADY IN THE AUDITORIUM?
YUP. ALREADY PRACTICING. THEY'RE MORE DETERMINED TO BE LIKE THE HOLOGRAMS THAN EVER.
KIMBER!
HEY, BA NEE.
YOU BEEN PRACTICING?
YEAH!
LELA SAYS IF I KEEP IT UP I CAN JOIN YOU GUYS SOON AND REALLY PLAY WITH THE STARLIGHTS!
YOU GONNA WATCH PRACTICE TODAY?
ALWAYS!
IT REALLY WAS WONDERFUL, JERRICA.
BUT WE ALL THOUGHT, WELL... THE GIRLS AND I THOUGHT THAT YOU WERE GOING TO SING?
NO. I WASN'T ABLE TO DO THAT.
WELL, THAT JEM IS INCREDIBLE. QUITE A FIND. CONGRATULATIONS TO YOU ALL.
THANK YOU, MS. BAILEY.
BEFORE YOU GO, COULD I ASK YOU A FAVOR?
OF COURSE.
WE'RE IN A BIT OF A PICKLE. THE FUNDRAISER BENEFIT ON SATURDAY, IT'S WHERE WE GET MOST OF THE FUNDS TO RUN STARLIGHT COMMUNITY CENTER FOR THE ENTIRE YEAR.
AND WELL, THE CELEBRITY M.C., OUR PRIMARY ENTERTAINMENT, REALLY, HAS HAD TO CANCEL.

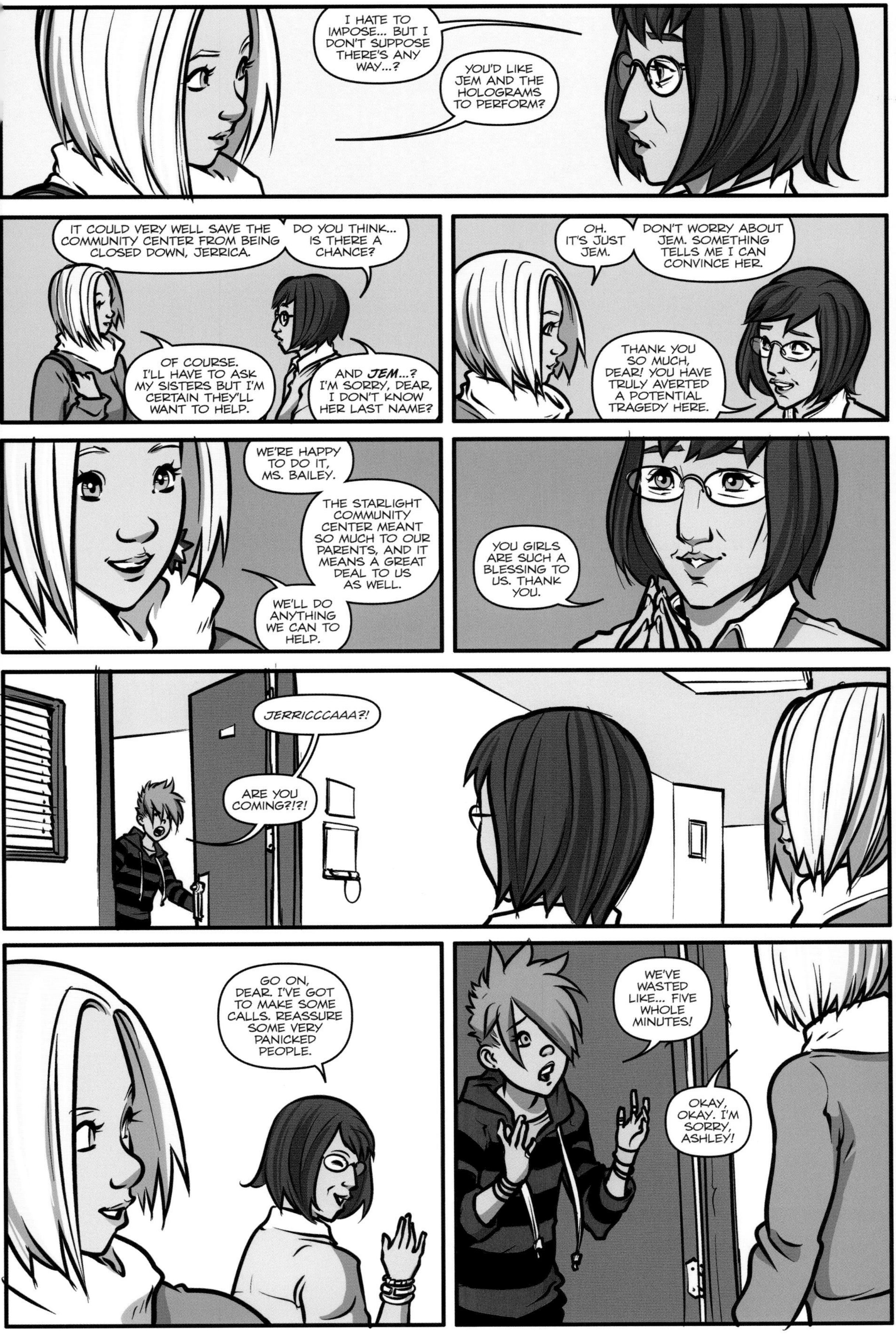
I HATE TO IMPOSE... BUT I DON'T SUPPOSE THERE'S ANY WAY...?
YOU'D LIKE JEM AND THE HOLOGRAMS TO PERFORM?
IT COULD VERY WELL SAVE THE COMMUNITY CENTER FROM BEING CLOSED DOWN, JERRICA.
DO YOU THINK... IS THERE A CHANCE?
OF COURSE. I'LL HAVE TO ASK MY SISTERS BUT I'M CERTAIN THEY'LL WANT TO HELP.
AND JEM...? I'M SORRY, DEAR, I DON'T KNOW HER LAST NAME?
OH. IT'S JUST JEM.
DON'T WORRY ABOUT JEM. SOMETHING TELLS ME I CAN CONVINCE HER.
THANK YOU SO MUCH, DEAR! YOU HAVE TRULY AVERTED A POTENTIAL TRAGEDY HERE.
WE'RE HAPPY TO DO IT, MS. BAILEY.
THE STARLIGHT COMMUNITY CENTER MEANT SO MUCH TO OUR PARENTS, AND IT MEANS A GREAT DEAL TO US AS WELL.
WE'LL DO ANYTHING WE CAN TO HELP.
YOU GIRLS ARE SUCH A BLESSING TO US. THANK YOU.
JERRICCCAAA?!
ARE YOU COMING?!?!
GO ON, DEAR. I'VE GOT TO MAKE SOME CALLS. REASSURE SOME VERY PANICKED PEOPLE.
WE'VE WASTED LIKE... FIVE WHOLE MINUTES!
OKAY, OKAY. I'M SORRY, ASHLEY!

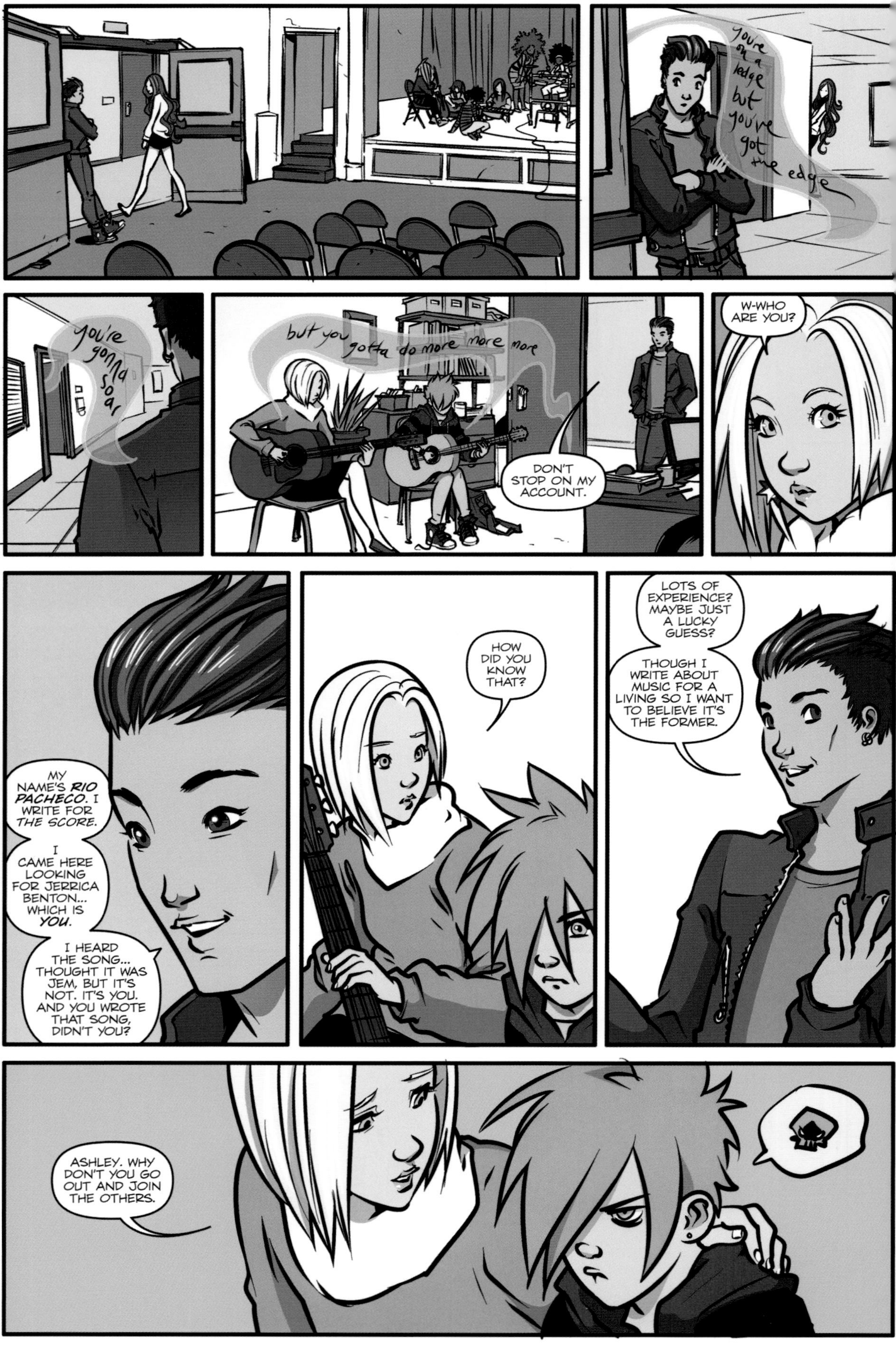
you're on a ledge but you've got the edge
you're gonna soar
but you gotta do more more more
DON'T STOP ON MY ACCOUNT.
W-WHO ARE YOU?
MY NAME'S RIO PACHECO. I WRITE FOR THE SCORE.
I CAME HERE LOOKING FOR JERRICA BENTON... WHICH IS YOU.
I HEARD THE SONG... THOUGHT IT WAS JEM, BUT IT'S NOT. IT'S YOU. AND YOU WROTE THAT SONG, DIDN'T YOU?
HOW DID YOU KNOW THAT?
LOTS OF EXPERIENCE? MAYBE JUST A LUCKY GUESS?
THOUGH I WRITE ABOUT MUSIC FOR A LIVING SO I WANT TO BELIEVE IT'S THE FORMER.
ASHLEY. WHY DON'T YOU GO OUT AND JOIN THE OTHERS.

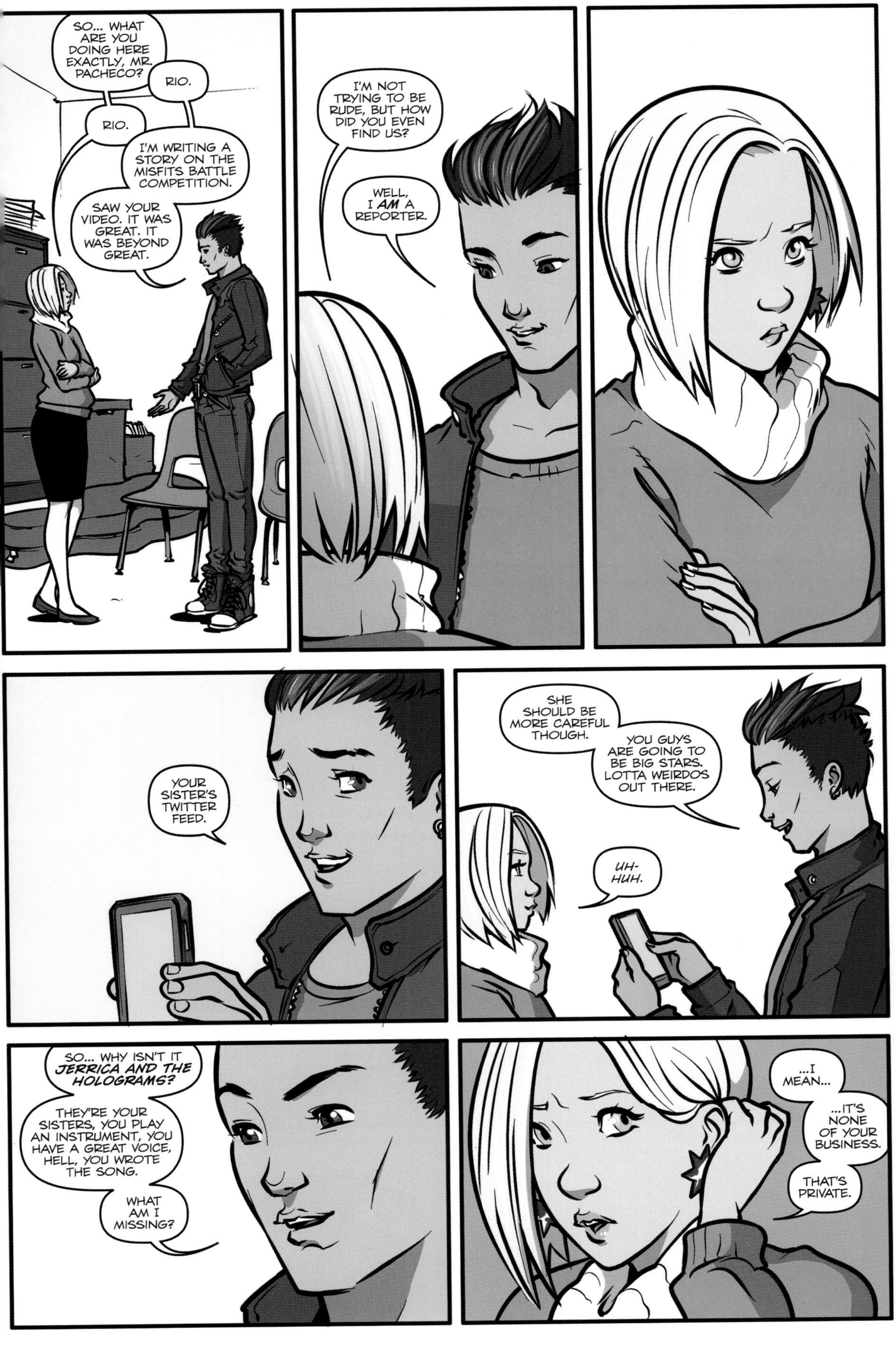
SO... WHAT ARE YOU DOING HERE EXACTLY, MR. PACHECO?
RIO.
RIO.
I'M WRITING A STORY ON THE MISFITS BATTLE COMPETITION.
SAW YOUR VIDEO. IT WAS GREAT. IT WAS BEYOND GREAT.
I'M NOT TRYING TO BE RUDE, BUT HOW DID YOU EVEN FIND US?
WELL, I *AM* A REPORTER.
YOUR SISTER'S TWITTER FEED.
SHE SHOULD BE MORE CAREFUL THOUGH.
YOU GUYS ARE GOING TO BE BIG STARS. LOTTA WEIRDOS OUT THERE.
UH-HUH.
SO... WHY ISN'T IT ***JERRICA AND THE HOLOGRAMS?***
THEY'RE YOUR SISTERS, YOU PLAY AN INSTRUMENT, YOU HAVE A GREAT VOICE, HELL, YOU WROTE THE SONG.
WHAT AM I MISSING?
...I MEAN...
...IT'S NONE OF YOUR BUSINESS.
THAT'S PRIVATE.

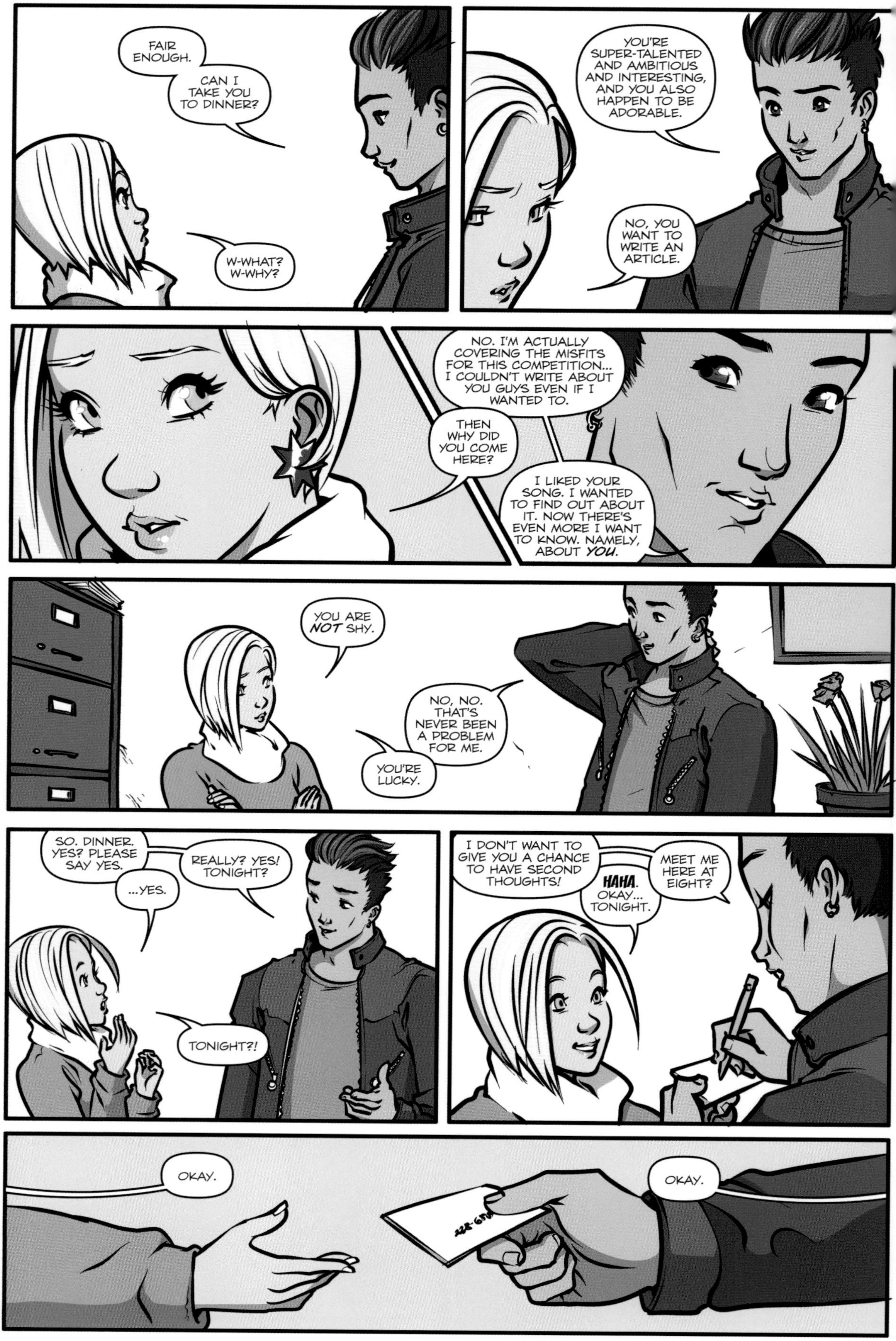
FAIR ENOUGH.
CAN I TAKE YOU TO DINNER?
W-WHAT? W-WHY?
YOU'RE SUPER-TALENTED AND AMBITIOUS AND INTERESTING, AND YOU ALSO HAPPEN TO BE ADORABLE.
NO, YOU WANT TO WRITE AN ARTICLE.
NO. I'M ACTUALLY COVERING THE MISFITS FOR THIS COMPETITION... I COULDN'T WRITE ABOUT YOU GUYS EVEN IF I WANTED TO.
THEN WHY DID YOU COME HERE?
I LIKED YOUR SONG. I WANTED TO FIND OUT ABOUT IT. NOW THERE'S EVEN MORE I WANT TO KNOW. NAMELY, ABOUT *YOU*.
YOU ARE *NOT* SHY.
NO, NO. THAT'S NEVER BEEN A PROBLEM FOR ME.
YOU'RE LUCKY.
SO. DINNER. YES? PLEASE SAY YES.
...YES.
REALLY? YES! TONIGHT?
TONIGHT?!
I DON'T WANT TO GIVE YOU A CHANCE TO HAVE SECOND THOUGHTS!
MEET ME HERE AT EIGHT?
HAHA. OKAY... TONIGHT.
OKAY.
OKAY.

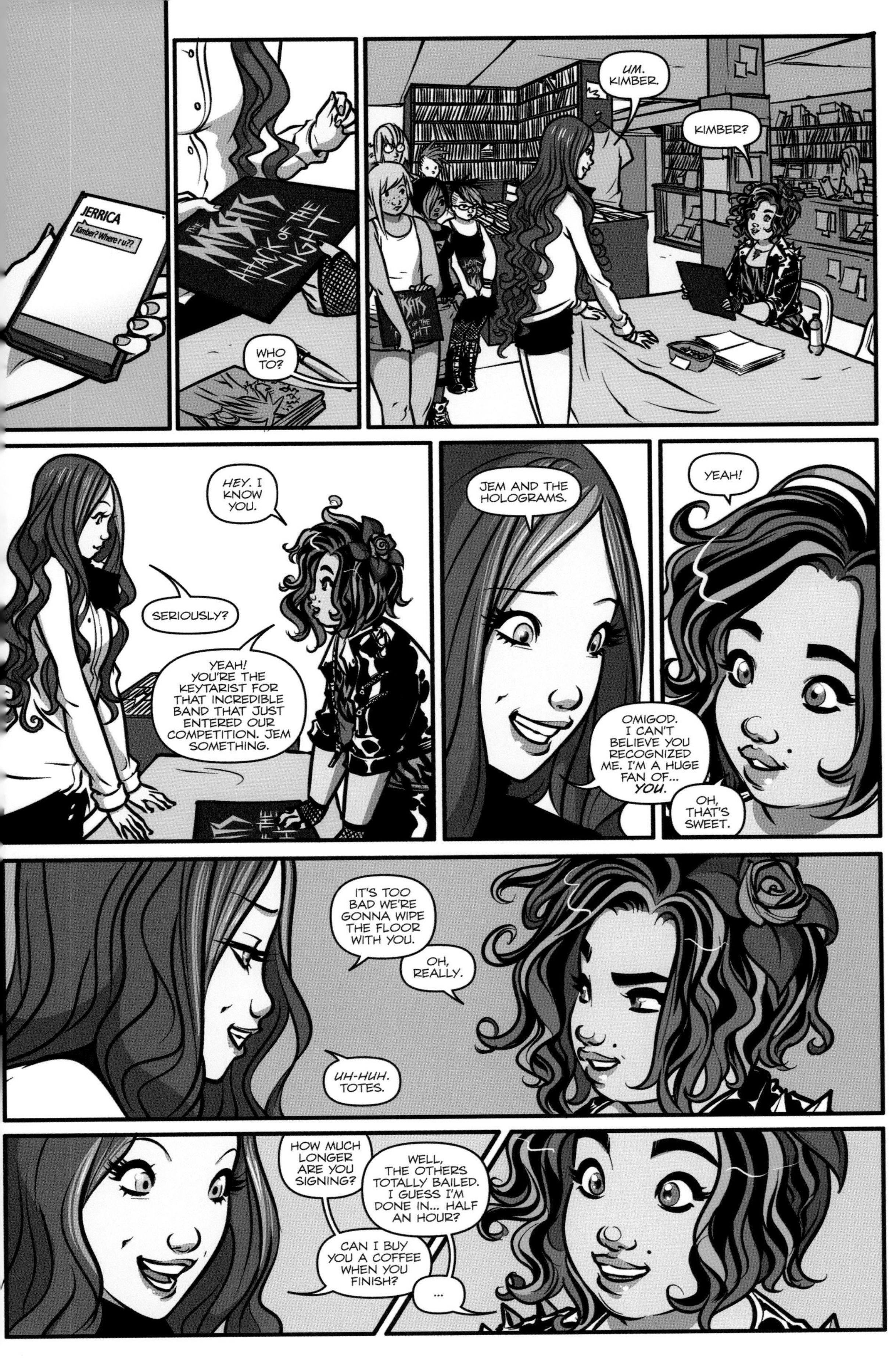

JERRICA
Kimber? Where r u??
WHO TO?
UM. KIMBER.
KIMBER?
HEY. I KNOW YOU.
SERIOUSLY?
YEAH! YOU'RE THE KEYTARIST FOR THAT INCREDIBLE BAND THAT JUST ENTERED OUR COMPETITION. JEM SOMETHING.
JEM AND THE HOLOGRAMS.
YEAH!
OMIGOD. I CAN'T BELIEVE YOU RECOGNIZED ME. I'M A HUGE FAN OF... YOU.
OH, THAT'S SWEET.
IT'S TOO BAD WE'RE GONNA WIPE THE FLOOR WITH YOU.
OH, REALLY.
UH-HUH. TOTES.
HOW MUCH LONGER ARE YOU SIGNING?
WELL, THE OTHERS TOTALLY BAILED. I GUESS I'M DONE IN... HALF AN HOUR?
CAN I BUY YOU A COFFEE WHEN YOU FINISH?
...

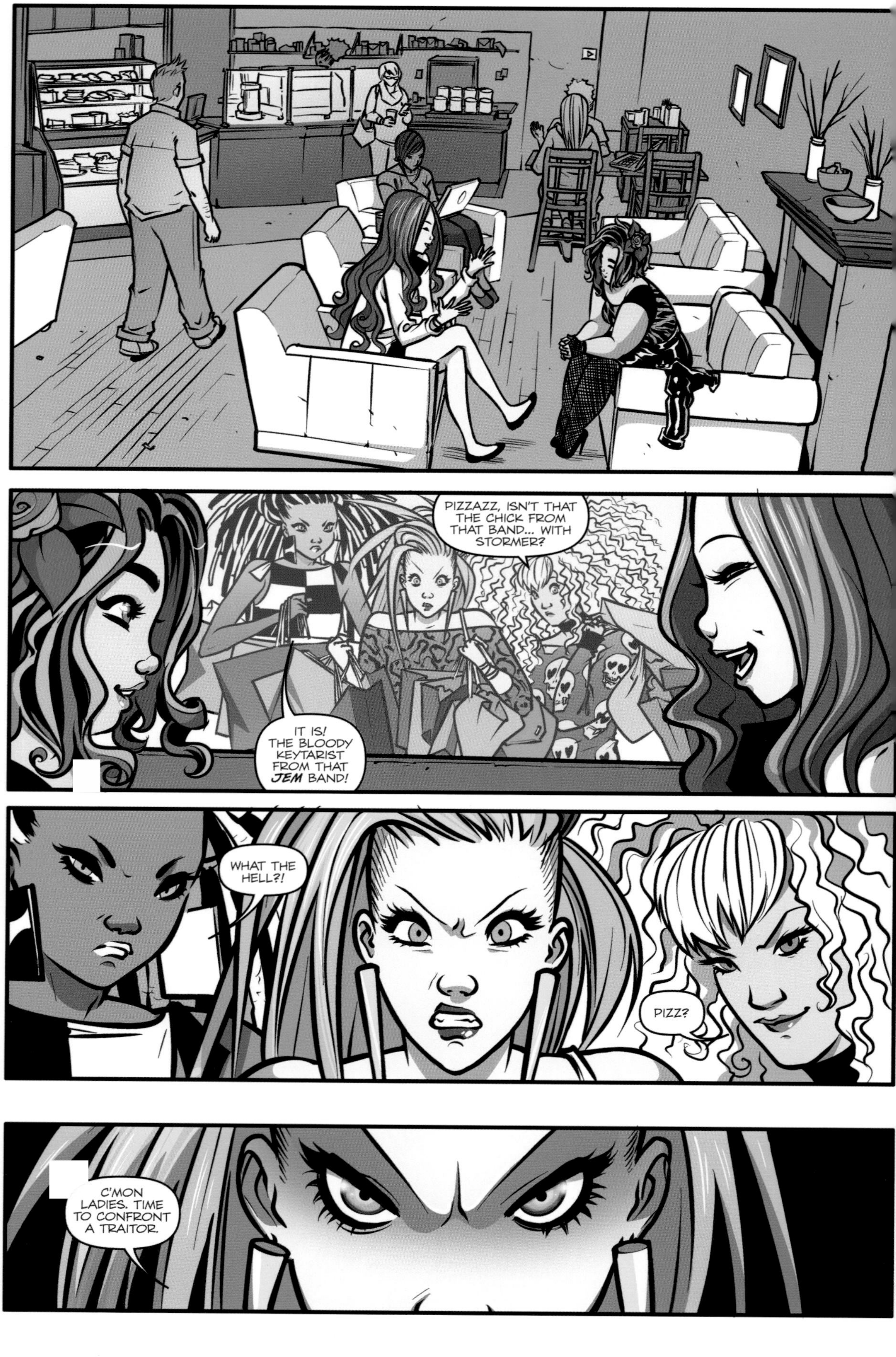
PIZZAZZ, ISN'T THAT THE CHICK FROM THAT BAND... WITH STORMER?
IT IS! THE BLOODY KEYTARIST FROM THAT JEM BAND!
WHAT THE HELL?!
PIZZ?
C'MON LADIES. TIME TO CONFRONT A TRAITOR.

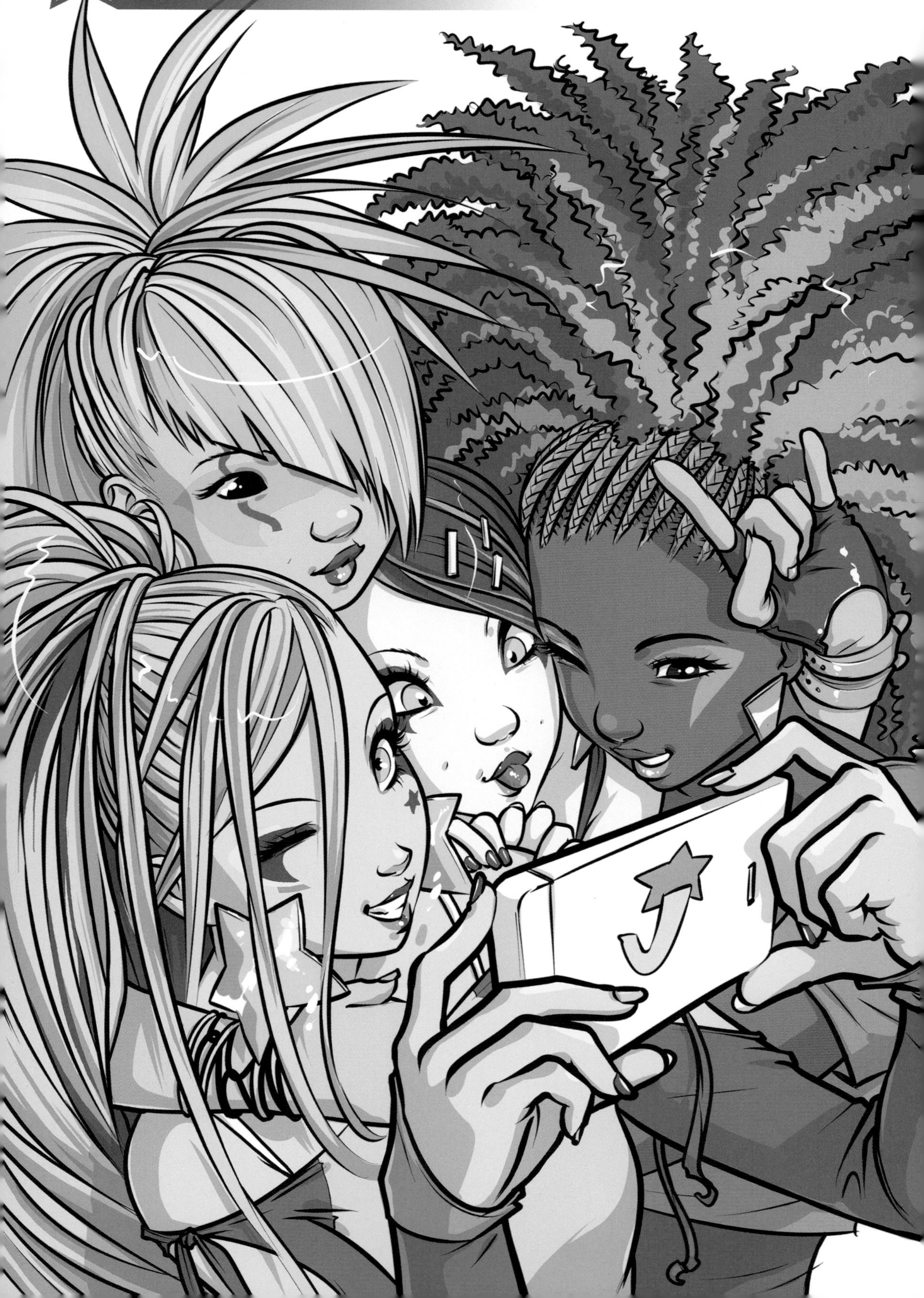

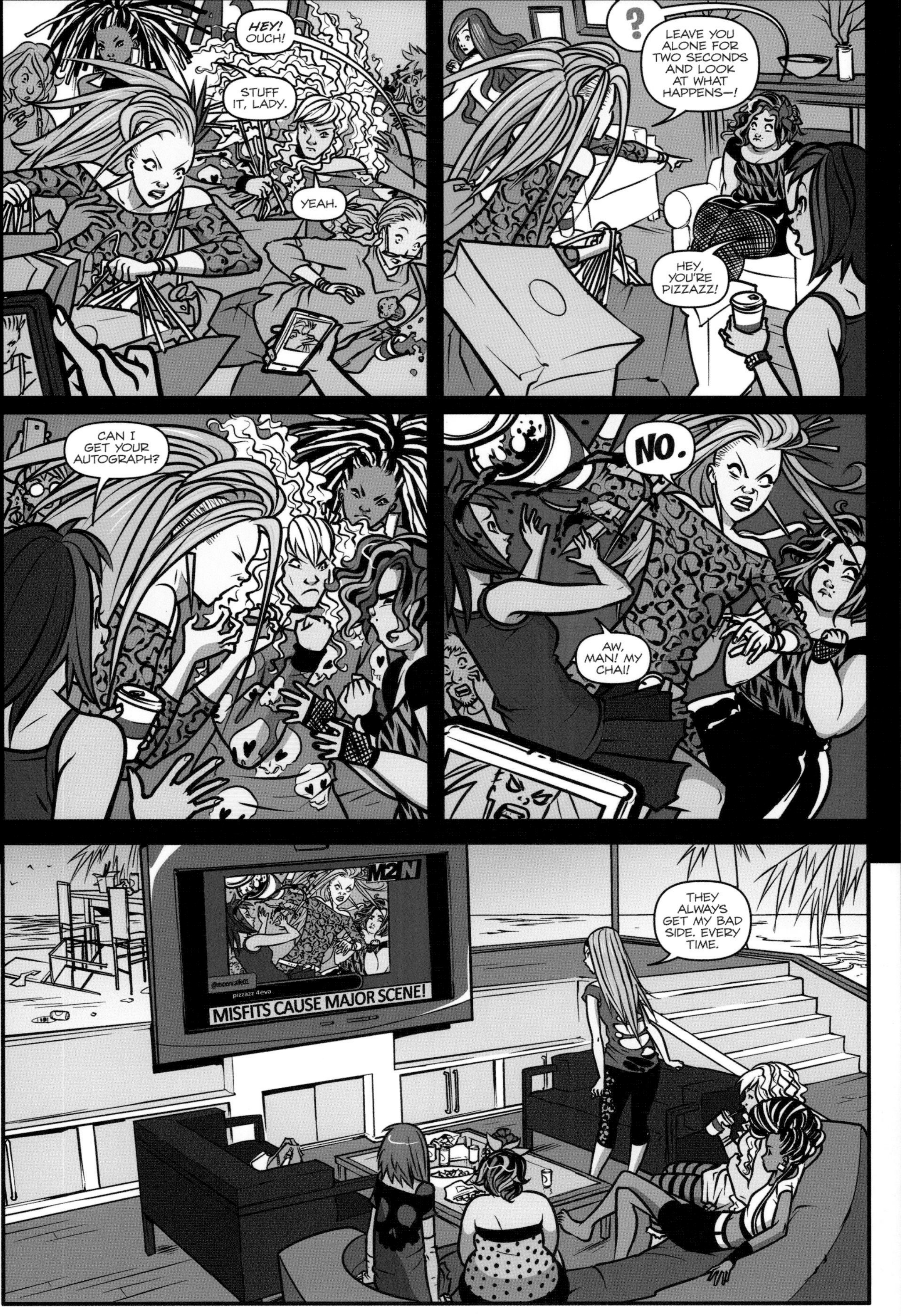
HEY! OUCH!
STUFF IT, LADY.
YEAH.
?
LEAVE YOU ALONE FOR TWO SECONDS AND LOOK AT WHAT HAPPENS—!
HEY, YOU'RE PIZZAZZ!
CAN I GET YOUR AUTOGRAPH?
NO.
AW, MAN! MY CHAI!
M2N
pizzazz 4eva
MISFITS CAUSE MAJOR SCENE!
THEY ALWAYS GET MY BAD SIDE. EVERY TIME.

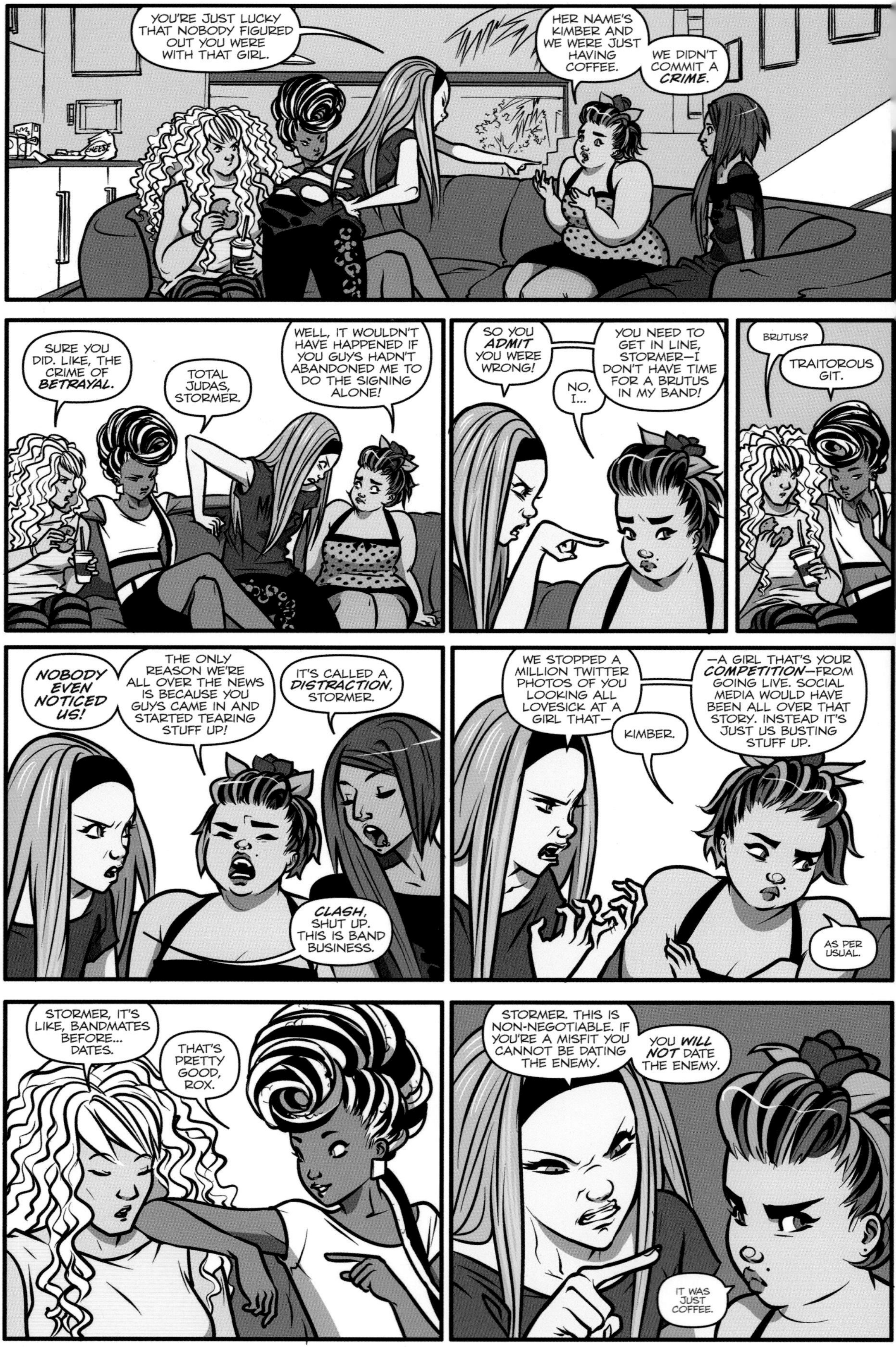

YOU'RE JUST LUCKY THAT NOBODY FIGURED OUT YOU WERE WITH THAT GIRL.
HER NAME'S KIMBER AND WE WERE JUST HAVING COFFEE.
WE DIDN'T COMMIT A *CRIME*.
SURE YOU DID. LIKE, THE CRIME OF *BETRAYAL*.
TOTAL JUDAS, STORMER.
WELL, IT WOULDN'T HAVE HAPPENED IF YOU GUYS HADN'T ABANDONED ME TO DO THE SIGNING ALONE!
SO YOU *ADMIT* YOU WERE WRONG!
YOU NEED TO GET IN LINE, STORMER—I DON'T HAVE TIME FOR A BRUTUS IN MY BAND!
NO, I...
BRUTUS?
TRAITOROUS GIT.
NOBODY EVEN NOTICED US!
THE ONLY REASON WE'RE ALL OVER THE NEWS IS BECAUSE YOU GUYS CAME IN AND STARTED TEARING STUFF UP!
IT'S CALLED A *DISTRACTION*, STORMER.
CLASH, SHUT UP. THIS IS BAND BUSINESS.
WE STOPPED A MILLION TWITTER PHOTOS OF YOU LOOKING ALL LOVESICK AT A GIRL THAT—
KIMBER.
—A GIRL THAT'S YOUR *COMPETITION*—FROM GOING LIVE. SOCIAL MEDIA WOULD HAVE BEEN ALL OVER THAT STORY. INSTEAD IT'S JUST US BUSTING STUFF UP.
AS PER USUAL.
STORMER, IT'S LIKE, BANDMATES BEFORE... DATES.
THAT'S PRETTY GOOD, ROX.
STORMER. THIS IS NON-NEGOTIABLE. IF YOU'RE A MISFIT YOU CANNOT BE DATING THE ENEMY.
YOU **WILL NOT** DATE THE ENEMY.
IT WAS JUST COFFEE.

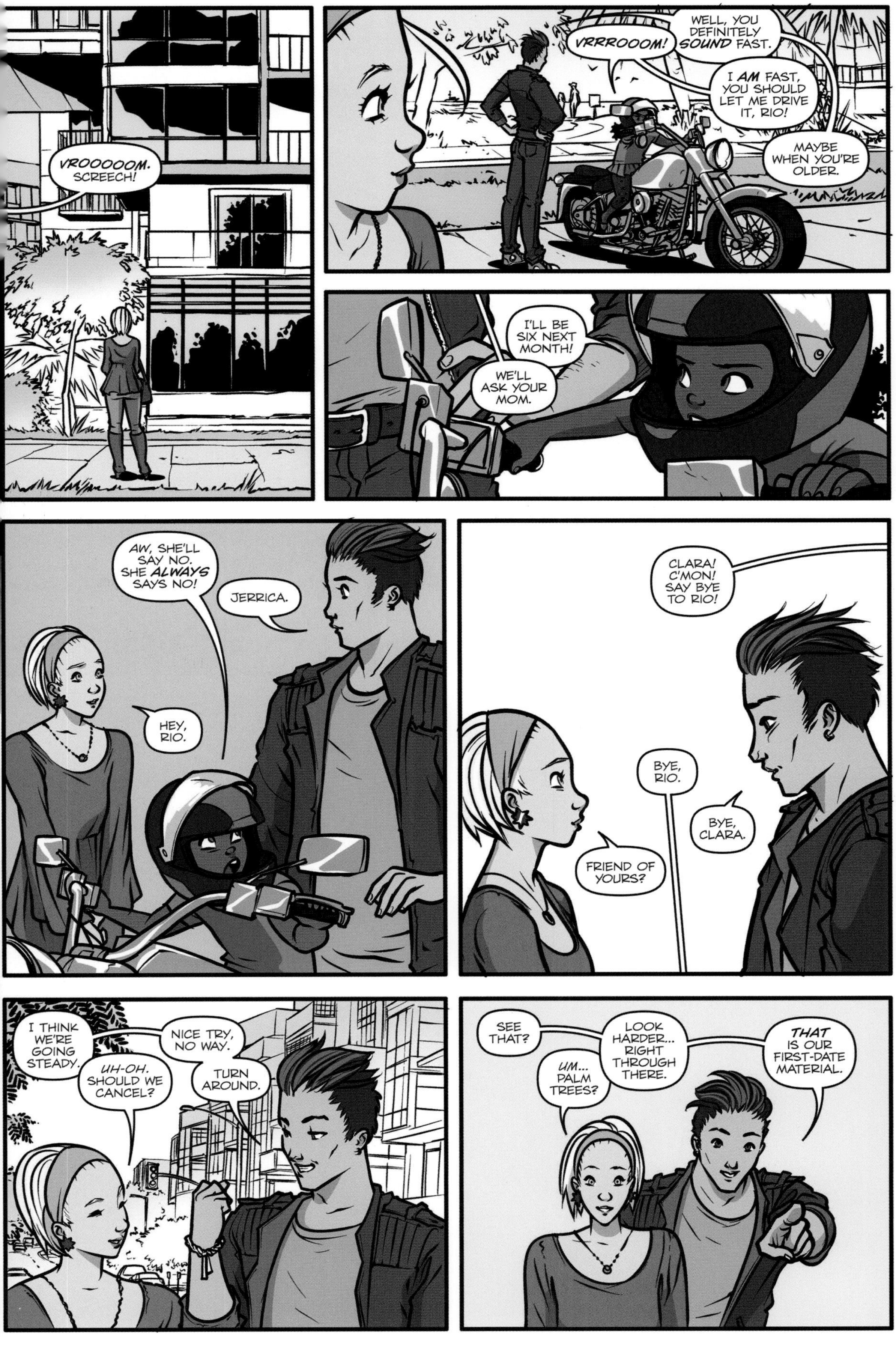
VROOOOOM. SCREECH!
VRRROOOM!
WELL, YOU DEFINITELY SOUND FAST.
I AM FAST, YOU SHOULD LET ME DRIVE IT, RIO!
MAYBE WHEN YOU'RE OLDER.
I'LL BE SIX NEXT MONTH!
WE'LL ASK YOUR MOM.
AW, SHE'LL SAY NO. SHE ALWAYS SAYS NO!
JERRICA.
HEY, RIO.
CLARA! C'MON! SAY BYE TO RIO!
BYE, RIO.
BYE, CLARA.
FRIEND OF YOURS?
I THINK WE'RE GOING STEADY.
UH-OH. SHOULD WE CANCEL?
NICE TRY, NO WAY.
TURN AROUND.
SEE THAT?
UM... PALM TREES?
LOOK HARDER... RIGHT THROUGH THERE.
THAT IS OUR FIRST-DATE MATERIAL.

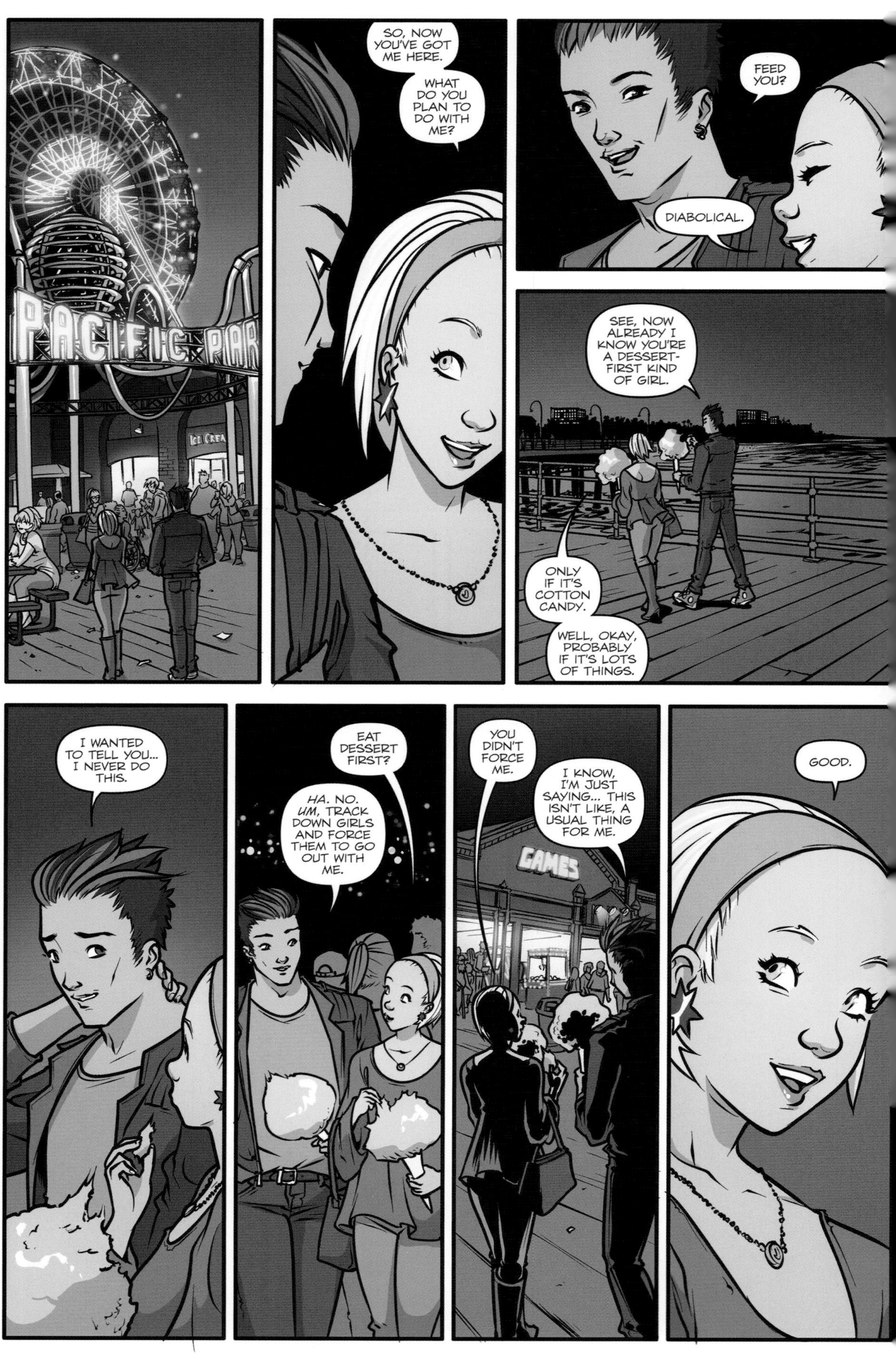
PACIFIC PAR
ICE CREA
SO, NOW YOU'VE GOT ME HERE.
WHAT DO YOU PLAN TO DO WITH ME?
FEED YOU?
DIABOLICAL.
SEE, NOW ALREADY I KNOW YOU'RE A DESSERT-FIRST KIND OF GIRL.
ONLY IF IT'S COTTON CANDY.
WELL, OKAY, PROBABLY IF IT'S LOTS OF THINGS.
I WANTED TO TELL YOU... I NEVER DO THIS.
EAT DESSERT FIRST?
HA. NO. UM, TRACK DOWN GIRLS AND FORCE THEM TO GO OUT WITH ME.
YOU DIDN'T FORCE ME.
GAMES
I KNOW, I'M JUST SAYING... THIS ISN'T LIKE, A USUAL THING FOR ME.
GOOD.

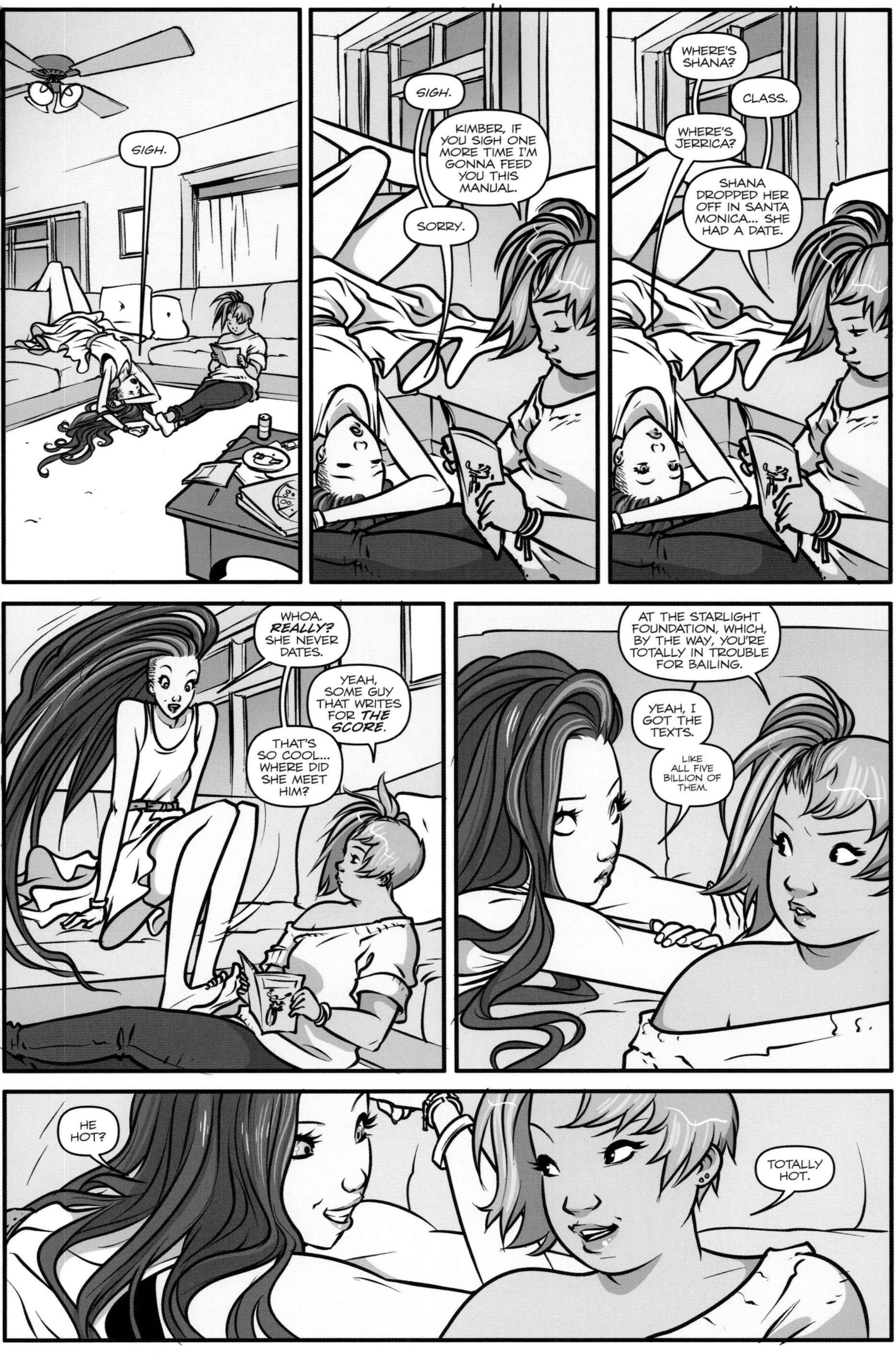
SIGH.
SIGH.
KIMBER, IF YOU SIGH ONE MORE TIME I'M GONNA FEED YOU THIS MANUAL.
SORRY.
WHERE'S SHANA?
CLASS.
WHERE'S JERRICA?
SHANA DROPPED HER OFF IN SANTA MONICA... SHE HAD A DATE.
WHOA. *REALLY?* SHE NEVER DATES.
YEAH, SOME GUY THAT WRITES FOR *THE SCORE*.
THAT'S SO COOL... WHERE DID SHE MEET HIM?
AT THE STARLIGHT FOUNDATION, WHICH, BY THE WAY, YOU'RE TOTALLY IN TROUBLE FOR BAILING.
YEAH, I GOT THE TEXTS.
LIKE ALL FIVE BILLION OF THEM.
HE HOT?
TOTALLY HOT.

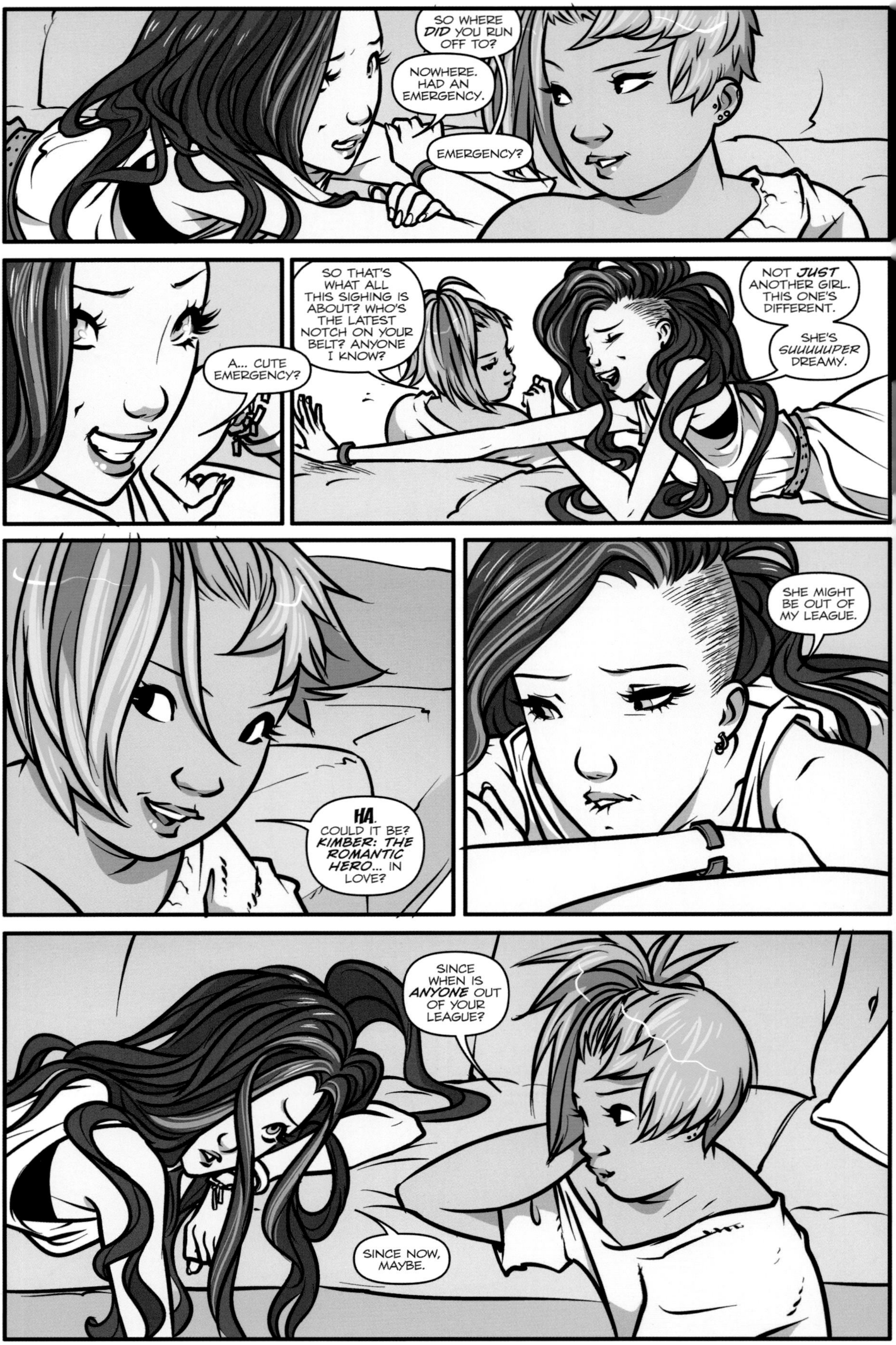
SO WHERE DID YOU RUN OFF TO?
NOWHERE. HAD AN EMERGENCY.
EMERGENCY?
A... CUTE EMERGENCY?
SO THAT'S WHAT ALL THIS SIGHING IS ABOUT? WHO'S THE LATEST NOTCH ON YOUR BELT? ANYONE I KNOW?
NOT JUST ANOTHER GIRL. THIS ONE'S DIFFERENT.
SHE'S SUUUUUPER DREAMY.
HA. COULD IT BE? KIMBER: THE ROMANTIC HERO... IN LOVE?
SHE MIGHT BE OUT OF MY LEAGUE.
SINCE WHEN IS ANYONE OUT OF YOUR LEAGUE?
SINCE NOW, MAYBE.

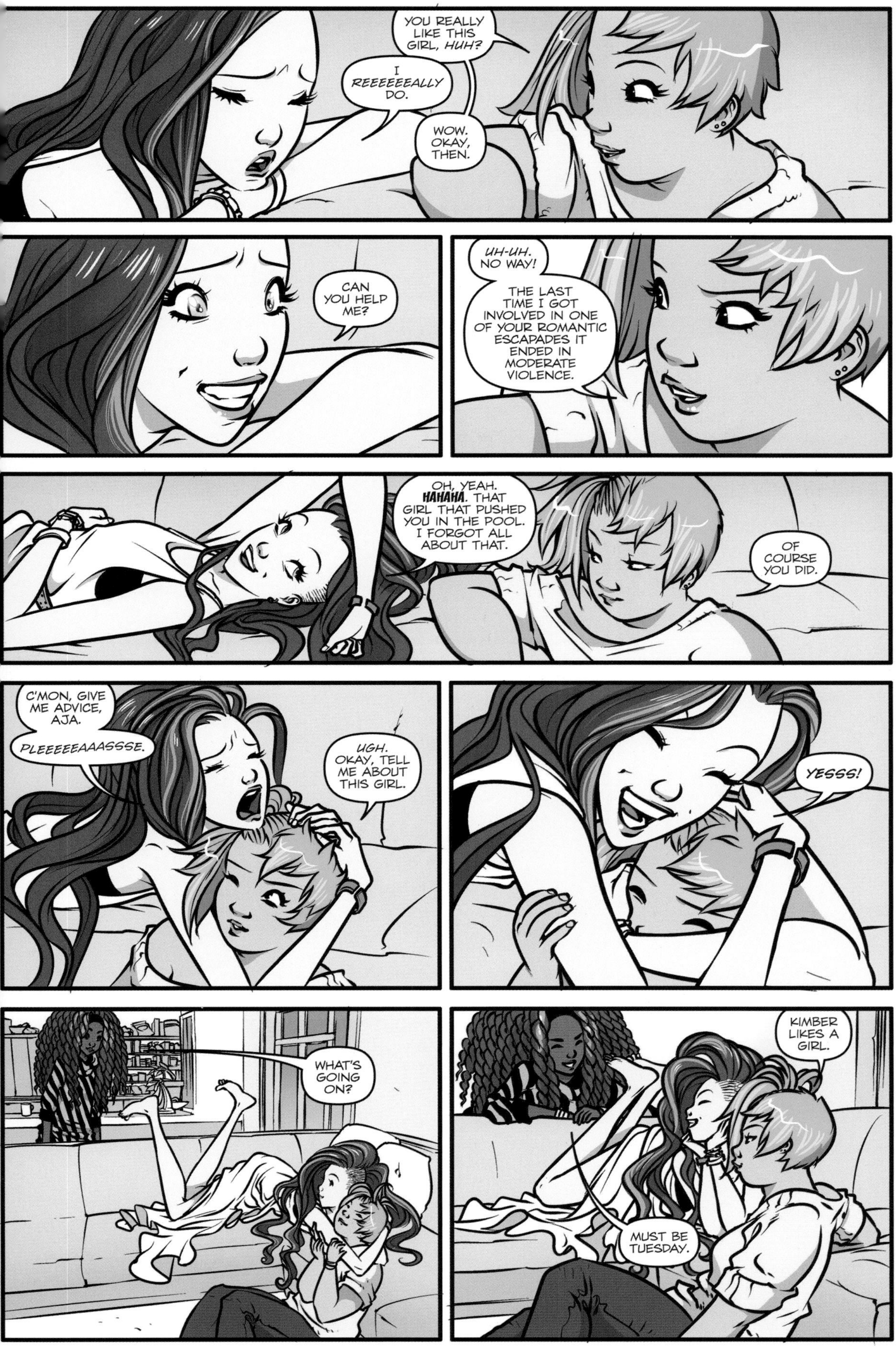
YOU REALLY LIKE THIS GIRL, HUH?
I REEEEEEALLY DO.
WOW. OKAY, THEN.
CAN YOU HELP ME?
UH-UH. NO WAY!
THE LAST TIME I GOT INVOLVED IN ONE OF YOUR ROMANTIC ESCAPADES IT ENDED IN MODERATE VIOLENCE.
OH, YEAH. HAHAHA. THAT GIRL THAT PUSHED YOU IN THE POOL. I FORGOT ALL ABOUT THAT.
OF COURSE YOU DID.
C'MON, GIVE ME ADVICE, AJA.
PLEEEEEAAASSSE.
UGH. OKAY, TELL ME ABOUT THIS GIRL.
YESSS!
WHAT'S GOING ON?
KIMBER LIKES A GIRL.
MUST BE TUESDAY.

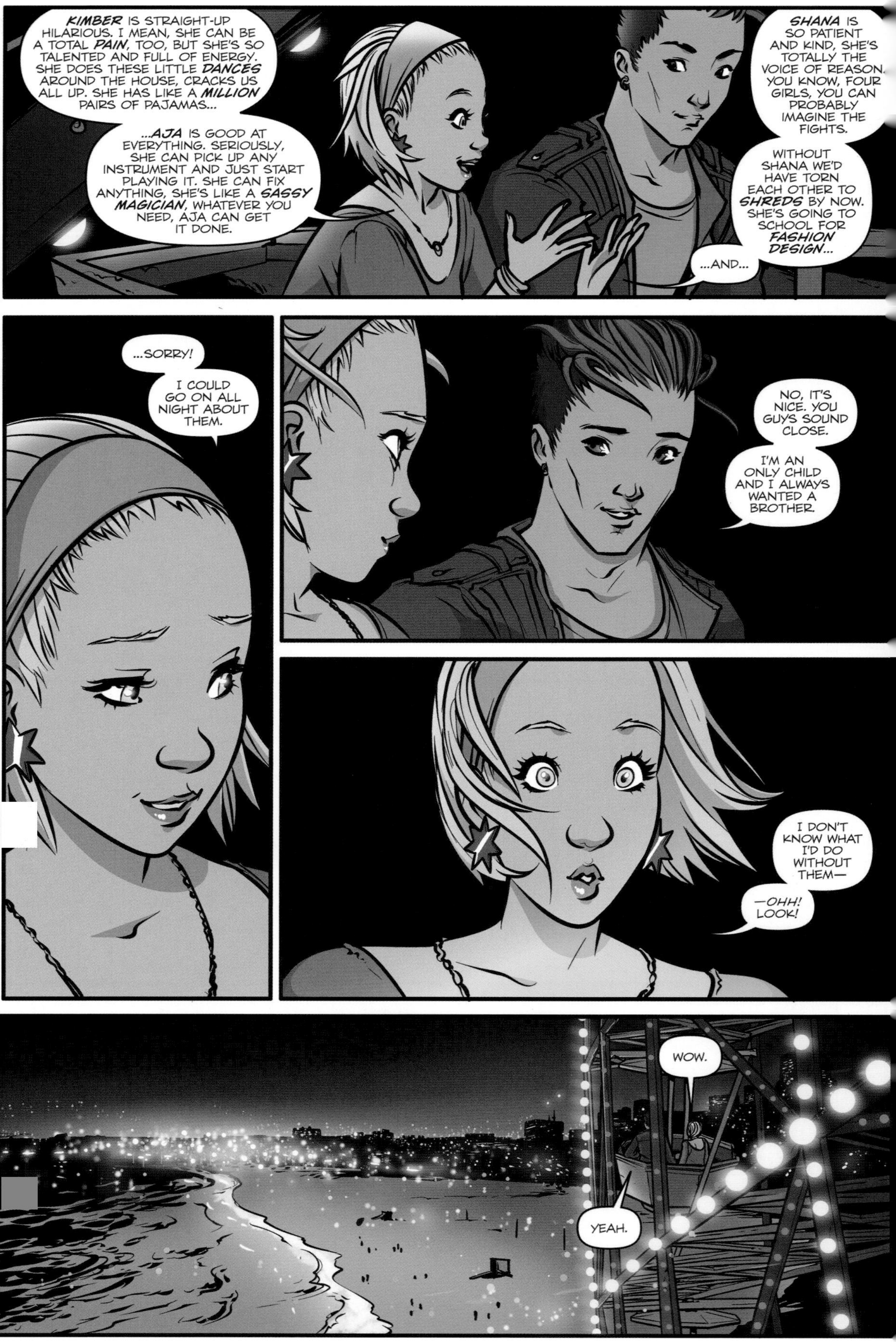
KIMBER IS STRAIGHT-UP HILARIOUS. I MEAN, SHE CAN BE A TOTAL PAIN, TOO, BUT SHE'S SO TALENTED AND FULL OF ENERGY. SHE DOES THESE LITTLE DANCES AROUND THE HOUSE, CRACKS US ALL UP. SHE HAS LIKE A MILLION PAIRS OF PAJAMAS...
...AJA IS GOOD AT EVERYTHING. SERIOUSLY, SHE CAN PICK UP ANY INSTRUMENT AND JUST START PLAYING IT. SHE CAN FIX ANYTHING, SHE'S LIKE A SASSY MAGICIAN, WHATEVER YOU NEED, AJA CAN GET IT DONE.
SHANA IS SO PATIENT AND KIND, SHE'S TOTALLY THE VOICE OF REASON. YOU KNOW, FOUR GIRLS, YOU CAN PROBABLY IMAGINE THE FIGHTS.
WITHOUT SHANA WE'D HAVE TORN EACH OTHER TO SHREDS BY NOW. SHE'S GOING TO SCHOOL FOR FASHION DESIGN...
...AND...
...SORRY!
I COULD GO ON ALL NIGHT ABOUT THEM.
NO, IT'S NICE. YOU GUYS SOUND CLOSE.
I'M AN ONLY CHILD AND I ALWAYS WANTED A BROTHER.
I DON'T KNOW WHAT I'D DO WITHOUT THEM—
—OHH! LOOK!
WOW.
YEAH.

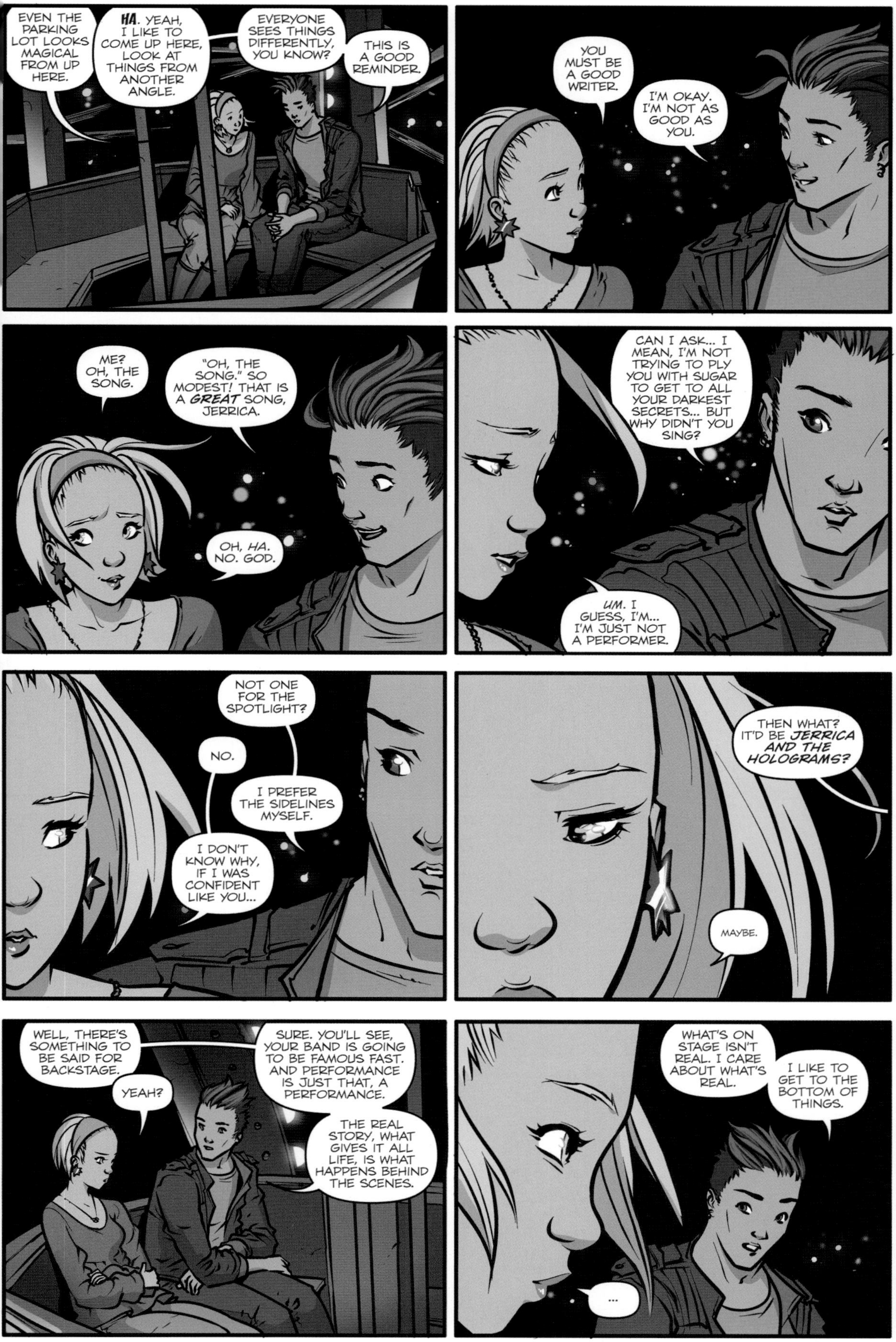
EVEN THE PARKING LOT LOOKS MAGICAL FROM UP HERE.
HA. YEAH, I LIKE TO COME UP HERE, LOOK AT THINGS FROM ANOTHER ANGLE.
EVERYONE SEES THINGS DIFFERENTLY, YOU KNOW?
THIS IS A GOOD REMINDER.
YOU MUST BE A GOOD WRITER.
I'M OKAY. I'M NOT AS GOOD AS YOU.
ME? OH, THE SONG.
"OH, THE SONG." SO MODEST! THAT IS A GREAT SONG, JERRICA.
OH, HA. NO. GOD.
CAN I ASK... I MEAN, I'M NOT TRYING TO PLY YOU WITH SUGAR TO GET TO ALL YOUR DARKEST SECRETS... BUT WHY DIDN'T YOU SING?
UM. I GUESS, I'M... I'M JUST NOT A PERFORMER.
NOT ONE FOR THE SPOTLIGHT?
NO.
I PREFER THE SIDELINES MYSELF.
I DON'T KNOW WHY, IF I WAS CONFIDENT LIKE YOU...
THEN WHAT? IT'D BE JERRICA AND THE HOLOGRAMS?
MAYBE.
WELL, THERE'S SOMETHING TO BE SAID FOR BACKSTAGE.
YEAH?
SURE. YOU'LL SEE, YOUR BAND IS GOING TO BE FAMOUS FAST. AND PERFORMANCE IS JUST THAT, A PERFORMANCE.
THE REAL STORY, WHAT GIVES IT ALL LIFE, IS WHAT HAPPENS BEHIND THE SCENES.
WHAT'S ON STAGE ISN'T REAL. I CARE ABOUT WHAT'S REAL.
I LIKE TO GET TO THE BOTTOM OF THINGS.
...

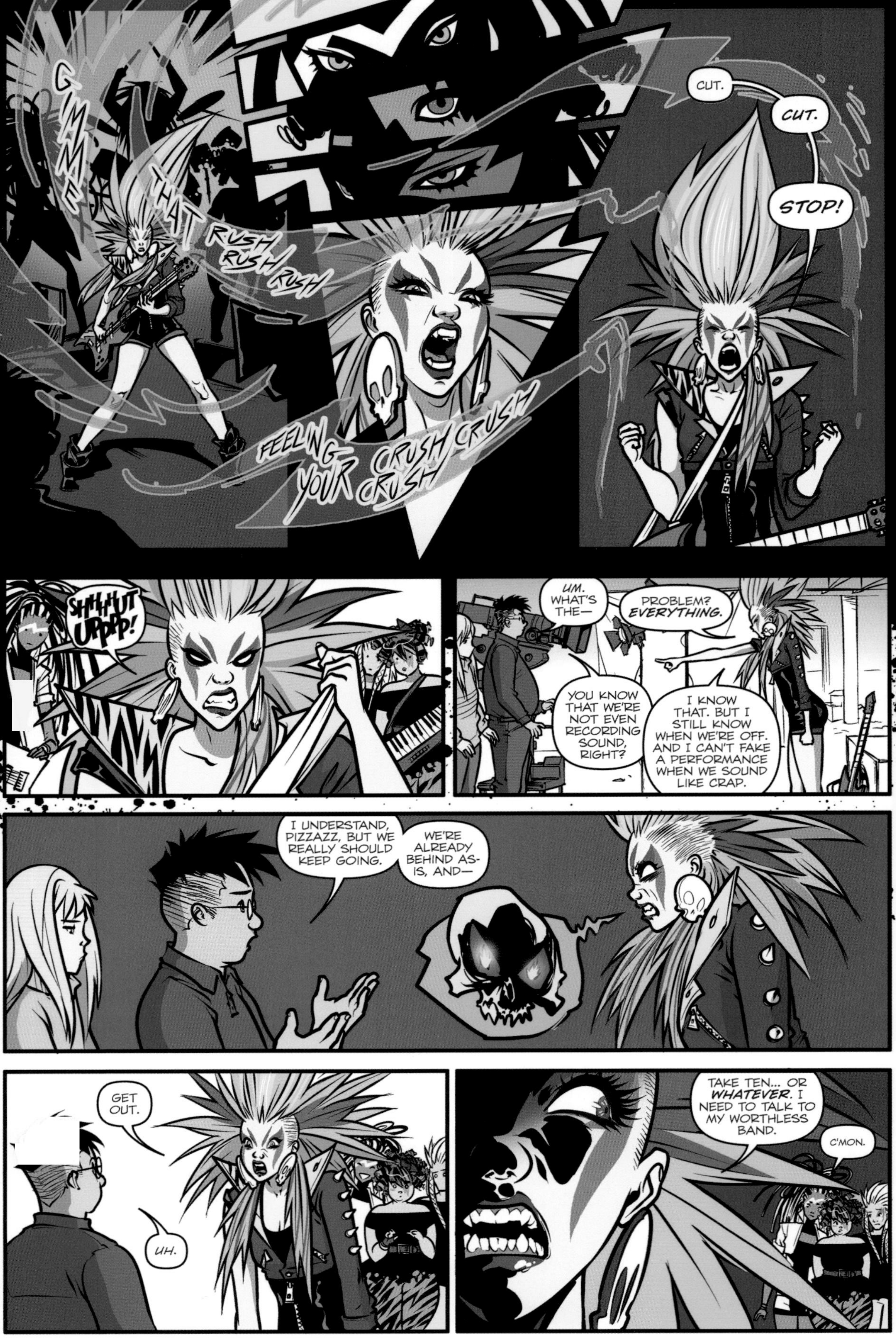
GIMME THAT RUSH RUSH RUSH
FEELING YOUR CRUSH CRUSH CRUSH CRUSH
CUT.
CUT.
STOP!
SHHHUT UPPP!
UM. WHAT'S THE—
PROBLEM? EVERYTHING.
YOU KNOW THAT WE'RE NOT EVEN RECORDING SOUND, RIGHT?
I KNOW THAT. BUT I STILL KNOW WHEN WE'RE OFF. AND I CAN'T FAKE A PERFORMANCE WHEN WE SOUND LIKE CRAP.
I UNDERSTAND, PIZZAZZ, BUT WE REALLY SHOULD KEEP GOING.
WE'RE ALREADY BEHIND AS-IS, AND—
GET OUT.
UH.
TAKE TEN... OR WHATEVER. I NEED TO TALK TO MY WORTHLESS BAND.
C'MON.

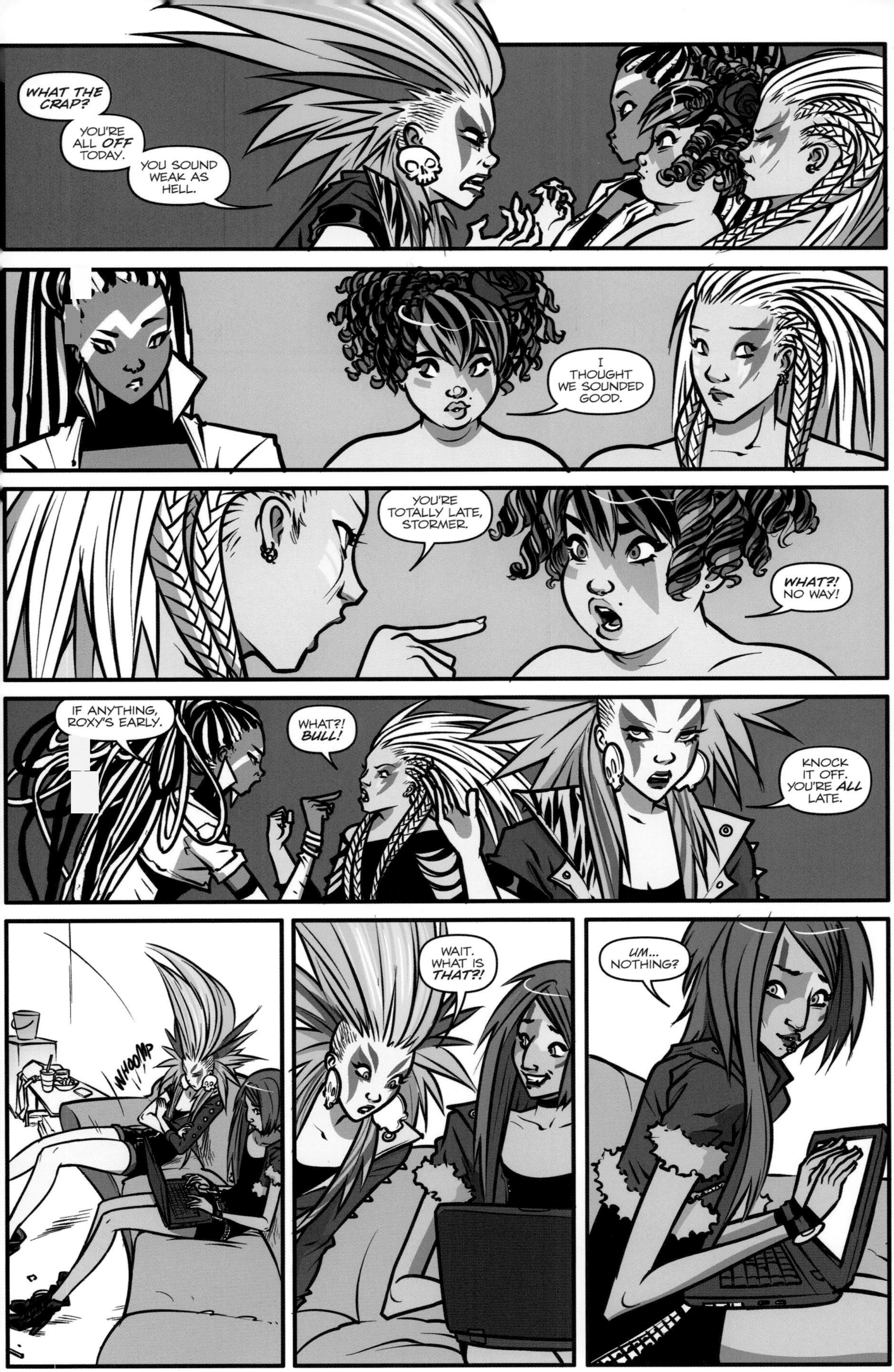

WHAT THE CRAP?
YOU'RE ALL OFF TODAY.
YOU SOUND WEAK AS HELL.
I THOUGHT WE SOUNDED GOOD.
YOU'RE TOTALLY LATE, STORMER.
WHAT?! NO WAY!
IF ANYTHING, ROXY'S EARLY.
WHAT?! BULL!
KNOCK IT OFF. YOU'RE ALL LATE.
WHOOMP
WAIT. WHAT IS THAT?!
UM... NOTHING?

WHAT THE HELL IS *THAT*?!

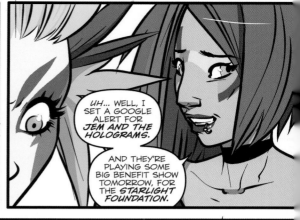

UH... WELL, I SET A GOOGLE ALERT FOR *JEM AND THE HOLOGRAMS*.

AND THEY'RE PLAYING SOME BIG BENEFIT SHOW TOMORROW, FOR THE *STARLIGHT FOUNDATION*.

WHAT.

UM... BENEFIT SHOW...?

WHO'S DOING A SHOW?

READ IT.

JEM AND THE HOLOGRAMS, A LOCAL BAND HOT OFF THEIR DEBUT VIDEO ENTERED IN THE VIRAL SENSATION *MISFITS VS! BAND* COMPETITION, WILL BE FILLING IN FOR EMCEE TINA PALER AT THE STARLIGHT FOUNDATION'S ANNUAL *FUNDRAISER BENEFIT*.

THE FRESHMAN BAND IS SEEING RECORD NUMBERS OF *VIEWS* AND *VOTES* IN THE ONLINE COMPETITION THAT HAVE ALL BUT GUARANTEED THEM A WIN FOR THE COMPETITION.

JEM AND THE HOLOGRAMS ARE A *LAST-MINUTE* ADDITION TO THE PROGRAM AFTER CELEBRITY-EMCEE TINA PALER WAS—

—FORCED TO PULL OUT OF THE STAR-STUDDED CELEBRITY ATTENDED EVENT. MEMBERS OF—

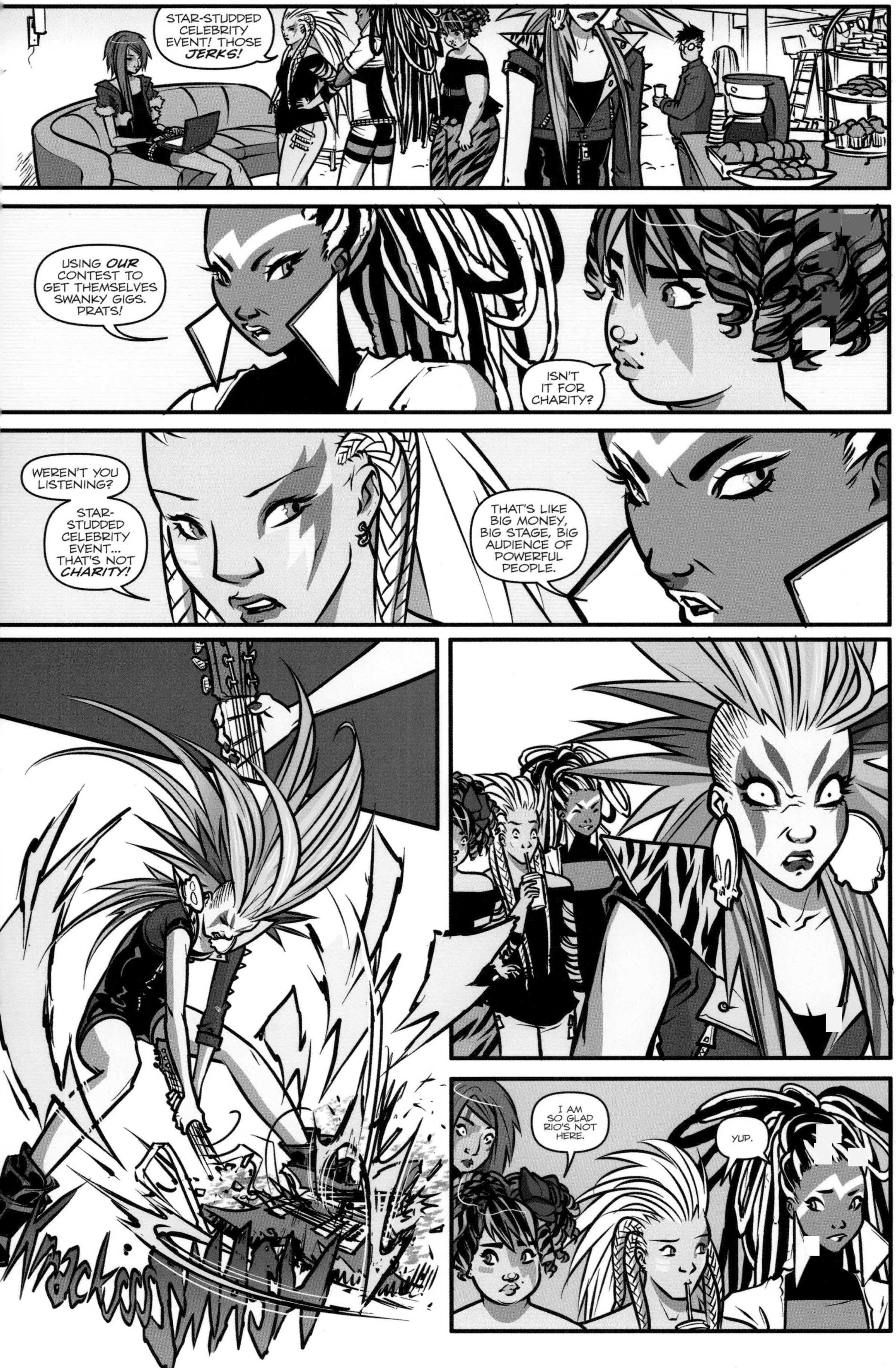
STAR-STUDDED CELEBRITY EVENT! THOSE JERKS!
USING OUR CONTEST TO GET THEMSELVES SWANKY GIGS. PRATS!
ISN'T IT FOR CHARITY?
WEREN'T YOU LISTENING?
STAR-STUDDED CELEBRITY EVENT... THAT'S NOT CHARITY!
THAT'S LIKE BIG MONEY, BIG STAGE, BIG AUDIENCE OF POWERFUL PEOPLE.
I AM SO GLAD RIO'S NOT HERE.
YUP.

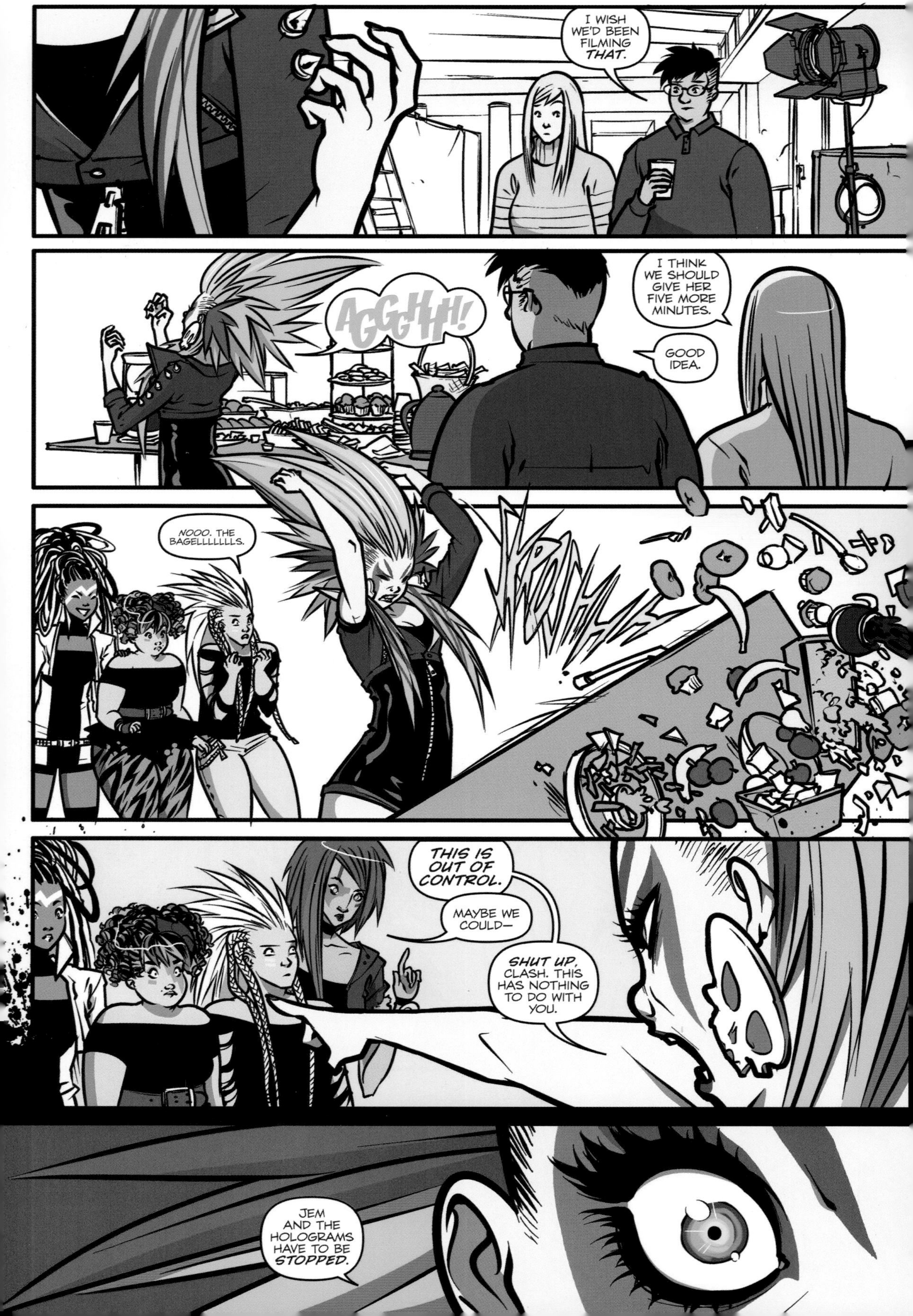
I WISH WE'D BEEN FILMING *THAT*.
AGGGHHH!
I THINK WE SHOULD GIVE HER FIVE MORE MINUTES.
GOOD IDEA.
NOOO. THE BAGELLLLLLLS.
THIS IS OUT OF CONTROL.
MAYBE WE COULD—
SHUT UP, CLASH. THIS HAS NOTHING TO DO WITH YOU.
JEM AND THE HOLOGRAMS HAVE TO BE *STOPPED*.

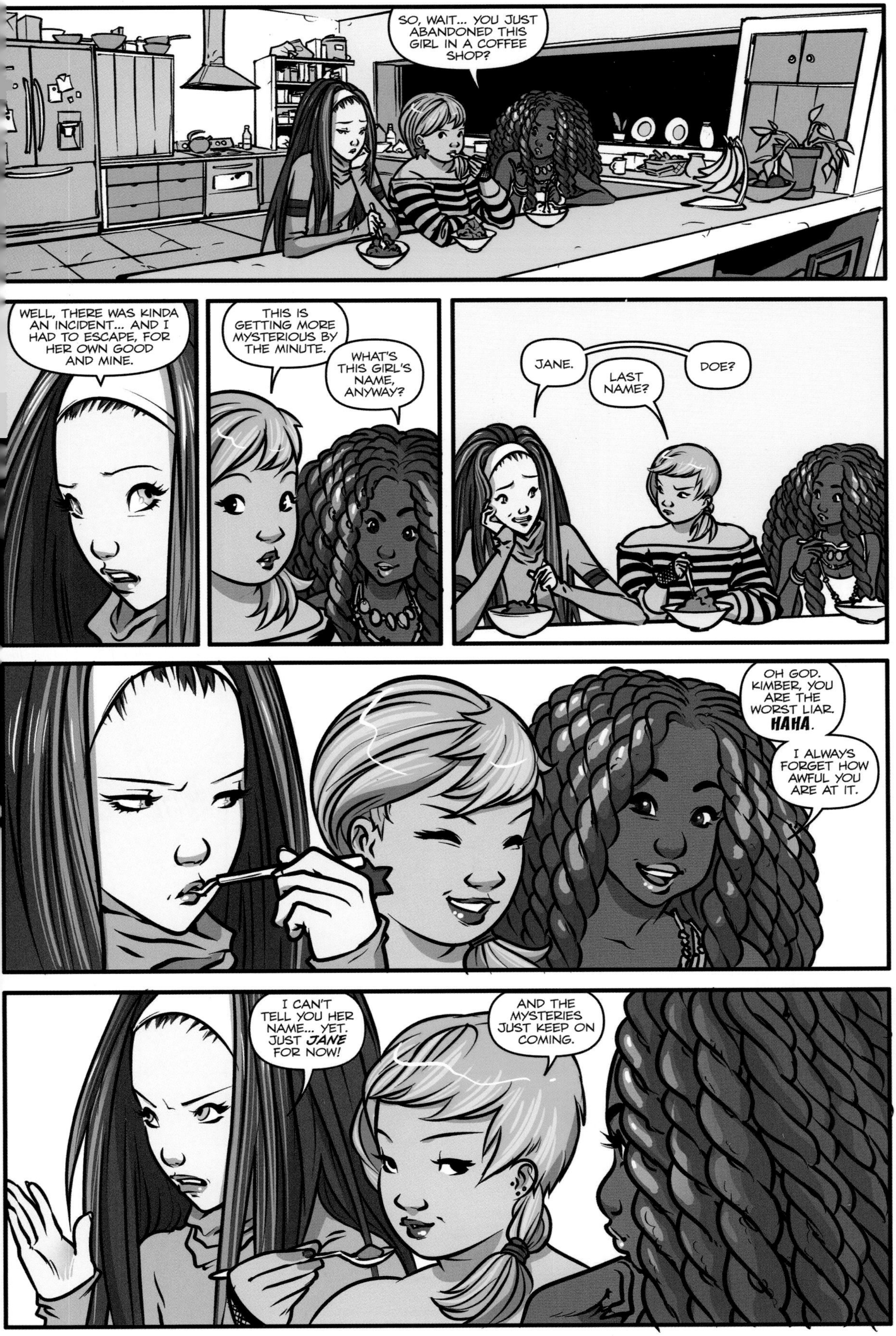
SO, WAIT... YOU JUST ABANDONED THIS GIRL IN A COFFEE SHOP?
WELL, THERE WAS KINDA AN INCIDENT... AND I HAD TO ESCAPE, FOR HER OWN GOOD AND MINE.
THIS IS GETTING MORE MYSTERIOUS BY THE MINUTE.
WHAT'S THIS GIRL'S NAME, ANYWAY?
JANE.
LAST NAME?
DOE?
OH GOD. KIMBER, YOU ARE THE WORST LIAR. HAHA.
I ALWAYS FORGET HOW AWFUL YOU ARE AT IT.
I CAN'T TELL YOU HER NAME... YET. JUST JANE FOR NOW!
AND THE MYSTERIES JUST KEEP ON COMING.

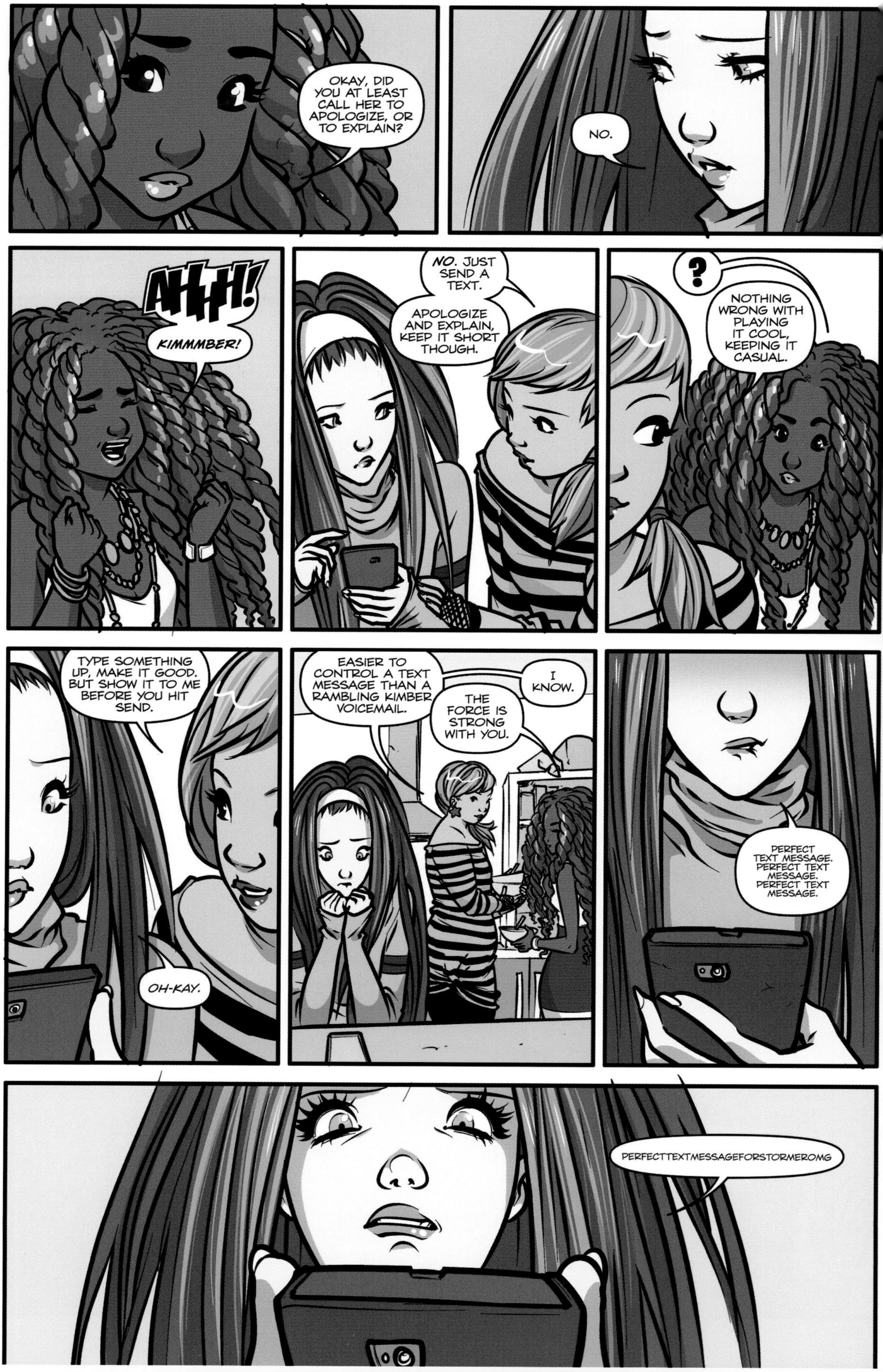
OKAY, DID YOU AT LEAST CALL HER TO APOLOGIZE, OR TO EXPLAIN?
NO.
AHHH!
KIMMMBER!
NO. JUST SEND A TEXT.
APOLOGIZE AND EXPLAIN, KEEP IT SHORT THOUGH.
?
NOTHING WRONG WITH PLAYING IT COOL, KEEPING IT CASUAL.
TYPE SOMETHING UP, MAKE IT GOOD. BUT SHOW IT TO ME BEFORE YOU HIT SEND.
OH-KAY.
EASIER TO CONTROL A TEXT MESSAGE THAN A RAMBLING KIMBER VOICEMAIL.
I KNOW.
THE FORCE IS STRONG WITH YOU.
PERFECT TEXT MESSAGE. PERFECT TEXT MESSAGE. PERFECT TEXT MESSAGE.
PERFECTTEXTMESSAGEFORSTORMEROMG

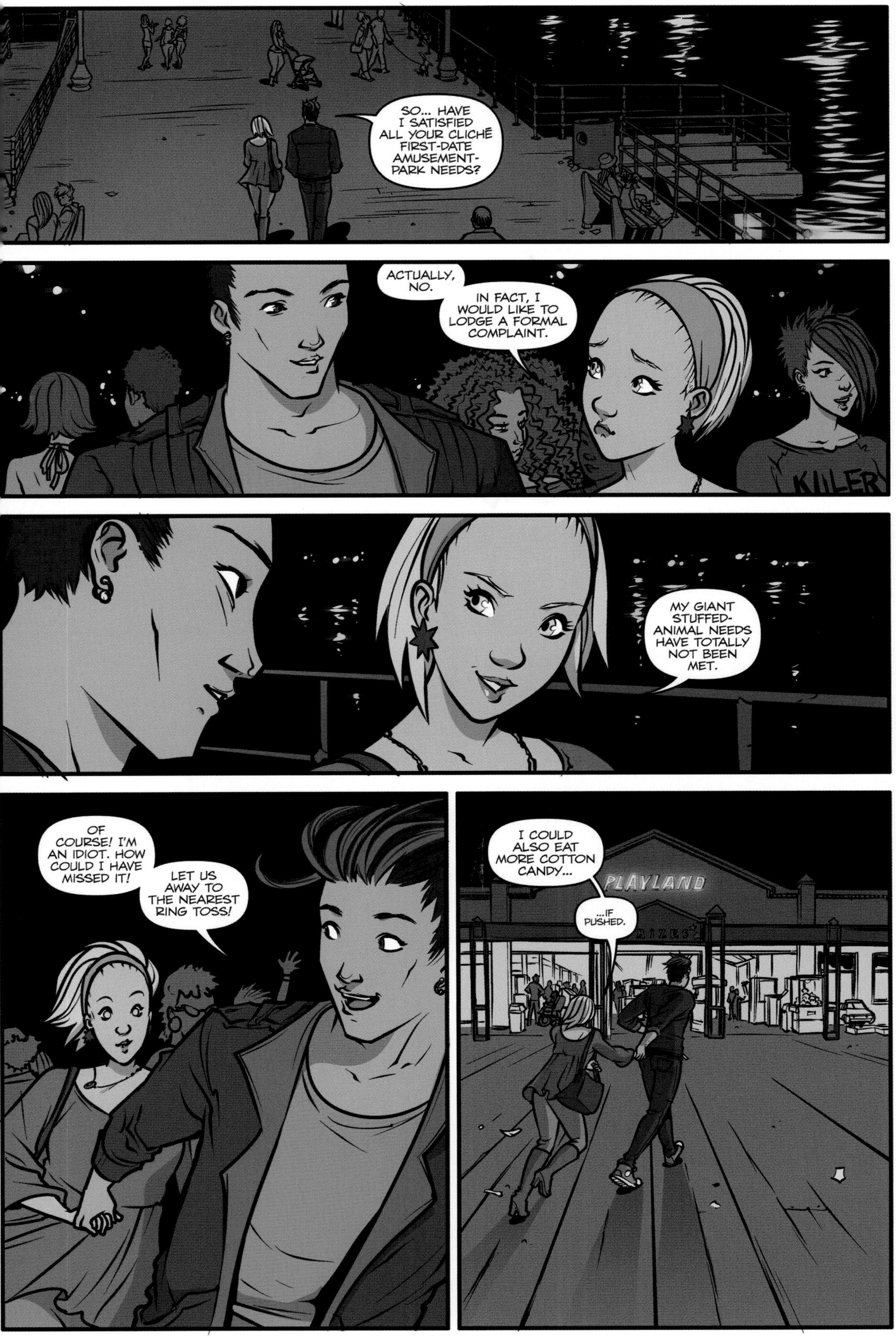
SO... HAVE I SATISFIED ALL YOUR CLICHÉ FIRST-DATE AMUSEMENT-PARK NEEDS?
ACTUALLY, NO.
IN FACT, I WOULD LIKE TO LODGE A FORMAL COMPLAINT.
KILLER
MY GIANT STUFFED-ANIMAL NEEDS HAVE TOTALLY NOT BEEN MET.
OF COURSE! I'M AN IDIOT. HOW COULD I HAVE MISSED IT!
LET US AWAY TO THE NEAREST RING TOSS!
I COULD ALSO EAT MORE COTTON CANDY...
PLAYLAND
...IF PUSHED.

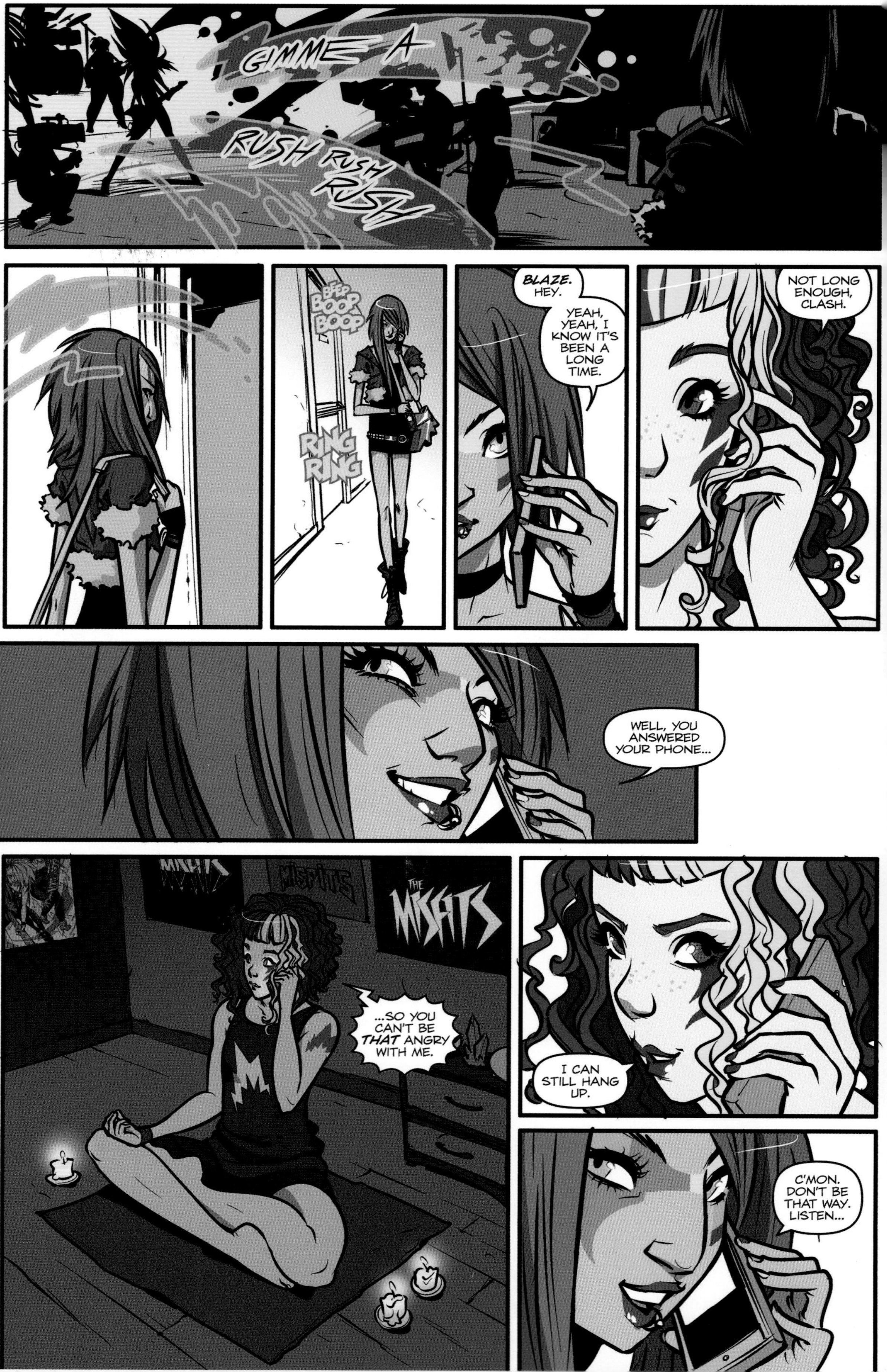
GIMME A
RUSH RUSH RUSH
BEEP BOOP BOOP
RING RING
BLAZE. HEY.
YEAH, YEAH, I KNOW IT'S BEEN A LONG TIME.
NOT LONG ENOUGH, CLASH.
WELL, YOU ANSWERED YOUR PHONE...
MISFITS
MISFITS
THE MISFITS
...SO YOU CAN'T BE THAT ANGRY WITH ME.
I CAN STILL HANG UP.
C'MON. DON'T BE THAT WAY. LISTEN...

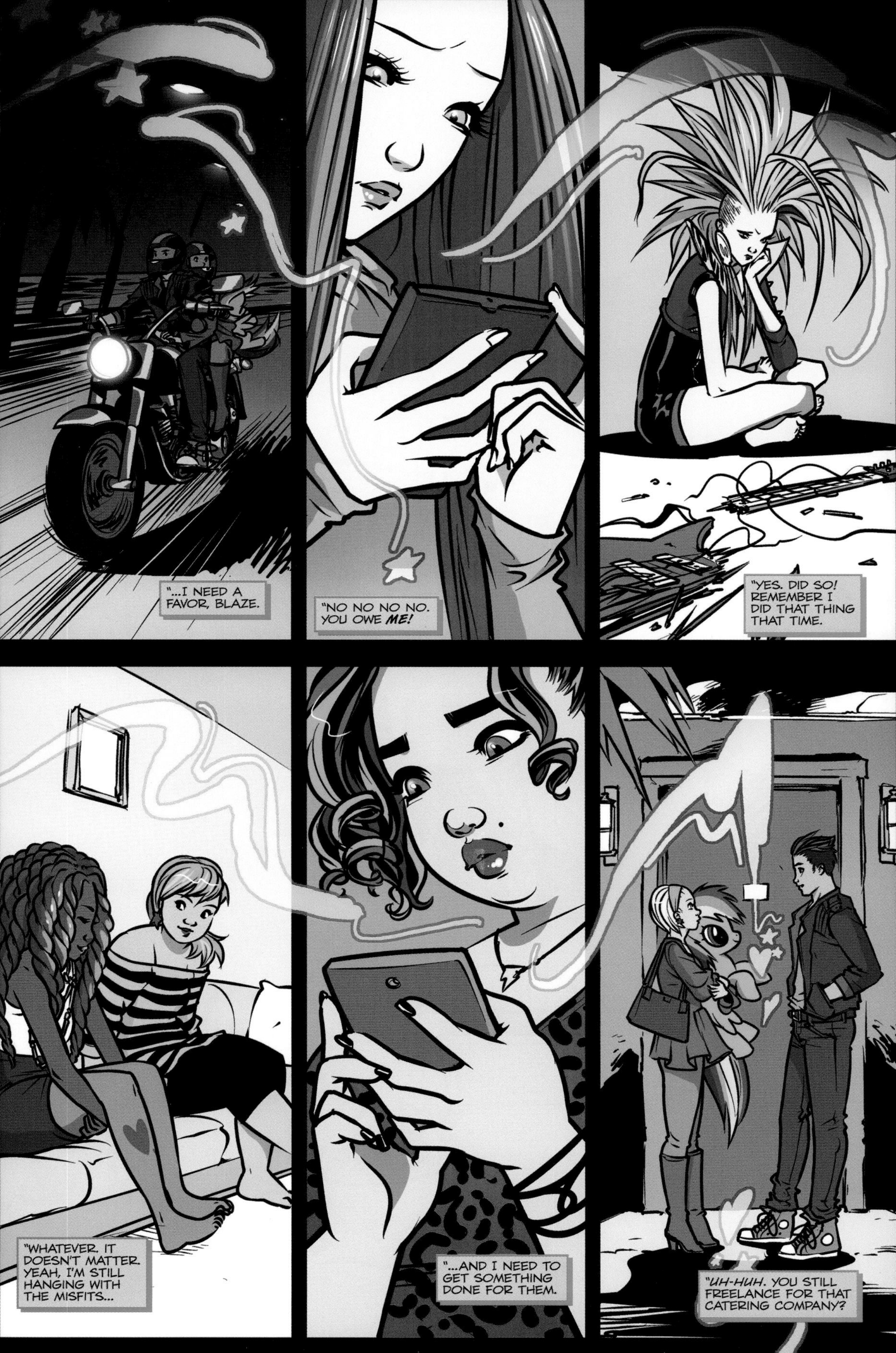
"...I NEED A FAVOR, BLAZE.
"NO NO NO NO. YOU OWE ME!
"YES. DID SO! REMEMBER I DID THAT THING THAT TIME.
"WHATEVER. IT DOESN'T MATTER. YEAH, I'M STILL HANGING WITH THE MISFITS...
"...AND I NEED TO GET SOMETHING DONE FOR THEM.
"UH-HUH. YOU STILL FREELANCE FOR THAT CATERING COMPANY?

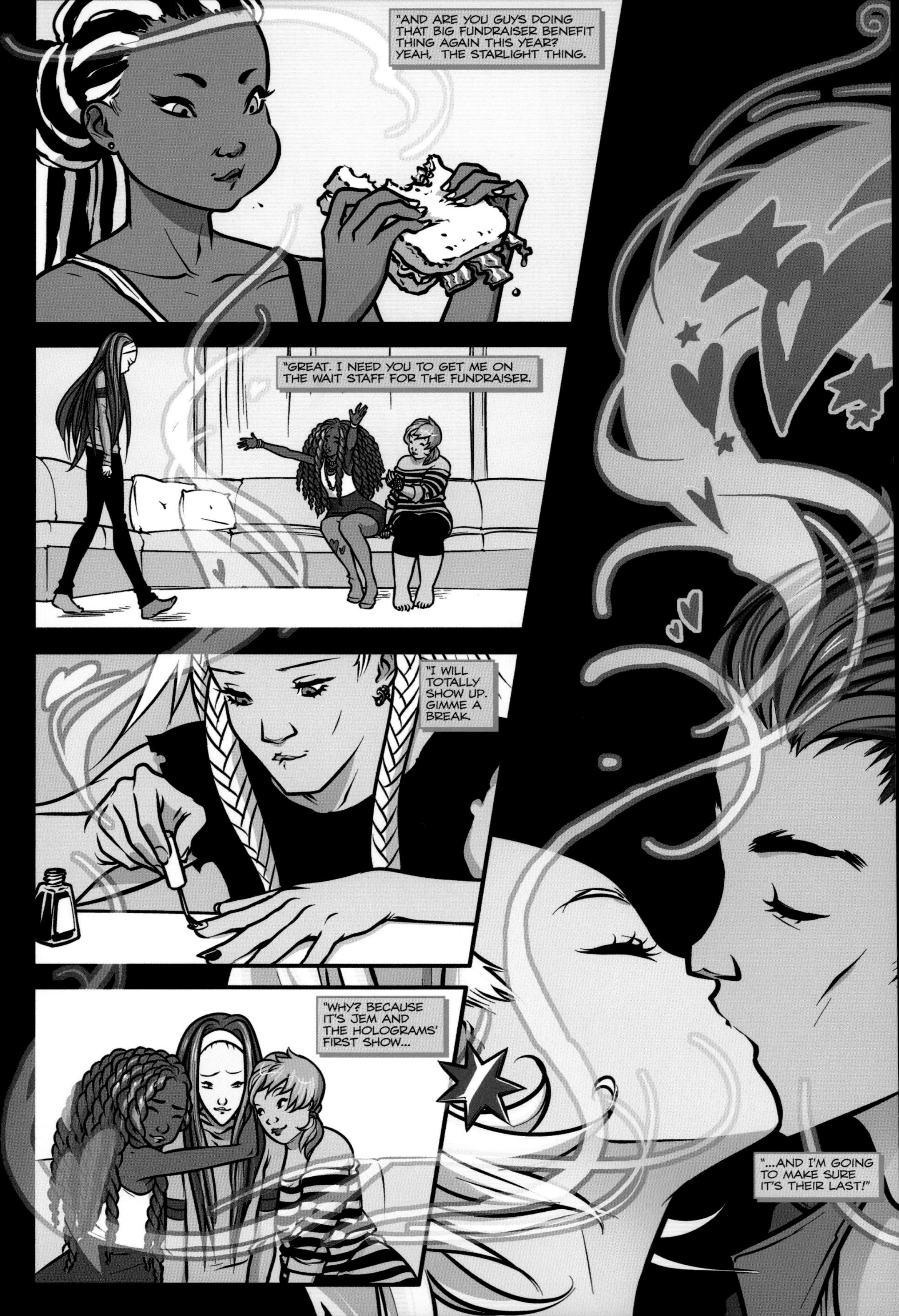
"AND ARE YOU GUYS DOING THAT BIG FUNDRAISER BENEFIT THING AGAIN THIS YEAR? YEAH, THE STARLIGHT THING.
"GREAT. I NEED YOU TO GET ME ON THE WAIT STAFF FOR THE FUNDRAISER.
"I WILL TOTALLY SHOW UP. GIMME A BREAK.
"WHY? BECAUSE IT'S JEM AND THE HOLOGRAMS' FIRST SHOW...
"...AND I'M GOING TO MAKE SURE IT'S THEIR LAST!"

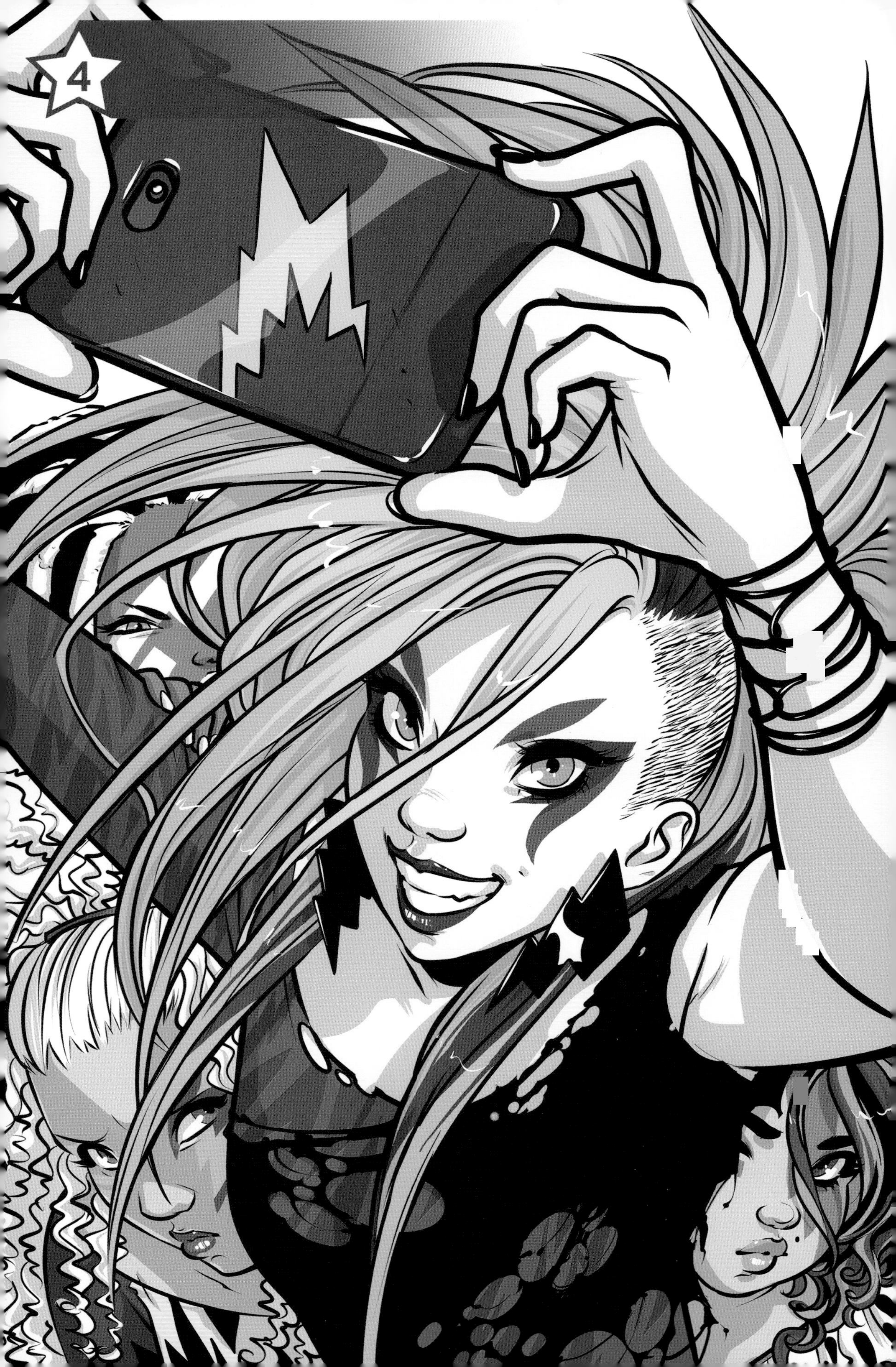
4

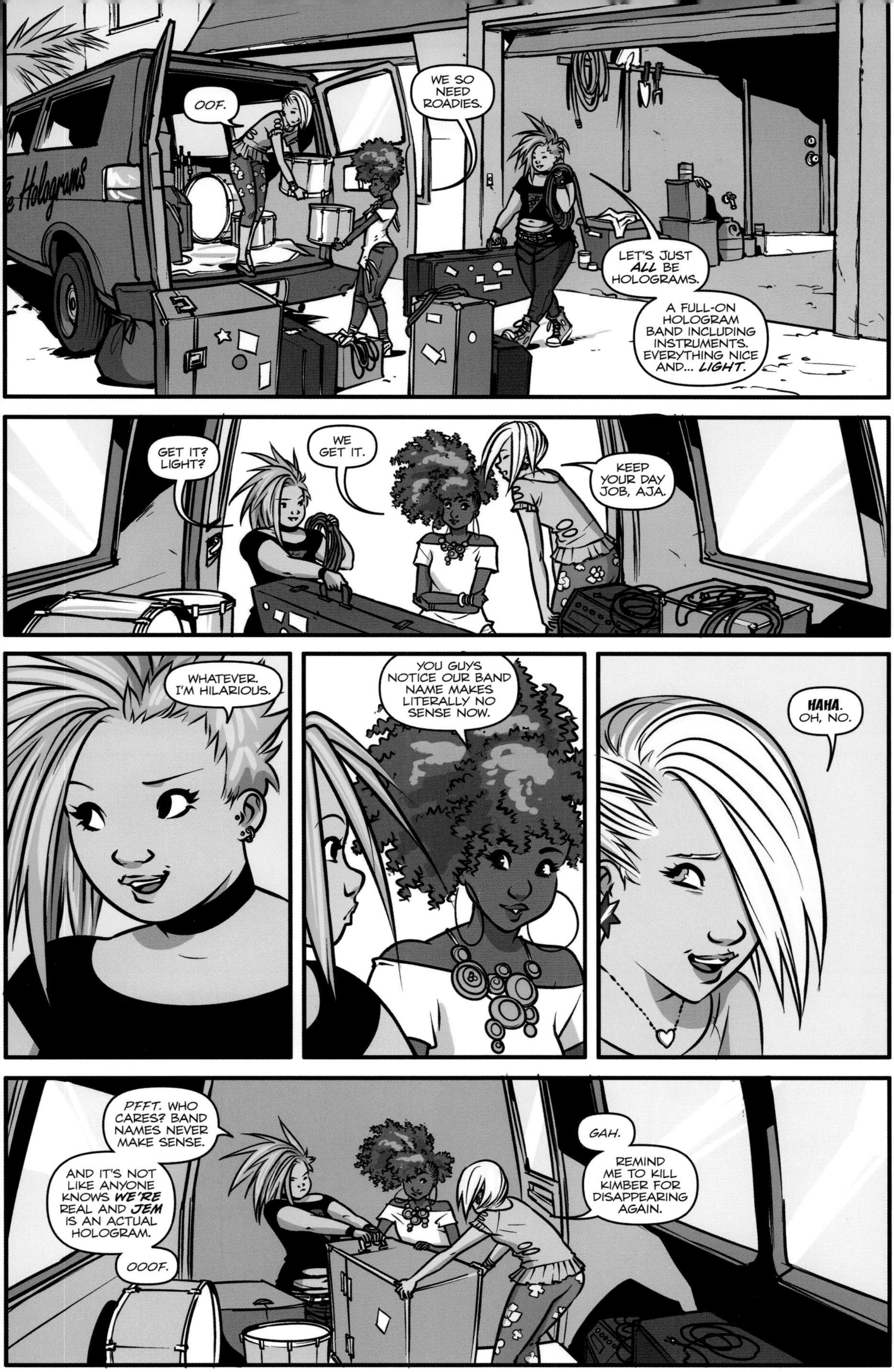
OOF.
WE SO NEED ROADIES.
LET'S JUST ***ALL*** BE HOLOGRAMS.
A FULL-ON HOLOGRAM BAND INCLUDING INSTRUMENTS. EVERYTHING NICE AND... ***LIGHT***.
GET IT? LIGHT?
WE GET IT.
KEEP YOUR DAY JOB, AJA.
WHATEVER. I'M HILARIOUS.
YOU GUYS NOTICE OUR BAND NAME MAKES LITERALLY NO SENSE NOW.
HAHA. OH, NO.
PFFT. WHO CARES? BAND NAMES NEVER MAKE SENSE.
AND IT'S NOT LIKE ANYONE KNOWS ***WE'RE*** REAL AND ***JEM*** IS AN ACTUAL HOLOGRAM.
OOOF.
GAH.
REMIND ME TO KILL KIMBER FOR DISAPPEARING AGAIN.

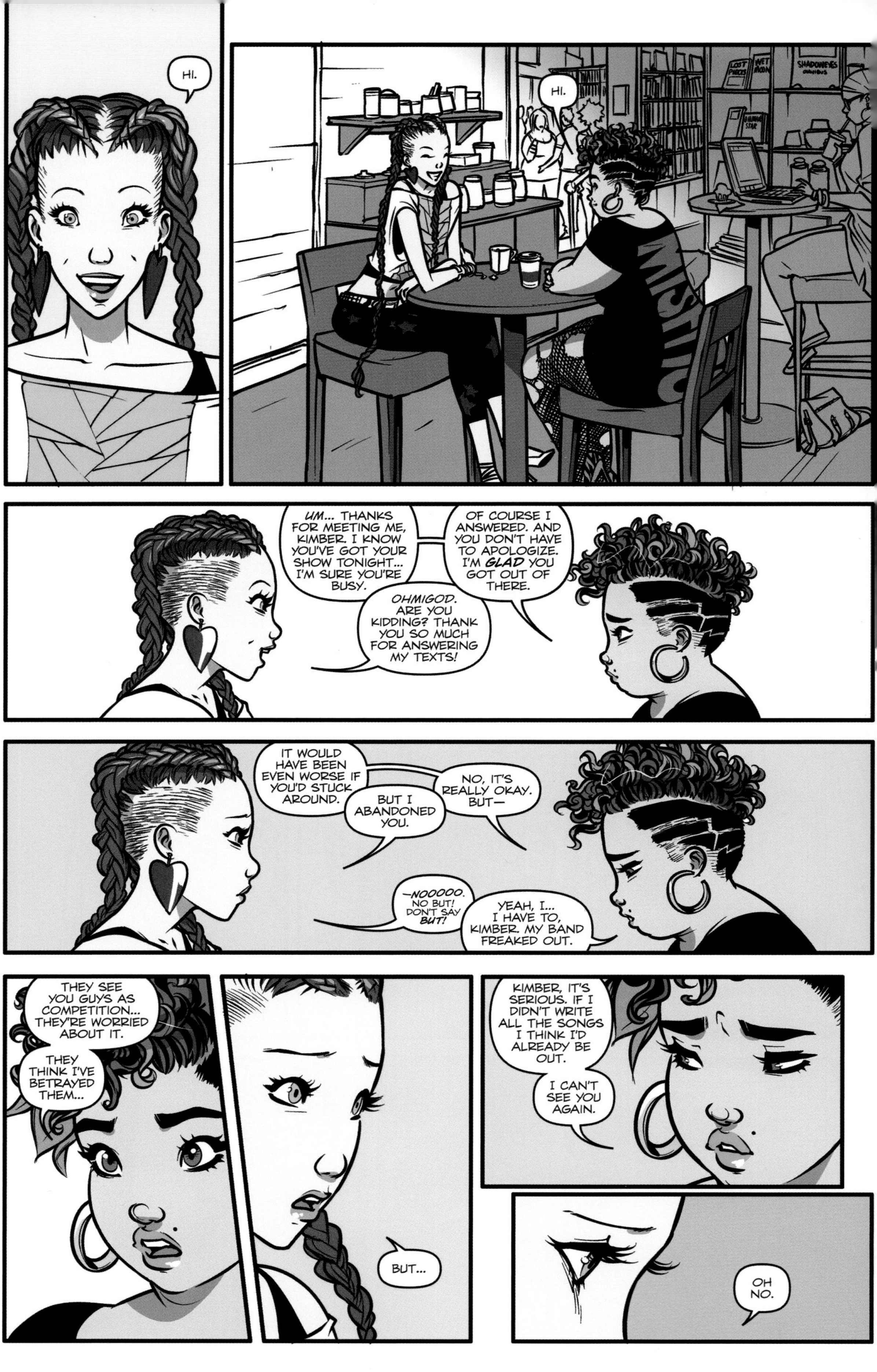
HI.
HI.
SHADOWEYES
LOST PIECES
WET MOON
UM... THANKS FOR MEETING ME, KIMBER. I KNOW YOU'VE GOT YOUR SHOW TONIGHT... I'M SURE YOU'RE BUSY.
OHMIGOD. ARE YOU KIDDING? THANK YOU SO MUCH FOR ANSWERING MY TEXTS!
OF COURSE I ANSWERED. AND YOU DON'T HAVE TO APOLOGIZE. I'M GLAD YOU GOT OUT OF THERE.
IT WOULD HAVE BEEN EVEN WORSE IF YOU'D STUCK AROUND.
BUT I ABANDONED YOU.
NO, IT'S REALLY OKAY. BUT—
—NOOOOO. NO BUT! DON'T SAY BUT!
YEAH, I... I HAVE TO, KIMBER. MY BAND FREAKED OUT.
THEY SEE YOU GUYS AS COMPETITION... THEY'RE WORRIED ABOUT IT.
THEY THINK I'VE BETRAYED THEM...
BUT...
KIMBER, IT'S SERIOUS. IF I DIDN'T WRITE ALL THE SONGS I THINK I'D ALREADY BE OUT.
I CAN'T SEE YOU AGAIN.
OH NO.

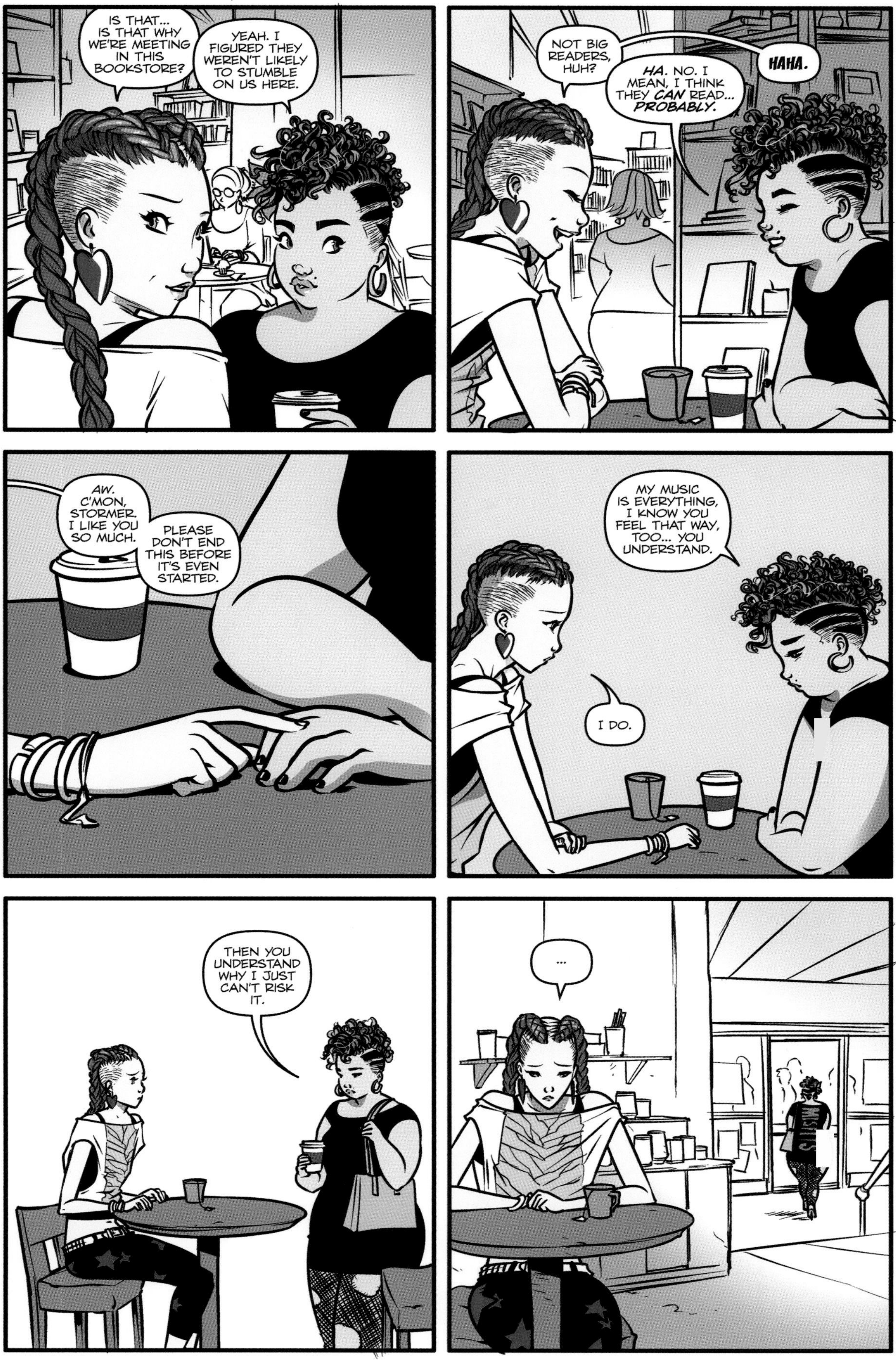
IS THAT... IS THAT WHY WE'RE MEETING IN THIS BOOKSTORE?
YEAH. I FIGURED THEY WEREN'T LIKELY TO STUMBLE ON US HERE.
NOT BIG READERS, HUH?
HA. NO. I MEAN, I THINK THEY CAN READ... PROBABLY.
HAHA.
AW. C'MON, STORMER. I LIKE YOU SO MUCH.
PLEASE DON'T END THIS BEFORE IT'S EVEN STARTED.
MY MUSIC IS EVERYTHING, I KNOW YOU FEEL THAT WAY, TOO... YOU UNDERSTAND.
I DO.
THEN YOU UNDERSTAND WHY I JUST CAN'T RISK IT.
...

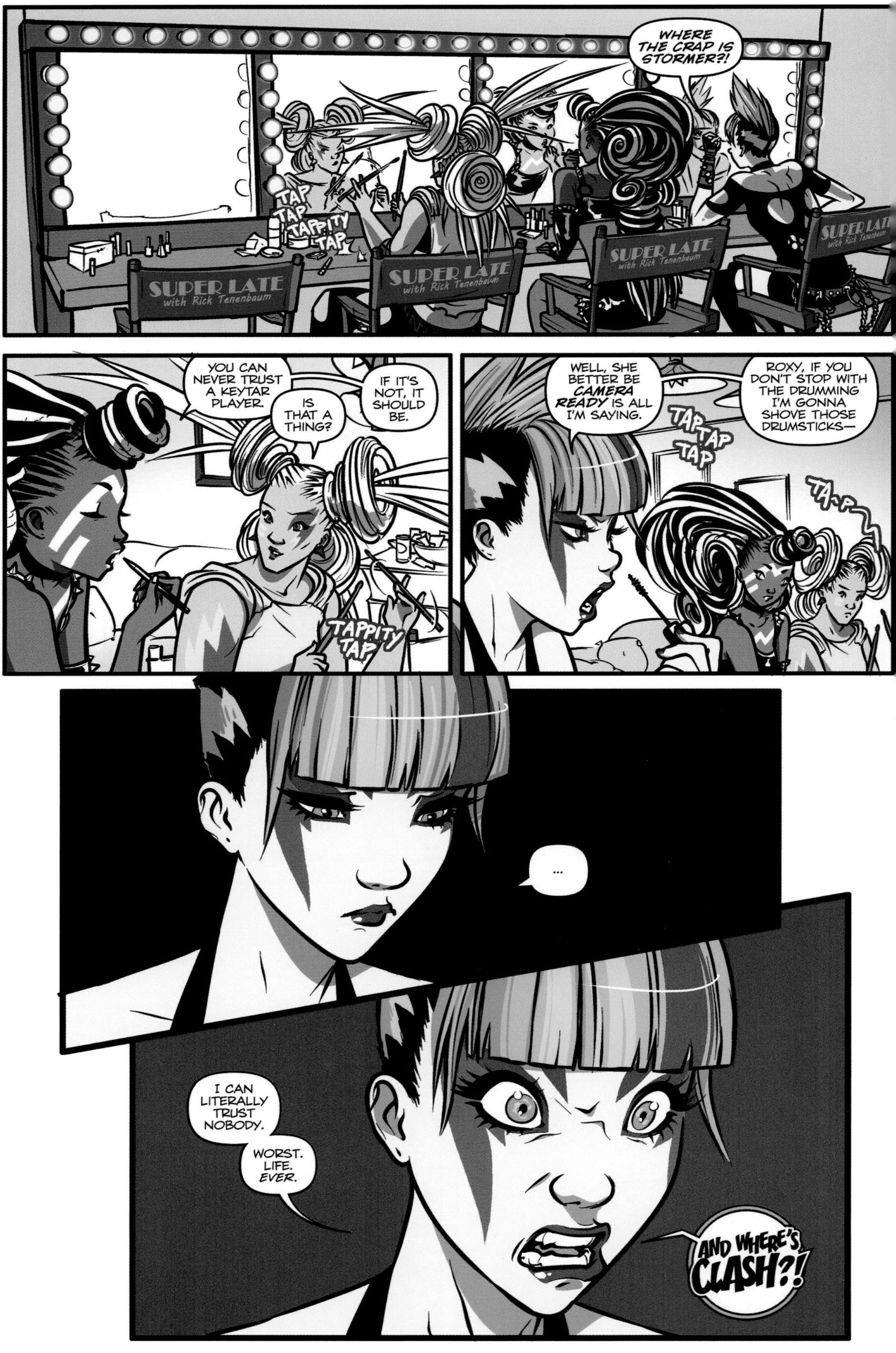

WHERE THE CRAP IS STORMER?!
TAP TAP TAPPITY TAP
SUPER LATE with Rick Tenenbaum
YOU CAN NEVER TRUST A KEYTAR PLAYER.
IS THAT A THING?
IF IT'S NOT, IT SHOULD BE.
TAPPITY TAP
WELL, SHE BETTER BE CAMERA READY IS ALL I'M SAYING.
ROXY, IF YOU DON'T STOP WITH THE DRUMMING I'M GONNA SHOVE THOSE DRUMSTICKS—
TAP TAP TAP
TA-P
...
I CAN LITERALLY TRUST NOBODY.
WORST. LIFE. EVER.
AND WHERE'S CLASH?!

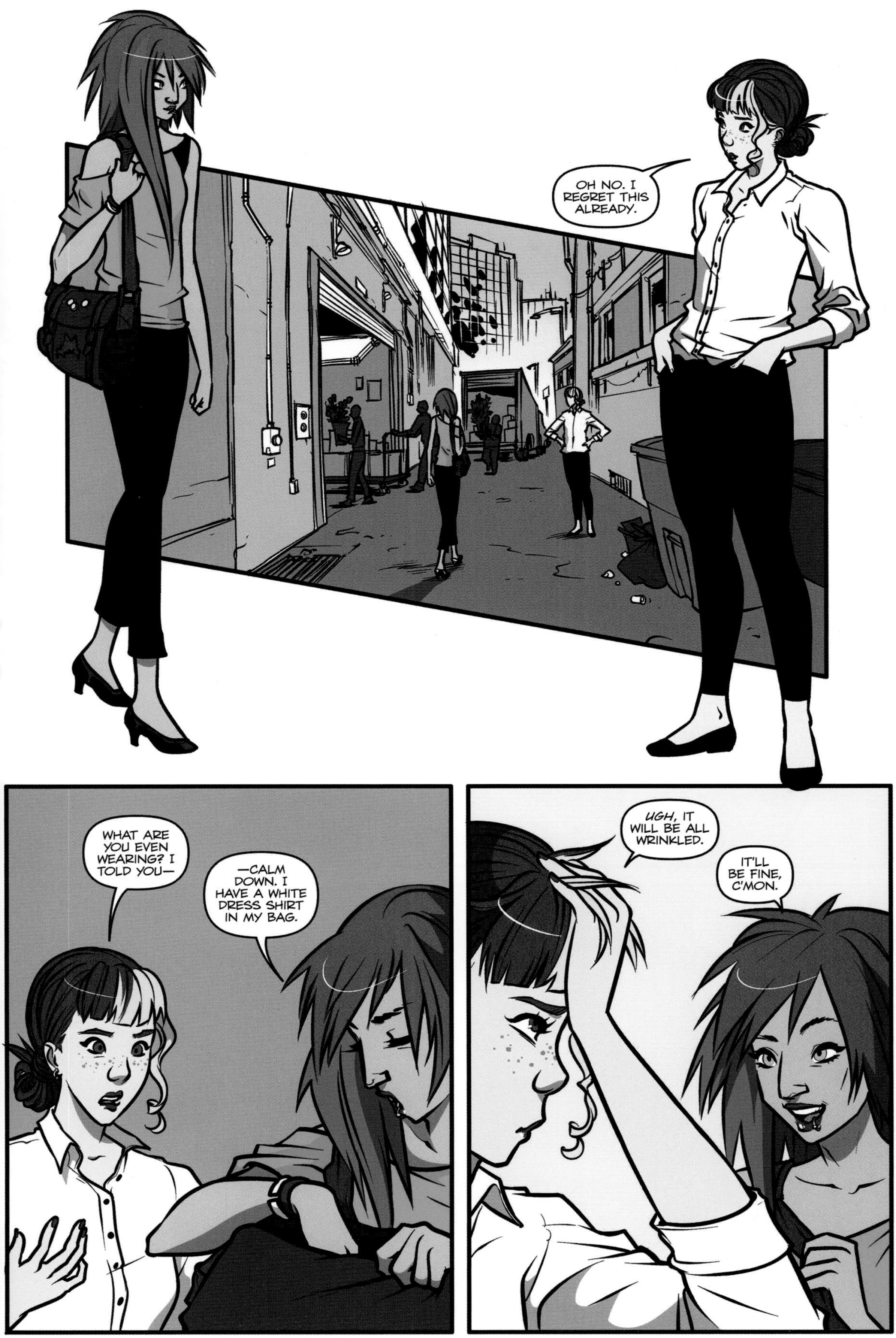
OH NO. I REGRET THIS ALREADY.
WHAT ARE YOU EVEN WEARING? I TOLD YOU—
—CALM DOWN. I HAVE A WHITE DRESS SHIRT IN MY BAG.
UGH, IT WILL BE ALL WRINKLED.
IT'LL BE FINE, C'MON.

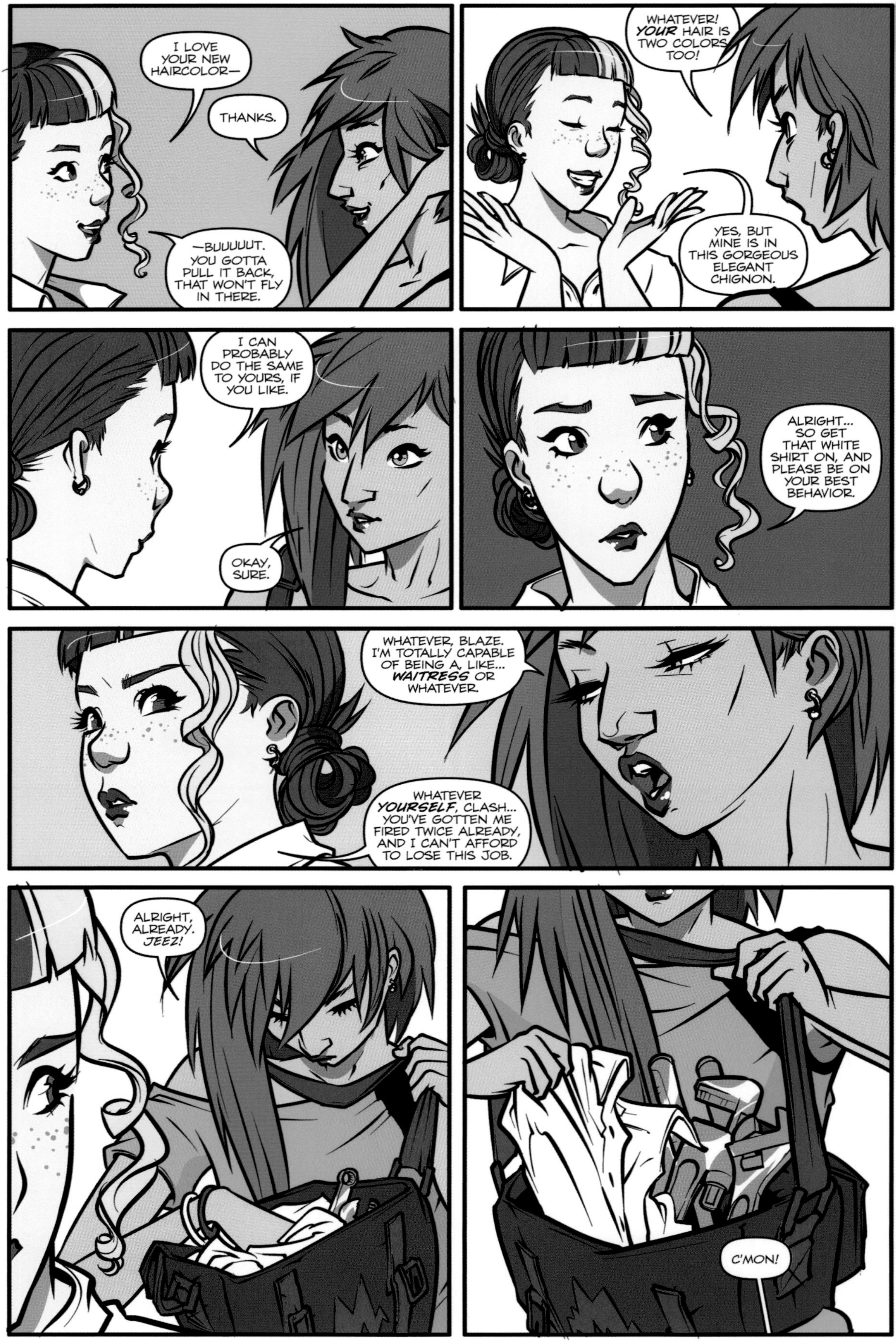
I LOVE YOUR NEW HAIRCOLOR—
THANKS.
—BUUUUUT. YOU GOTTA PULL IT BACK, THAT WON'T FLY IN THERE.
WHATEVER! *YOUR* HAIR IS TWO COLORS TOO!
YES, BUT MINE IS IN THIS GORGEOUS ELEGANT CHIGNON.
I CAN PROBABLY DO THE SAME TO YOURS, IF YOU LIKE.
OKAY, SURE.
ALRIGHT... SO GET THAT WHITE SHIRT ON, AND PLEASE BE ON YOUR BEST BEHAVIOR.
WHATEVER, BLAZE. I'M TOTALLY CAPABLE OF BEING A, LIKE... *WAITRESS* OR WHATEVER.
WHATEVER *YOURSELF*, CLASH... YOU'VE GOTTEN ME FIRED TWICE ALREADY, AND I CAN'T AFFORD TO LOSE THIS JOB.
ALRIGHT, ALREADY. *JEEZ!*
C'MON!

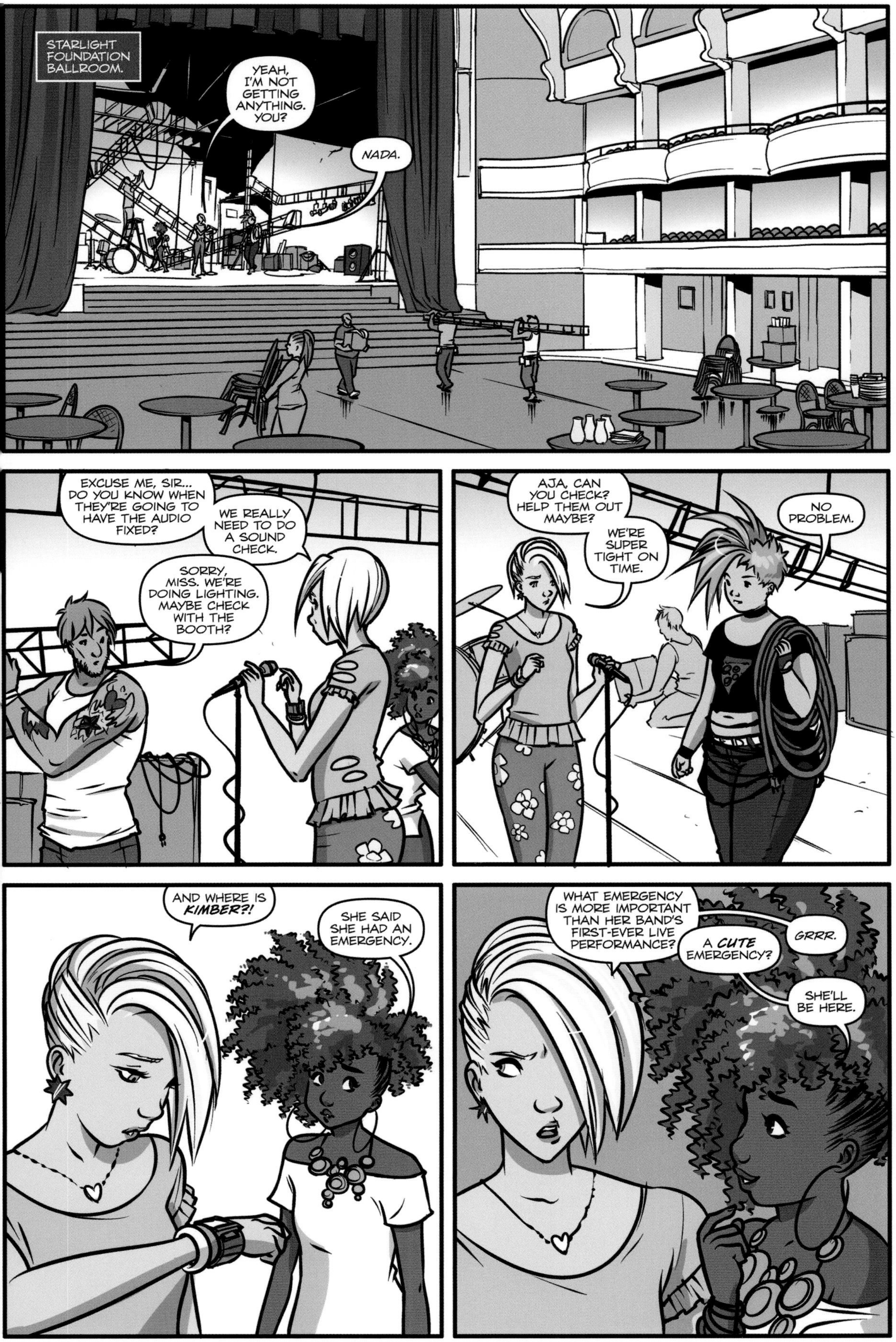
STARLIGHT FOUNDATION BALLROOM.
YEAH, I'M NOT GETTING ANYTHING. YOU?
NADA.
EXCUSE ME, SIR... DO YOU KNOW WHEN THEY'RE GOING TO HAVE THE AUDIO FIXED?
WE REALLY NEED TO DO A SOUND CHECK.
SORRY, MISS. WE'RE DOING LIGHTING. MAYBE CHECK WITH THE BOOTH?
AJA, CAN YOU CHECK? HELP THEM OUT MAYBE?
WE'RE SUPER TIGHT ON TIME.
NO PROBLEM.
AND WHERE IS KIMBER?!
SHE SAID SHE HAD AN EMERGENCY.
WHAT EMERGENCY IS MORE IMPORTANT THAN HER BAND'S FIRST-EVER LIVE PERFORMANCE?
A CUTE EMERGENCY?
GRRR.
SHE'LL BE HERE.

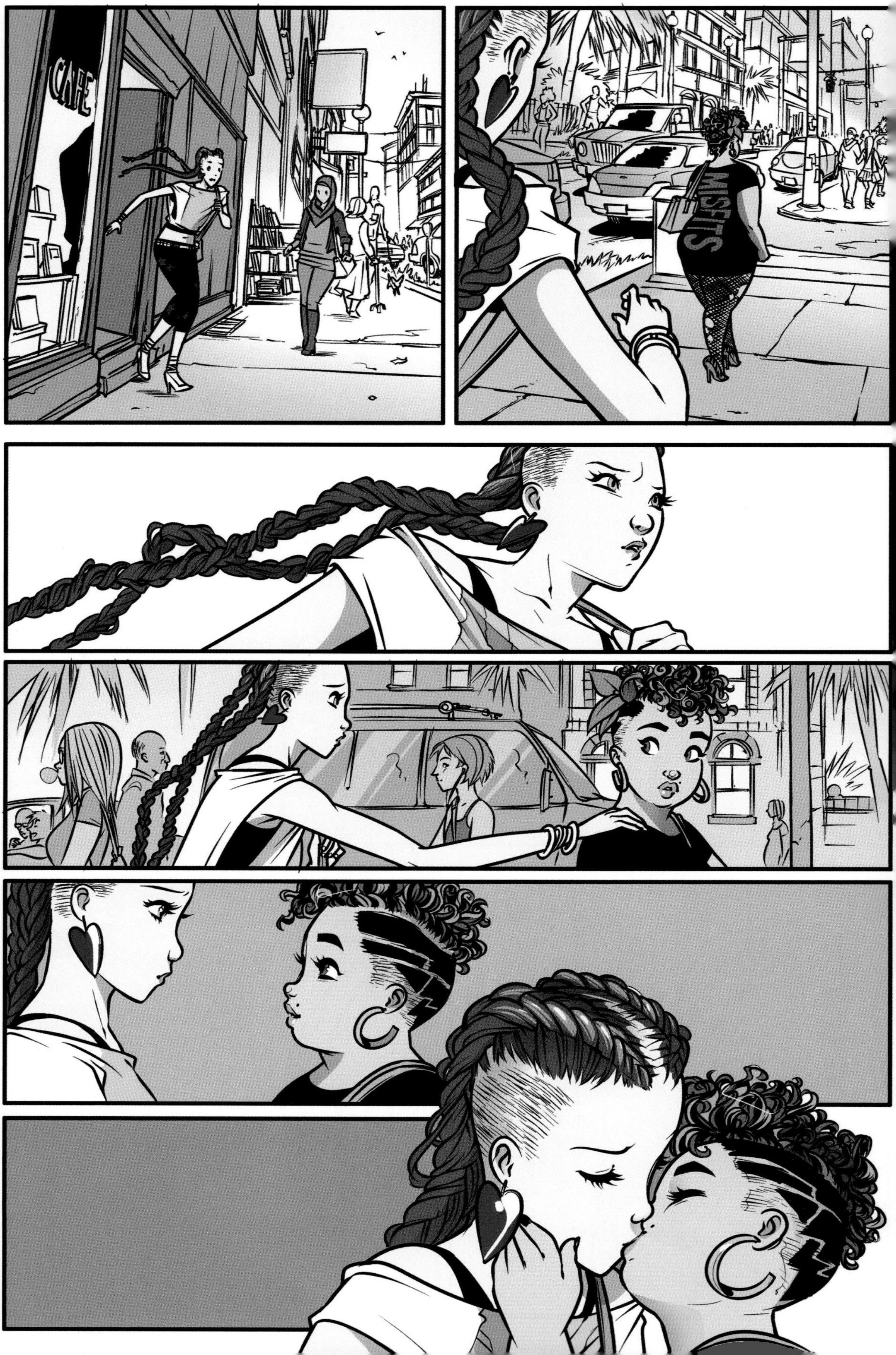
CAFE
MISFITS

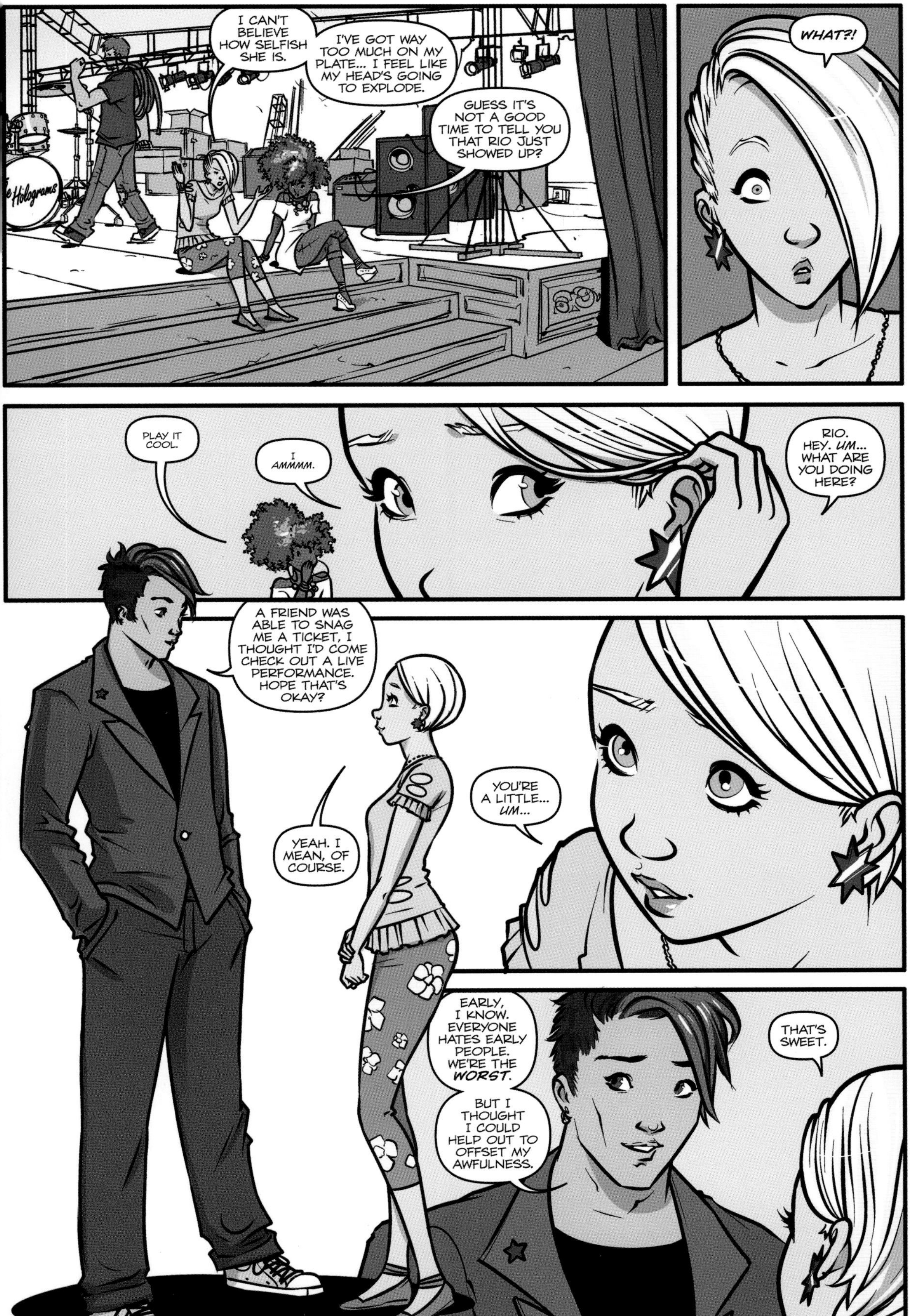
I CAN'T BELIEVE HOW SELFISH SHE IS.
I'VE GOT WAY TOO MUCH ON MY PLATE... I FEEL LIKE MY HEAD'S GOING TO EXPLODE.
GUESS IT'S NOT A GOOD TIME TO TELL YOU THAT RIO JUST SHOWED UP?
WHAT?!
PLAY IT COOL.
I *AMMMM.*
RIO. HEY. *UM*... WHAT ARE YOU DOING HERE?
A FRIEND WAS ABLE TO SNAG ME A TICKET, I THOUGHT I'D COME CHECK OUT A LIVE PERFORMANCE. HOPE THAT'S OKAY?
YEAH. I MEAN, OF COURSE.
YOU'RE A LITTLE... *UM*...
EARLY, I KNOW. EVERYONE HATES EARLY PEOPLE. WE'RE THE ***WORST***.
BUT I THOUGHT I COULD HELP OUT TO OFFSET MY AWFULNESS.
THAT'S SWEET.

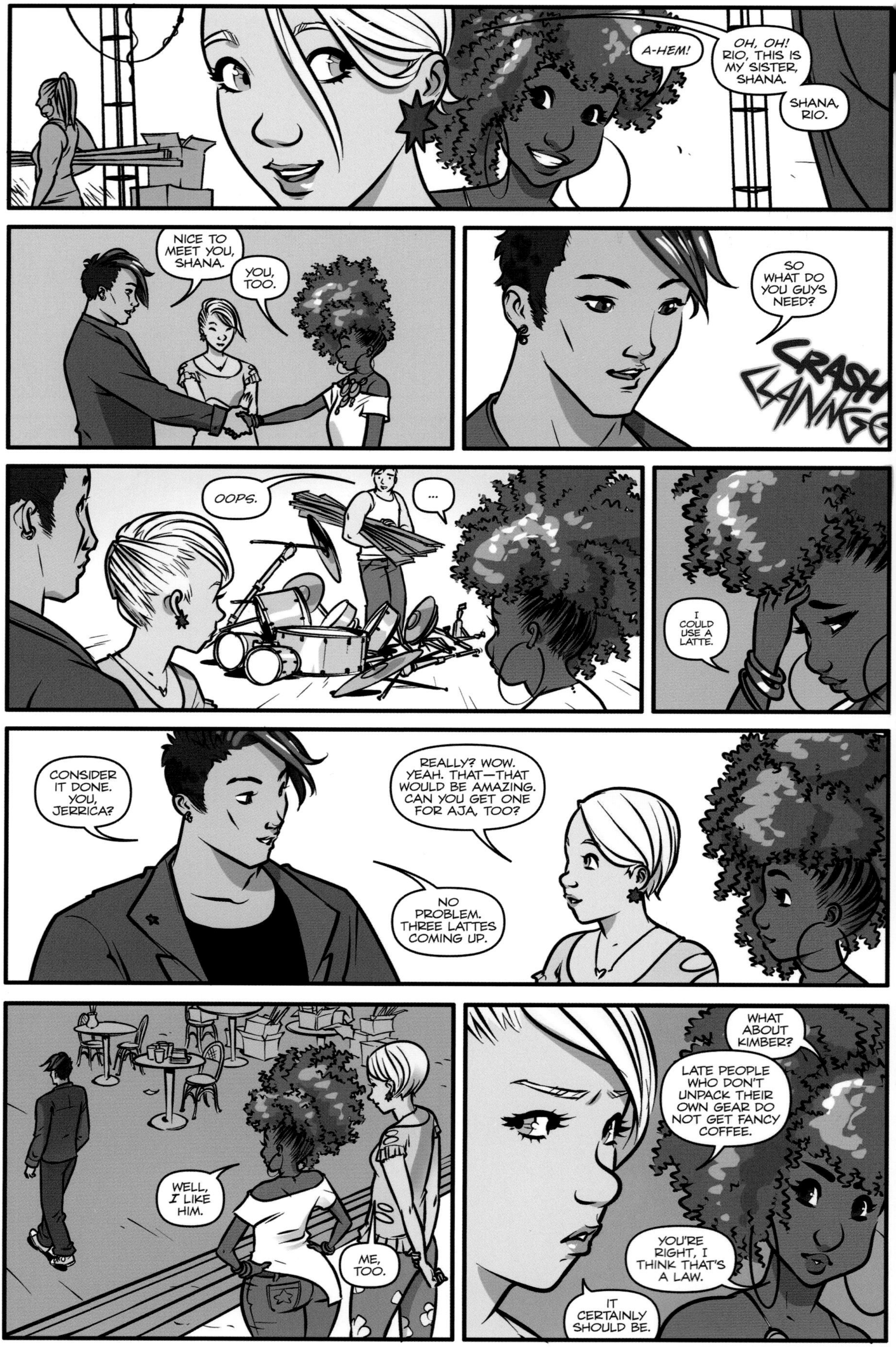
A-HEM!
OH, OH! RIO, THIS IS MY SISTER, SHANA.
SHANA, RIO.
NICE TO MEET YOU, SHANA.
YOU, TOO.
SO WHAT DO YOU GUYS NEED?
CRASH CLANNGG
OOPS.
...
I COULD USE A LATTE.
CONSIDER IT DONE. YOU, JERRICA?
REALLY? WOW. YEAH. THAT—THAT WOULD BE AMAZING. CAN YOU GET ONE FOR AJA, TOO?
NO PROBLEM. THREE LATTES COMING UP.
WELL, I LIKE HIM.
ME, TOO.
WHAT ABOUT KIMBER?
LATE PEOPLE WHO DON'T UNPACK THEIR OWN GEAR DO NOT GET FANCY COFFEE.
YOU'RE RIGHT, I THINK THAT'S A LAW.
IT CERTAINLY SHOULD BE.

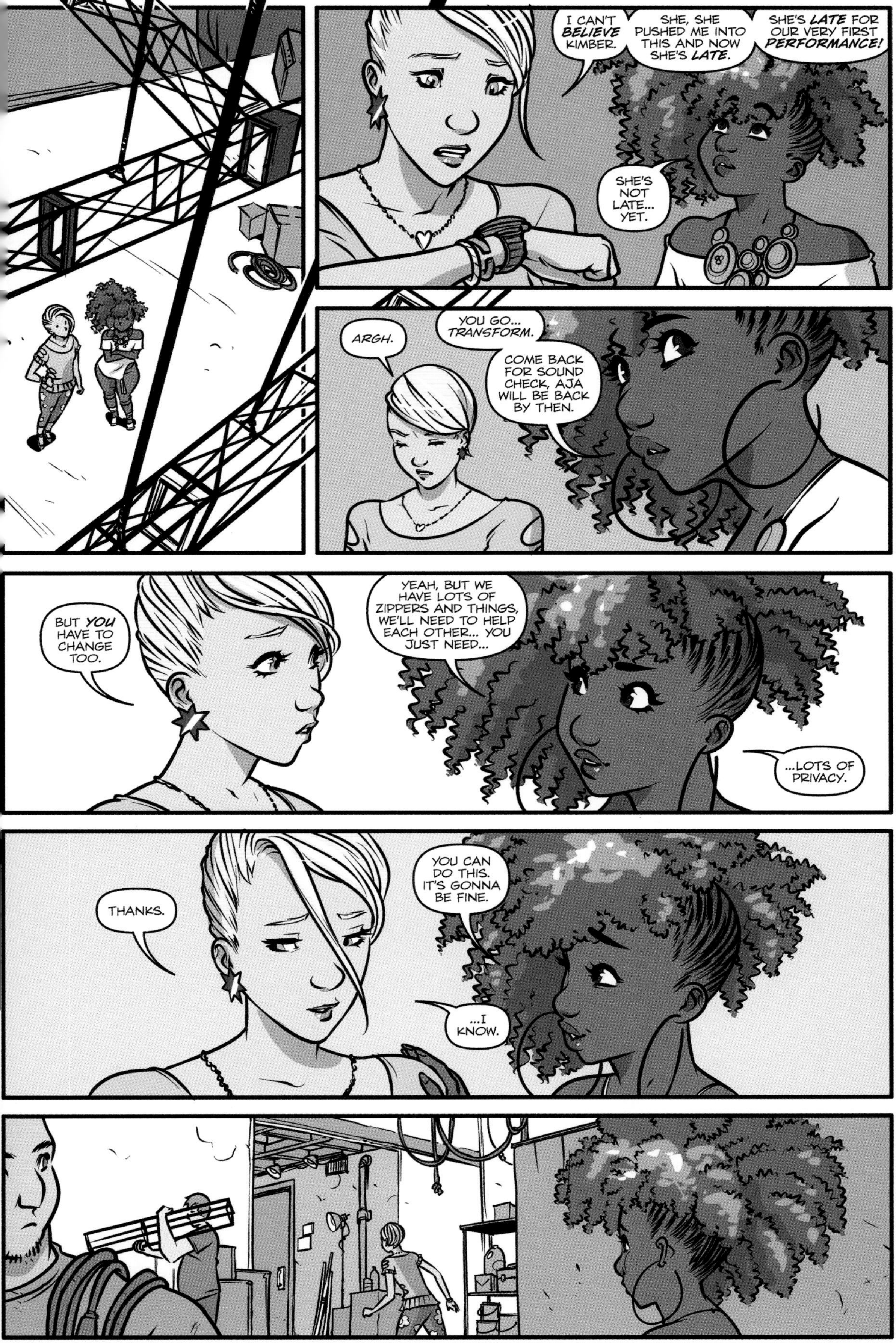

I CAN'T *BELIEVE* KIMBER.
SHE, SHE PUSHED ME INTO THIS AND NOW SHE'S *LATE*.
SHE'S *LATE* FOR OUR VERY FIRST *PERFORMANCE!*
SHE'S NOT LATE... YET.
ARGH.
YOU GO... *TRANSFORM*.
COME BACK FOR SOUND CHECK, AJA WILL BE BACK BY THEN.
BUT *YOU* HAVE TO CHANGE TOO.
YEAH, BUT WE HAVE LOTS OF ZIPPERS AND THINGS, WE'LL NEED TO HELP EACH OTHER... YOU JUST NEED...
...LOTS OF PRIVACY.
THANKS.
YOU CAN DO THIS. IT'S GONNA BE FINE.
...I KNOW.

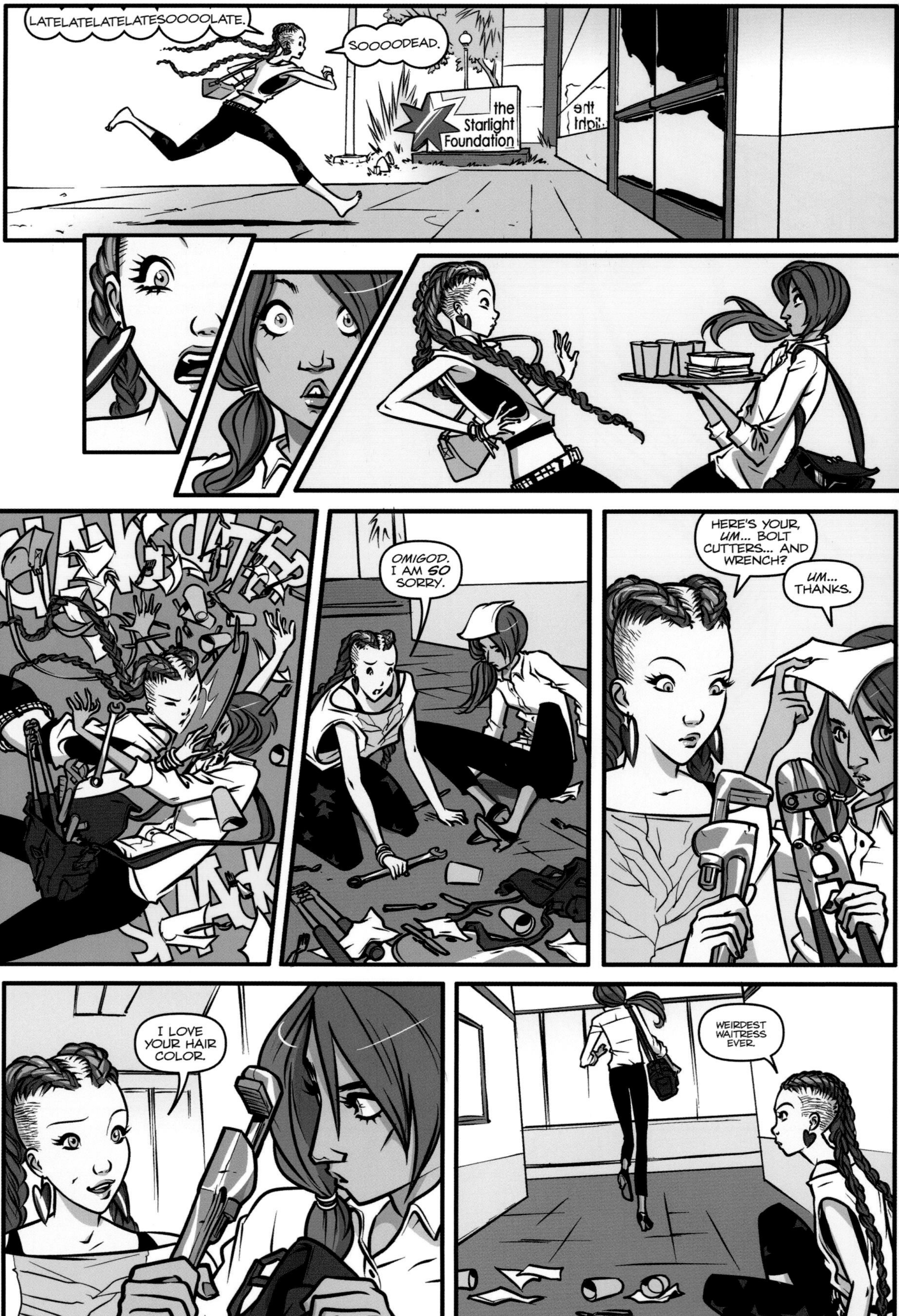
LATELATELATELATESOOOOLATE.
SOOOODEAD.
the Starlight Foundation
OMIGOD. I AM SO SORRY.
HERE'S YOUR, UM... BOLT CUTTERS... AND WRENCH?
UM... THANKS.
I LOVE YOUR HAIR COLOR.
WEIRDEST WAITRESS EVER.

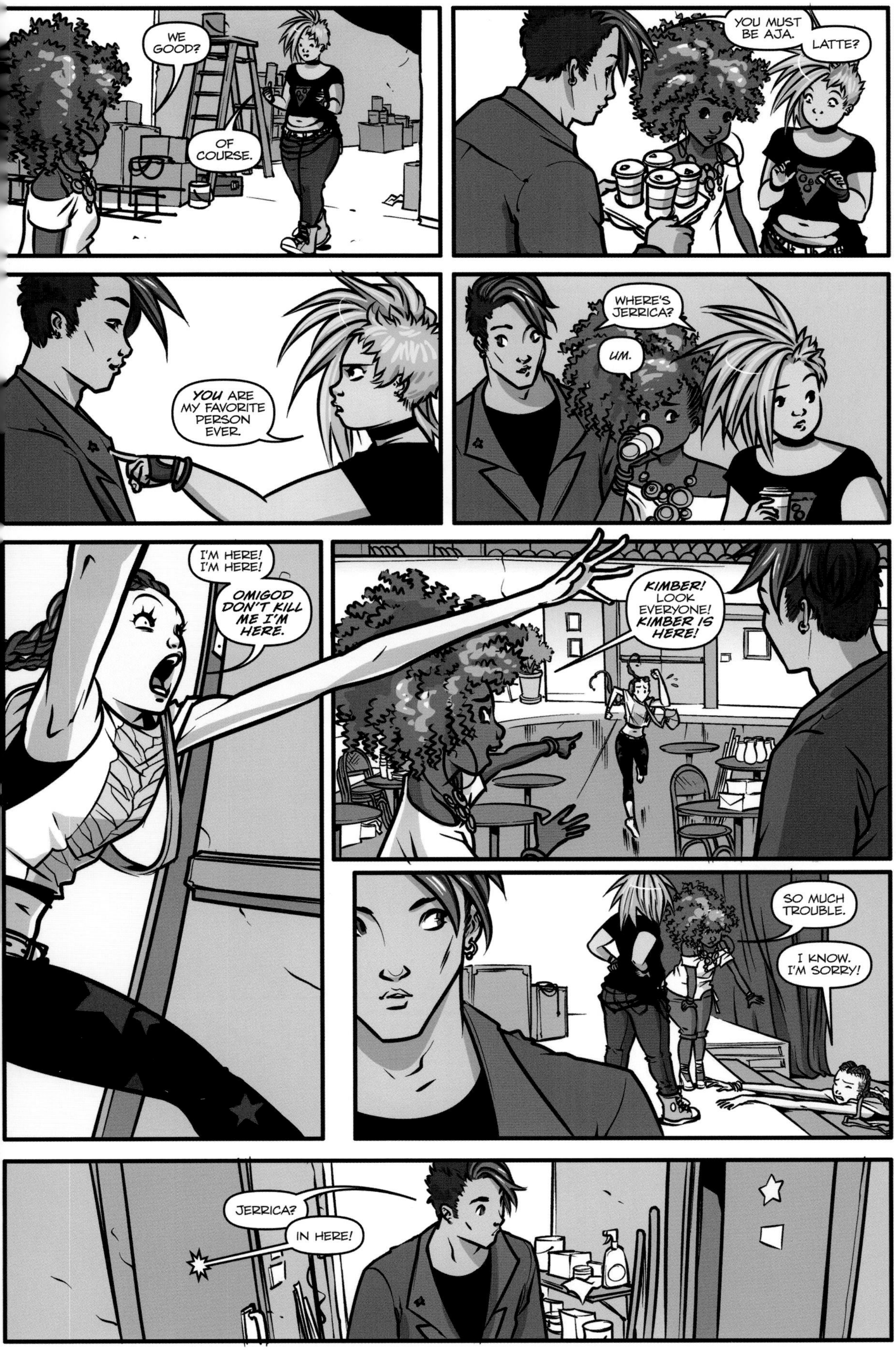
WE GOOD?
OF COURSE.
YOU MUST BE AJA.
LATTE?
YOU ARE MY FAVORITE PERSON EVER.
WHERE'S JERRICA?
UM.
I'M HERE! I'M HERE!
OMIGOD DON'T KILL ME I'M HERE.
KIMBER! LOOK EVERYONE! KIMBER IS HERE!
SO MUCH TROUBLE.
I KNOW. I'M SORRY!
JERRICA?
IN HERE!

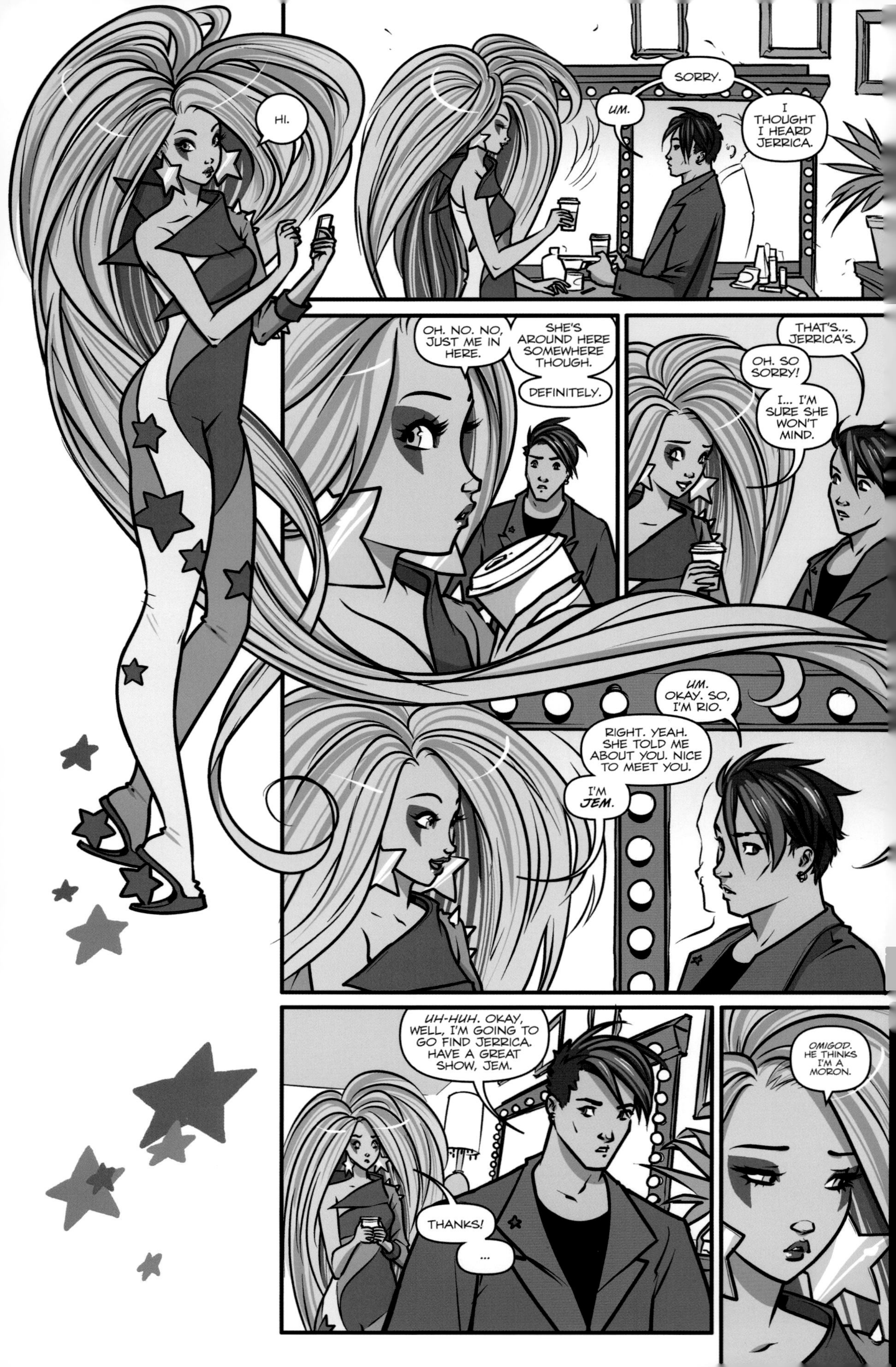
HI.
UM.
SORRY.
I THOUGHT I HEARD JERRICA.
OH. NO. NO, JUST ME IN HERE.
SHE'S AROUND HERE SOMEWHERE THOUGH.
DEFINITELY.
THAT'S... JERRICA'S.
OH. SO SORRY!
I... I'M SURE SHE WON'T MIND.
UM. OKAY. SO, I'M RIO.
RIGHT. YEAH. SHE TOLD ME ABOUT YOU. NICE TO MEET YOU.
I'M JEM.
UH-HUH. OKAY, WELL, I'M GOING TO GO FIND JERRICA. HAVE A GREAT SHOW, JEM.
THANKS!
...
OMIGOD. HE THINKS I'M A MORON.

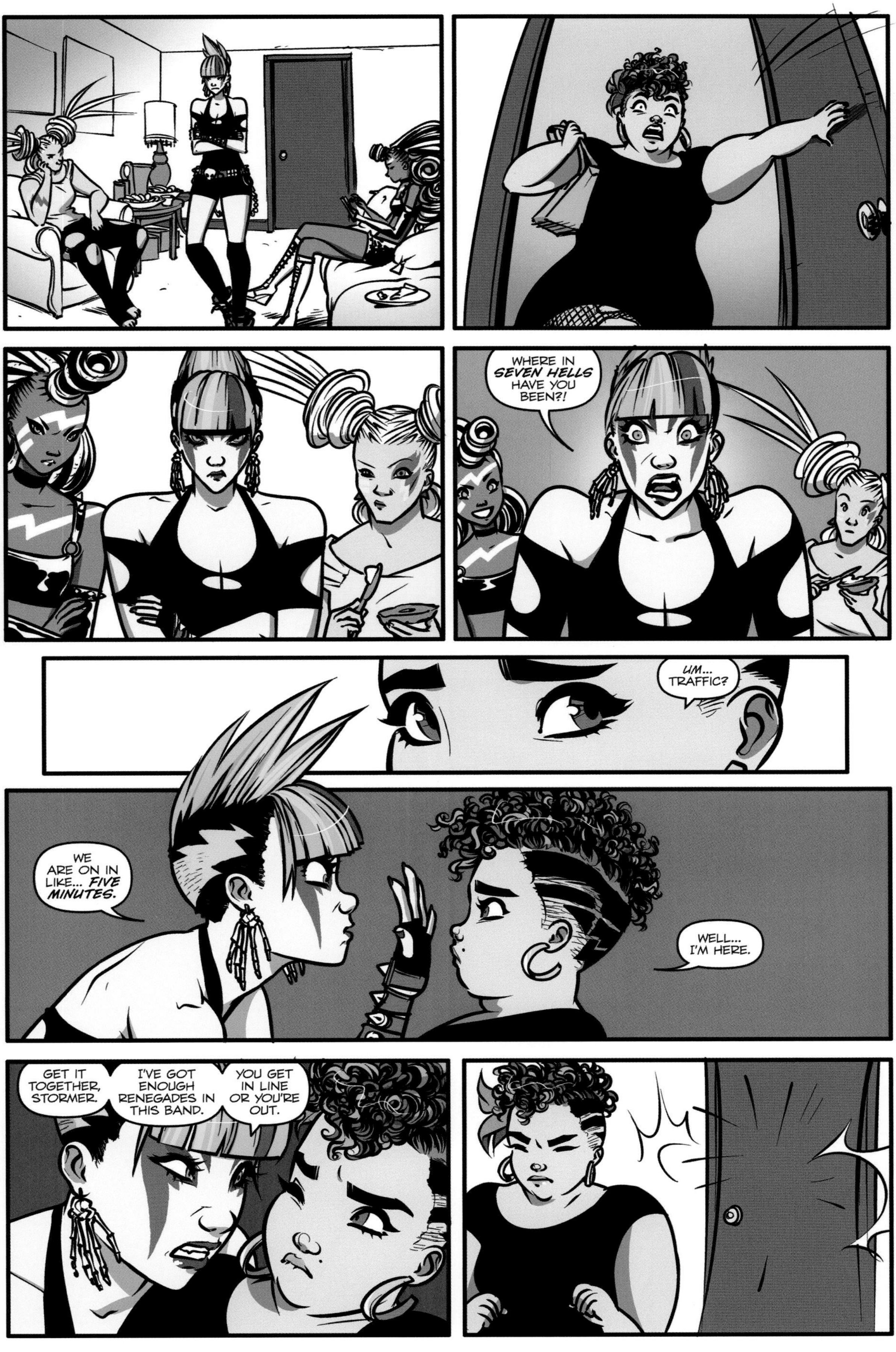
WHERE IN *SEVEN HELLS* HAVE YOU BEEN?!
UM... TRAFFIC?
WE ARE ON IN LIKE... *FIVE MINUTES.*
WELL... I'M HERE.
GET IT TOGETHER, STORMER.
I'VE GOT ENOUGH RENEGADES IN THIS BAND.
YOU GET IN LINE OR YOU'RE OUT.

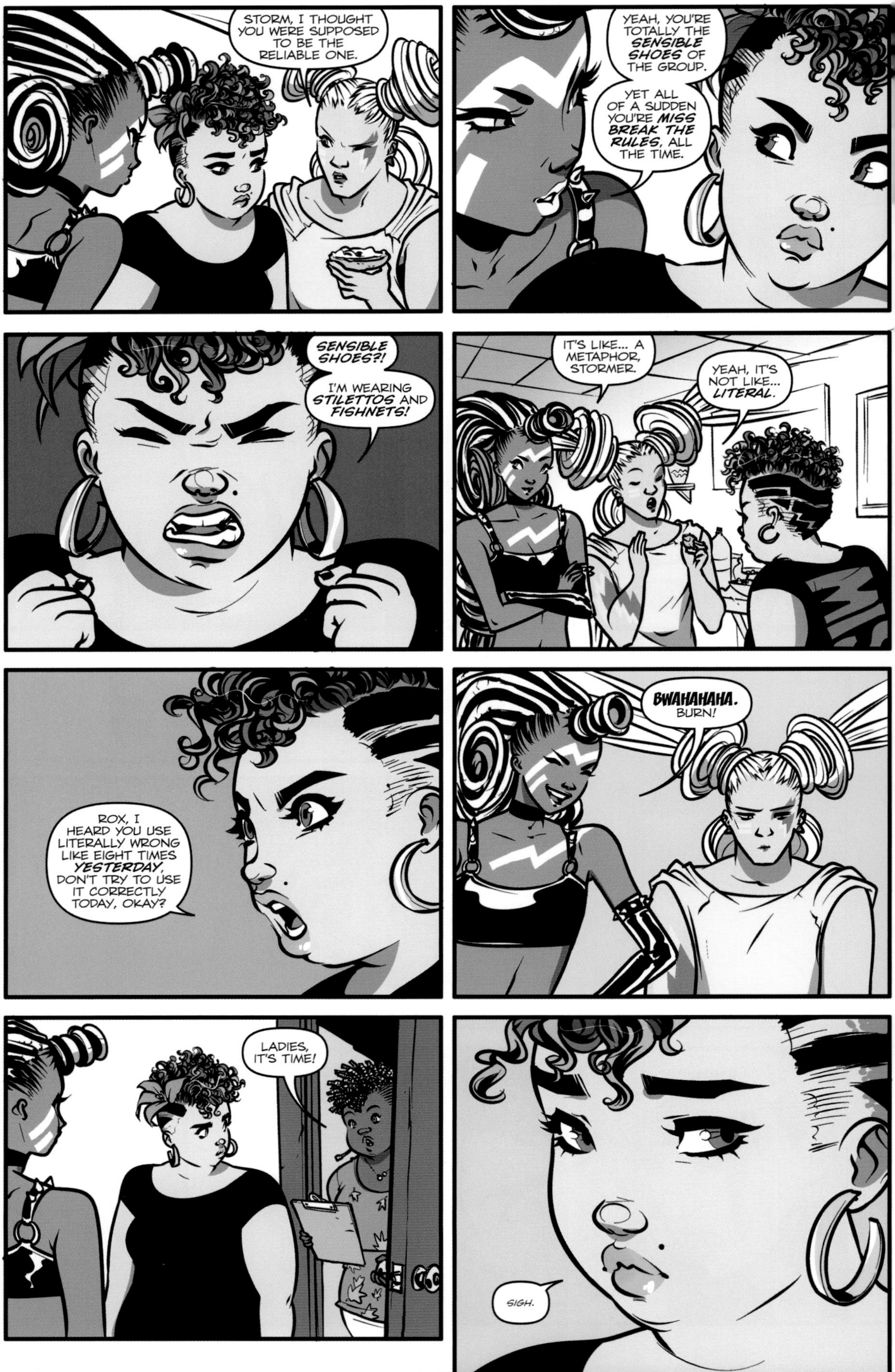
STORM, I THOUGHT YOU WERE SUPPOSED TO BE THE RELIABLE ONE.
YEAH, YOU'RE TOTALLY THE SENSIBLE SHOES OF THE GROUP.
YET ALL OF A SUDDEN YOU'RE MISS BREAK THE RULES, ALL THE TIME.
SENSIBLE SHOES?!
I'M WEARING STILETTOS AND FISHNETS!
IT'S LIKE... A METAPHOR, STORMER.
YEAH, IT'S NOT LIKE... LITERAL.
ROX, I HEARD YOU USE LITERALLY WRONG LIKE EIGHT TIMES YESTERDAY, DON'T TRY TO USE IT CORRECTLY TODAY, OKAY?
BWAHAHAHA. BURN!
LADIES, IT'S TIME!
SIGH.

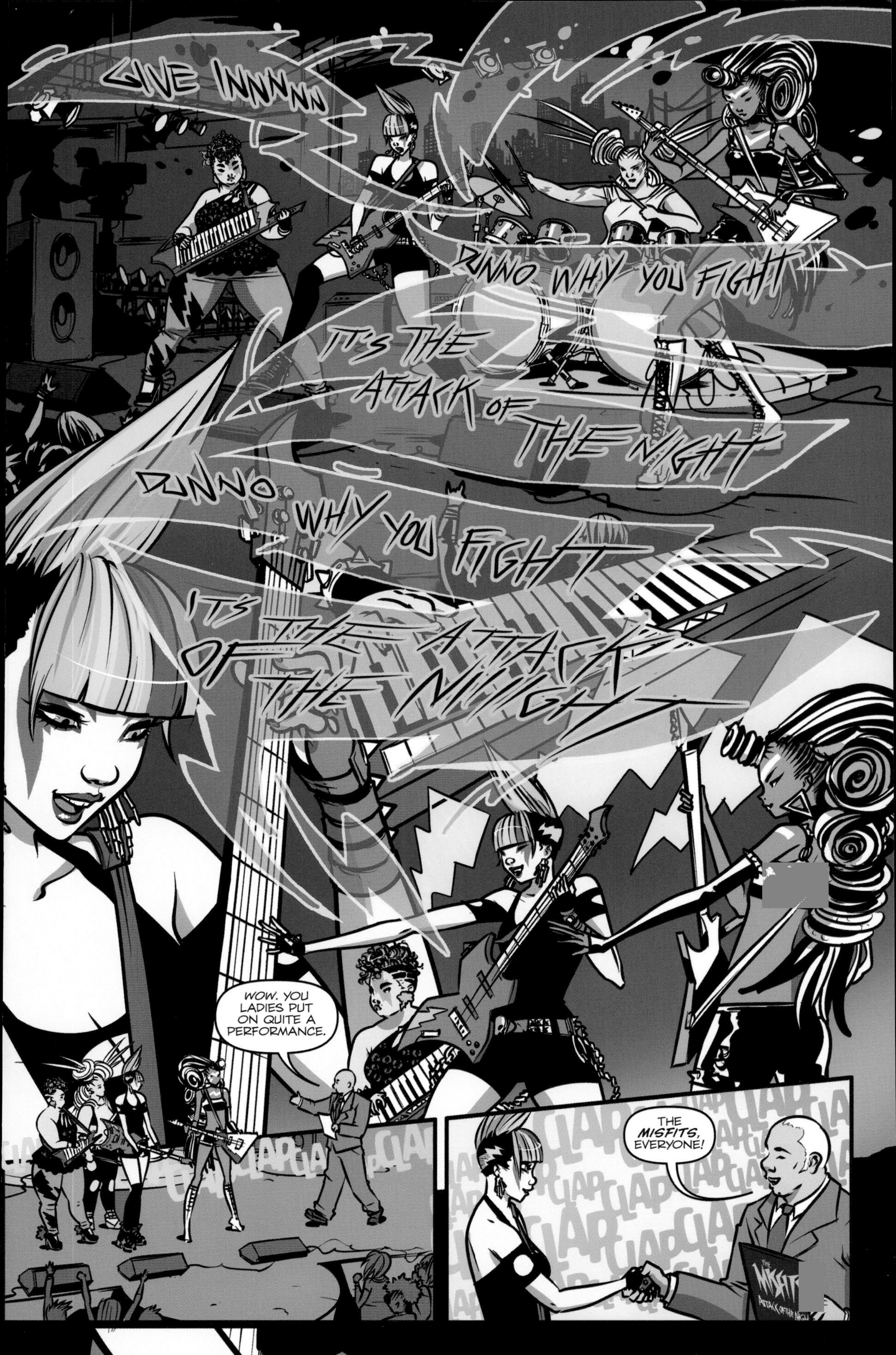
GIVE INNNNN
DUNNO WHY YOU FIGHT
IT'S THE ATTACK OF THE NIGHT
DUNNO WHY YOU FIGHT
IT'S THE ATTACK OF THE NIGHT
WOW. YOU LADIES PUT ON QUITE A PERFORMANCE.
CLAP CLAP CLAP
THE *MISFITS,* EVERYONE!
CLAP CLAP CLAP CLAP

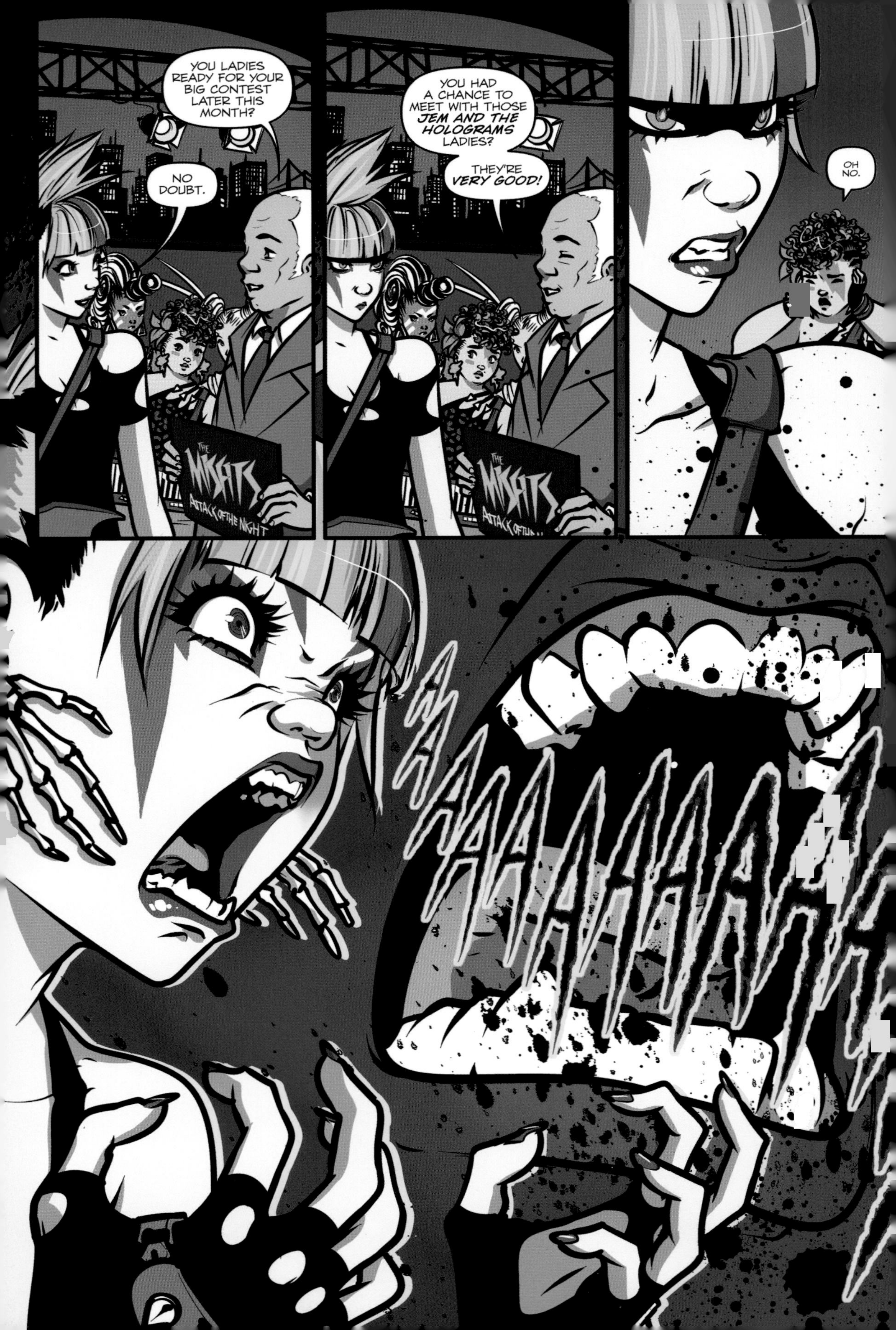
YOU LADIES READY FOR YOUR BIG CONTEST LATER THIS MONTH?
NO DOUBT.
THE MISFITS ATTACK OF THE NIGHT
YOU HAD A CHANCE TO MEET WITH THOSE JEM AND THE HOLOGRAMS LADIES?
THEY'RE VERY GOOD!
OH NO.
AAAAAAAAAAH

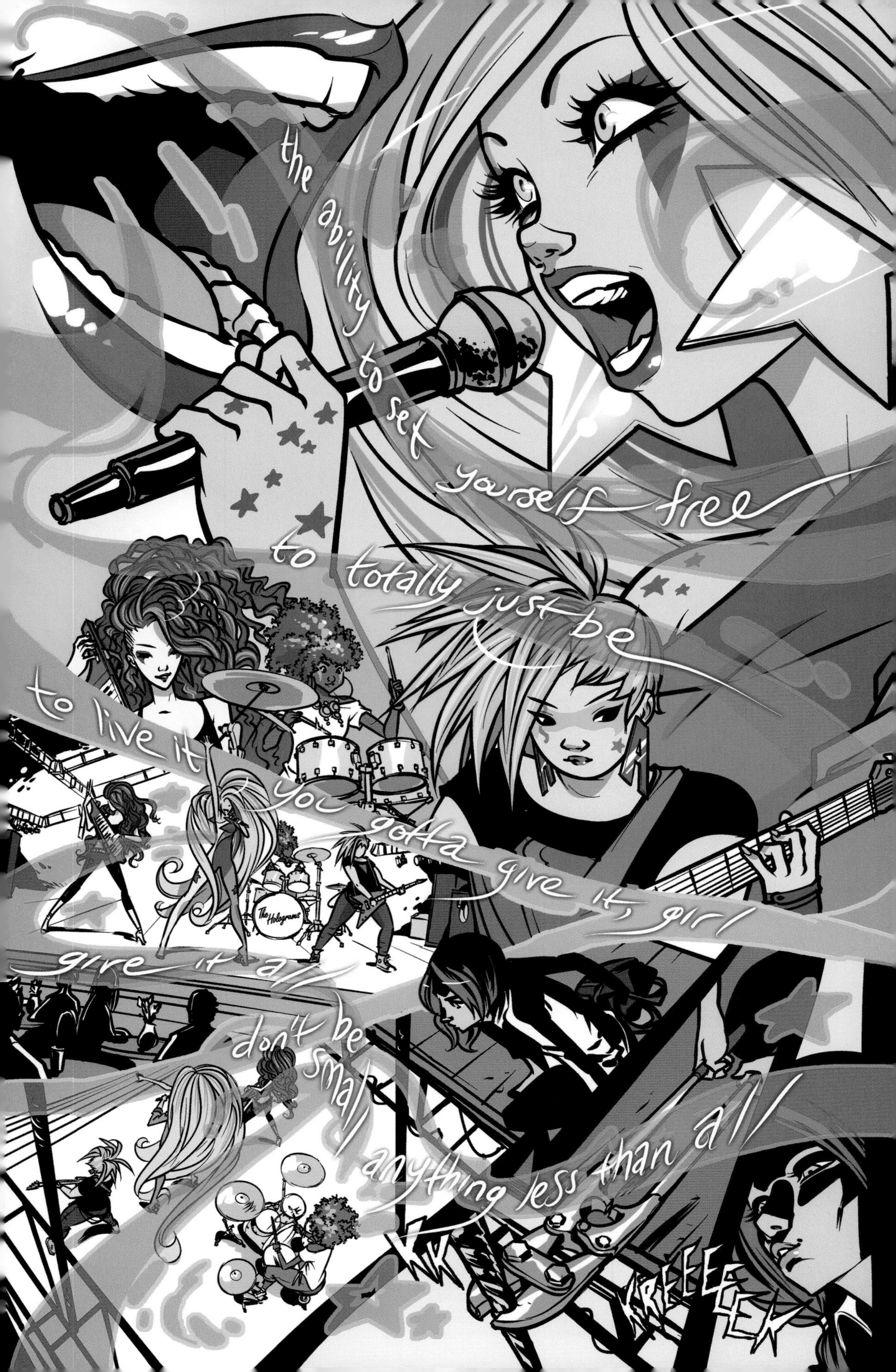

the ability to set yourself free
to totally just be
to live it you gotta give it, girl
give it all
don't be small
anything less than all
The Holograms
KRREEEEEEK

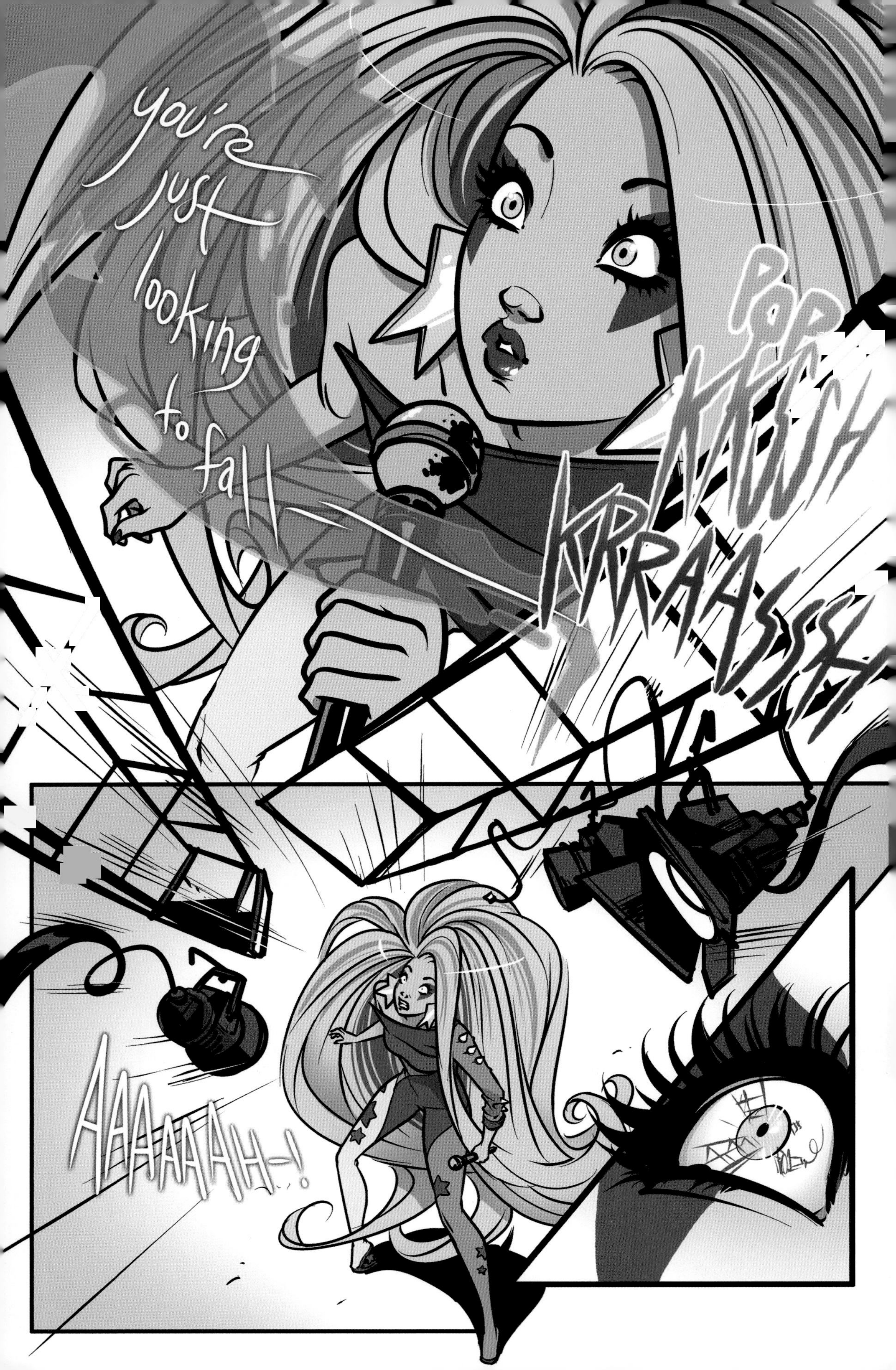
you're just looking to fall!
POP KECH
KRRAASSH
AAAAAAH-!

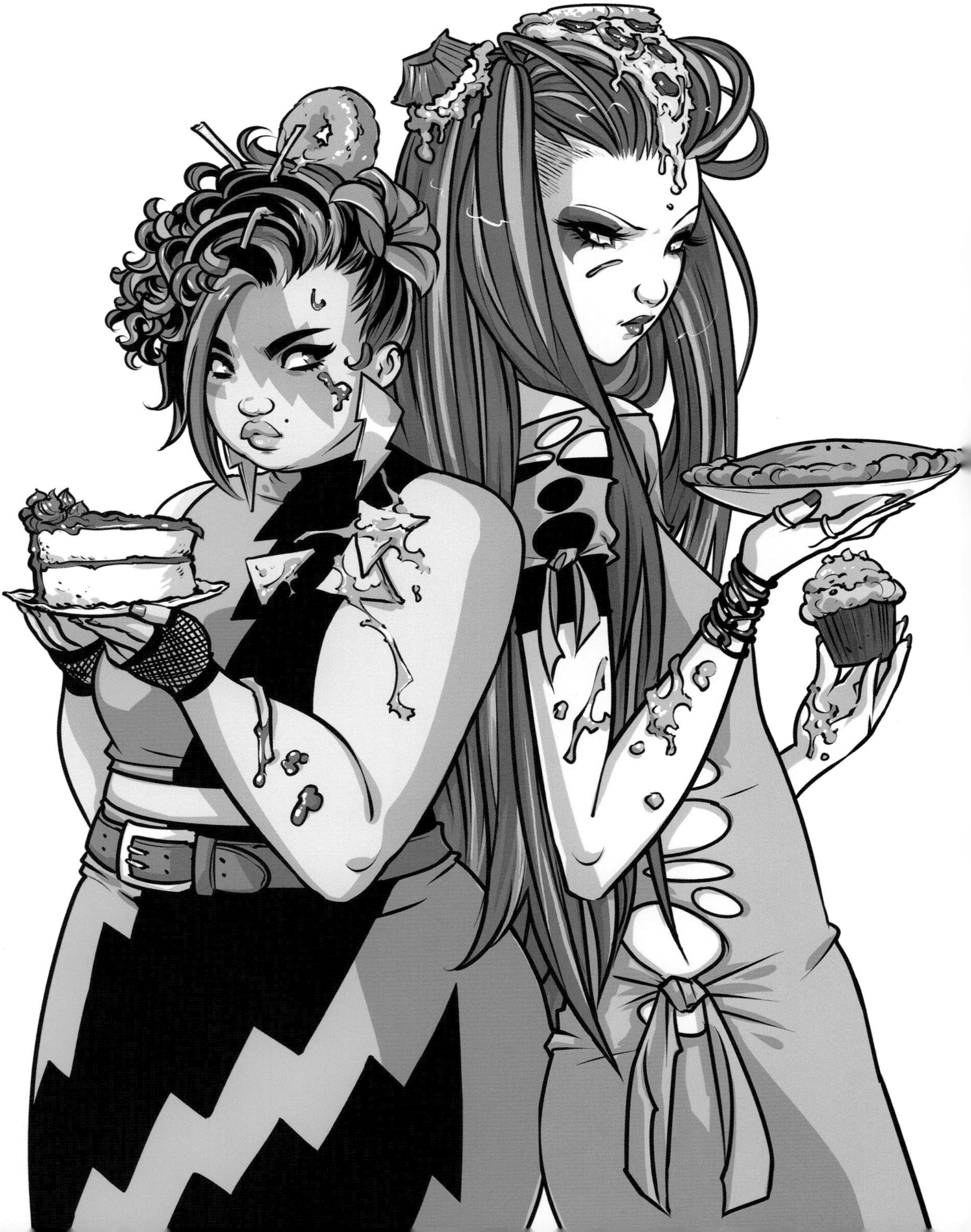

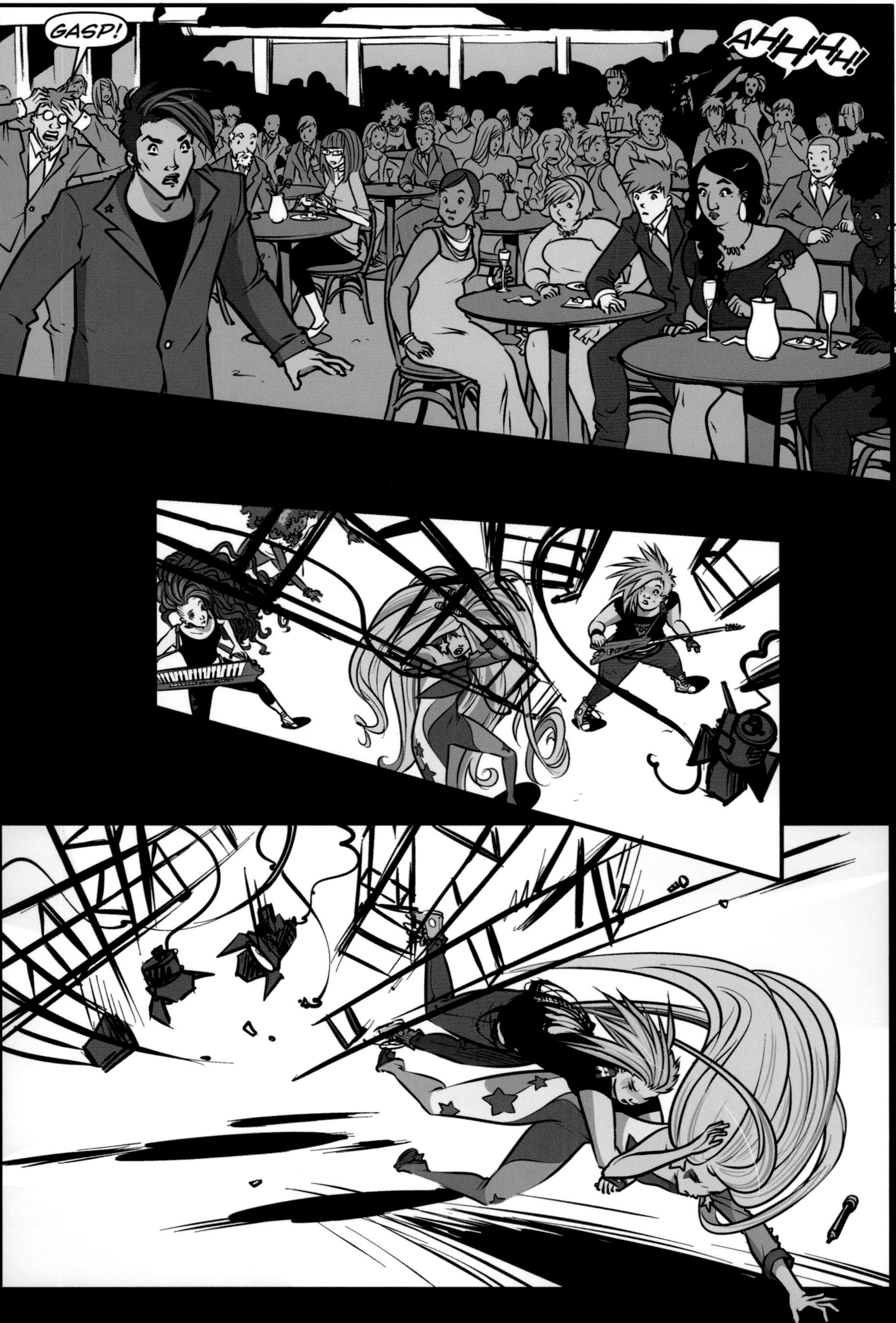
GASP!
AHHHH!

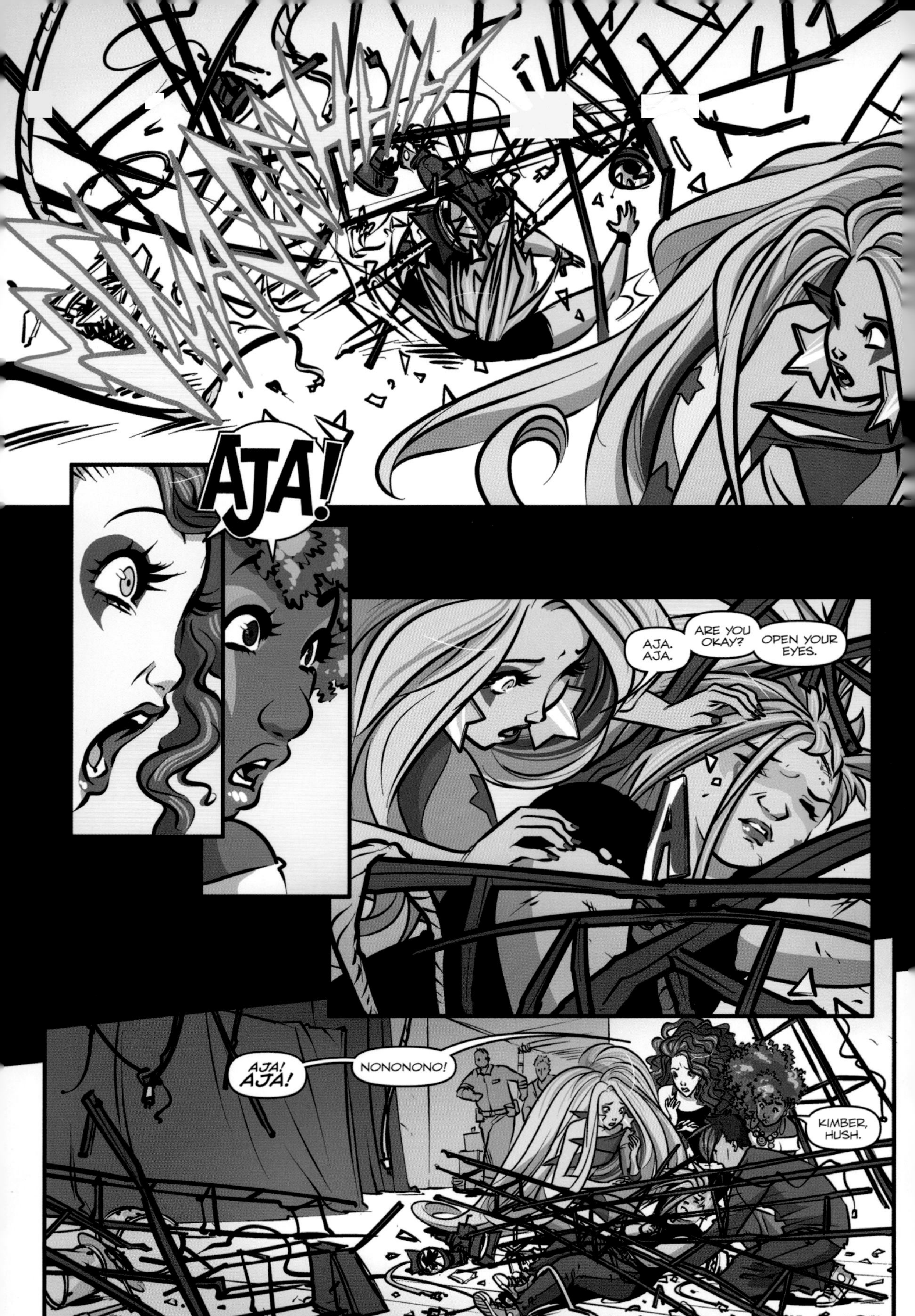
AJA!
AJA. AJA.
ARE YOU OKAY?
OPEN YOUR EYES.
AJA! AJA!
NONONONO!
KIMBER, HUSH.

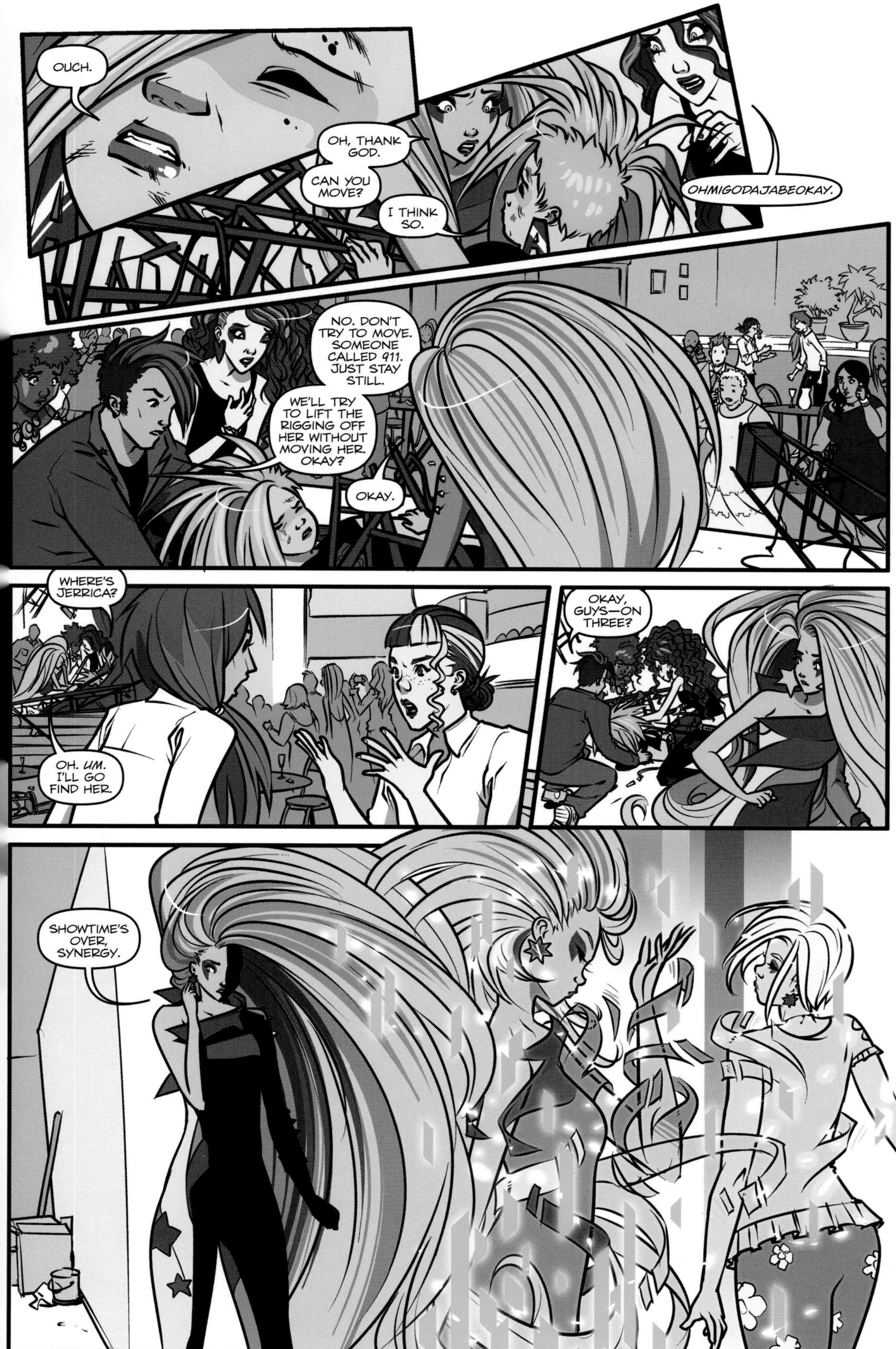
OUCH.
OH, THANK GOD.
CAN YOU MOVE?
I THINK SO.
OHMIGODAJABEOKAY.
NO. DON'T TRY TO MOVE. SOMEONE CALLED 911. JUST STAY STILL.
WE'LL TRY TO LIFT THE RIGGING OFF HER WITHOUT MOVING HER. OKAY?
OKAY.
WHERE'S JERRICA?
OH. UM. I'LL GO FIND HER.
OKAY, GUYS—ON THREE?
SHOWTIME'S OVER, SYNERGY.

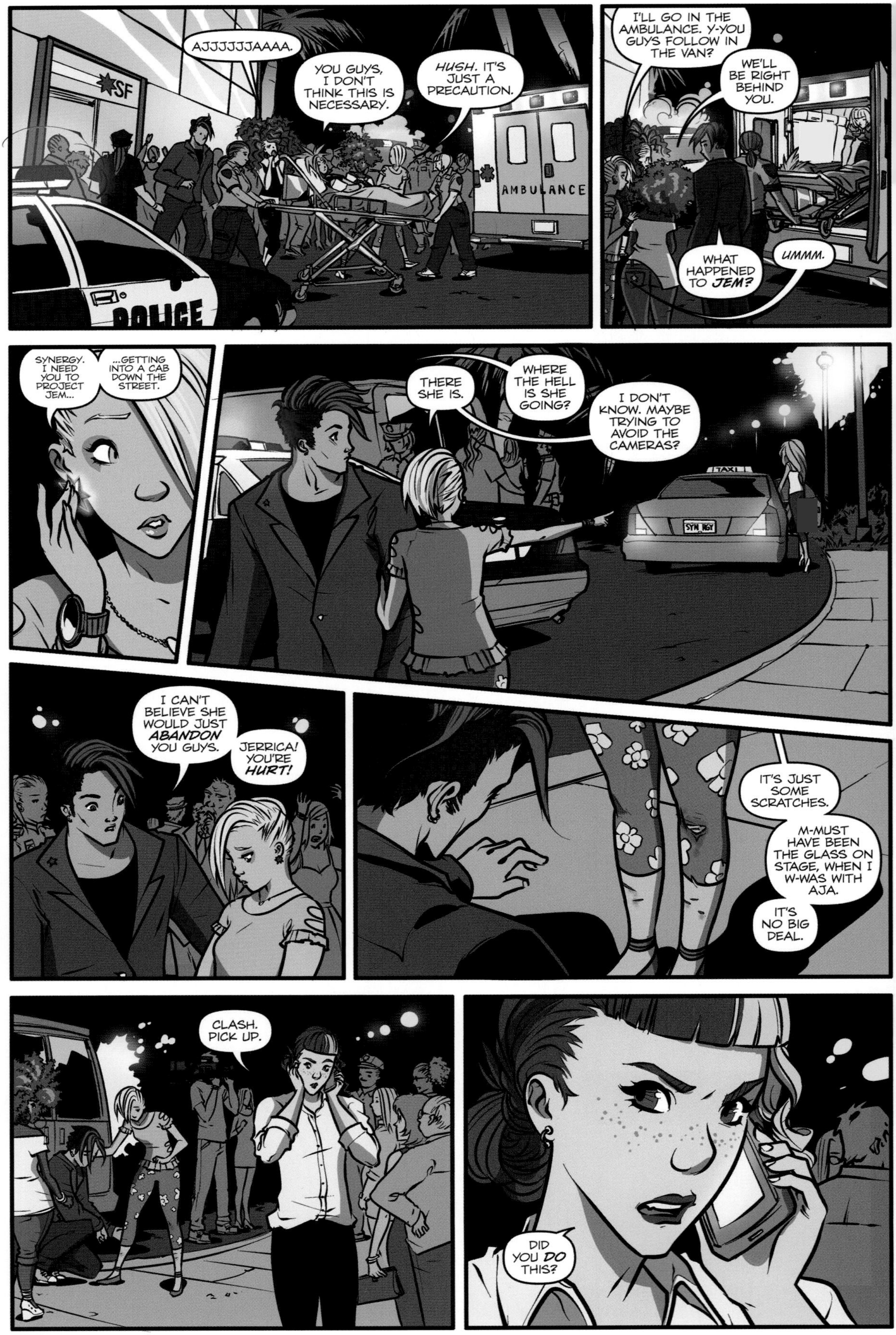

SF
AJJJJJJAAAA.
YOU GUYS, I DON'T THINK THIS IS NECESSARY.
HUSH. IT'S JUST A PRECAUTION.
AMBULANCE
POLICE
I'LL GO IN THE AMBULANCE. Y-YOU GUYS FOLLOW IN THE VAN?
WE'LL BE RIGHT BEHIND YOU.
WHAT HAPPENED TO ***JEM?***
UMMM.
SYNERGY. I NEED YOU TO PROJECT JEM...
...GETTING INTO A CAB DOWN THE STREET.
THERE SHE IS.
WHERE THE HELL IS SHE GOING?
I DON'T KNOW. MAYBE TRYING TO AVOID THE CAMERAS?
TAXI
SYN RGY
I CAN'T BELIEVE SHE WOULD JUST ***ABANDON*** YOU GUYS.
JERRICA! YOU'RE ***HURT!***
IT'S JUST SOME SCRATCHES.
M-MUST HAVE BEEN THE GLASS ON STAGE, WHEN I W-WAS WITH AJA.
IT'S NO BIG DEAL.
CLASH. PICK UP.
DID YOU ***DO*** THIS?

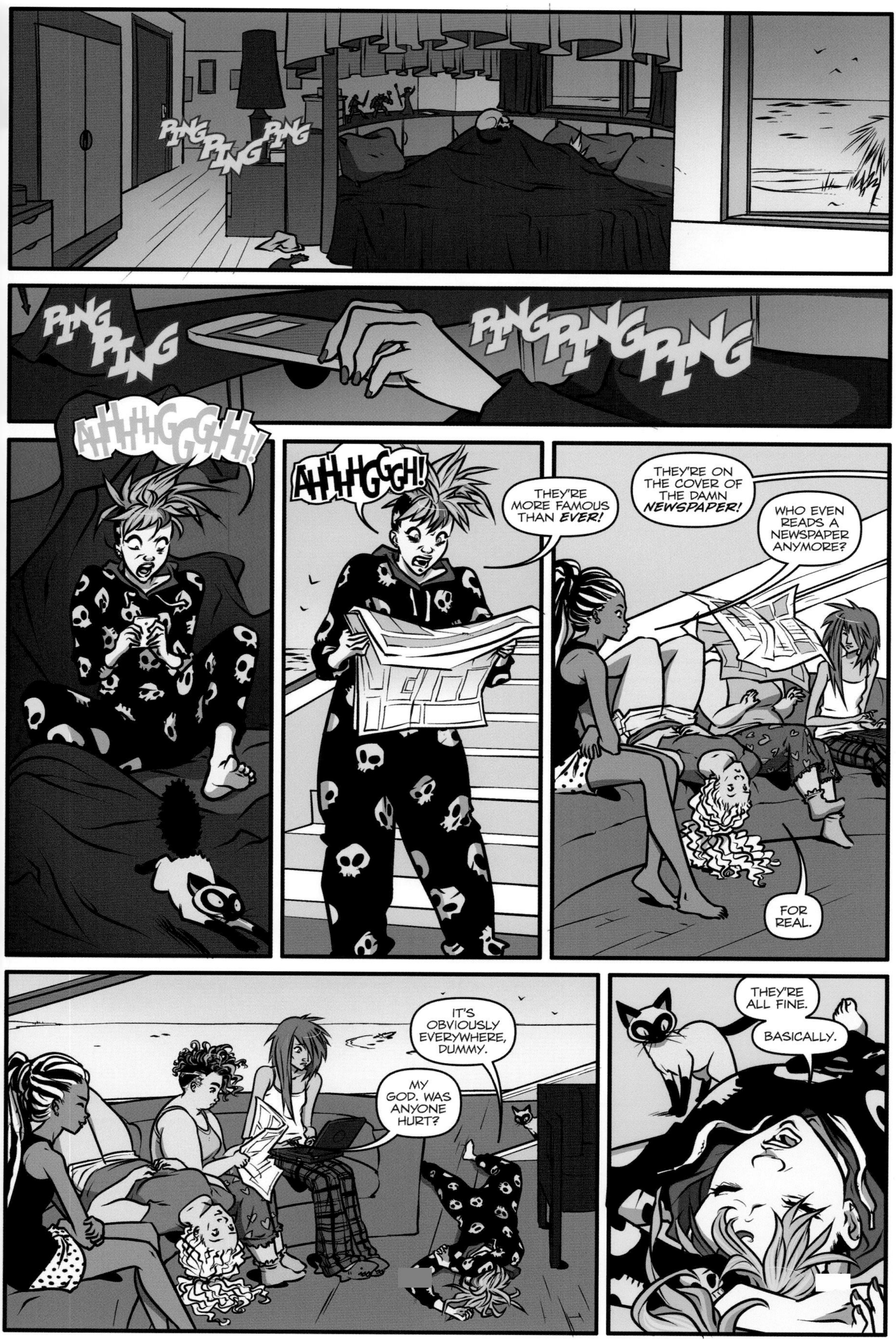
PING PING PING
PING PING
PING PING PING
AHHHHGGGHHH!
AHHHHGGGH!
THEY'RE MORE FAMOUS THAN *EVER!*
THEY'RE ON THE COVER OF THE DAMN *NEWSPAPER!*
WHO EVEN READS A NEWSPAPER ANYMORE?
FOR REAL.
IT'S OBVIOUSLY EVERYWHERE, DUMMY.
MY GOD. WAS ANYONE HURT?
THEY'RE ALL FINE.
BASICALLY.

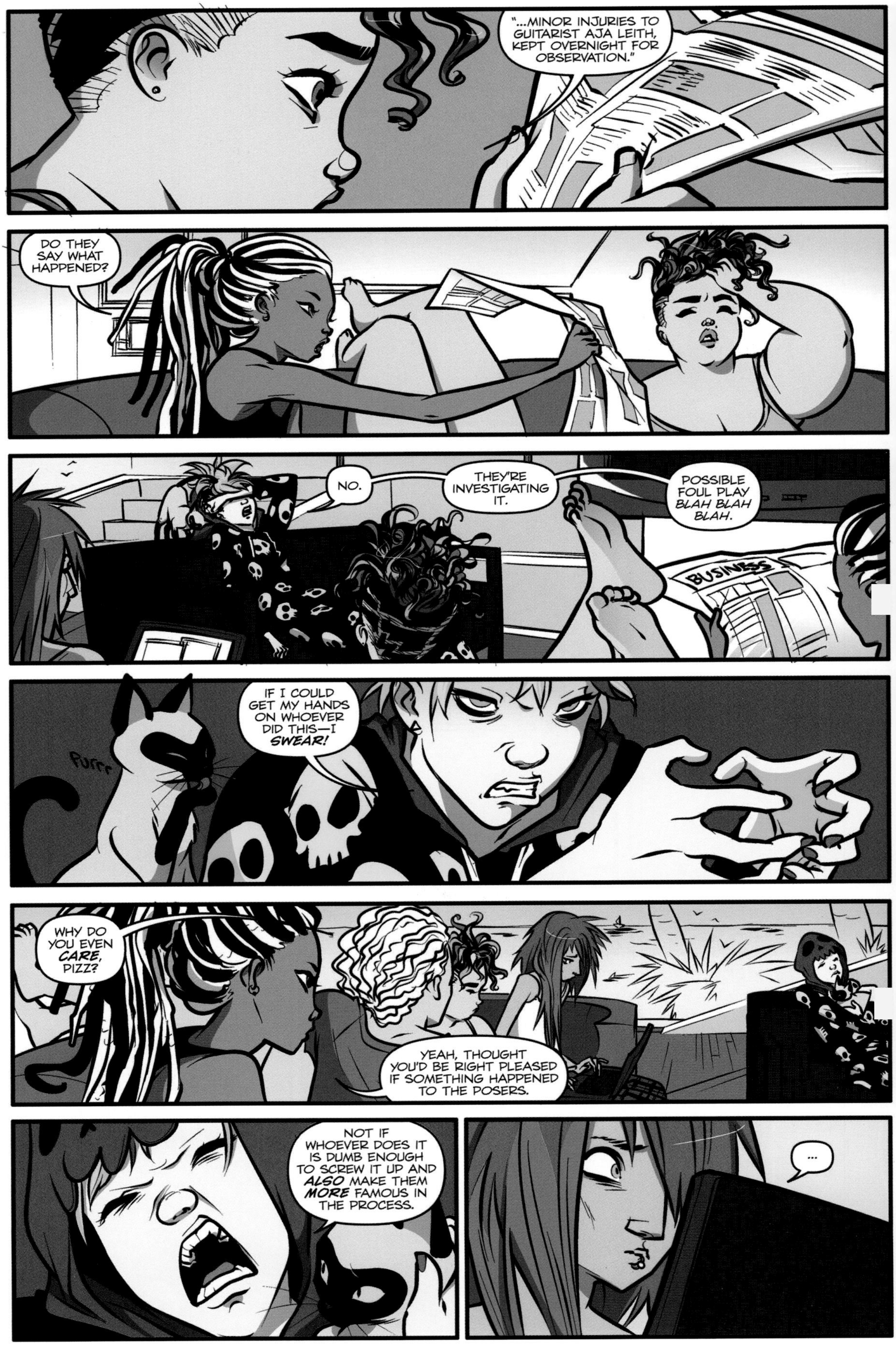
"...MINOR INJURIES TO GUITARIST AJA LEITH, KEPT OVERNIGHT FOR OBSERVATION."
DO THEY SAY WHAT HAPPENED?
NO.
THEY'RE INVESTIGATING IT.
POSSIBLE FOUL PLAY *BLAH BLAH BLAH*.
BUSINESS
IF I COULD GET MY HANDS ON WHOEVER DID THIS—I ***SWEAR!***
PURRR
WHY DO YOU EVEN ***CARE***, PIZZ?
YEAH, THOUGHT YOU'D BE RIGHT PLEASED IF SOMETHING HAPPENED TO THE POSERS.
NOT IF WHOEVER DOES IT IS DUMB ENOUGH TO SCREW IT UP AND ***ALSO*** MAKE THEM ***MORE*** FAMOUS IN THE PROCESS.
...

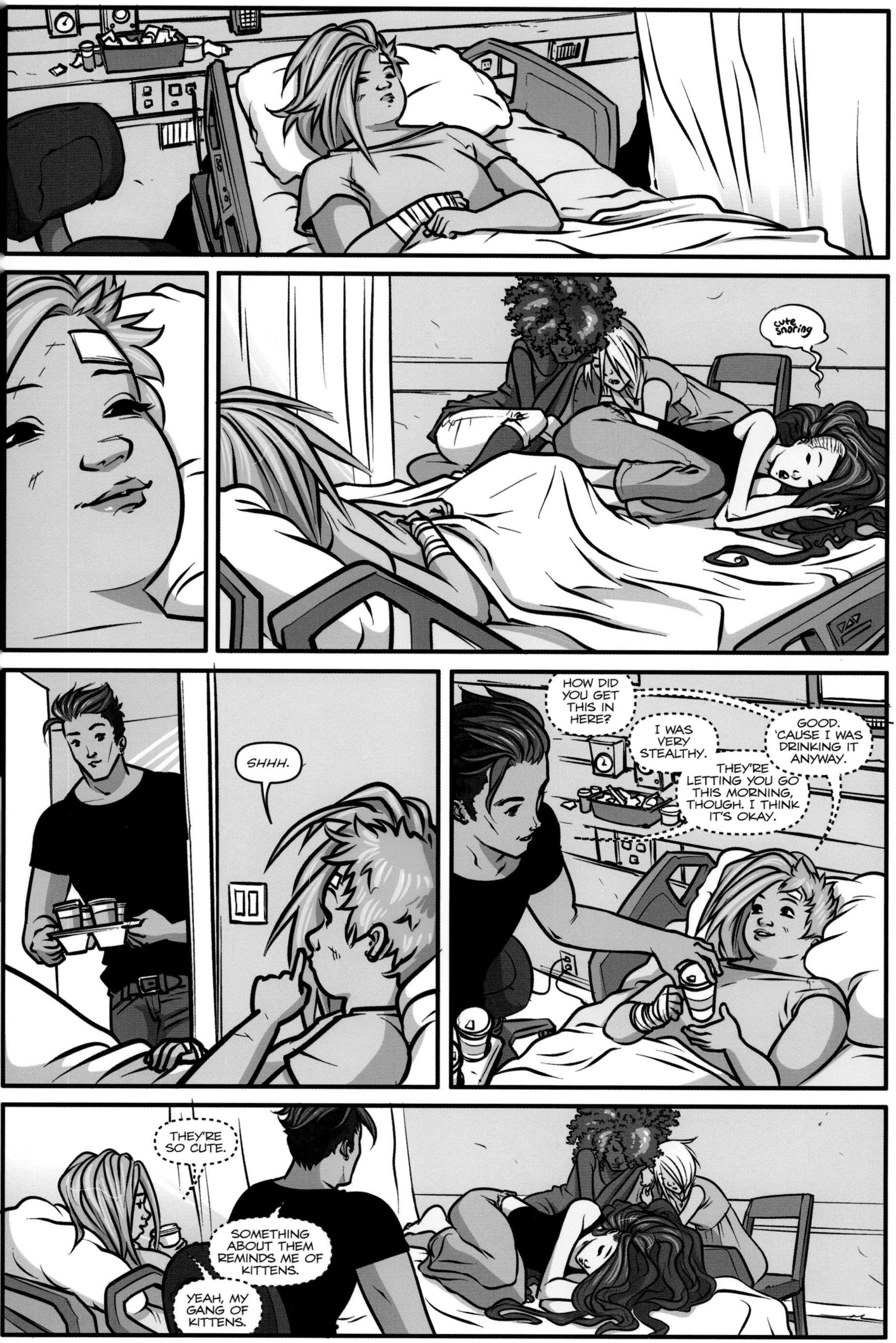
cute snoring
SHHH.
HOW DID YOU GET THIS IN HERE?
I WAS VERY STEALTHY.
THEY'RE LETTING YOU GO THIS MORNING, THOUGH. I THINK IT'S OKAY.
GOOD. 'CAUSE I WAS DRINKING IT ANYWAY.
THEY'RE SO CUTE.
SOMETHING ABOUT THEM REMINDS ME OF KITTENS.
YEAH, MY GANG OF KITTENS.

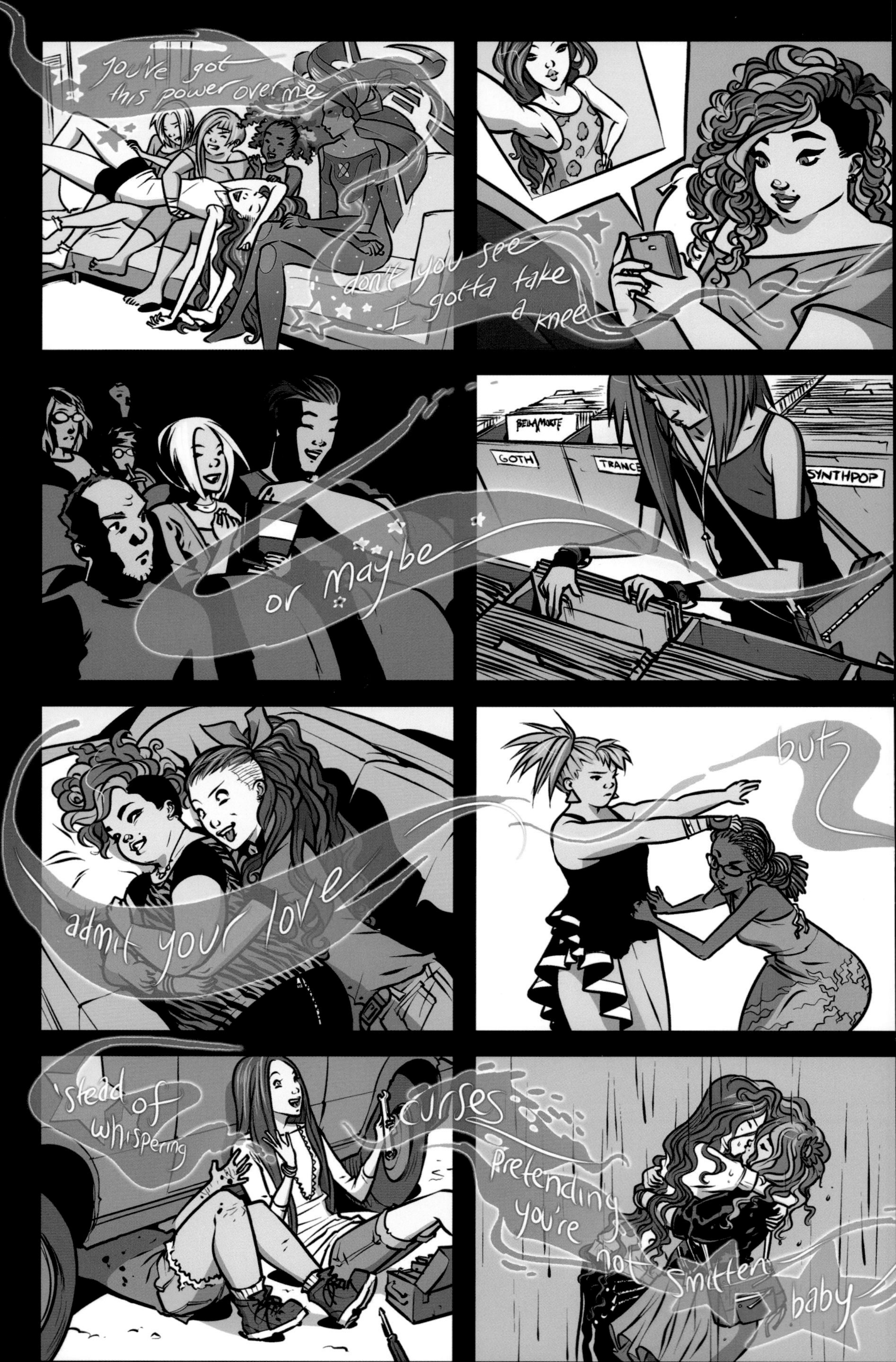

you've got this power over me
don't you see I gotta take a knee
BELLAMORTE
GOTH
TRANCE
SYNTHPOP
or maybe
admit your love
but
'stead of whispering
curses
pretending you're not smitten
baby

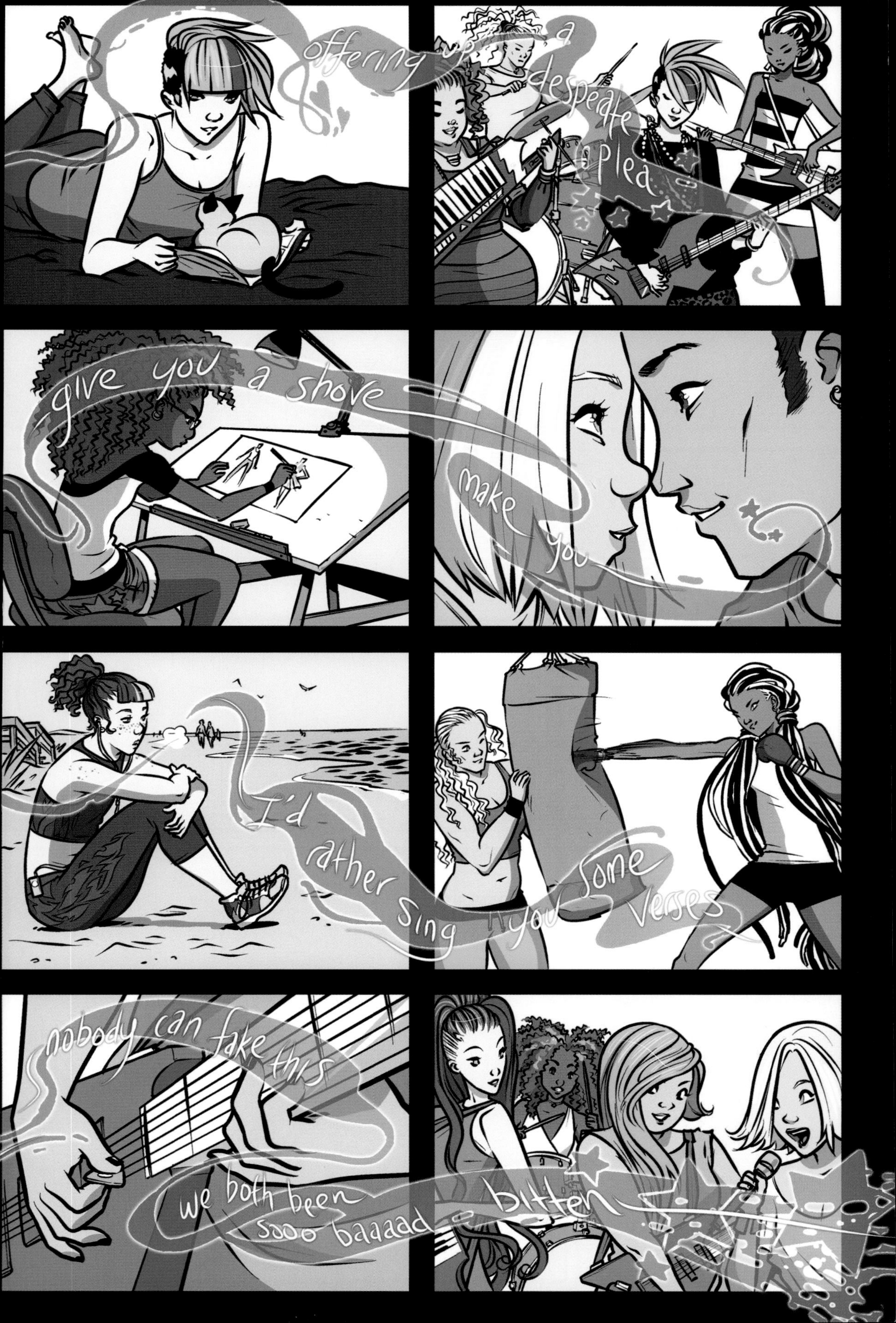
offering up a
despeate
plea
give you a shove
make you
I'd rather sing you some verses
nobody can fake this
we both been sooo baaaad bitten

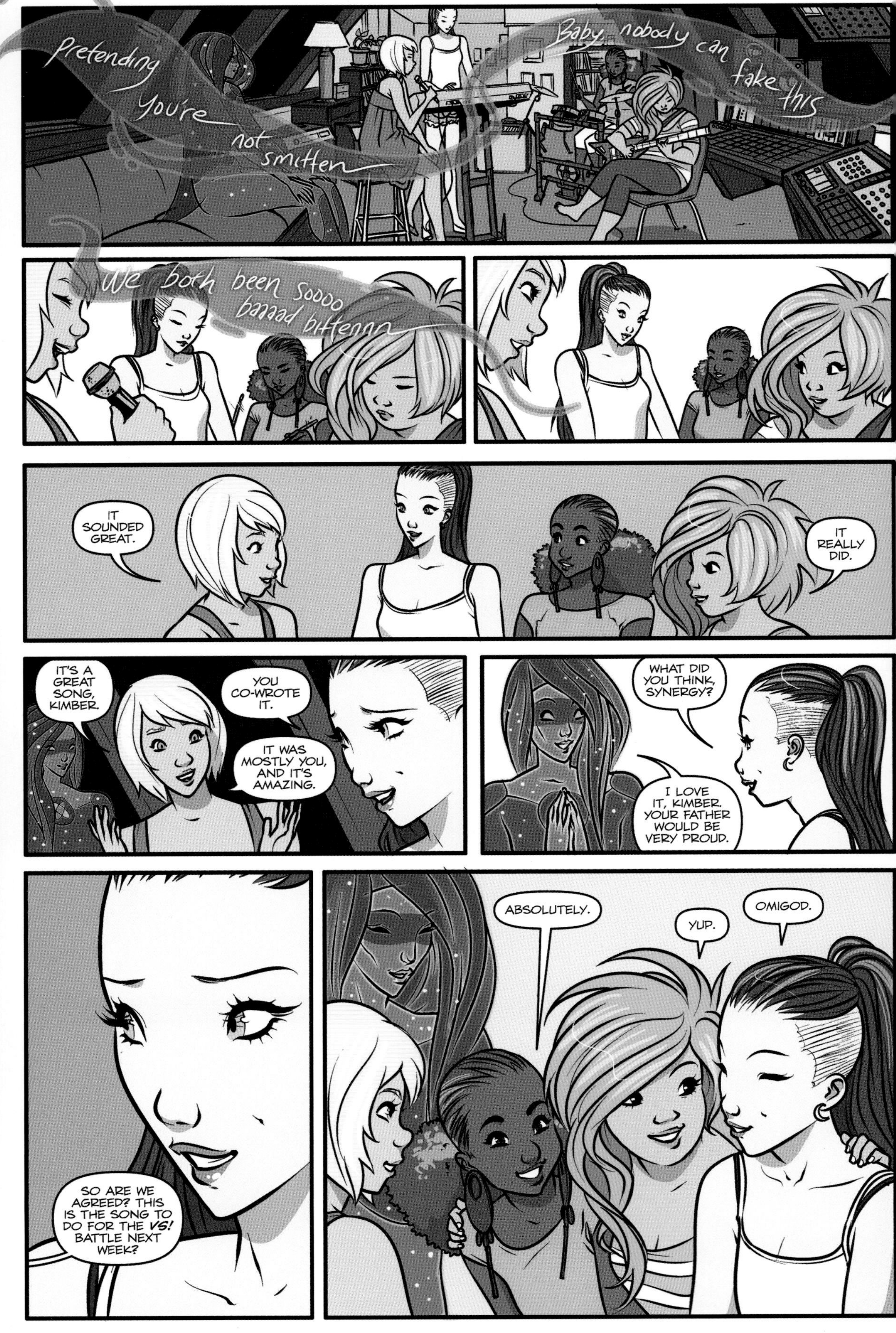
Pretending you're not smitten
Baby, nobody can fake this
We both been soooo baaaad bittennn
IT SOUNDED GREAT.
IT REALLY DID.
IT'S A GREAT SONG, KIMBER.
YOU CO-WROTE IT.
IT WAS MOSTLY YOU, AND IT'S AMAZING.
WHAT DID YOU THINK, SYNERGY?
I LOVE IT, KIMBER. YOUR FATHER WOULD BE VERY PROUD.
SO ARE WE AGREED? THIS IS THE SONG TO DO FOR THE VS! BATTLE NEXT WEEK?
ABSOLUTELY.
YUP.
OMIGOD.

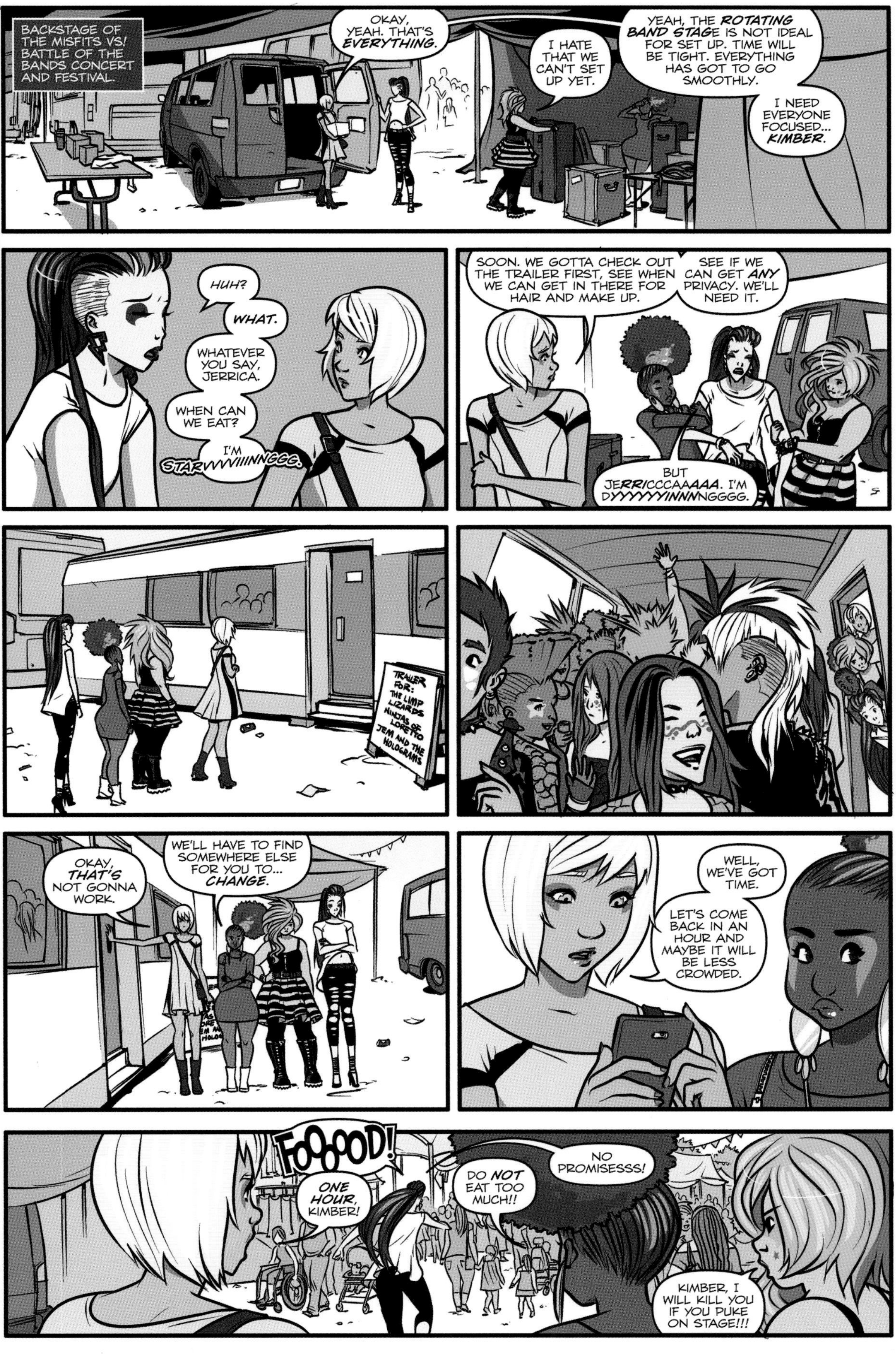
BACKSTAGE OF THE MISFITS VS! BATTLE OF THE BANDS CONCERT AND FESTIVAL.
OKAY, YEAH. THAT'S *EVERYTHING*.
I HATE THAT WE CAN'T SET UP YET.
YEAH, THE *ROTATING BAND STAGE* IS NOT IDEAL FOR SET UP. TIME WILL BE TIGHT. EVERYTHING HAS GOT TO GO SMOOTHLY.
I NEED EVERYONE FOCUSED... *KIMBER*.
HUH?
WHAT.
WHATEVER YOU SAY, JERRICA.
WHEN CAN WE EAT?
I'M STARVVVVIIINNGGG.
SOON. WE GOTTA CHECK OUT THE TRAILER FIRST, SEE WHEN WE CAN GET IN THERE FOR HAIR AND MAKE UP.
SEE IF WE CAN GET *ANY* PRIVACY. WE'LL NEED IT.
BUT JERRICCCAAAAA. I'M DYYYYYYINNNNGGGG.
TRAILER FOR: THE LIMP LIZARDS NINJAS OF LORETTO JEM AND THE HOLOGRAMS
OKAY, *THAT'S* NOT GONNA WORK.
WE'LL HAVE TO FIND SOMEWHERE ELSE FOR YOU TO... *CHANGE*.
WELL, WE'VE GOT TIME.
LET'S COME BACK IN AN HOUR AND MAYBE IT WILL BE LESS CROWDED.
FOOOOOD!
ONE HOUR, KIMBER!
DO *NOT* EAT TOO MUCH!!
NO PROMISESSS!
KIMBER, I WILL KILL YOU IF YOU PUKE ON STAGE!!!

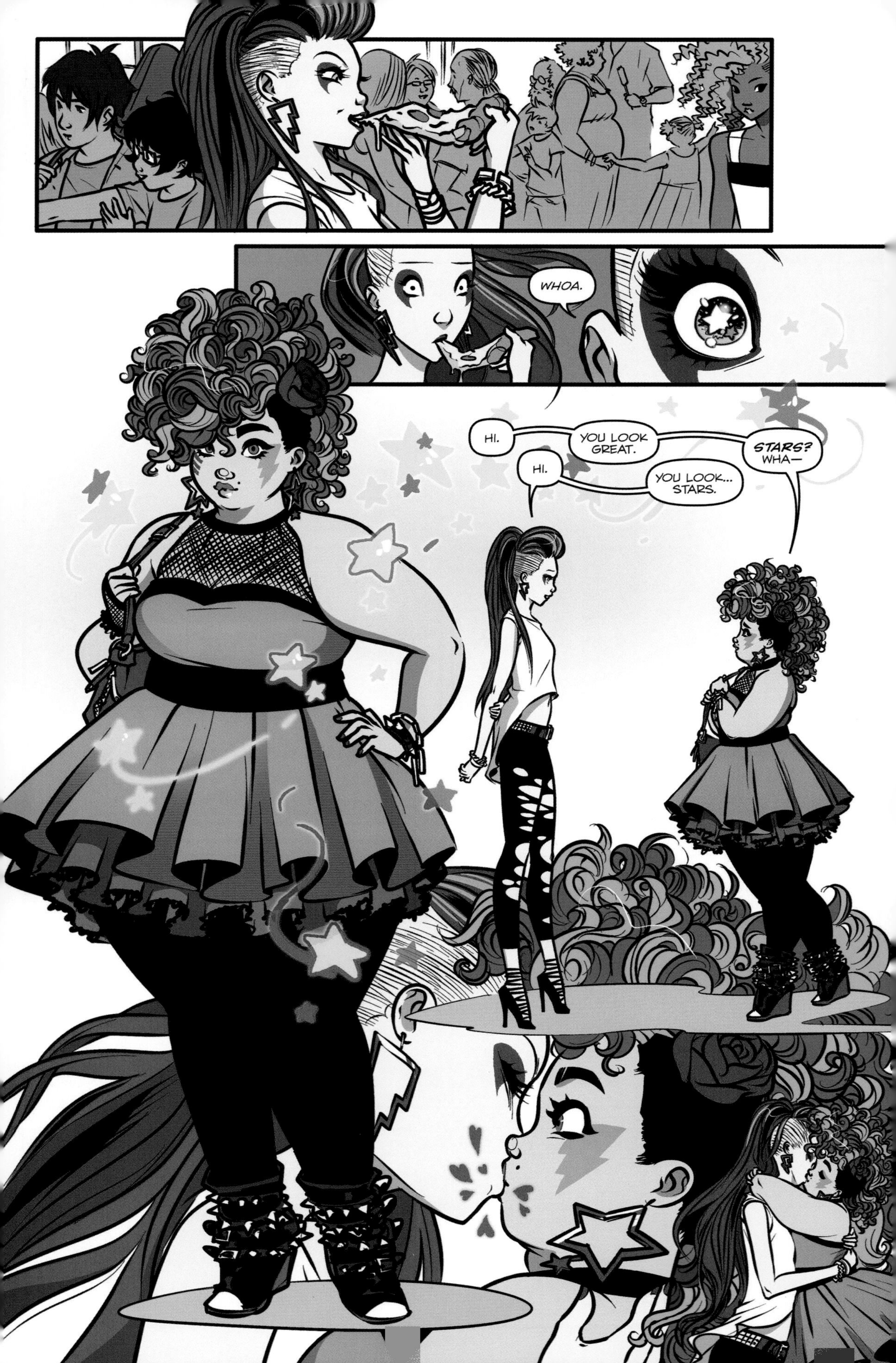
WHOA.
HI.
YOU LOOK GREAT.
STARS? WHA—
HI.
YOU LOOK... STARS.

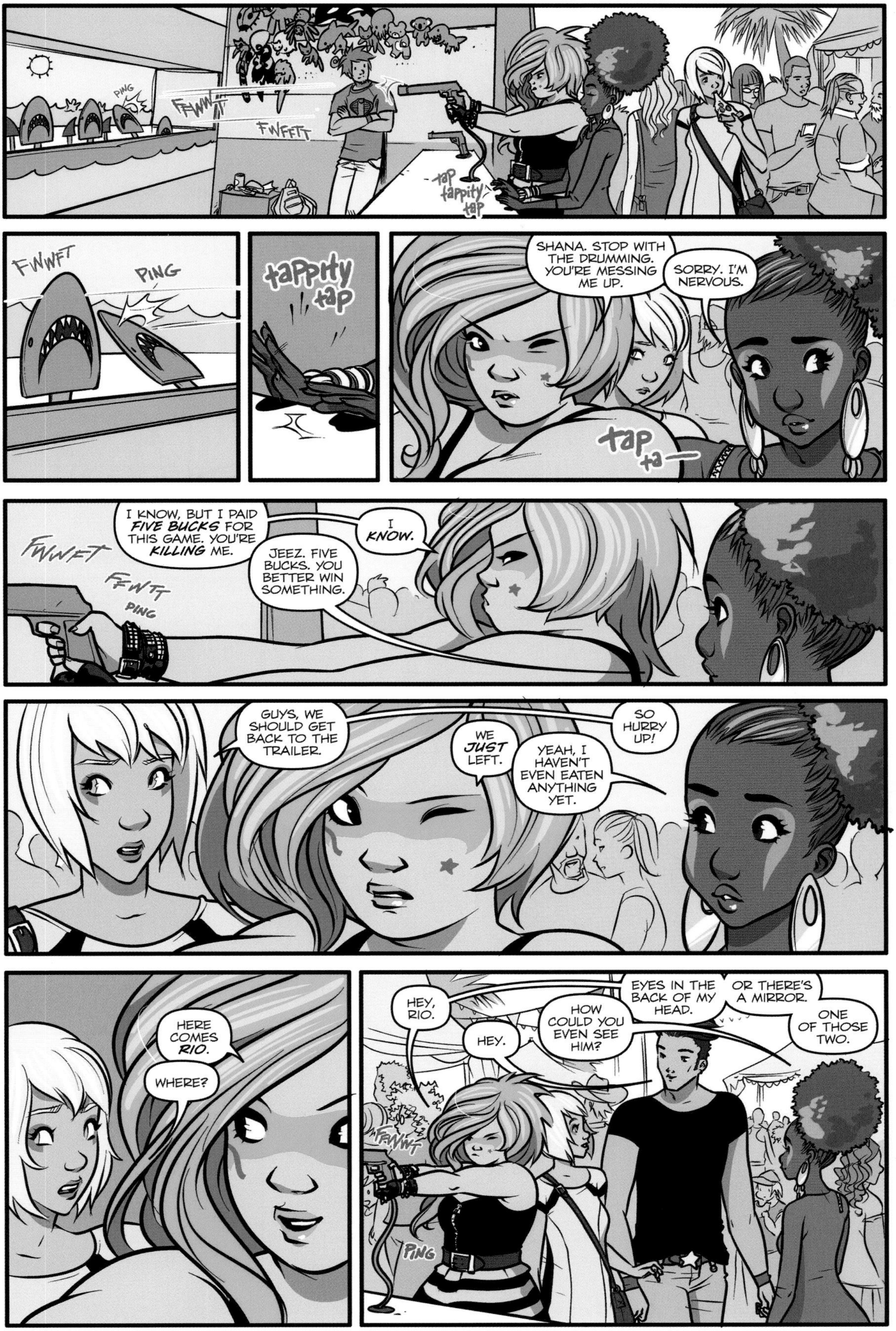
PING
FFWWT
FWFFTT
-tap tappity tap
FWWFT
PING
tappity tap
SHANA. STOP WITH THE DRUMMING. YOU'RE MESSING ME UP.
SORRY. I'M NERVOUS.
tap ta—
I KNOW, BUT I PAID FIVE BUCKS FOR THIS GAME. YOU'RE KILLING ME.
I KNOW.
JEEZ. FIVE BUCKS. YOU BETTER WIN SOMETHING.
FWWFT
FFWTT
PING
GUYS, WE SHOULD GET BACK TO THE TRAILER.
WE JUST LEFT.
YEAH, I HAVEN'T EVEN EATEN ANYTHING YET.
SO HURRY UP!
HERE COMES RIO.
WHERE?
HEY, RIO.
HEY.
HOW COULD YOU EVEN SEE HIM?
EYES IN THE BACK OF MY HEAD.
OR THERE'S A MIRROR.
ONE OF THOSE TWO.
FFWWT
PING

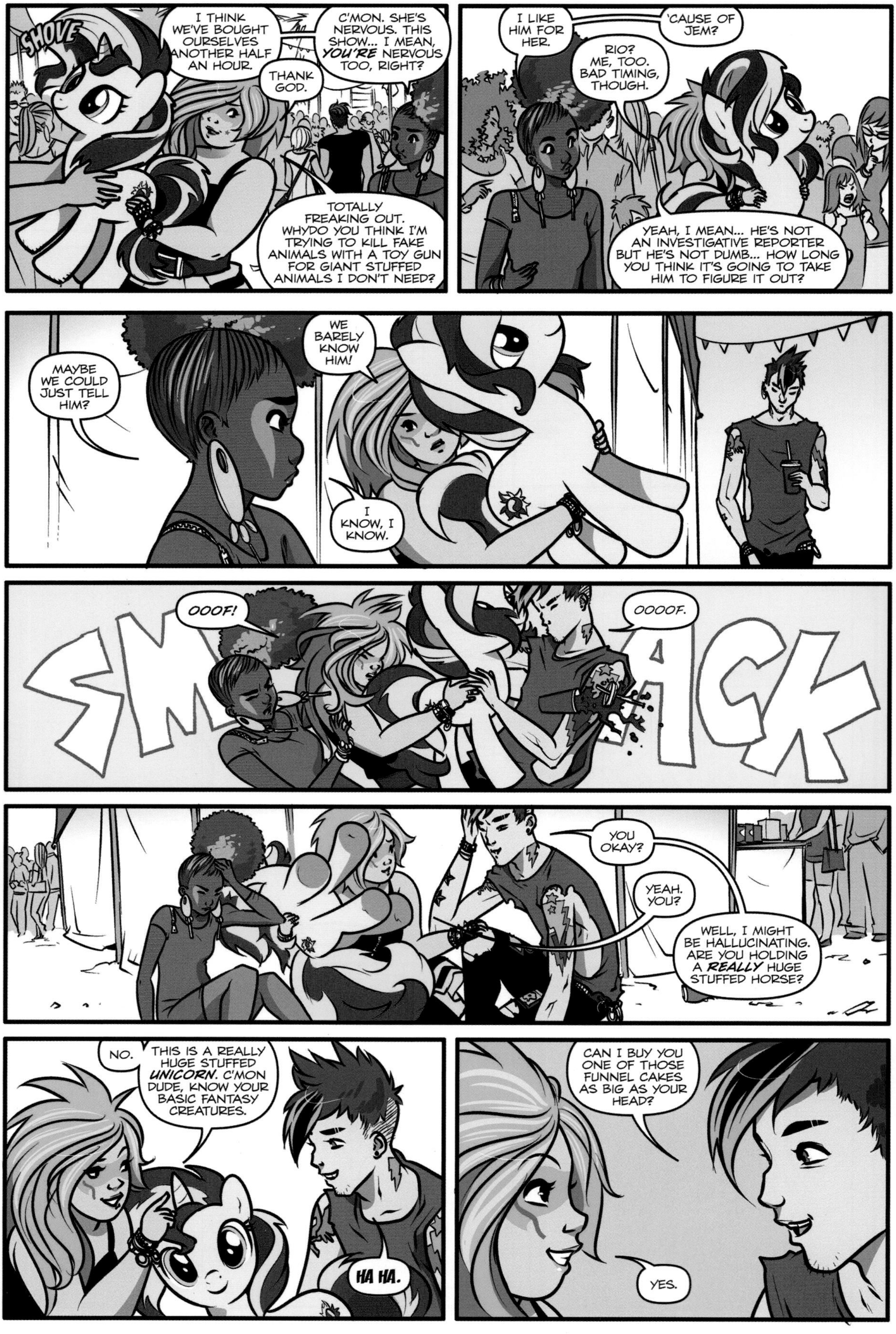
SHOVE
I THINK WE'VE BOUGHT OURSELVES ANOTHER HALF AN HOUR.
THANK GOD.
C'MON. SHE'S NERVOUS. THIS SHOW... I MEAN, YOU'RE NERVOUS TOO, RIGHT?
TOTALLY FREAKING OUT. WHYDO YOU THINK I'M TRYING TO KILL FAKE ANIMALS WITH A TOY GUN FOR GIANT STUFFED ANIMALS I DON'T NEED?
I LIKE HIM FOR HER.
'CAUSE OF JEM?
RIO? ME, TOO. BAD TIMING, THOUGH.
YEAH, I MEAN... HE'S NOT AN INVESTIGATIVE REPORTER BUT HE'S NOT DUMB... HOW LONG YOU THINK IT'S GOING TO TAKE HIM TO FIGURE IT OUT?
MAYBE WE COULD JUST TELL HIM?
WE BARELY KNOW HIM!
I KNOW, I KNOW.
SMACK
OOOF!
OOOOF.
YOU OKAY?
YEAH. YOU?
WELL, I MIGHT BE HALLUCINATING. ARE YOU HOLDING A REALLY HUGE STUFFED HORSE?
NO.
THIS IS A REALLY HUGE STUFFED UNICORN. C'MON DUDE, KNOW YOUR BASIC FANTASY CREATURES.
HA HA.
CAN I BUY YOU ONE OF THOSE FUNNEL CAKES AS BIG AS YOUR HEAD?
YES.

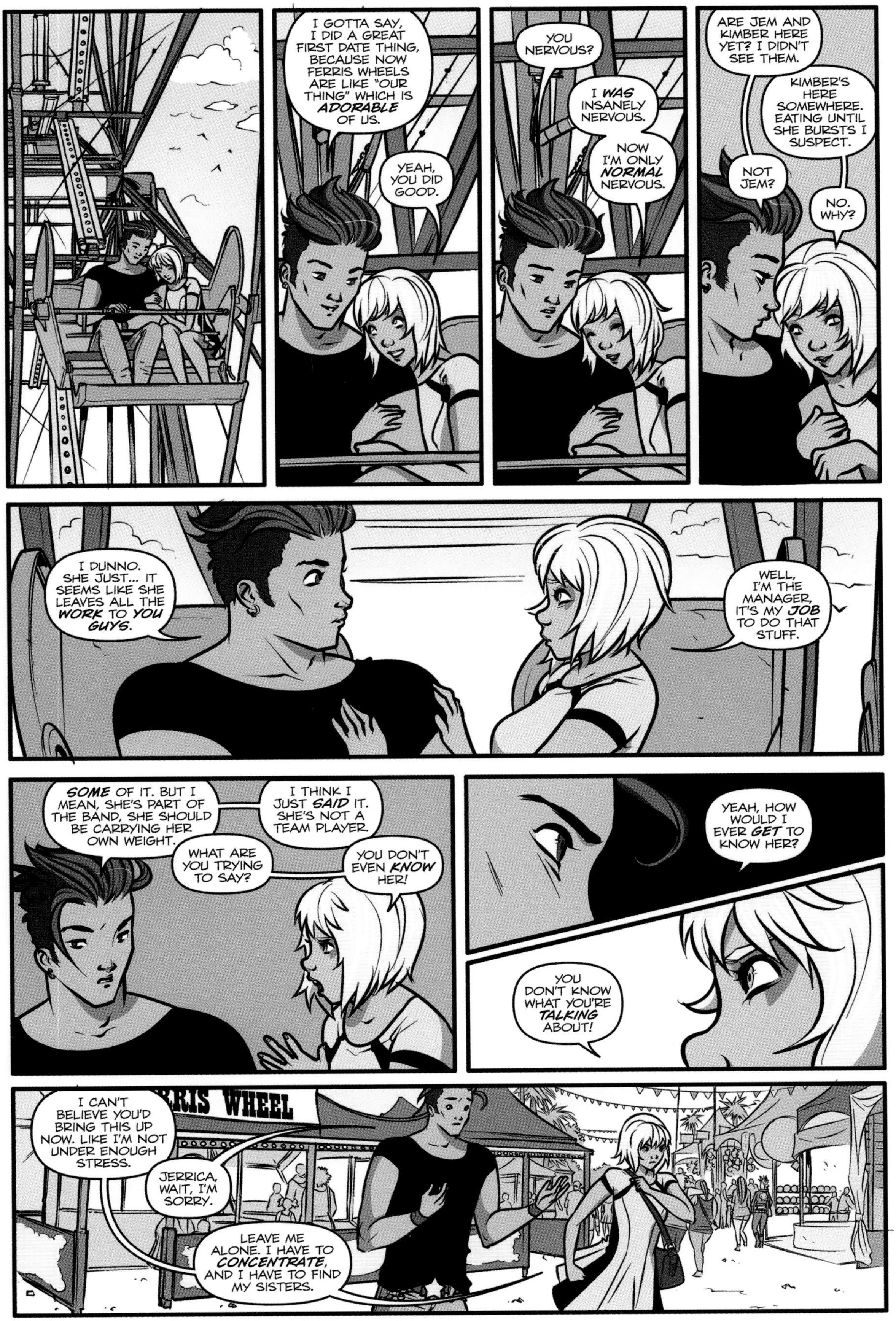
I GOTTA SAY, I DID A GREAT FIRST DATE THING, BECAUSE NOW FERRIS WHEELS ARE LIKE "OUR THING" WHICH IS ADORABLE OF US.
YEAH, YOU DID GOOD.
YOU NERVOUS?
I WAS INSANELY NERVOUS.
NOW I'M ONLY NORMAL NERVOUS.
ARE JEM AND KIMBER HERE YET? I DIDN'T SEE THEM.
KIMBER'S HERE SOMEWHERE. EATING UNTIL SHE BURSTS I SUSPECT.
NOT JEM?
NO. WHY?
I DUNNO. SHE JUST... IT SEEMS LIKE SHE LEAVES ALL THE WORK TO YOU GUYS.
WELL, I'M THE MANAGER, IT'S MY JOB TO DO THAT STUFF.
SOME OF IT. BUT I MEAN, SHE'S PART OF THE BAND, SHE SHOULD BE CARRYING HER OWN WEIGHT.
WHAT ARE YOU TRYING TO SAY?
I THINK I JUST SAID IT. SHE'S NOT A TEAM PLAYER.
YOU DON'T EVEN KNOW HER!
YEAH, HOW WOULD I EVER GET TO KNOW HER?
YOU DON'T KNOW WHAT YOU'RE TALKING ABOUT!
RRIS WHEEL
I CAN'T BELIEVE YOU'D BRING THIS UP NOW. LIKE I'M NOT UNDER ENOUGH STRESS.
JERRICA, WAIT, I'M SORRY.
LEAVE ME ALONE. I HAVE TO CONCENTRATE, AND I HAVE TO FIND MY SISTERS.

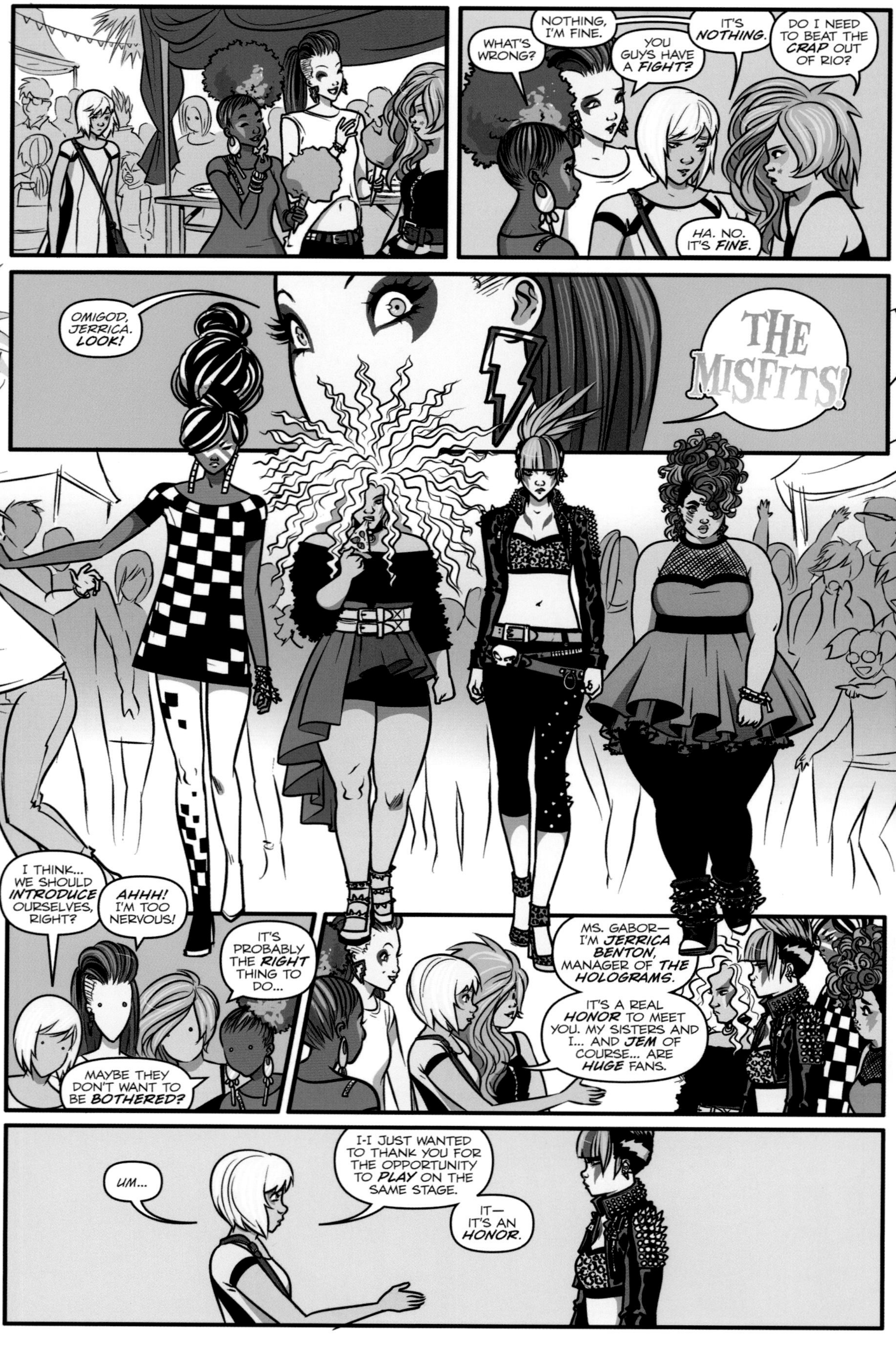

WHAT'S WRONG?
NOTHING, I'M FINE.
YOU GUYS HAVE A *FIGHT?*
IT'S *NOTHING*.
DO I NEED TO BEAT THE *CRAP* OUT OF RIO?
HA. NO. IT'S *FINE*.
OMIGOD, JERRICA. *LOOK!*
THE MISFITS!
I THINK... WE SHOULD *INTRODUCE* OURSELVES, RIGHT?
AHHH! I'M TOO NERVOUS!
IT'S PROBABLY THE *RIGHT* THING TO DO...
MAYBE THEY DON'T WANT TO BE *BOTHERED?*
MS. GABOR— I'M *JERRICA BENTON*, MANAGER OF *THE HOLOGRAMS*.
IT'S A REAL *HONOR* TO MEET YOU. MY SISTERS AND I... AND *JEM* OF COURSE... ARE *HUGE* FANS.
UM...
I-I JUST WANTED TO THANK YOU FOR THE OPPORTUNITY TO *PLAY* ON THE SAME STAGE.
IT— IT'S AN *HONOR*.

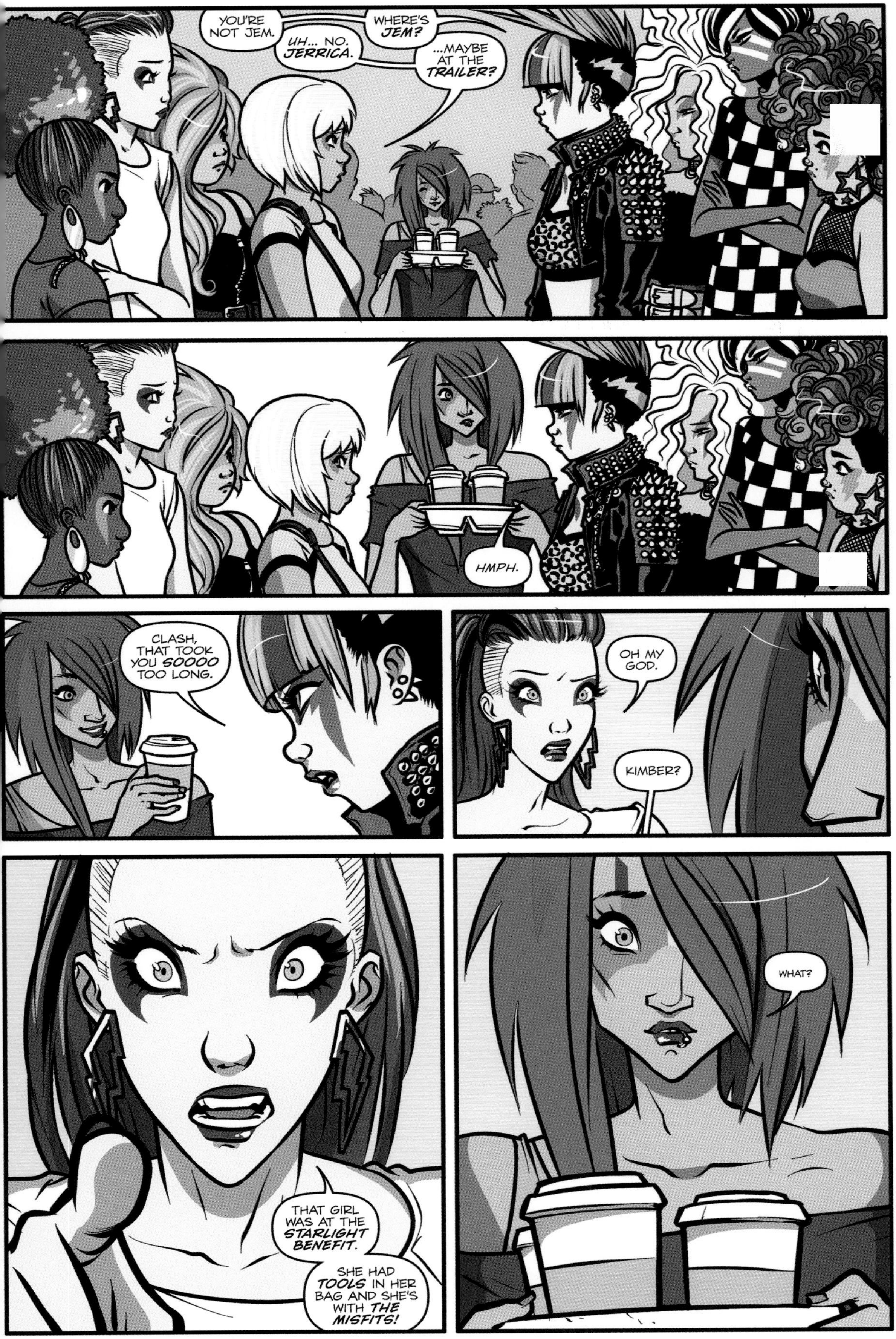
YOU'RE NOT JEM.
UH... NO. JERRICA.
WHERE'S JEM?
...MAYBE AT THE TRAILER?
HMPH.
CLASH, THAT TOOK YOU SOOOO TOO LONG.
OH MY GOD.
KIMBER?
THAT GIRL WAS AT THE STARLIGHT BENEFIT.
SHE HAD TOOLS IN HER BAG AND SHE'S WITH THE MISFITS!
WHAT?

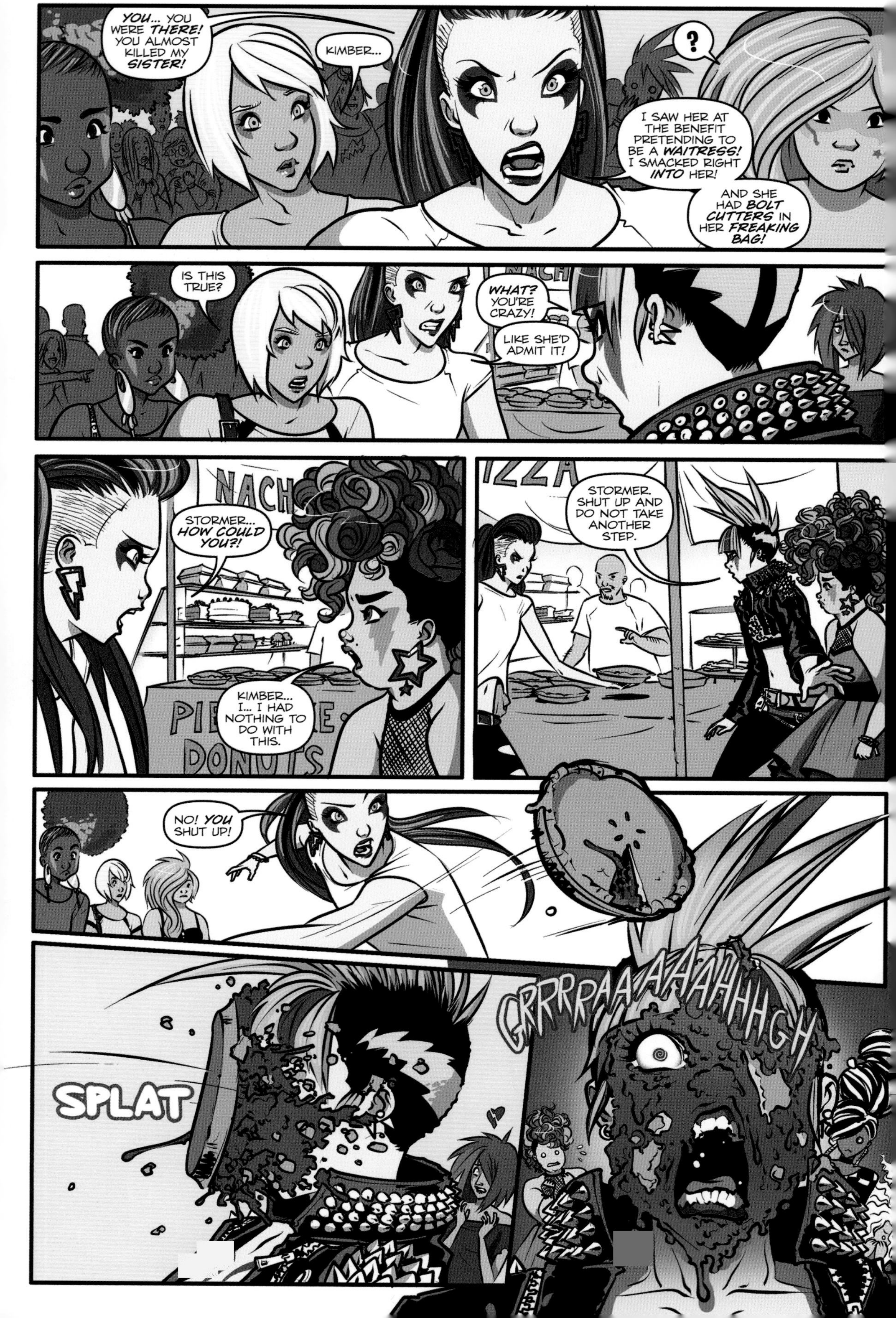
YOU... YOU WERE THERE! YOU ALMOST KILLED MY SISTER!
KIMBER...
?
I SAW HER AT THE BENEFIT PRETENDING TO BE A WAITRESS! I SMACKED RIGHT INTO HER!
AND SHE HAD BOLT CUTTERS IN HER FREAKING BAG!
IS THIS TRUE?
WHAT? YOU'RE CRAZY!
LIKE SHE'D ADMIT IT!
NACH
STORMER... HOW COULD YOU?!
KIMBER... I... I HAD NOTHING TO DO WITH THIS.
PIE
DONUTS
IZZA
STORMER. SHUT UP AND DO NOT TAKE ANOTHER STEP.
NO! YOU SHUT UP!
SPLAT
GRRRRAAAAAAHHHHGH

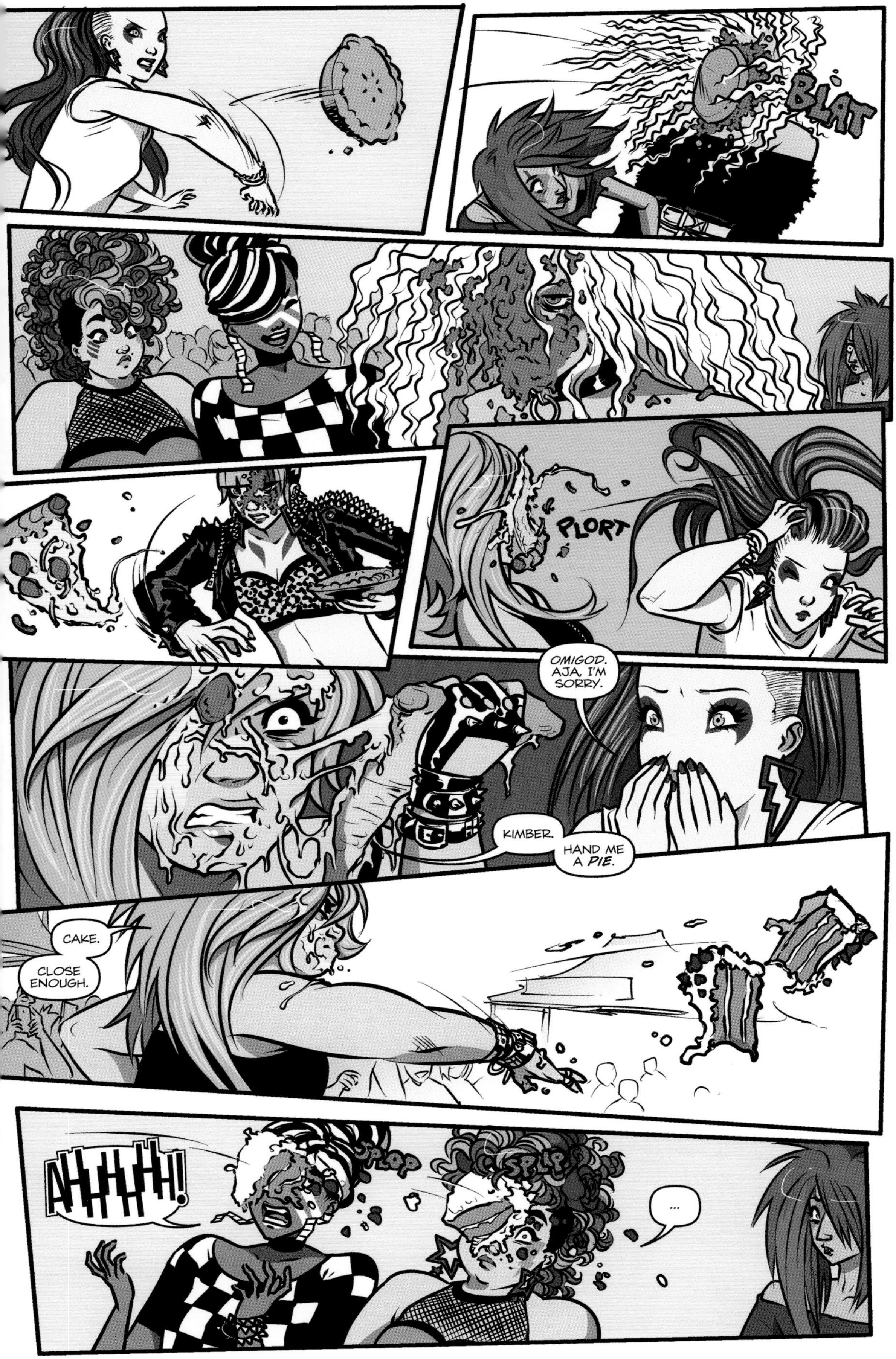
BLAT
PLORT
OMIGOD. AJA, I'M SORRY.
KIMBER.
HAND ME A *PIE*.
CAKE.
CLOSE ENOUGH.
AHHHHH!
SPLOP
SPLOP
...

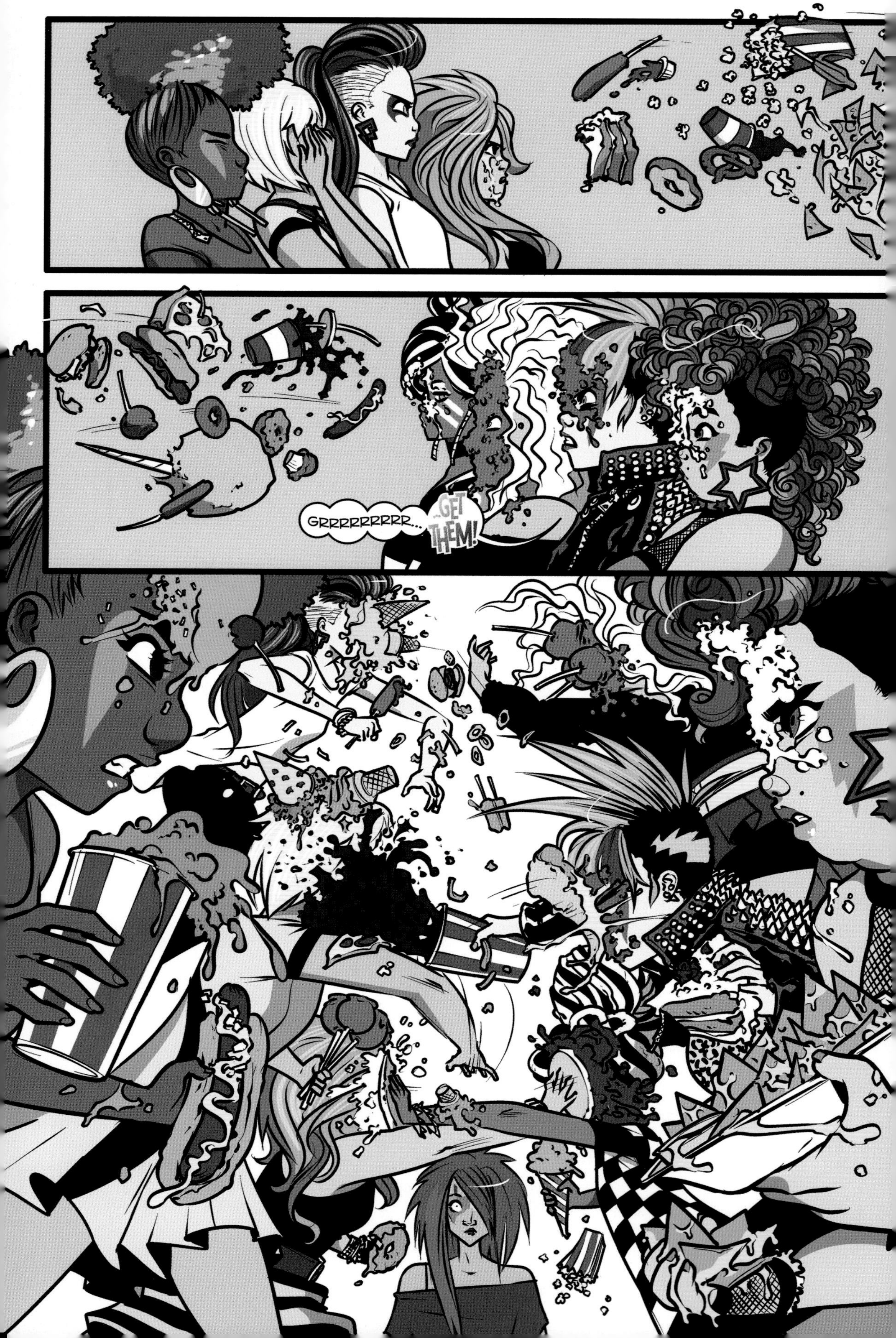
GRRRRRRRRR...
...GET THEM!

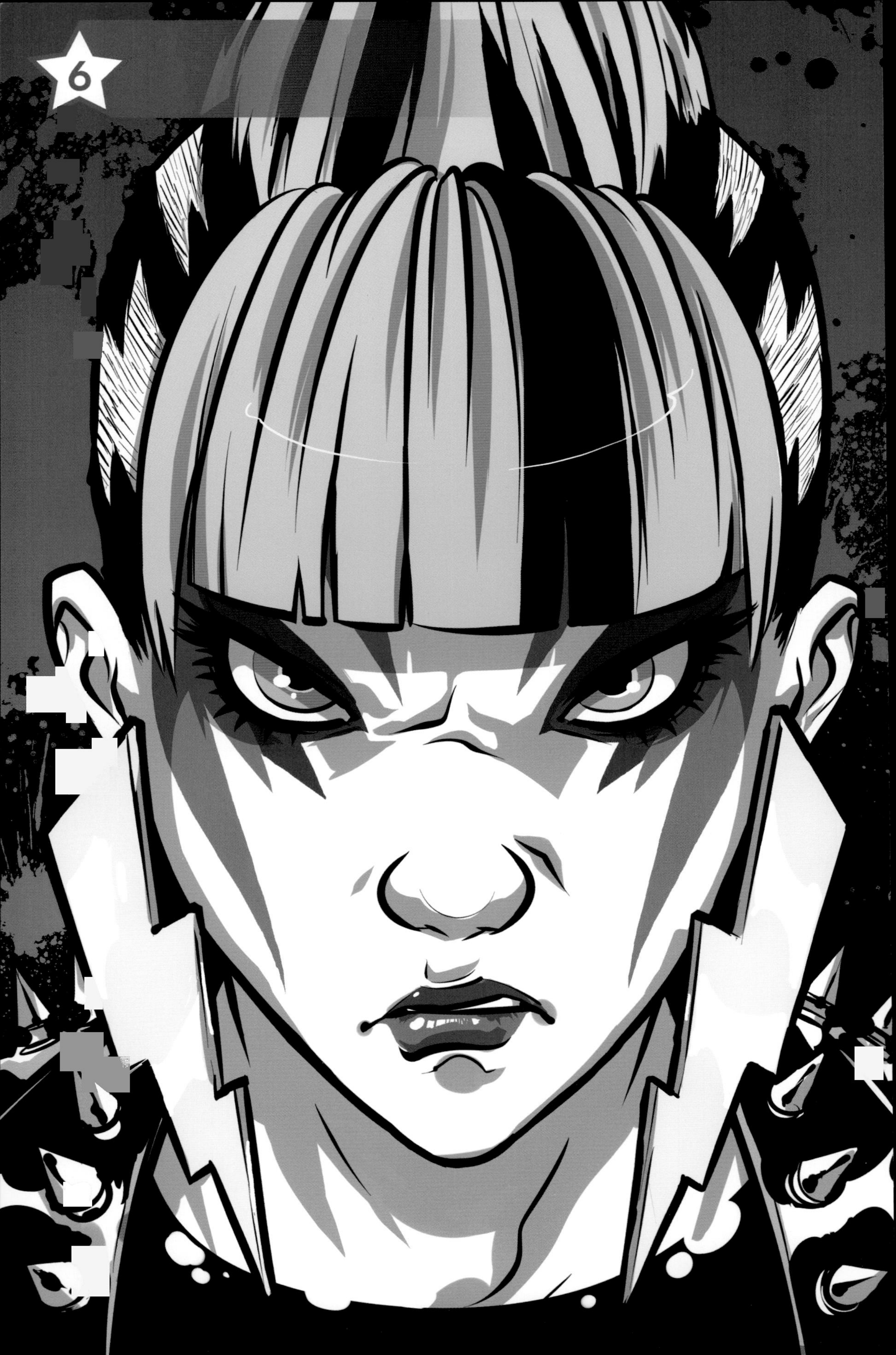
6

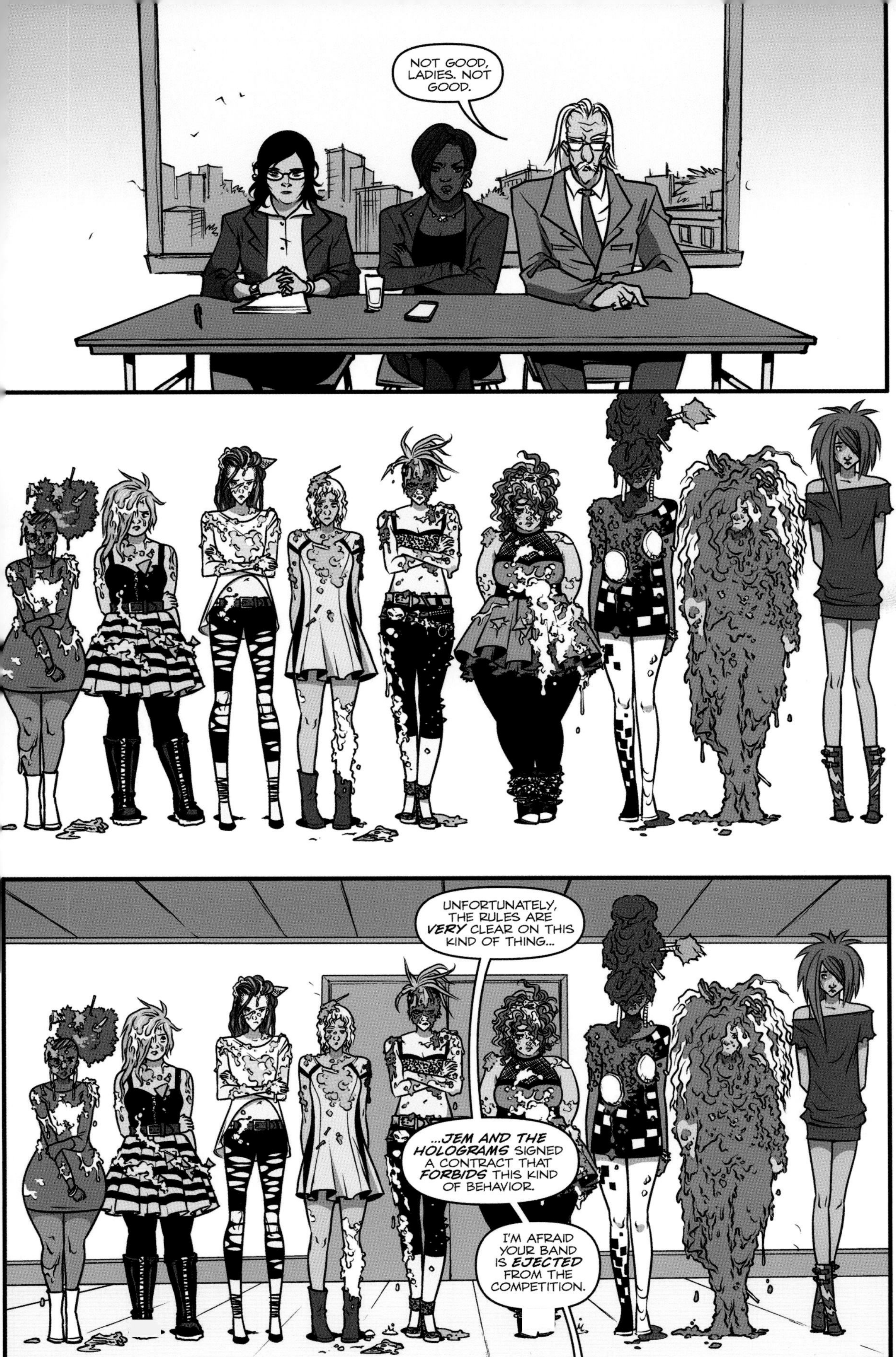

NOT GOOD, LADIES. NOT GOOD.
UNFORTUNATELY, THE RULES ARE VERY CLEAR ON THIS KIND OF THING...
...JEM AND THE HOLOGRAMS SIGNED A CONTRACT THAT FORBIDS THIS KIND OF BEHAVIOR.
I'M AFRAID YOUR BAND IS EJECTED FROM THE COMPETITION.

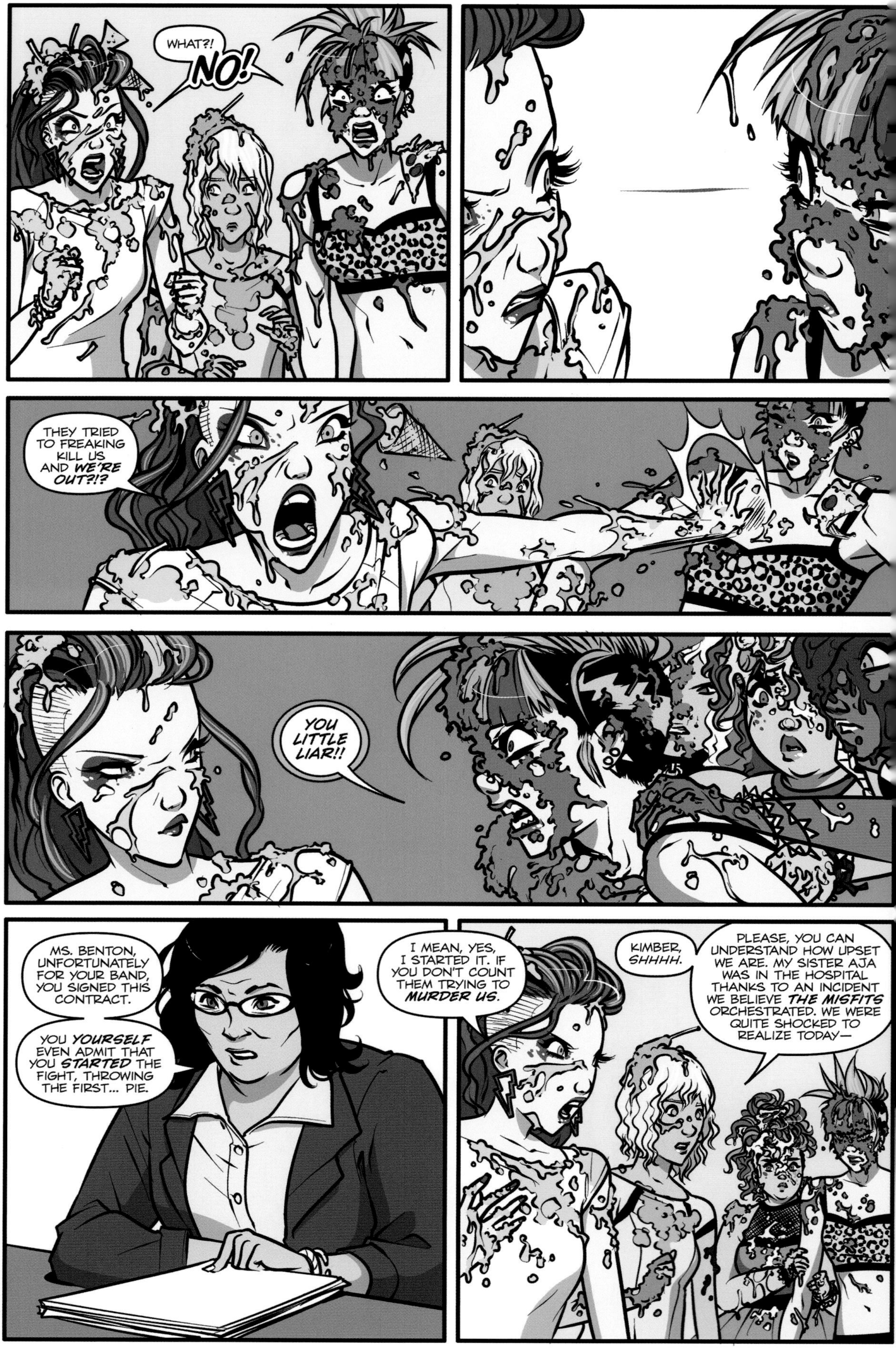
WHAT?! NO!
THEY TRIED TO FREAKING KILL US AND WE'RE OUT?!?
YOU LITTLE LIAR!!
MS. BENTON, UNFORTUNATELY FOR YOUR BAND, YOU SIGNED THIS CONTRACT.
YOU YOURSELF EVEN ADMIT THAT YOU STARTED THE FIGHT, THROWING THE FIRST... PIE.
I MEAN, YES, I STARTED IT. IF YOU DON'T COUNT THEM TRYING TO MURDER US.
KIMBER, SHHHH.
PLEASE, YOU CAN UNDERSTAND HOW UPSET WE ARE. MY SISTER AJA WAS IN THE HOSPITAL THANKS TO AN INCIDENT WE BELIEVE THE MISFITS ORCHESTRATED. WE WERE QUITE SHOCKED TO REALIZE TODAY—

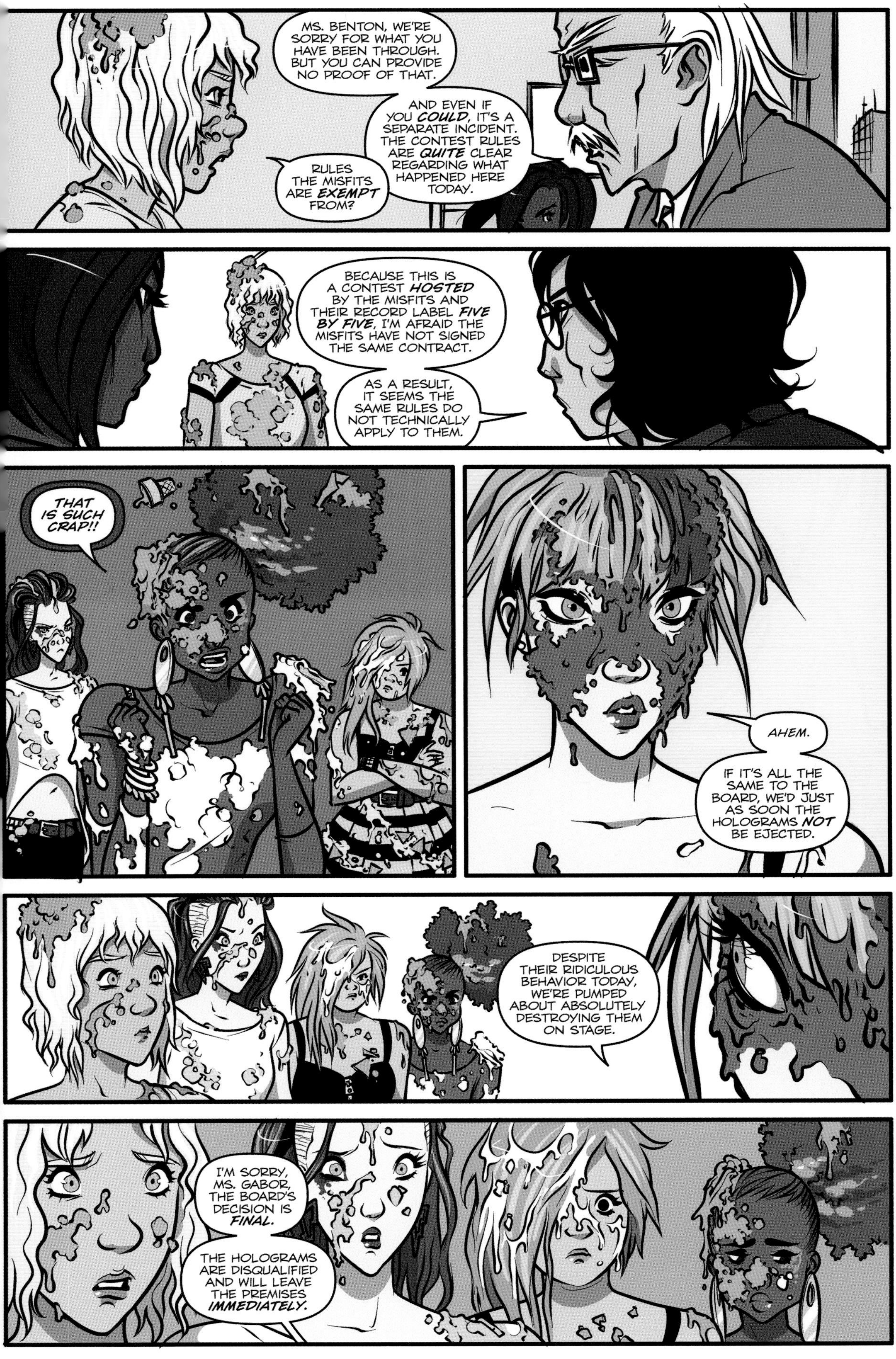
MS. BENTON, WE'RE SORRY FOR WHAT YOU HAVE BEEN THROUGH. BUT YOU CAN PROVIDE NO PROOF OF THAT.
AND EVEN IF YOU **COULD**, IT'S A SEPARATE INCIDENT. THE CONTEST RULES ARE **QUITE** CLEAR REGARDING WHAT HAPPENED HERE TODAY.
RULES THE MISFITS ARE **EXEMPT** FROM?
BECAUSE THIS IS A CONTEST **HOSTED** BY THE MISFITS AND THEIR RECORD LABEL **FIVE BY FIVE**, I'M AFRAID THE MISFITS HAVE NOT SIGNED THE SAME CONTRACT.
AS A RESULT, IT SEEMS THE SAME RULES DO NOT TECHNICALLY APPLY TO THEM.
THAT IS SUCH CRAP!!
AHEM.
IF IT'S ALL THE SAME TO THE BOARD, WE'D JUST AS SOON THE HOLOGRAMS **NOT** BE EJECTED.
DESPITE THEIR RIDICULOUS BEHAVIOR TODAY, WE'RE PUMPED ABOUT ABSOLUTELY DESTROYING THEM ON STAGE.
I'M SORRY, MS. GABOR, THE BOARD'S DECISION IS **FINAL**.
THE HOLOGRAMS ARE DISQUALIFIED AND WILL LEAVE THE PREMISES **IMMEDIATELY**.

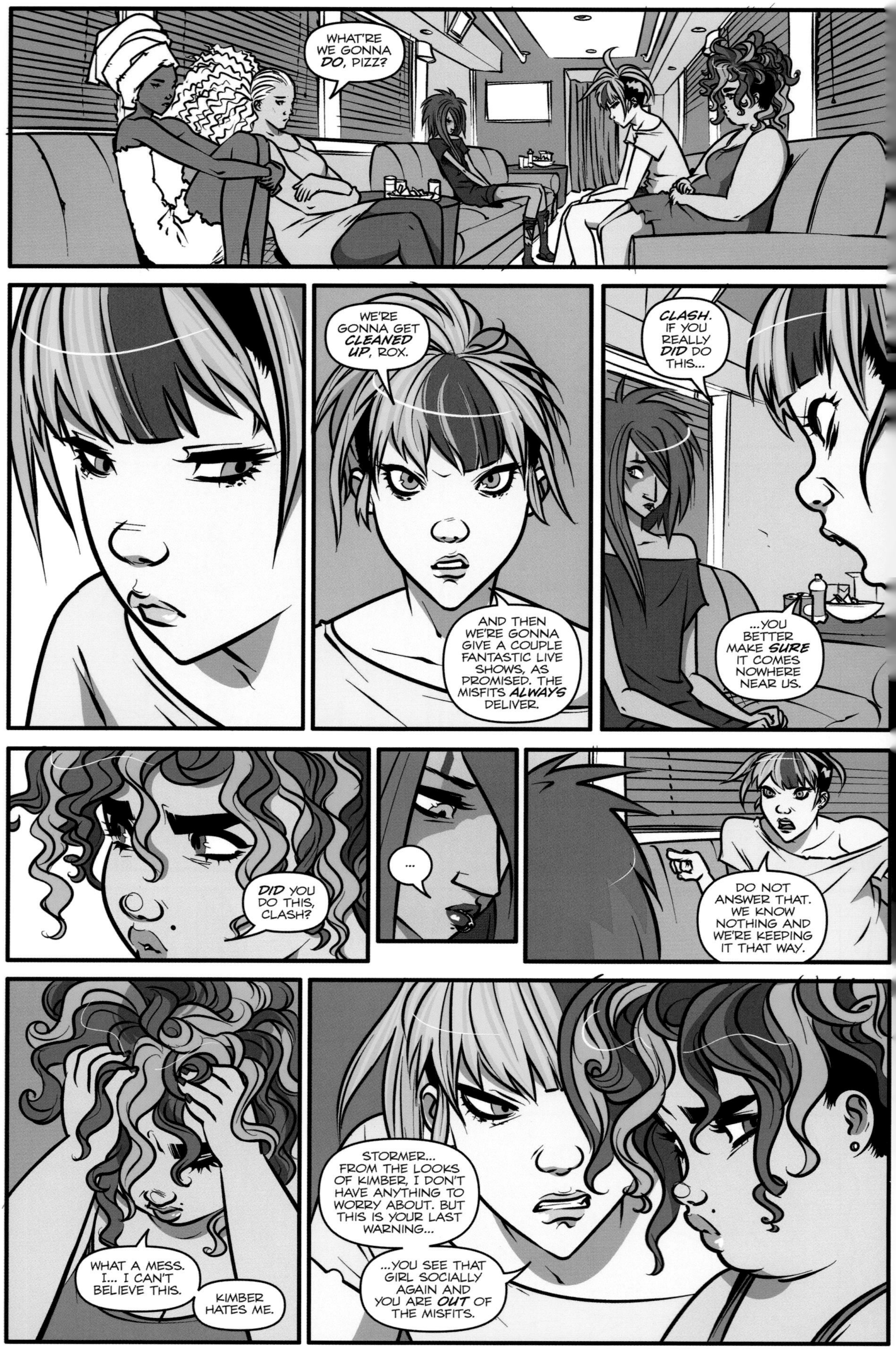
WHAT'RE WE GONNA DO, PIZZ?
WE'RE GONNA GET CLEANED UP, ROX.
AND THEN WE'RE GONNA GIVE A COUPLE FANTASTIC LIVE SHOWS, AS PROMISED. THE MISFITS ALWAYS DELIVER.
CLASH. IF YOU REALLY DID DO THIS...
...YOU BETTER MAKE SURE IT COMES NOWHERE NEAR US.
DID YOU DO THIS, CLASH?
...
DO NOT ANSWER THAT. WE KNOW NOTHING AND WE'RE KEEPING IT THAT WAY.
WHAT A MESS. I... I CAN'T BELIEVE THIS.
KIMBER HATES ME.
STORMER... FROM THE LOOKS OF KIMBER, I DON'T HAVE ANYTHING TO WORRY ABOUT. BUT THIS IS YOUR LAST WARNING...
...YOU SEE THAT GIRL SOCIALLY AGAIN AND YOU ARE OUT OF THE MISFITS.

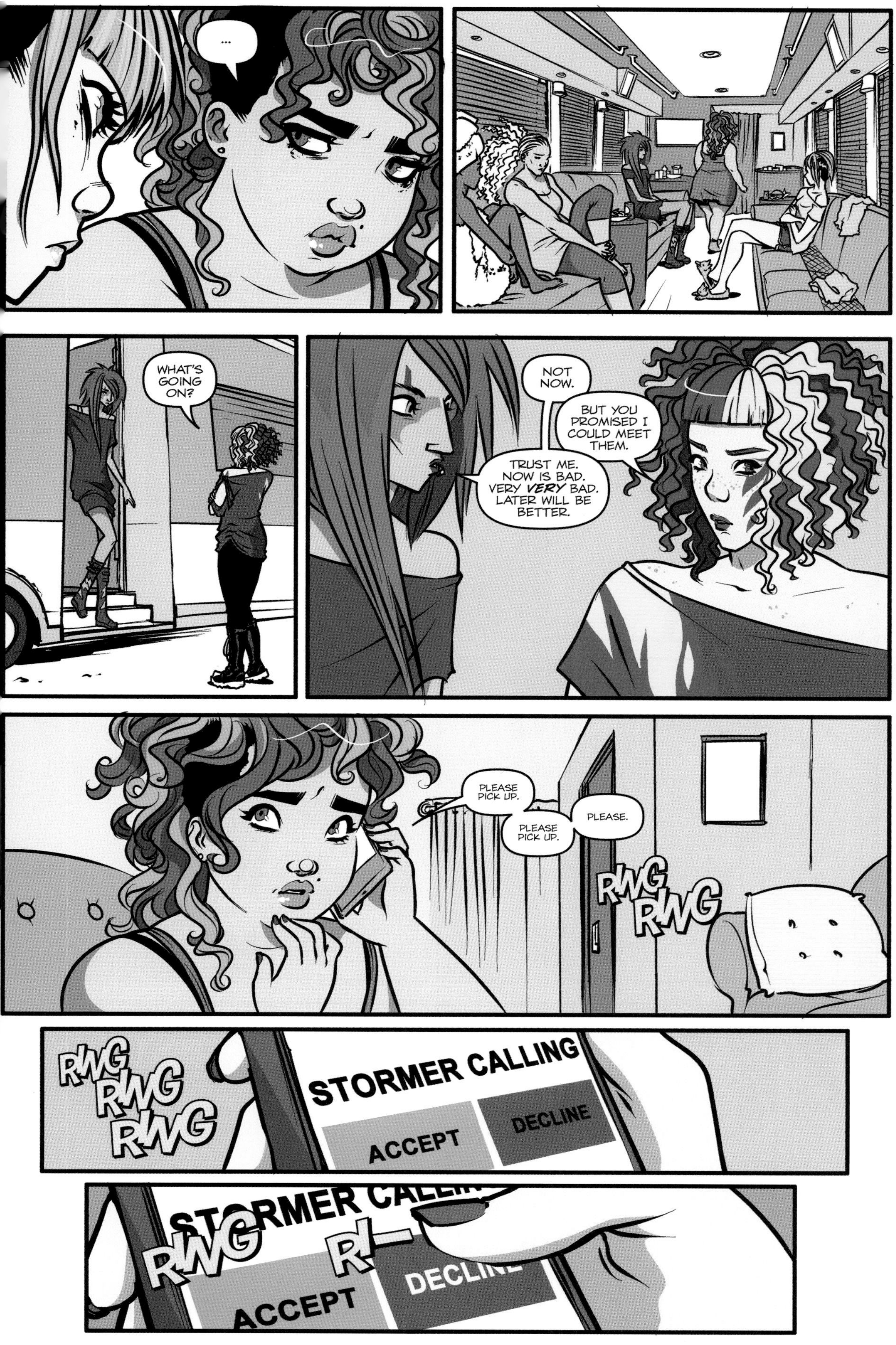

...
WHAT'S GOING ON?
NOT NOW.
BUT YOU PROMISED I COULD MEET THEM.
TRUST ME. NOW IS BAD. VERY *VERY* BAD. LATER WILL BE BETTER.
PLEASE PICK UP.
PLEASE PICK UP.
PLEASE.
RING RING
RING RING RING
STORMER CALLING
ACCEPT
DECLINE
RING
RI—
ACCEPT
DECLINE

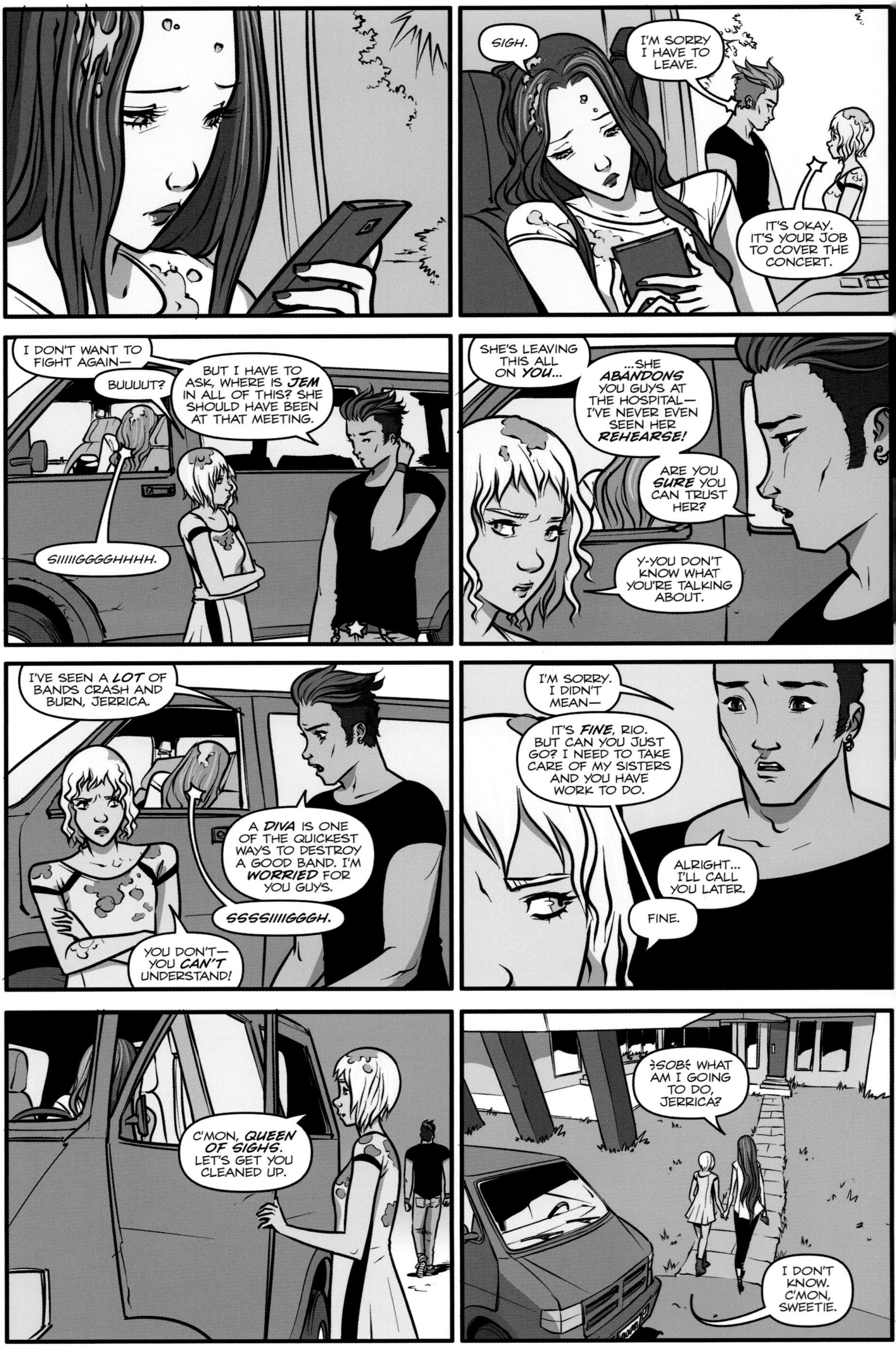
SIGH.
I'M SORRY I HAVE TO LEAVE.
IT'S OKAY. IT'S YOUR JOB TO COVER THE CONCERT.
I DON'T WANT TO FIGHT AGAIN—
BUUUUT?
BUT I HAVE TO ASK, WHERE IS JEM IN ALL OF THIS? SHE SHOULD HAVE BEEN AT THAT MEETING.
SIIIIGGGGHHHH.
SHE'S LEAVING THIS ALL ON YOU...
...SHE ABANDONS YOU GUYS AT THE HOSPITAL— I'VE NEVER EVEN SEEN HER REHEARSE!
ARE YOU SURE YOU CAN TRUST HER?
Y-YOU DON'T KNOW WHAT YOU'RE TALKING ABOUT.
I'VE SEEN A LOT OF BANDS CRASH AND BURN, JERRICA.
A DIVA IS ONE OF THE QUICKEST WAYS TO DESTROY A GOOD BAND. I'M WORRIED FOR YOU GUYS.
SSSSIIIIGGGH.
YOU DON'T— YOU CAN'T UNDERSTAND!
I'M SORRY. I DIDN'T MEAN—
IT'S FINE, RIO. BUT CAN YOU JUST GO? I NEED TO TAKE CARE OF MY SISTERS AND YOU HAVE WORK TO DO.
ALRIGHT... I'LL CALL YOU LATER.
FINE.
C'MON, QUEEN OF SIGHS. LET'S GET YOU CLEANED UP.
SOB WHAT AM I GOING TO DO, JERRICA?
I DON'T KNOW. C'MON, SWEETIE.

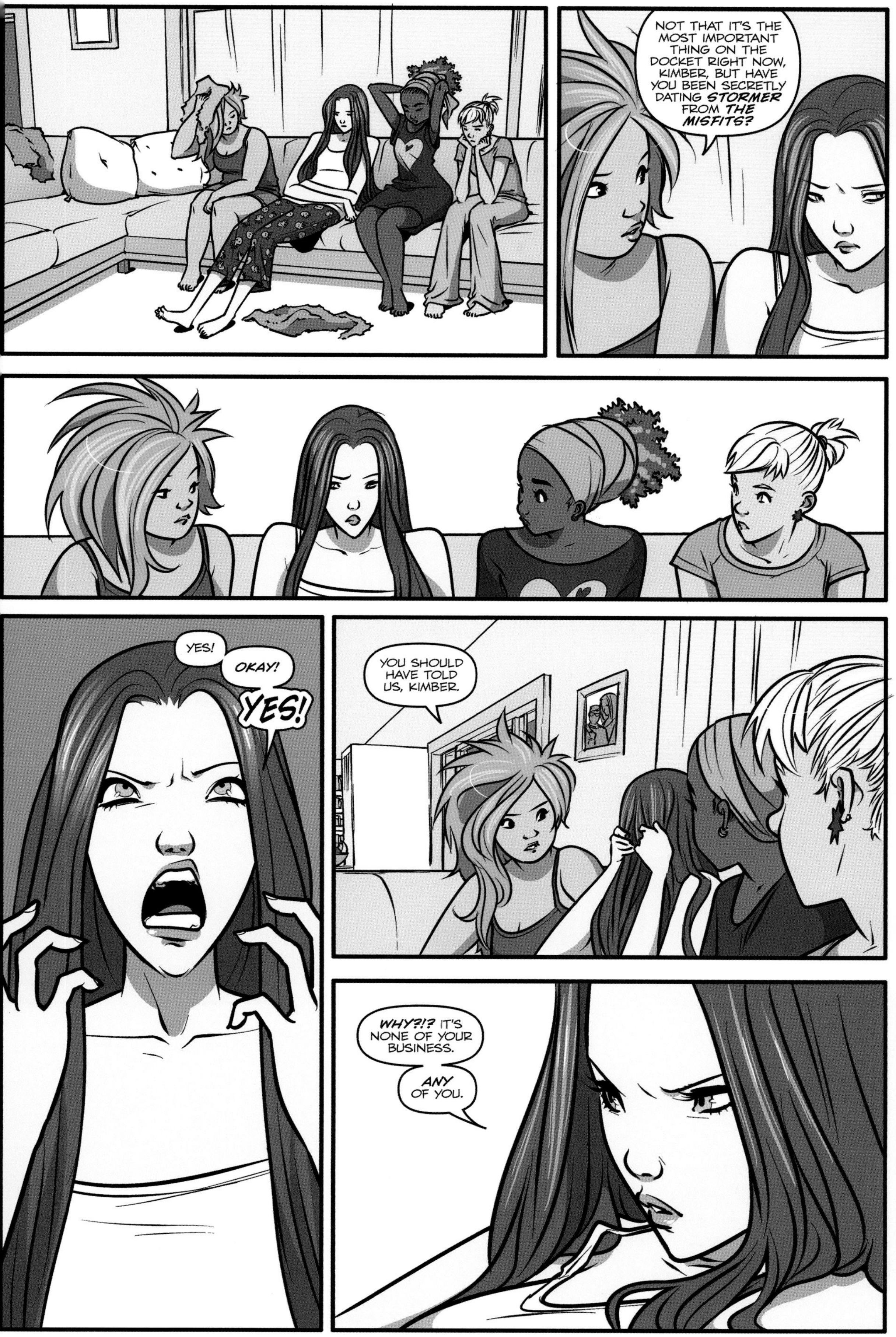
NOT THAT IT'S THE MOST IMPORTANT THING ON THE DOCKET RIGHT NOW, KIMBER, BUT HAVE YOU BEEN SECRETLY DATING STORMER FROM THE MISFITS?
YES!
OKAY!
YES!
YOU SHOULD HAVE TOLD US, KIMBER.
WHY?!? IT'S NONE OF YOUR BUSINESS.
ANY OF YOU.

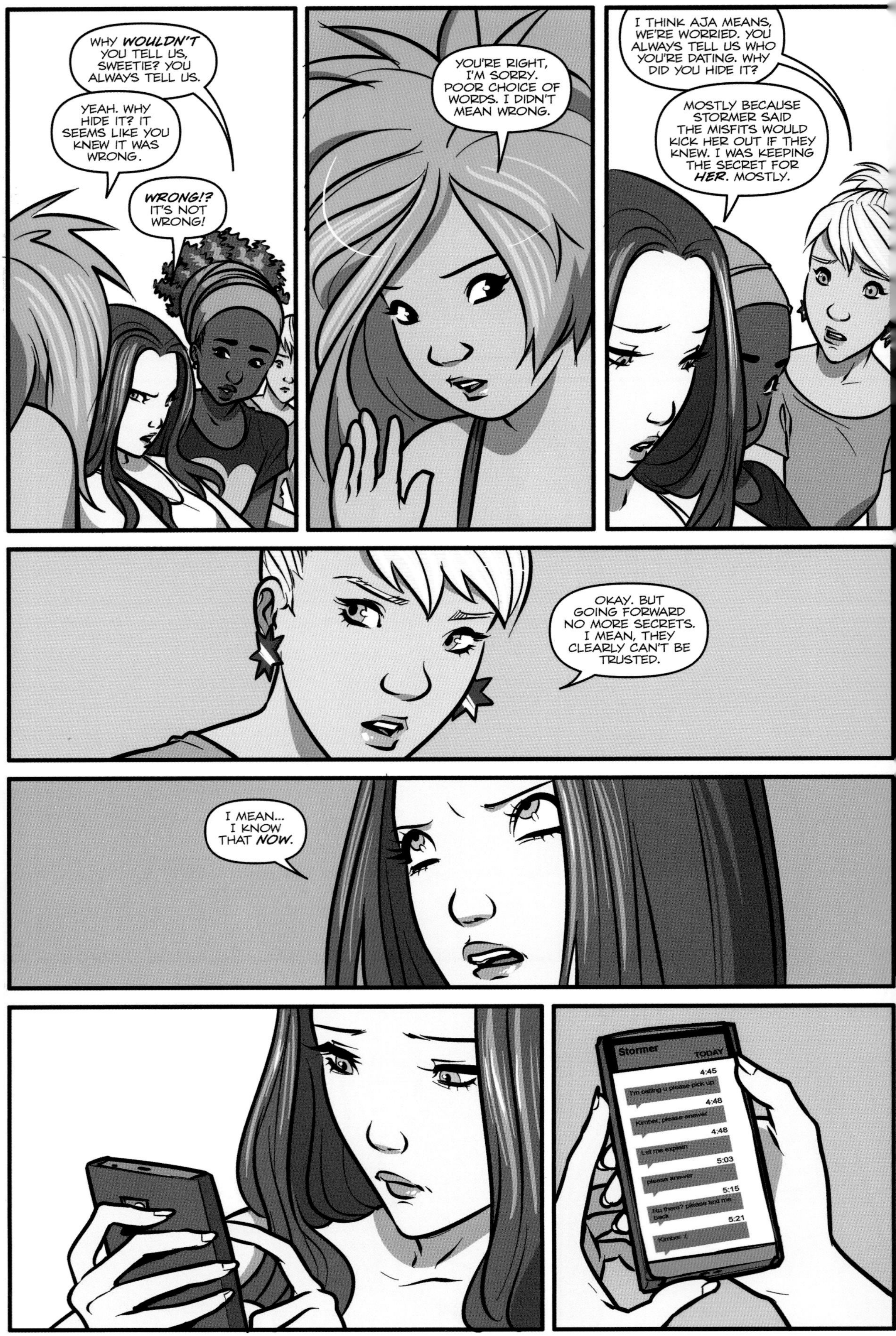
WHY *WOULDN'T* YOU TELL US, SWEETIE? YOU ALWAYS TELL US.
YEAH. WHY HIDE IT? IT SEEMS LIKE YOU KNEW IT WAS WRONG.
WRONG!? IT'S NOT WRONG!
YOU'RE RIGHT, I'M SORRY. POOR CHOICE OF WORDS. I DIDN'T MEAN WRONG.
I THINK AJA MEANS, WE'RE WORRIED. YOU ALWAYS TELL US WHO YOU'RE DATING. WHY DID YOU HIDE IT?
MOSTLY BECAUSE STORMER SAID THE MISFITS WOULD KICK HER OUT IF THEY KNEW. I WAS KEEPING THE SECRET FOR *HER*. MOSTLY.
OKAY. BUT GOING FORWARD NO MORE SECRETS. I MEAN, THEY CLEARLY CAN'T BE TRUSTED.
I MEAN... I KNOW THAT *NOW*.
Stormer
TODAY
4:45
I'm calling u please pick up
4:48
Kimber, please answer
4:48
Let me explain
5:03
please answer
5:15
Ru there? please text me back
5:21
Kimber :(

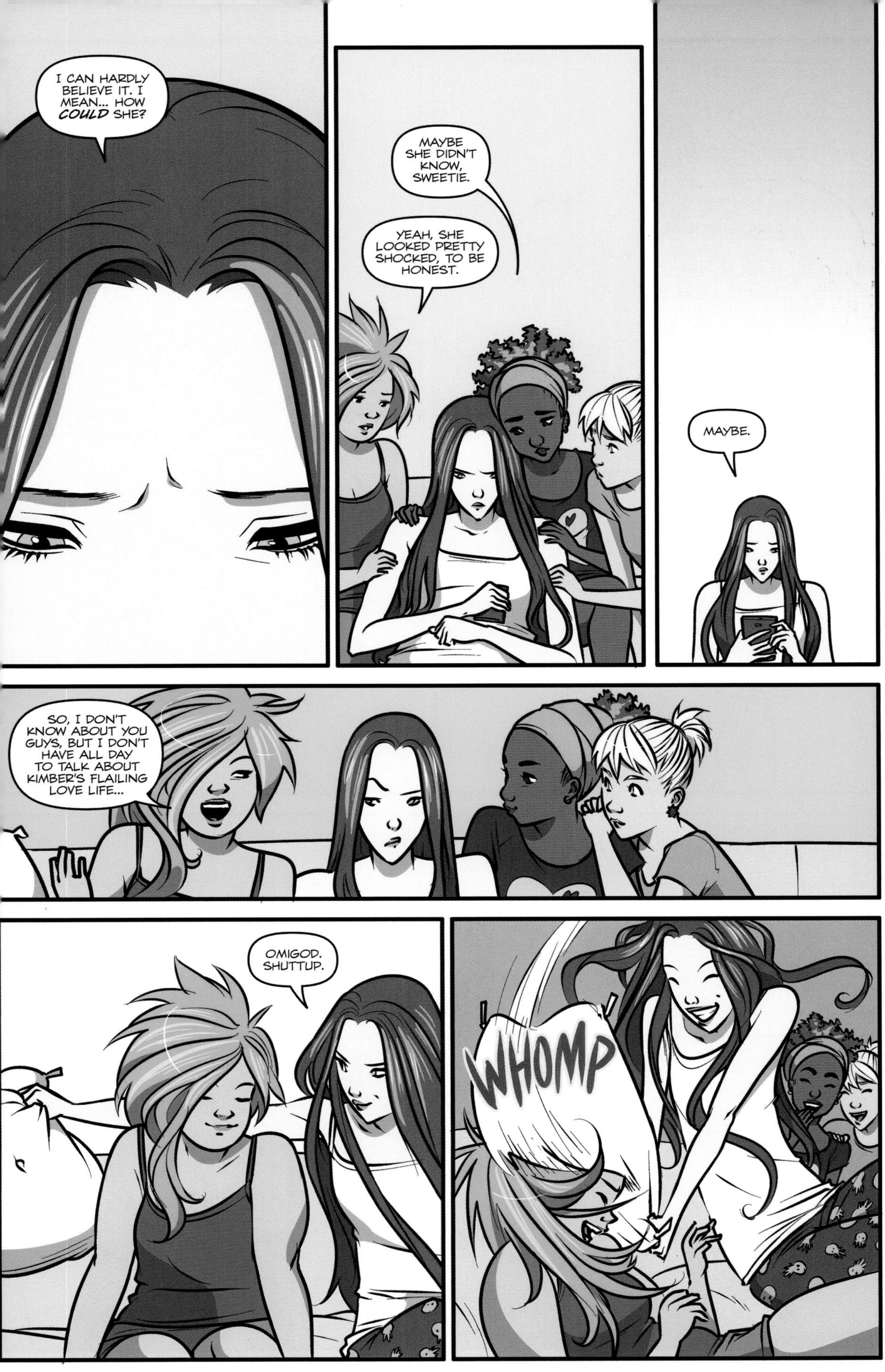
I CAN HARDLY BELIEVE IT. I MEAN... HOW COULD SHE?
MAYBE SHE DIDN'T KNOW, SWEETIE.
YEAH, SHE LOOKED PRETTY SHOCKED, TO BE HONEST.
MAYBE.
SO, I DON'T KNOW ABOUT YOU GUYS, BUT I DON'T HAVE ALL DAY TO TALK ABOUT KIMBER'S FLAILING LOVE LIFE...
OMIGOD. SHUTTUP.
WHOMP

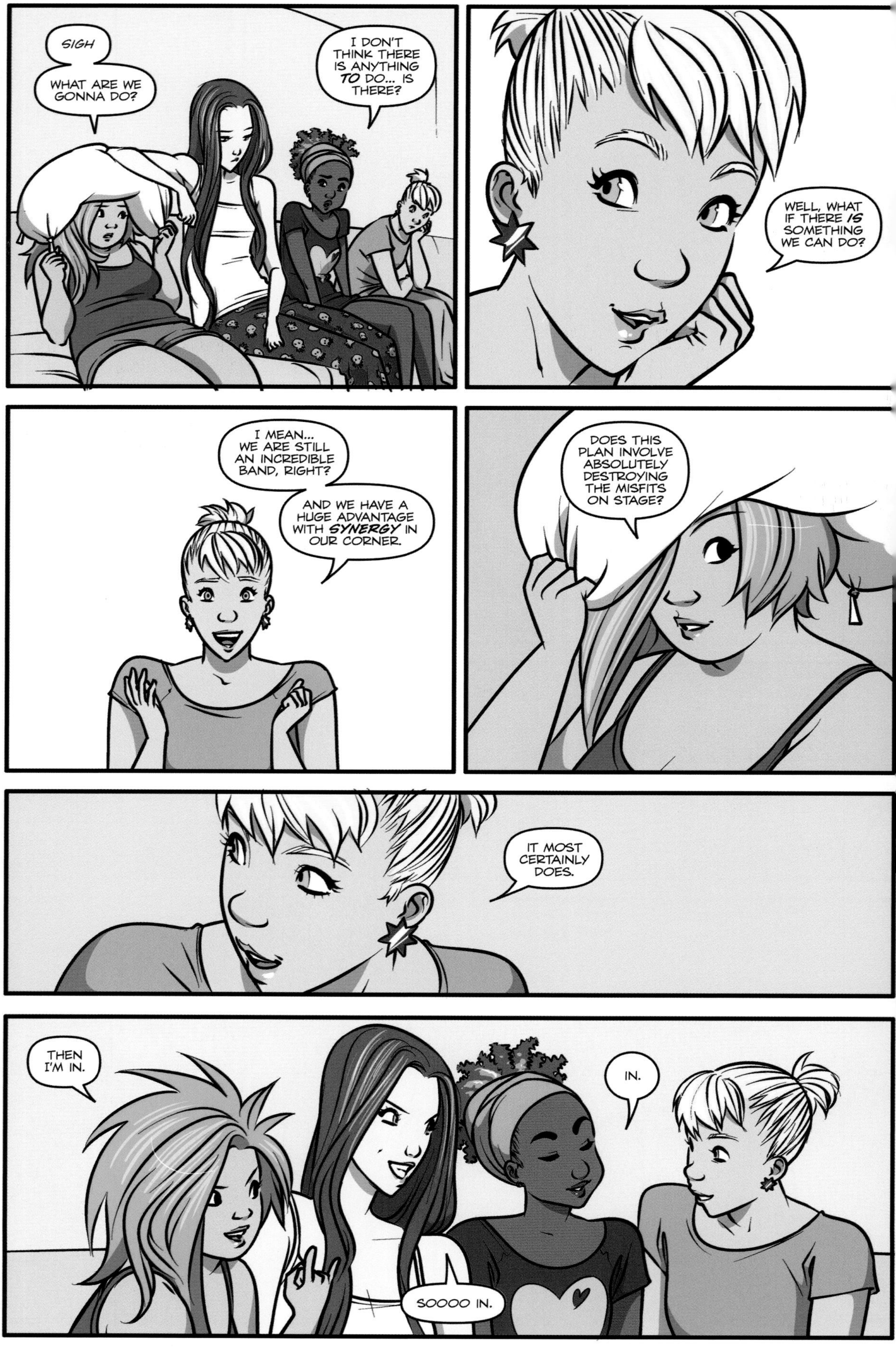
SIGH
WHAT ARE WE GONNA DO?
I DON'T THINK THERE IS ANYTHING TO DO... IS THERE?
WELL, WHAT IF THERE IS SOMETHING WE CAN DO?
I MEAN... WE ARE STILL AN INCREDIBLE BAND, RIGHT?
AND WE HAVE A HUGE ADVANTAGE WITH SYNERGY IN OUR CORNER.
DOES THIS PLAN INVOLVE ABSOLUTELY DESTROYING THE MISFITS ON STAGE?
IT MOST CERTAINLY DOES.
THEN I'M IN.
SOOOO IN.
IN.

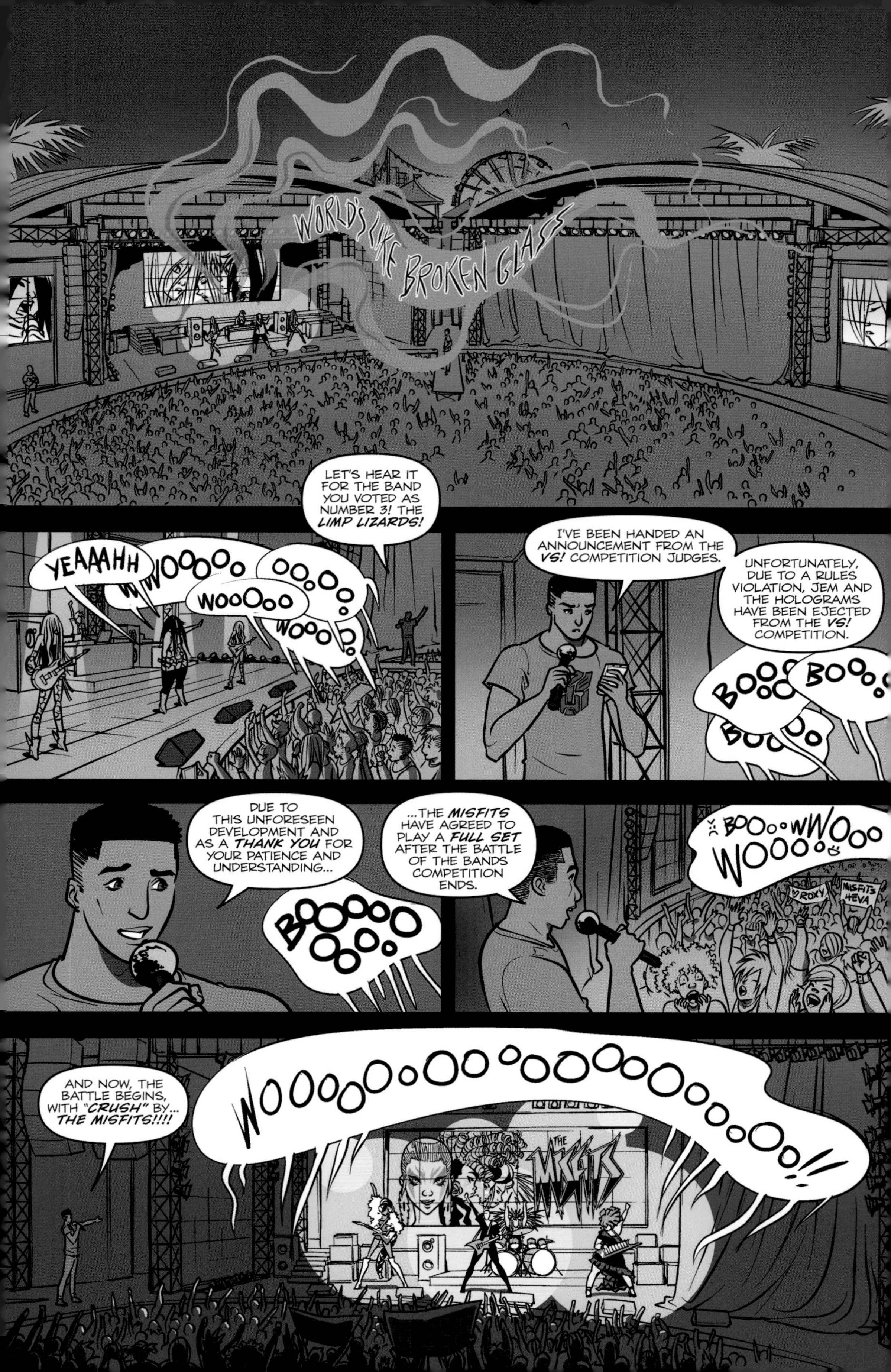
WORLD'S LIKE BROKEN GLASS
LET'S HEAR IT FOR THE BAND YOU VOTED AS NUMBER 3! THE *LIMP LIZARDS!*
YEAAAHH
WWOOOOo
OOoOo
WOOOoo
WOOoO
I'VE BEEN HANDED AN ANNOUNCEMENT FROM THE *VS!* COMPETITION JUDGES.
UNFORTUNATELY, DUE TO A RULES VIOLATION, JEM AND THE HOLOGRAMS HAVE BEEN EJECTED FROM THE *VS!* COMPETITION.
BOOOO
BOOoo
BOOOO
DUE TO THIS UNFORESEEN DEVELOPMENT AND AS A ***THANK YOU*** FOR YOUR PATIENCE AND UNDERSTANDING...
BOOOOO OOOo
...THE ***MISFITS*** HAVE AGREED TO PLAY A ***FULL SET*** AFTER THE BATTLE OF THE BANDS COMPETITION ENDS.
BOOo∘WWOoo WOOOo∘
♥ROXY
MISFITS 4EVA
AND NOW, THE BATTLE BEGINS, WITH "***CRUSH***" BY... ***THE MISFITS!!!!***
WOOOOOoOO oOOOOOOOOOooOOo!!
THE MISFITS

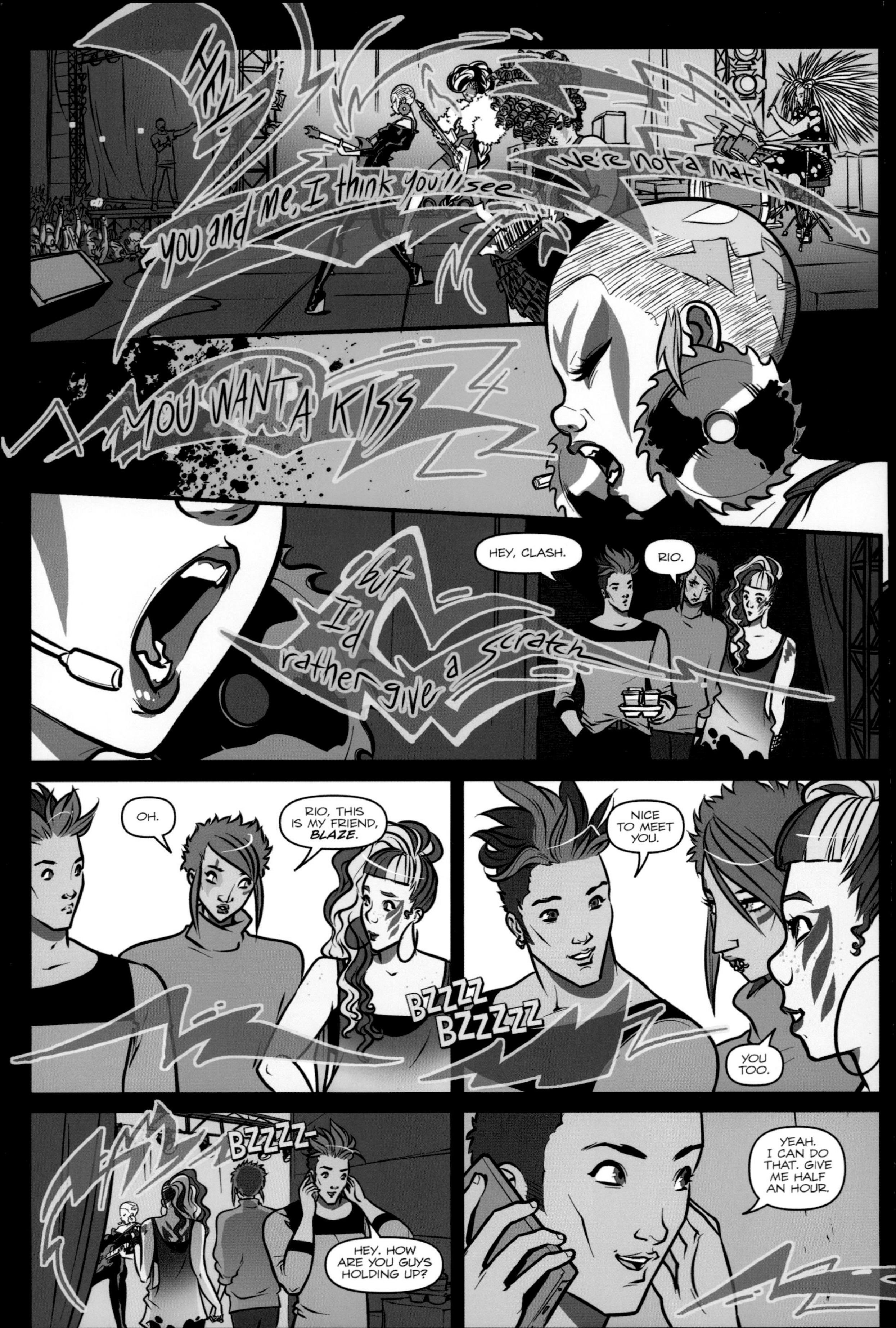
HEY!
you and me, I think you'll see
we're not a match
YOU WANT A KISS
but I'd rather give a scratch
HEY, CLASH.
RIO.
OH.
RIO, THIS IS MY FRIEND, *BLAZE*.
NICE TO MEET YOU.
BZZZZ BZZZZZ
YOU TOO.
BZZZZ-
HEY. HOW ARE YOU GUYS HOLDING UP?
YEAH. I CAN DO THAT. GIVE ME HALF AN HOUR.

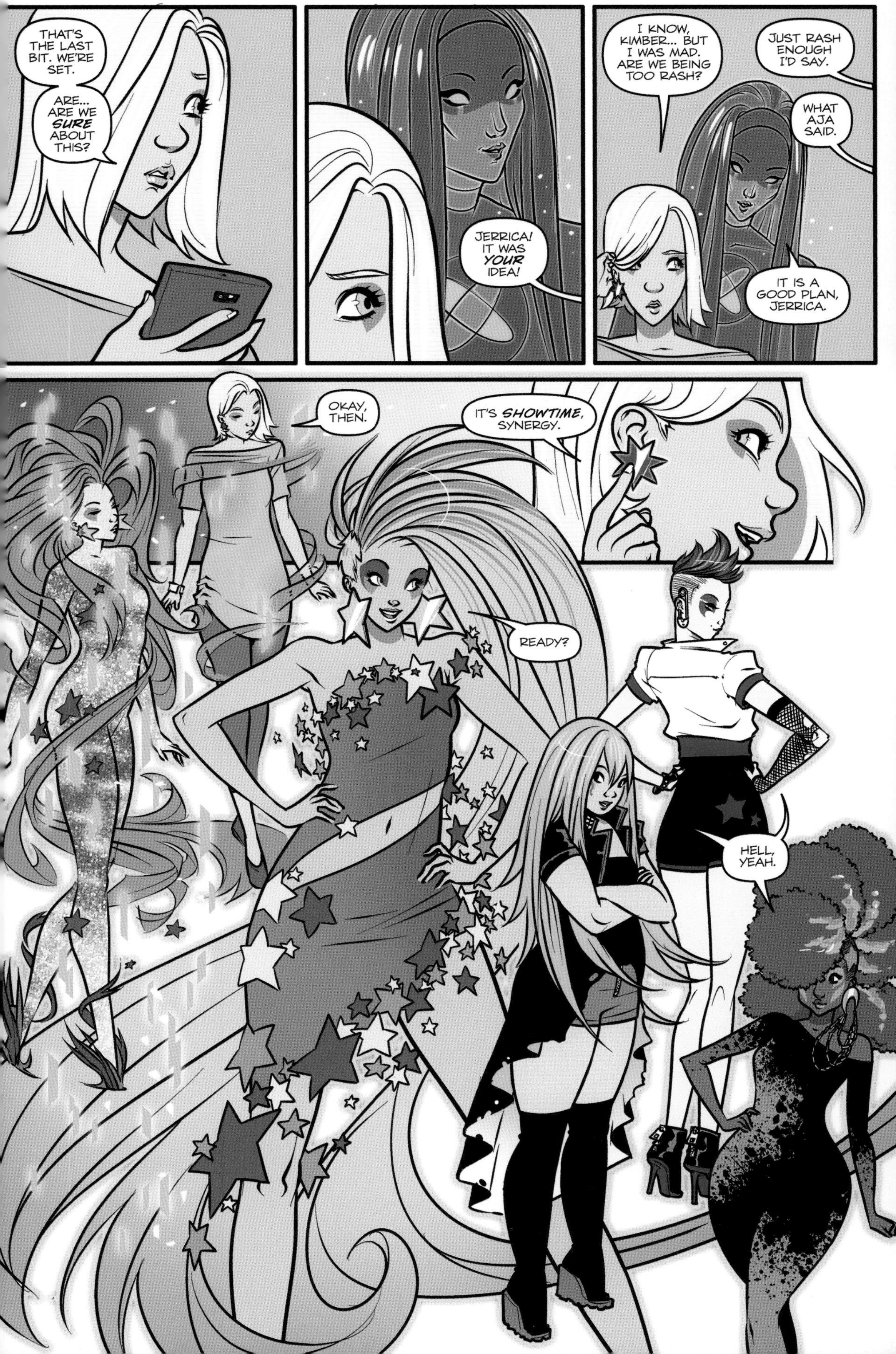

THAT'S THE LAST BIT. WE'RE SET.
ARE... ARE WE *SURE* ABOUT THIS?
JERRICA! IT WAS *YOUR* IDEA!
I KNOW, KIMBER... BUT I WAS MAD. ARE WE BEING TOO RASH?
JUST RASH ENOUGH I'D SAY.
WHAT AJA SAID.
IT IS A GOOD PLAN, JERRICA.
OKAY, THEN.
IT'S *SHOWTIME*, SYNERGY.
READY?
HELL, YEAH.

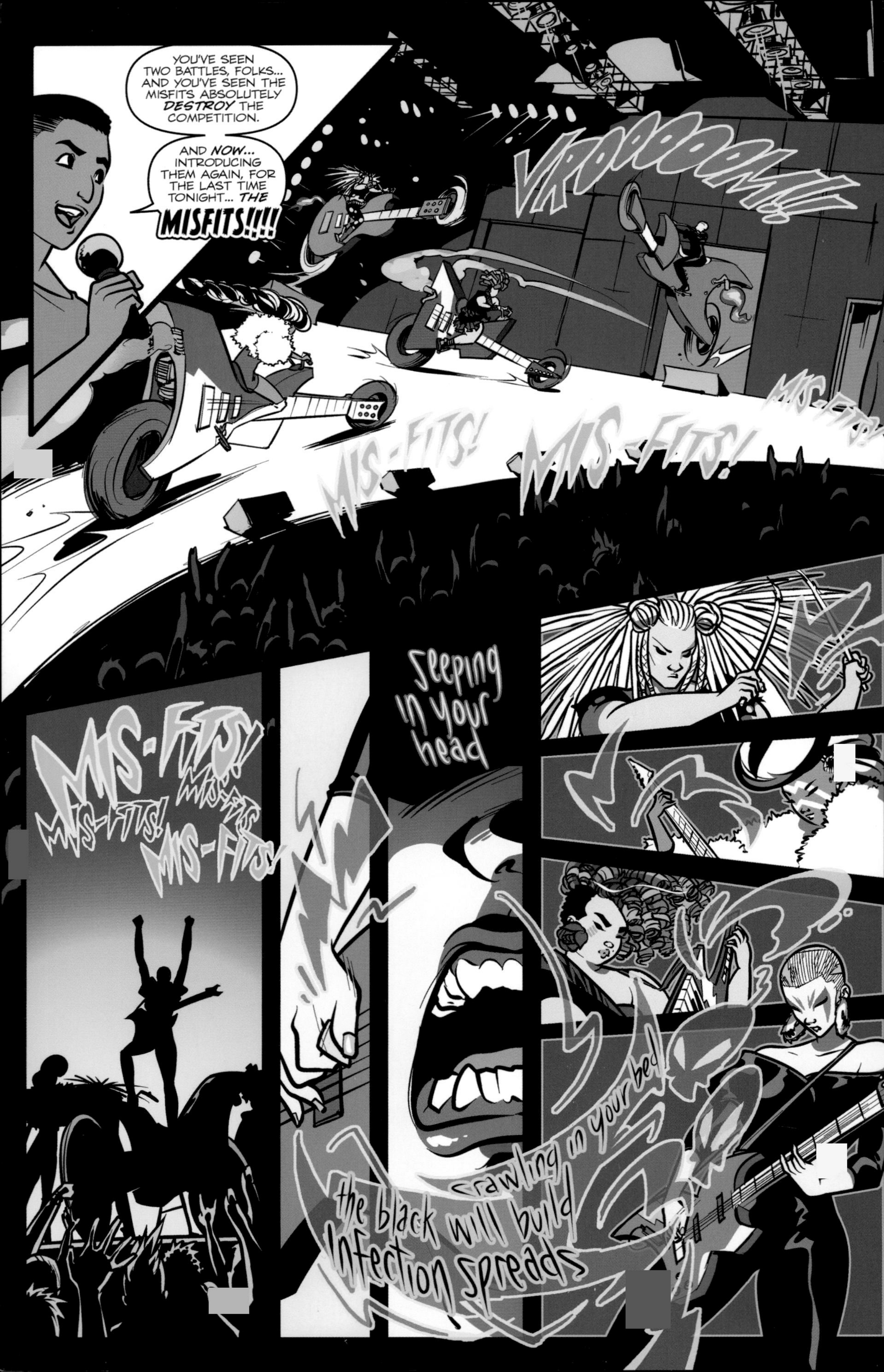
YOU'VE SEEN TWO BATTLES, FOLKS... AND YOU'VE SEEN THE MISFITS ABSOLUTELY DESTROY THE COMPETITION.
AND NOW... INTRODUCING THEM AGAIN, FOR THE LAST TIME TONIGHT... THE MISFITS!!!!!
VROOOOOOM!!!
MIS-FITS!
MIS-FITS!
MIS-FITS!
MIS-FITS!
MIS-FITS!
MIS-FITS!
MIS-FITS!
Sleeping in your head
Crawling in your bed
the black will build
Infection spreads

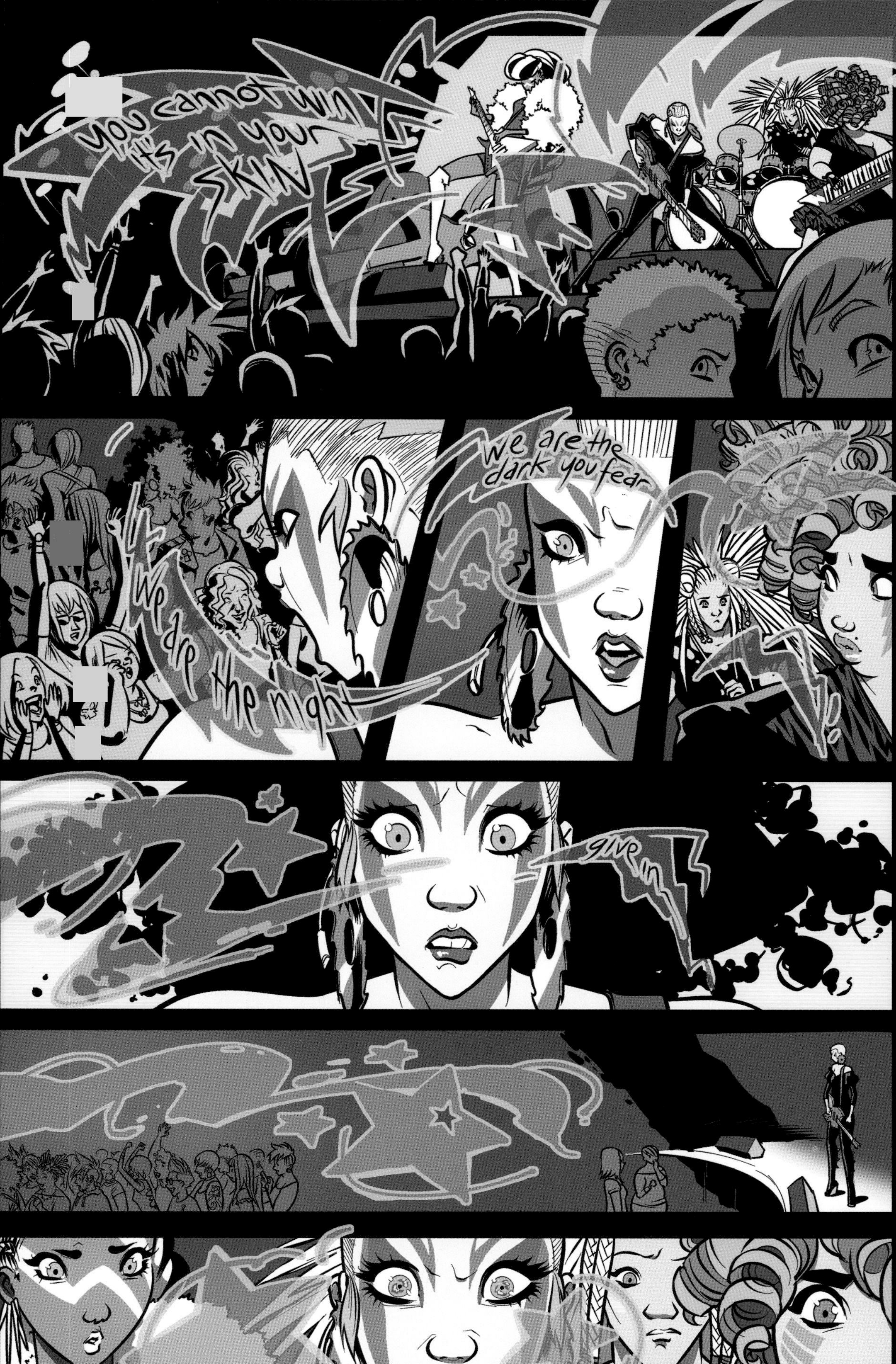
you cannot win
it's in your SKIN
we are the dark you fear
We are the night
give in

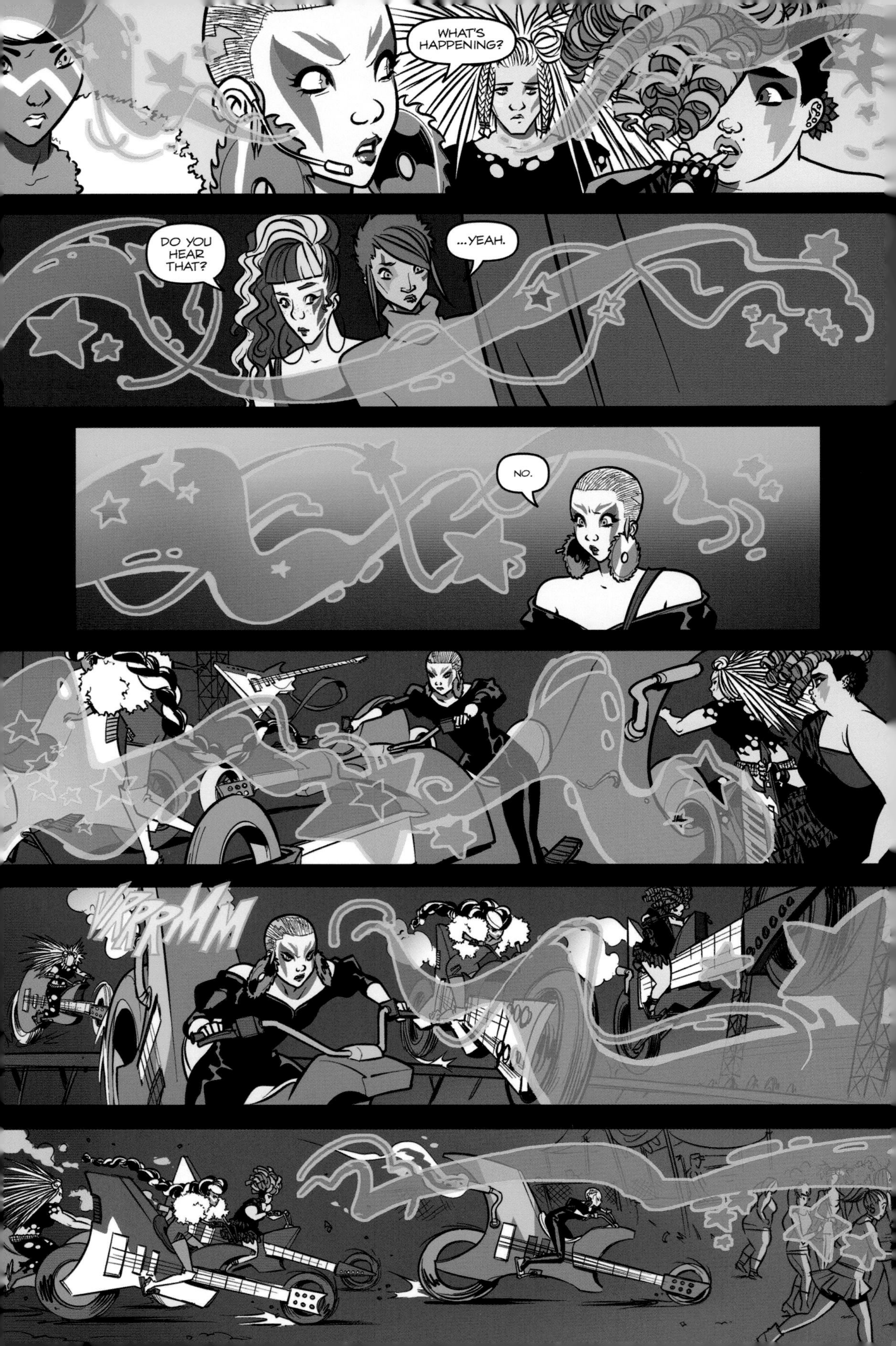
WHAT'S HAPPENING?
DO YOU HEAR THAT?
...YEAH.
NO.
VRRRMM

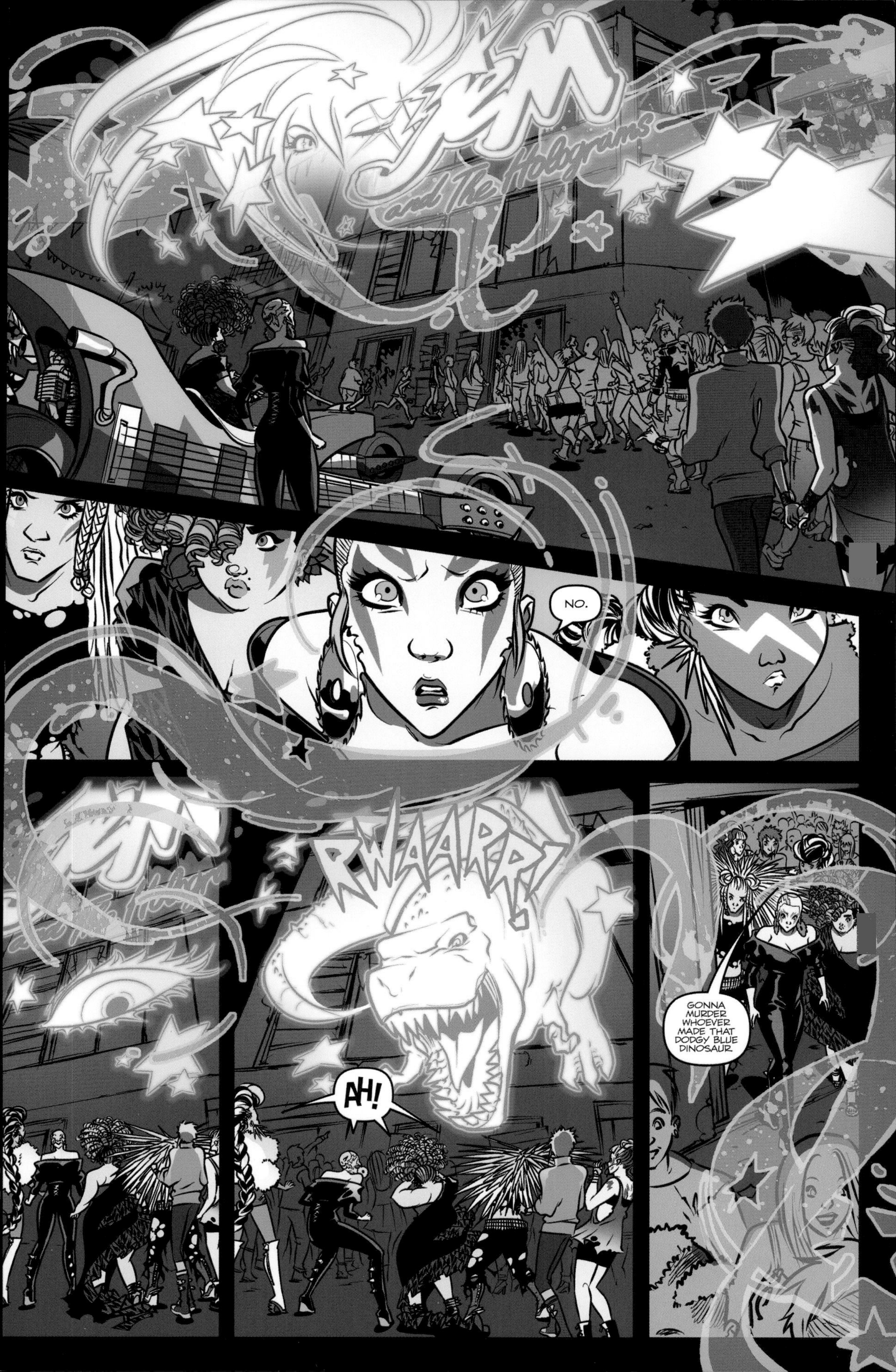
Jem and The Holograms
NO.
RWAARR!
AH!
GONNA MURDER WHOEVER MADE THAT DODGY BLUE DINOSAUR

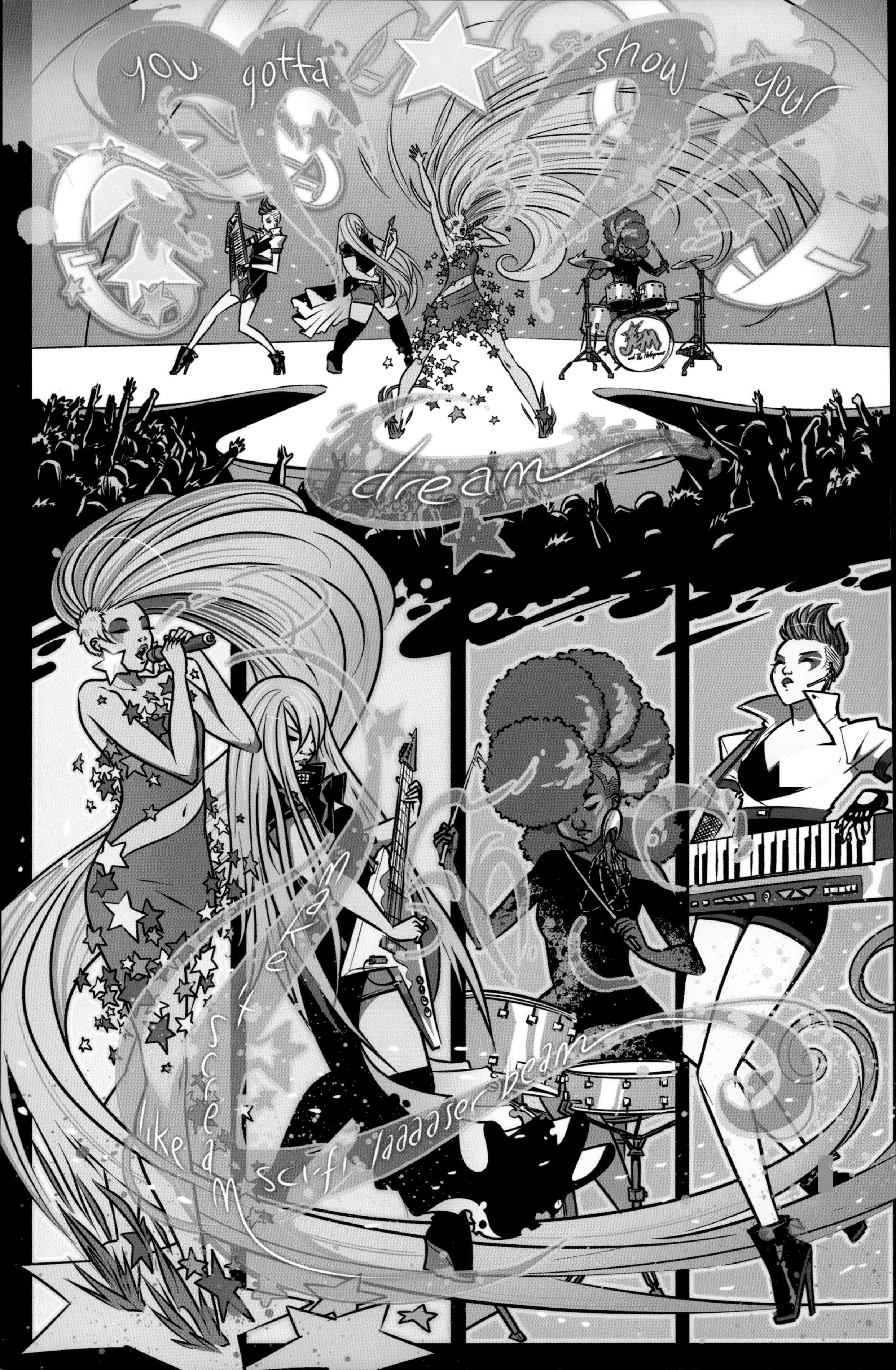

you gotta show your
dream
make it scream like a sci-fi laaaaser beam

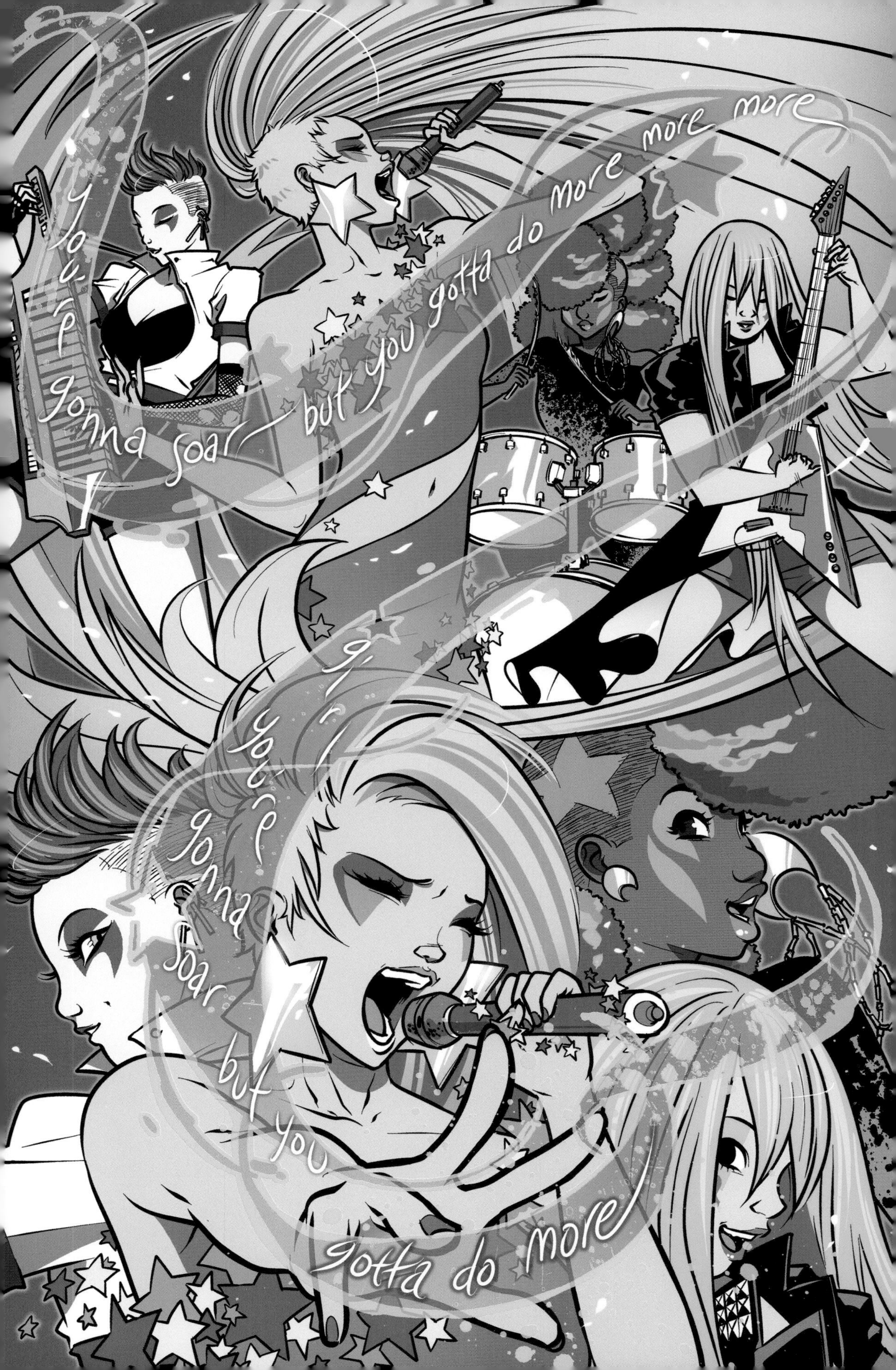
you're gonna soar— but you gotta do more more more
girl you're gonna soar but you gotta do more

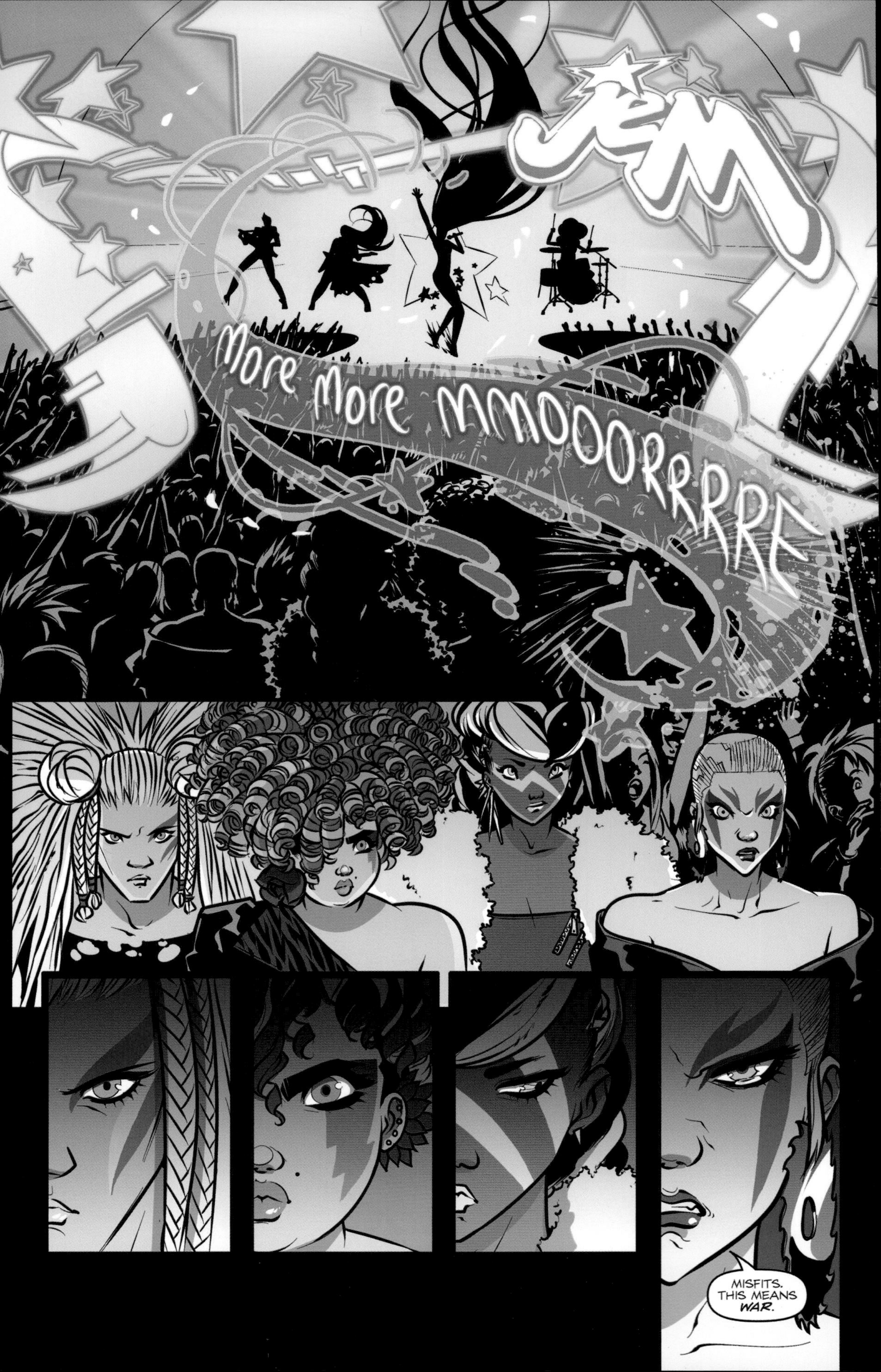
JEM
More More MMOOORRRRE
MISFITS. THIS MEANS *WAR*.

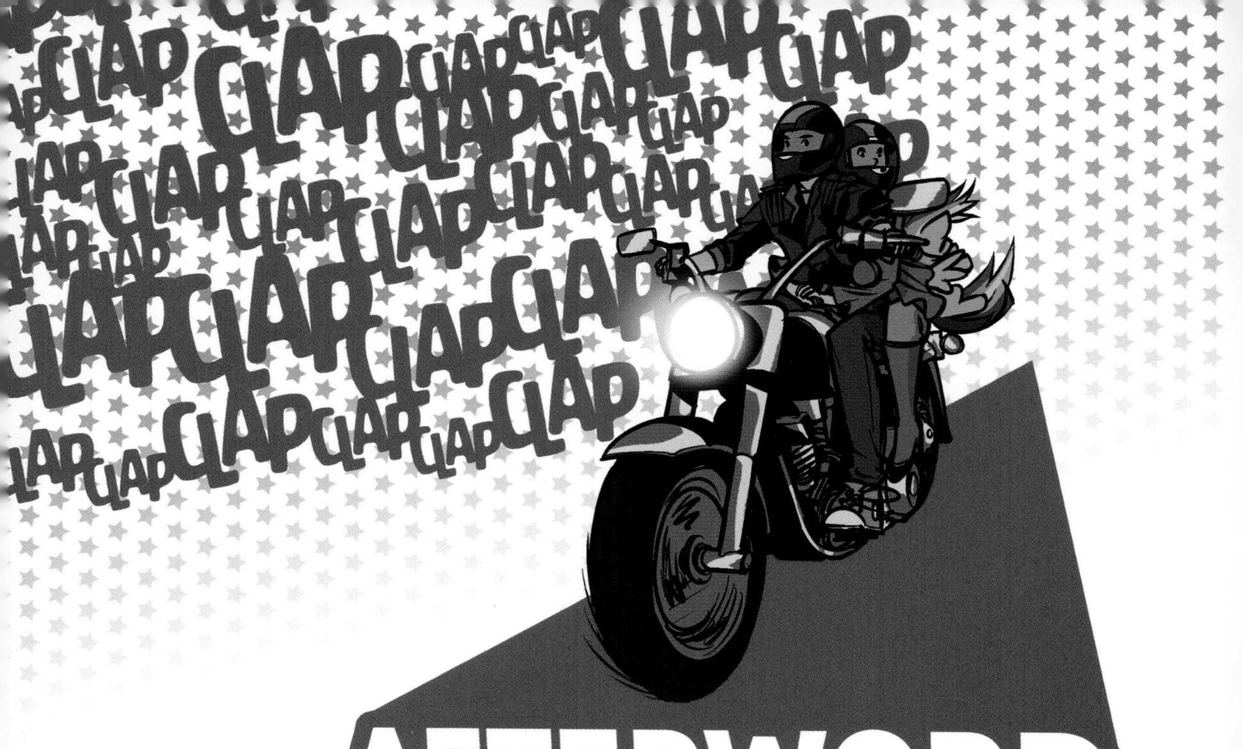
CLAP CLAP CLAP CLAP CLAP
CLAP CLAP CLAP CLAP CLAP
CLAP CLAP CLAP CLAP CLAP
CLAP CLAP CLAP CLAP
CLAP CLAP CLAP CLAP CLAP

AFTERWORD

Wow, those six months really flew by.

It's still kind of weird to me that I'm drawing *Jem and the Holograms,* and even weirder that it's been such a great experience–I'm such a pessimist that I was sure it was going to be stressful. The fans have been great and Hasbro has been awesome; it's been an absolute dream job. I get to take part in a whole new version of *Jem*, I get paid to come up with outfits and hairstyles all day, and most importantly I get to work with Kelly. We talk all the time anyway, so now talking about *Jem* is just another conversation topic. And she's been very patient and nice when dealing with me being a diva and putting up with me teasing her and burying her under all my stupid story ideas. I can be quite a handful sometimes.

Anyway, I honestly never thought there'd be a *Jem* comic. Years ago I came up with random ideas for a make-believe *Jem* revamp, I did a bunch of fan-art back in 2011, and I used to brainstorm possible storylines with friends just for fun (in fact one of those ideas will actually happen in this comic in an upcoming story!). So, of course, when I heard there was going to be a comic, I jumped on it.

Jem and the Holograms is an unusual brand, in that unlike most other '80s franchises there was never another incarnation of it. There've never been any other versions beyond the cartoon and the doll line, so all I had to work with were the original designs and my own sensibilities. I love the original character designs, of course, but I think when a person works on an established property that they should bring themselves to it as much as possible. You have to make it personal. By doing that and bringing your own style to the characters, you show your love for them and the material in a way that only you can. I threw myself into the comic and didn't hold back–I put myself into every character, every design, every idea. I feel such a connection to it and to the characters, I care about them as if they were my own, especially Pizzazz–she's basically me if I were to let my dark side run amok!

Jem has also been a new, strange experience for me because I finally came out as transgender after I finished the first issue. I'd considered coming out before issue #1, but decided not to because I was really scared about my bosses' reactions. I felt like I was pulling the rug out from under them after the comic had already begun, and I was afraid of fan reaction and afraid of destroying my career–basically I was scared of literally everything… but it all turned out better than I could have imagined. *Jem* is even more personal to me than it would've otherwise been; it's the first comic I've done as my true self and in some ways I feel like *Jem* is where I've finally cut loose and the floodgates were opened artistically and emotionally. In my mind *Jem* will be forever associated with all that and how totally amazingly supportive everyone has been.

Thank you to all the fans, especially the ones who reached out to me in support and who have written in to us about the comic. Thank you to Christy Marx and Samantha Newark. Thank you to all my colleagues and friends in the comics industry. Thank you to the *Jem* team: Kelly, John, Victoria, Shawn, Rosalind, Michael, and everyone at Hasbro. Thank you to IDW and the *TMNT* team: Chris, Bobby, Tom, and Kevin. Thank you to my friends who were there for me through this: Zach, James, Yhasmine, Amy, Candace, Jessi, Marisa, and Maureen. Thank you to my team of medical professionals: Carrie, Shahida, Steven, and Diane. Thank you to everyone at the Quatela Medical Spa: Bridget, Nicole, Karen, and Kelly (different Kelly!). And most of all, thank you to Erin, who is more important to me than I can say.

So that's it for now. I'll see all of you again when I return!

Thank you so much everyone.

Sophie Campbell
Artist

ART BY **AMY MEBBERSON**

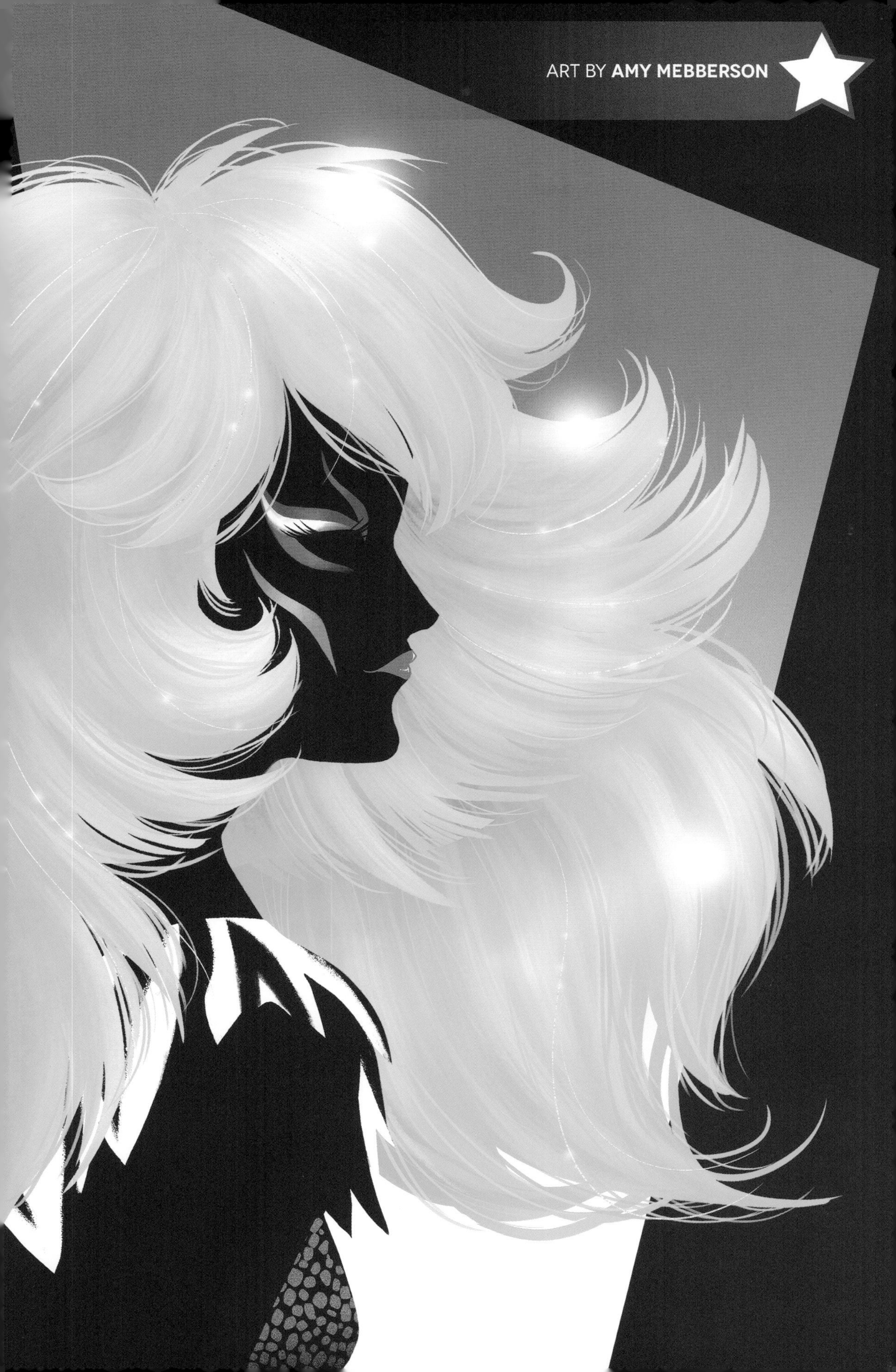

Jem

REAL NAME: Jerrica Benton

AGE: 23

HEIGHT: As Jerrica -5'5"; as Jem - 5'11"

INSTRUMENT(S): Lead vocals, guitar, songwriter.

LOVES: Her sisters, writing, the smell of old books, the sound of waves and rain, peaches, and chocolate!

HATES: Public speaking, dog-eared books, cold showers, tabloids, and onions.

GUILTY PLEASURE: Bubble baths.

PRIZED POSSESSION: Jemstar earrings.

VOTED MOST LIKELY TO: Do the right thing.

DEEPEST SECRET: Jem is the secret holographic alter-ego of Jerrica Benton, created with the help of Synergy.

Aja

NAME: Aja Leith

AGE: 23

HEIGHT: 5'5"

INSTRUMENT(S): Lead guitar, backup vocals. Also plays piano and drums.

LOVES: Sports, motorcycles, vintage cars, shoes, photography, the latest tech gadgets, and fish tacos.

HATES: Whiners, incompetents, texting, and rats. Gross.

GUILTY PLEASURE: Extreme Nachos.

PRIZED POSSESSION: Limited Ed. Les Paul Supreme Guitar, Caribbean Blue.

VOTED MOST LIKELY TO: Be the next MacGyver.

DEEPEST SECRET: Sometimes feels like a jack of all trades but a master of nothing.

Shana

NAME: Shana Elmsford

AGE: 22

HEIGHT: 5'2"

INSTRUMENT(S): Drums and backup vocals. Also plays bass.

LOVES: Fashion, New York, Paris, sci-fi movies, British period dramas, long baths, and sushi.

HATES: Alarm clocks, flying, baking, and snakes.

GUILTY PLEASURE: See's dark chocolate bordeaux candies.

PRIZED POSSESSION: Revenge of the Jedi poster! Totally rare!!

VOTED MOST LIKELY TO: Be the next Lagerfeld, but way prettier and not a dude!

DEEPEST SECRET: Not compleeeetely sure she wants to be in a world-famous band.

Kimber

NAME: Kimber Benton

AGE: 18

HEIGHT: 5'9"

INSTRUMENT(S): Keytar, backup vocals, songwriter. Also plays piano and guitar.

LOVES: Writing, girls, lawyer shows, animals, swimming, surfing, also pizza, coffee ice-cream, and red velvet cake.

HATES: Political shows, spiders, heights, and fish. Fish are so weird and gross. What are gills, even?! So gross.

GUILTY PLEASURE: Binge shoe shopping.

PRIZED POSSESSION: Extensive pajama collection.

VOTED MOST LIKELY TO: Get whatever she wants.

DEEPEST SECRET: Loves trashy romance novels, but doesn't hide it. She's an open book.

Pizzazz

NAME: Phyllis Gabor

AGE: 24

HEIGHT: 5'11"

INSTRUMENT(S): Lead vocals. Also plays guitar.

LOVES: Music, leather, and curly fries.

HATES: Jem and The Holograms and, well... too many things to list.

GUILTY PLEASURE: Extravagant spa days.

PRIZED POSSESSION: 1951 Fender Stratocaster.

VOTED MOST LIKELY TO: Totally dominate.

DEEPEST SECRET: Was in beauty pageants as a child. Her talent was singing, but she only sang country songs.

Jetta

NAME: Sheila Burns

AGE: 22

HEIGHT: 5'9"

INSTRUMENT(S): Bass, backup vocals. Also plays saxophone.

LOVES: Good pubs, vintage cars, bacon sandwiches, bowling, boxing, cookie dough, and Manchester United.

HATES: Sneezing, umbrellas, weddings, and swans (all geese, really). Geese are total prats.

GUILTY PLEASURE: Target. Target for everything.

PRIZED POSSESSION: U.S. Work Visa, she REALLY doesn't want to go back to the U.K.

VOTED MOST LIKELY TO: Throw a punch.

DEEPEST SECRET: She comes from a poor British family, which is the opposite of what she tells everyone.

Stormer

NAME: Mary Phillips

AGE: 20

HEIGHT: 5'5"

INSTRUMENT(S): Keytar and backup vocals, songwriter. Also plays guitar.

LOVES: Old first edition books, fishnets, flowers, thunderstorms, Super Bowl dancing sharks, Halloween, and chai lattes.

HATES: Doing laundry, going to the beach, mornings, red meat, and bears.

VOTED MOST LIKELY TO: Be a famous writer.

GUILTY PLEASURE: Binge shoe shopping.

PRIZED POSSESSION: First edition *To Kill a Mockingbird*.

DEEPEST SECRET: She's not sure she has what it takes to make it as a solo artist.

Roxy

NAME: Roxy Pelligrini

AGE: 22

HEIGHT: 5'6"

INSTRUMENT(S): Drums, backup vocals. Also plays guitar.

LOVES: Neil Peart, boxing, nail polish, funny gross-out movies, dinosaurs, The Sixers, and mocha frappuccinos.

HATES: Twitter, Facebook, and stupid Tumblr! And hangnails. The worst!

GUILTY PLEASURE: All-day movie marathons.

PRIZED POSSESSION: Neil Peart autographed drumsticks.

VOTED MOST LIKELY TO: Get arrested.

DEEPEST SECRET: She's a high-functioning illiterate.

Rio

NAME: Rio Pacheco

AGE: 24

HEIGHT: 6'2"

INSTRUMENT(S): Plays guitar, badly.

LOVES: Motorcycles, sci-fi, classic horror movies, snowboarding, surfing, comics, vintage t-shirts, cat gifs, and cereal.

HATES: Divas, Hawaiian pizza, hospitals, bullies, and marshmallow peeps.

PRIZED POSSESSION: Custom motorcycle he's building from both vintage and new parts - a bike worthy of Mad Max!

VOTED MOST LIKELY TO: Discover your secrets.

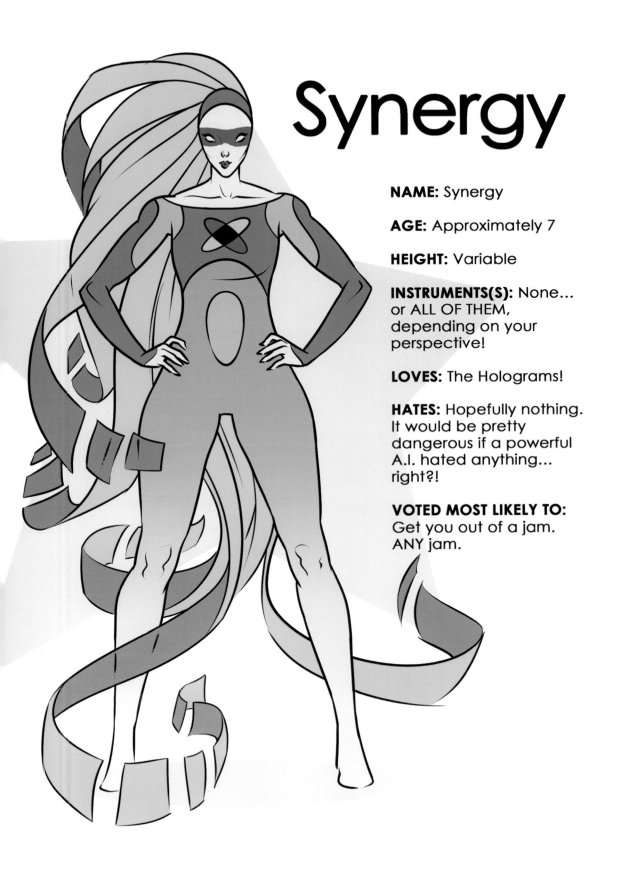

Synergy

NAME: Synergy

AGE: Approximately 7

HEIGHT: Variable

INSTRUMENTS(S): None... or ALL OF THEM, depending on your perspective!

LOVES: The Holograms!

HATES: Hopefully nothing. It would be pretty dangerous if a powerful A.I. hated anything... right?!

VOTED MOST LIKELY TO: Get you out of a jam. ANY jam.

Clash

NAME: Constance Montgomery

AGE: 21

HEIGHT: 6'1"

INSTRUMENT(S): None. Wants to be a singer.

LOVES: The Misfits... especially Pizzazz. Also vintage vinyl, faux fur, and cake!

HATES: Everything Pizzazz hates. (...which is a lot).

PRIZED POSSESSION: Tech 12 Turntable.

VOTED MOST LIKELY TO: Sell you out, unless you're the Misfits.

Blaze

NAME: Leah Dwyer

AGE: 22

HEIGHT: 5'10"

INSTRUMENT(S): Vocals.

LOVES: Yoga, lacrosse, hugs, mysticism, milkshakes, the beach, and old photo albums.

HATES: Jellybeans, ghosts, horror movies, and sharks.

PRIZED POSSESSION: The Misfits' first album vinyl signed by all four band members!

VOTED MOST LIKELY TO: Race you (and win!).

BEHIND THE SCENES

Since I was about 10 years old, I've wanted to do a *Jem and the Holograms* comic.

A few years ago I was writing *Transformers* comics at IDW and the first thing I suggested to my editor was "we should do a *Jem* comic."

A couple years later, I got hired to be Senior Editor here. And my first panel at San Diego Comic-Con 2011, I said how much I wanted to do a *Jem* comic.

And every once in a while, when I talked to Hasbro's Michael Kelly, or to freelance creators, I'd talk about how much I wanted to do that *Jem* comic.

Well, it took a while, but the time for wanting is over... and if you've just read this, I think you'll agree that all the waiting paid off because it got us Kelly Thompson writing, Sophie Campbell drawing, and M. Victoria Robado coloring what I like to think is the book of the year!

For my part—in case you want to hear the editor ramble on—I always loved *Jem*. When I was a kid, I watched it every weekend, sandwiched between episodes of *Inhumanoids* and *Big Foot and the Muscle Machines*.

I *guess* it was a "girls'" cartoon. There was more pink than in *G.I. Joe*. I dunno. For me, *Jem* was music and adventure for everybody, inclusive of me. It was cartoons for the music-video generation. There were a handful of other shows on thematically similar ground—I devoured them, too—but nothing had the same sense of style and friendship and camp and seriousness. What Christy Marx and company put on the screen in the 1980s stuck with me.

I grew up, got more into music, got really into comics, and spent most of my adulthood making comics for a living. And, like I may have mentioned, wanting to do a *Jem* comic.

Then, finally, the path to making a *Jem* comic became clear... and I was editing it! The dream was about to become a reality... and that meant if it got messed up, it was my fault.

I didn't have a particular vision—that had to come from the writer and artist. But I did know there was a certain *feeling* we needed. *Jem* needed honesty and integrity—to be true to her roots while reaching for the sky. Which sounds lame, but... well, there I was.

I gave a few interested creators the same speech: the source material is a really strong foundation but this new series (like the original series) would be set in the *now*. And I think there are two big questions inherent in bringing *Jem* to 2015's version of *now*:

1) How does the Jerrica/Jem secret identity work? In today's world, it really didn't feel right having the head of a record label who turns into a pop superstar... so, what *is* the split between the character's alter egos?

2) How does music get played on the comics page? Because that's a tricky one. You can't hear anything in a comic. That, *uh*, that makes music tricky.

Several talented people put real effort into working this through, and pitched their hearts out. Some of the pitches were reverential to the original cartoon and toys—sticking very close to the classic roots. Some strayed far in an effort to modernize the concept for the YouTube/Tumblr generation. Some of these were very, very good pitches.

But there was actually a third trick: for new fans, this comic had to come out of the gate and be engaging without requiring the reader to know the original; *and*, at the same time, for fans of the classic *Jem*, this comic had to be as good—not as *Jem was*—but as good as they *remember* it being. Which can be a nigh-impossible task.

Fellow IDW editor Sarah Gaydos introduced me to Kelly Thompson and Sophie Campbell. I knew Sophie a little—a couple years earlier, she'd done some fan-art redesigns of the Holograms and the Misfits that were really, really exciting. Plus she was doing amazing work on IDW's *Teenage Mutant Ninja Turtles* comic, and she'd drawn one of my favorite comics in recent years, the Joe Keating-written *Glory*. I didn't know Kelly yet, but I'd heard of her novel, *The Girl Who Would Be King*, and after giving that and her follow-up, *Storykiller*, a read, I knew I had to talk to them.

Their pitch landed exactly where it needed to be. Kelly and Sophie had sharp, smart ideas on how to put the music on the page; how to carry the melodrama of *Jem* into the 21st century; what dual identities could mean to somebody in a world where everybody's on social media 24 hours a day... plus the new designs from Sophie were beautiful. And more than anything else—they came at *Jem* from a place of honesty and integrity. These characters felt real, their world felt important. And it walked that line of being new *and* classic at once. It honored the past while carrying the story forward.

Hasbro agreed: Kelly and Sophie were the right people. Once Victoria came onboard on colors—hitting the perfect visual tone—we were off to the races.

Thanks to everybody who pitched—there wasn't a dud in the bunch, and at least two of those pitches led to somebody getting hired to work on other comics I edit. Thanks to Michael Kelly, Heather Hopkins, Ed Lane, Kristina Coppola, and Andrea Hopelain (and everybody else!) at Hasbro for being great about everything. Thanks for Christy Marx for making *Jem* sing, literally and figuratively, in the first place. Thanks to all the amazing cover artists we've had and will have in the coming months. Thanks to *you* for taking a chance. The best—as they say—is still to come.

But biggest thanks to Kelly and Sophie for making 10-year-old John's dream come true.

John Barber
Senior Editor

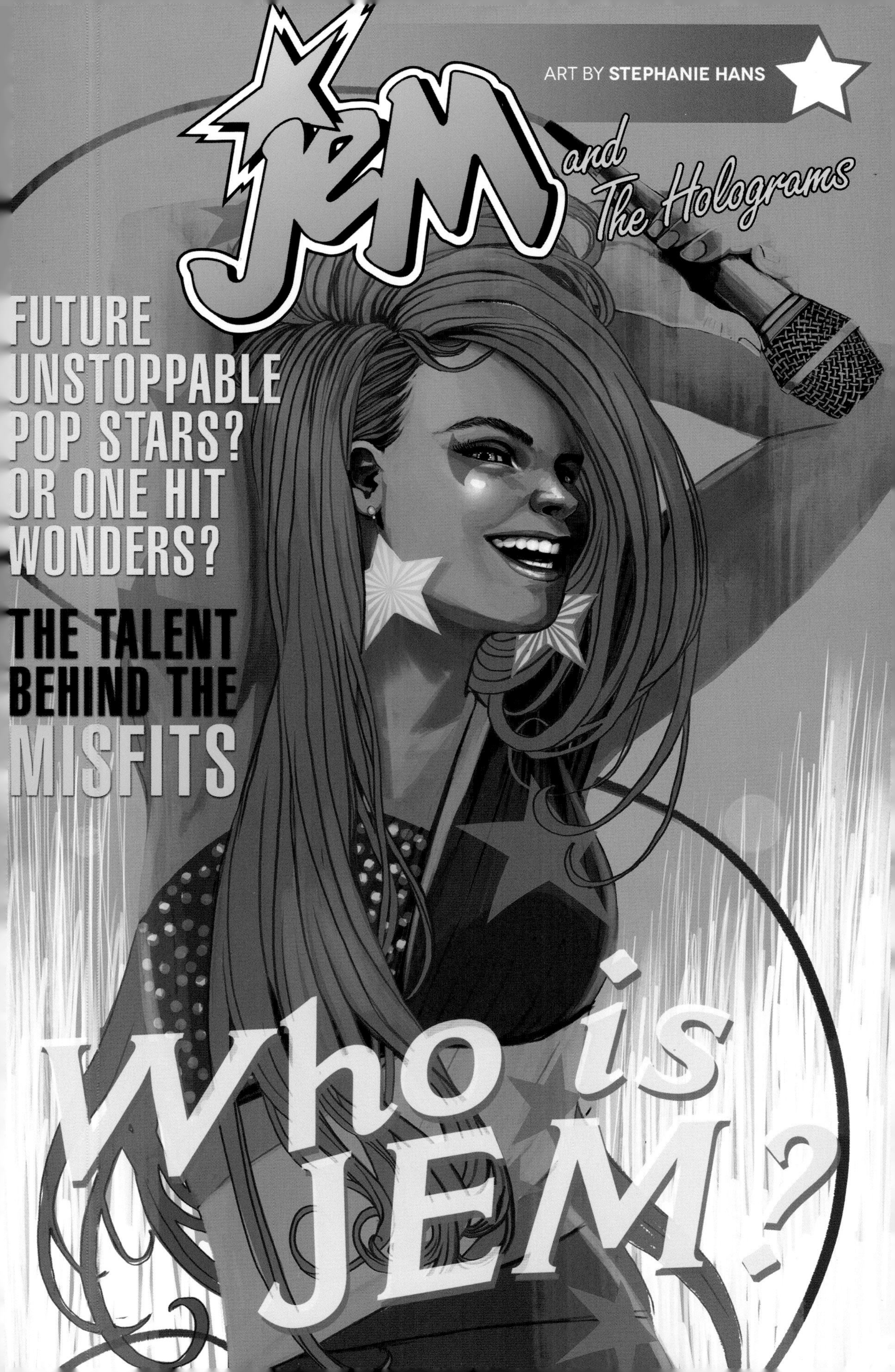
ART BY STEPHANIE HANS
JEM and The Holograms
FUTURE UNSTOPPABLE POP STARS? OR ONE HIT WONDERS?
THE TALENT BEHIND THE MISFITS
Who is JEM?

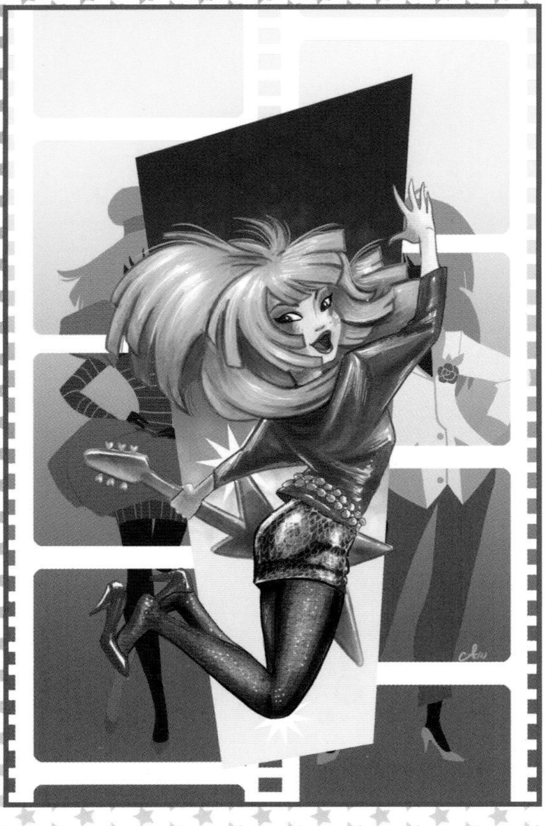

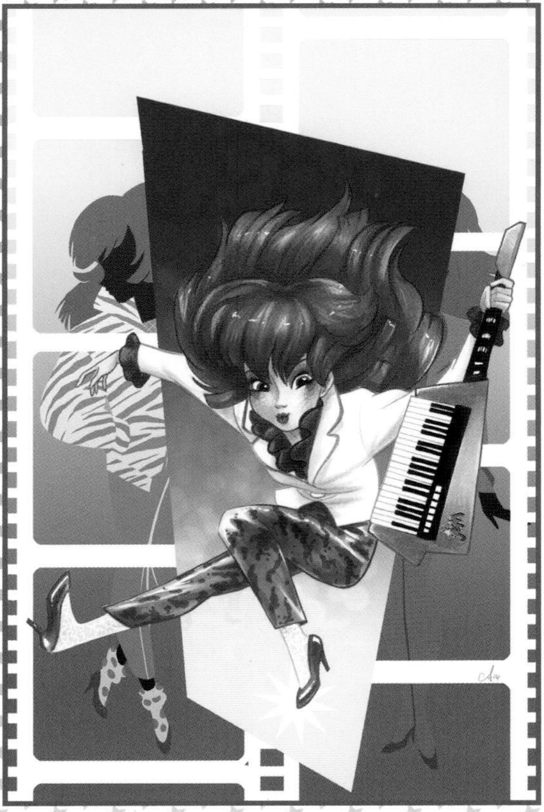

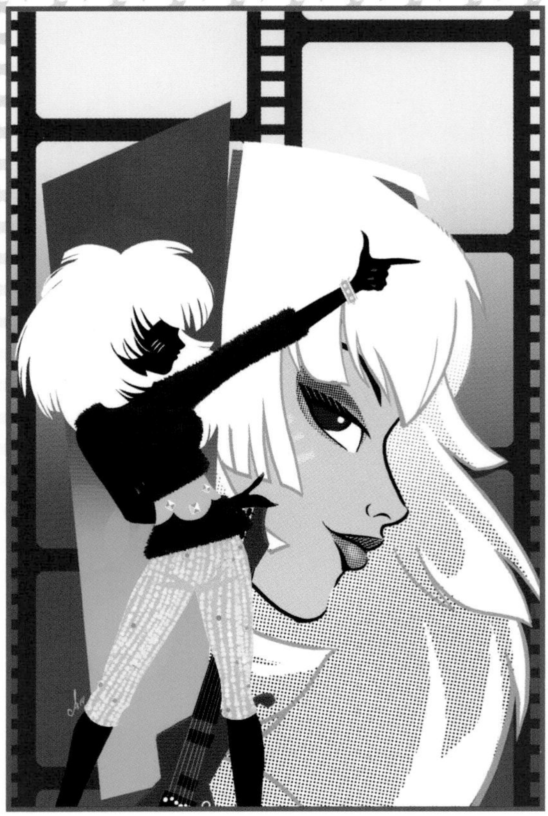

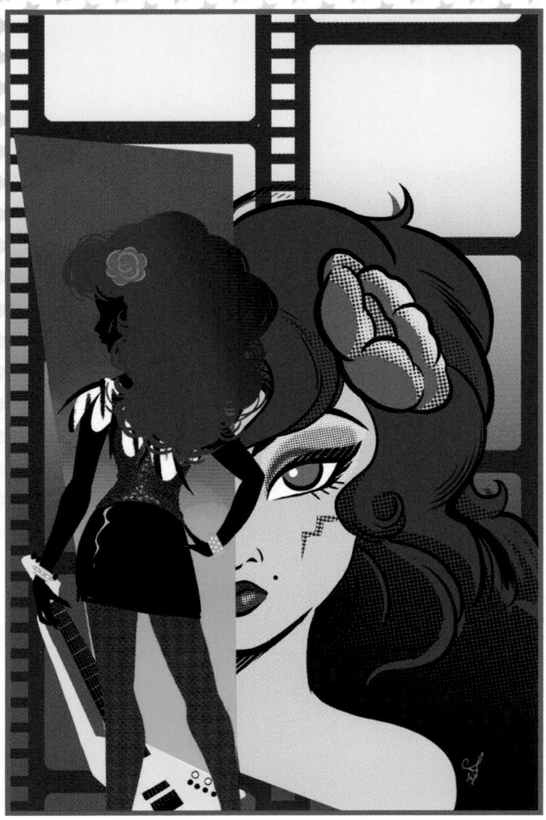

ART BY **AMY MEBBERSON**

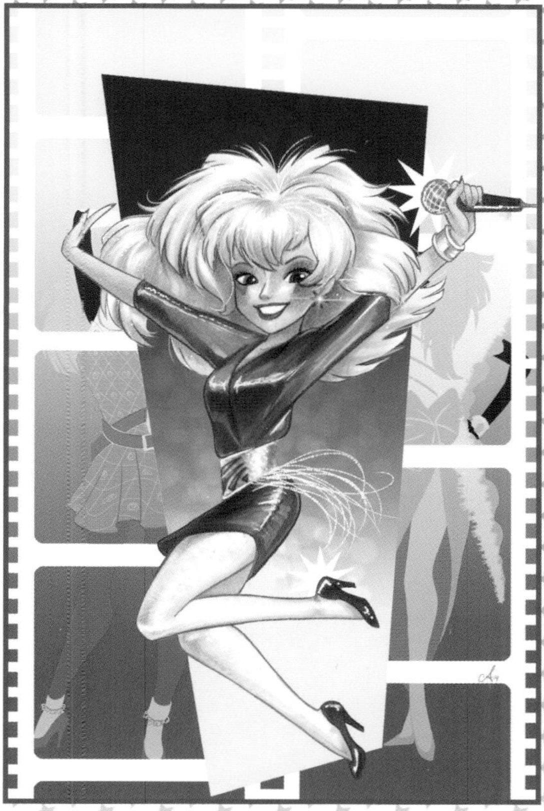
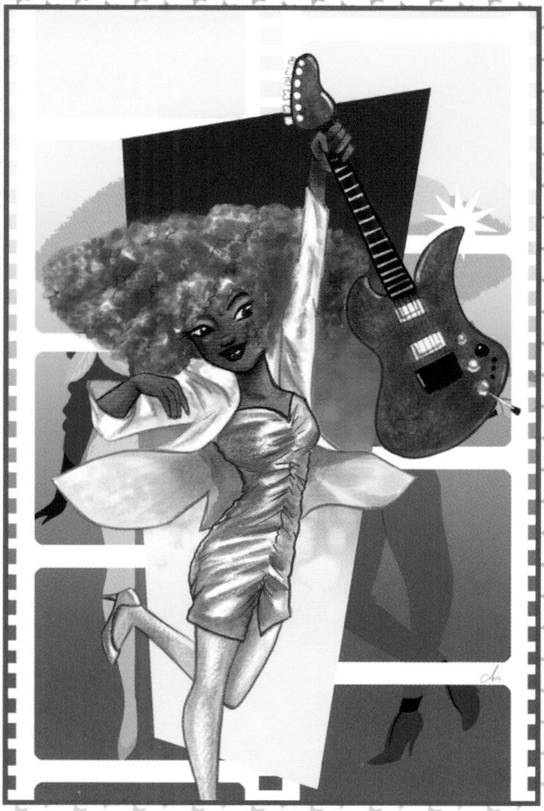
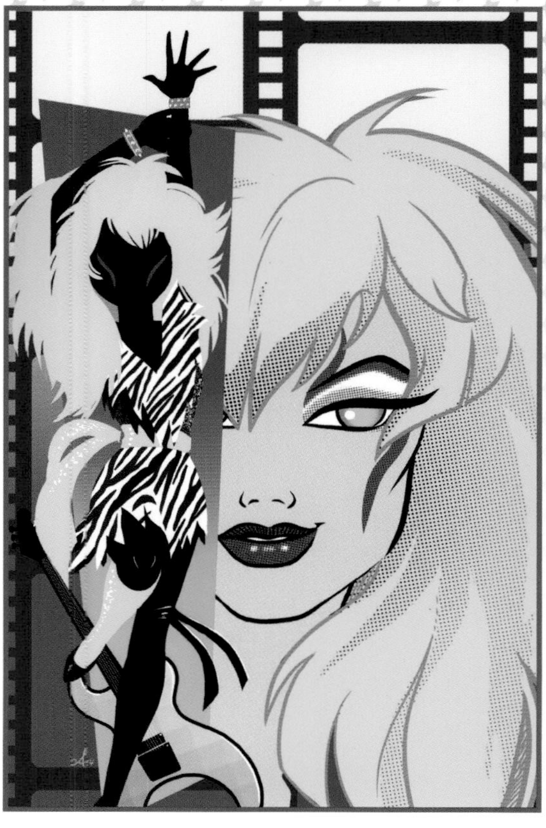
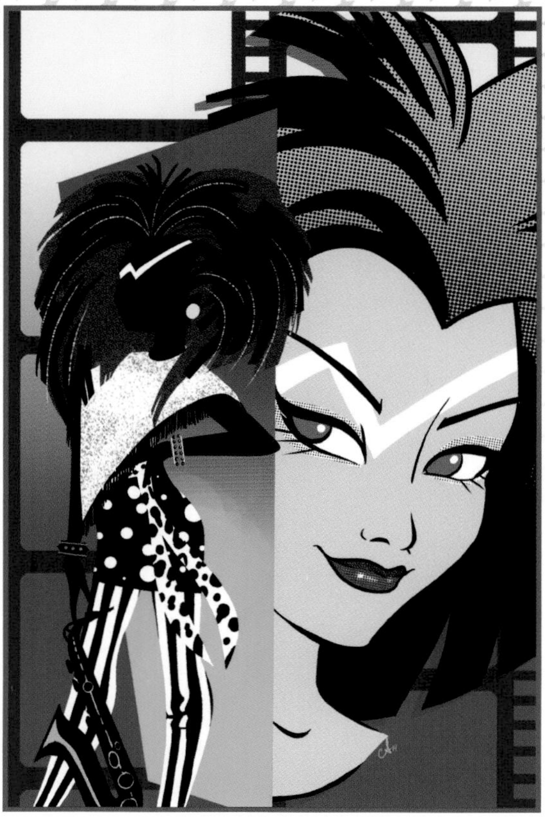

ART BY **SARA RICHARD**

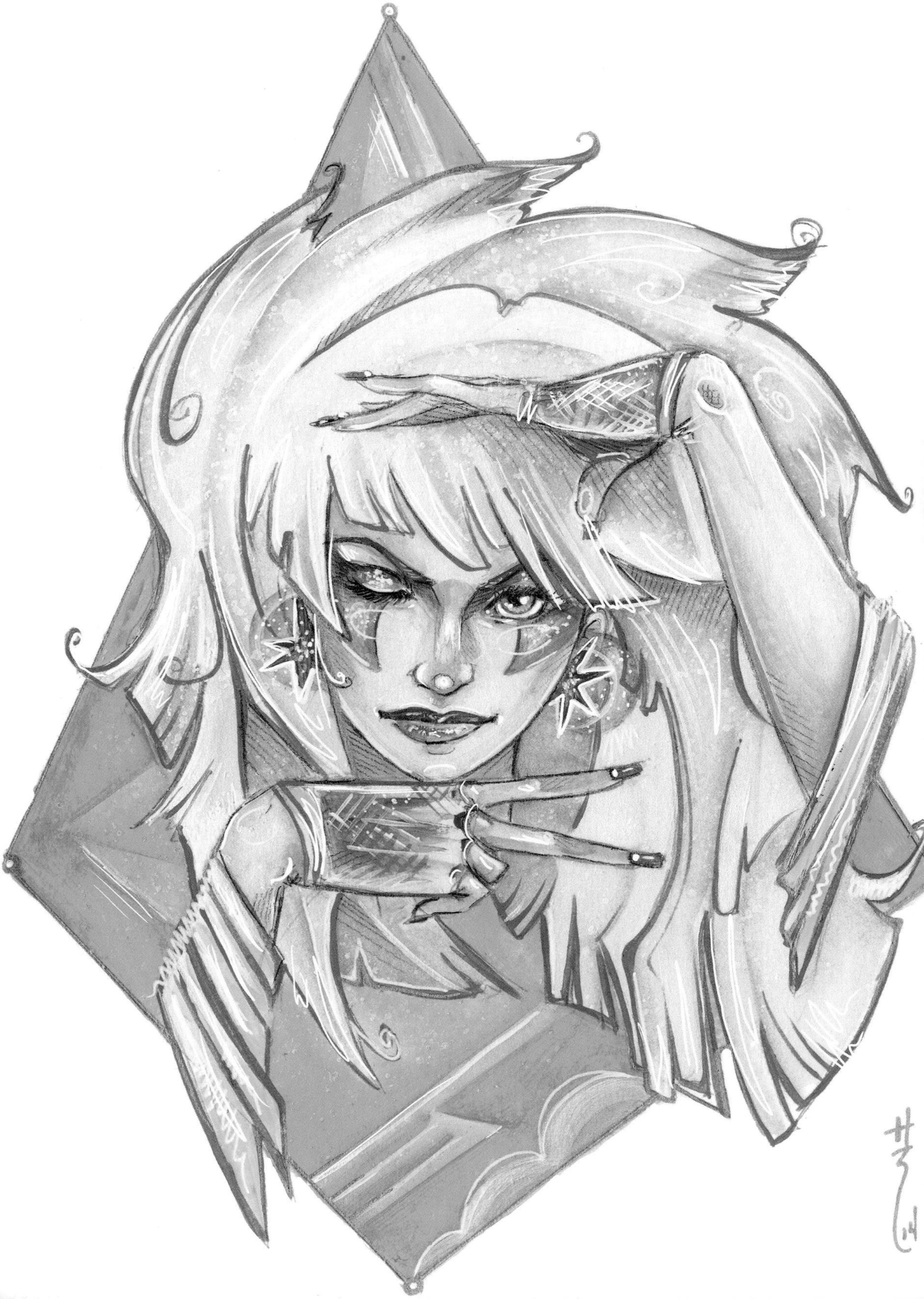

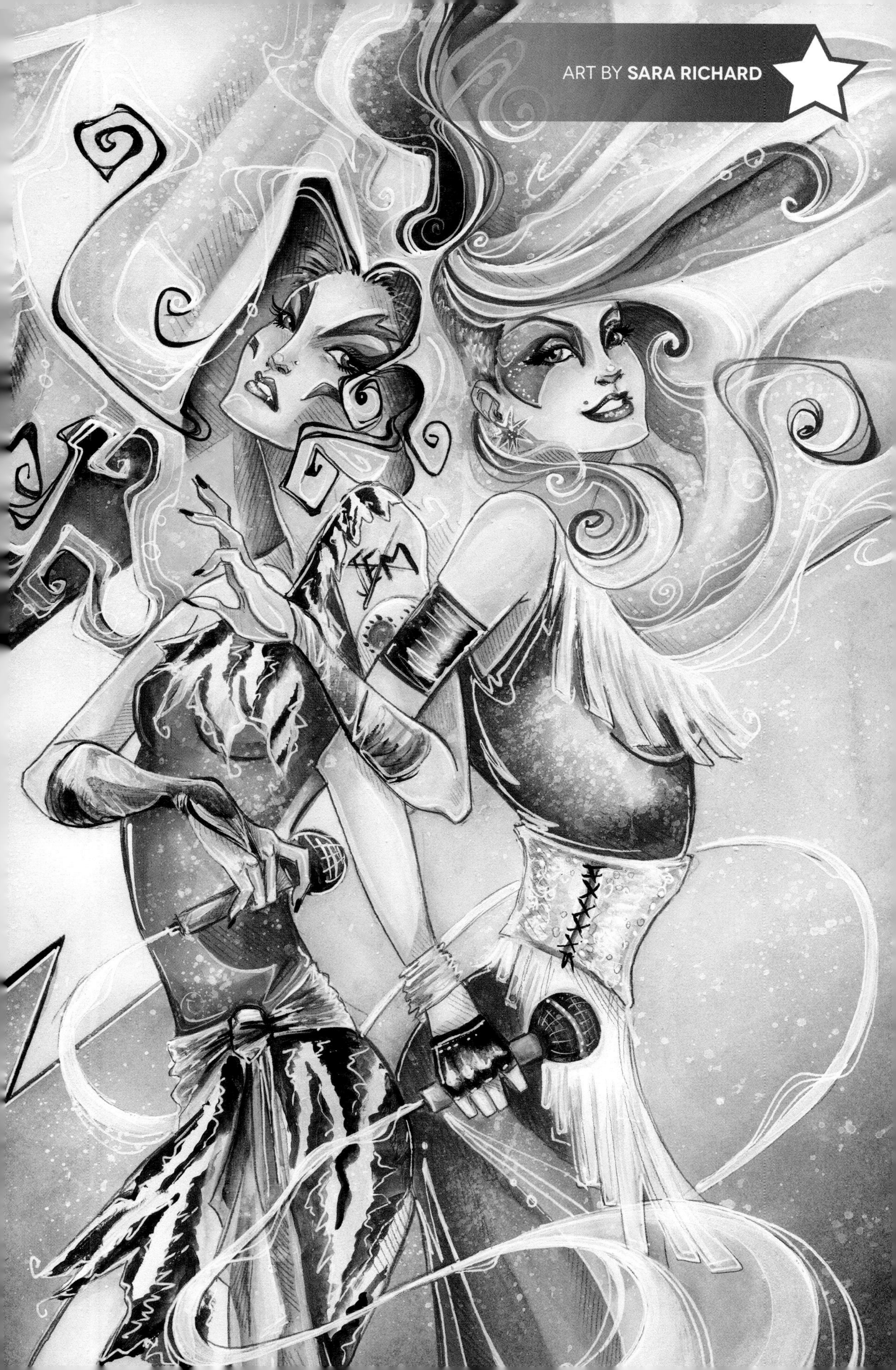

ART BY **SARA RICHARD**

ART BY **SARA RICHARD**

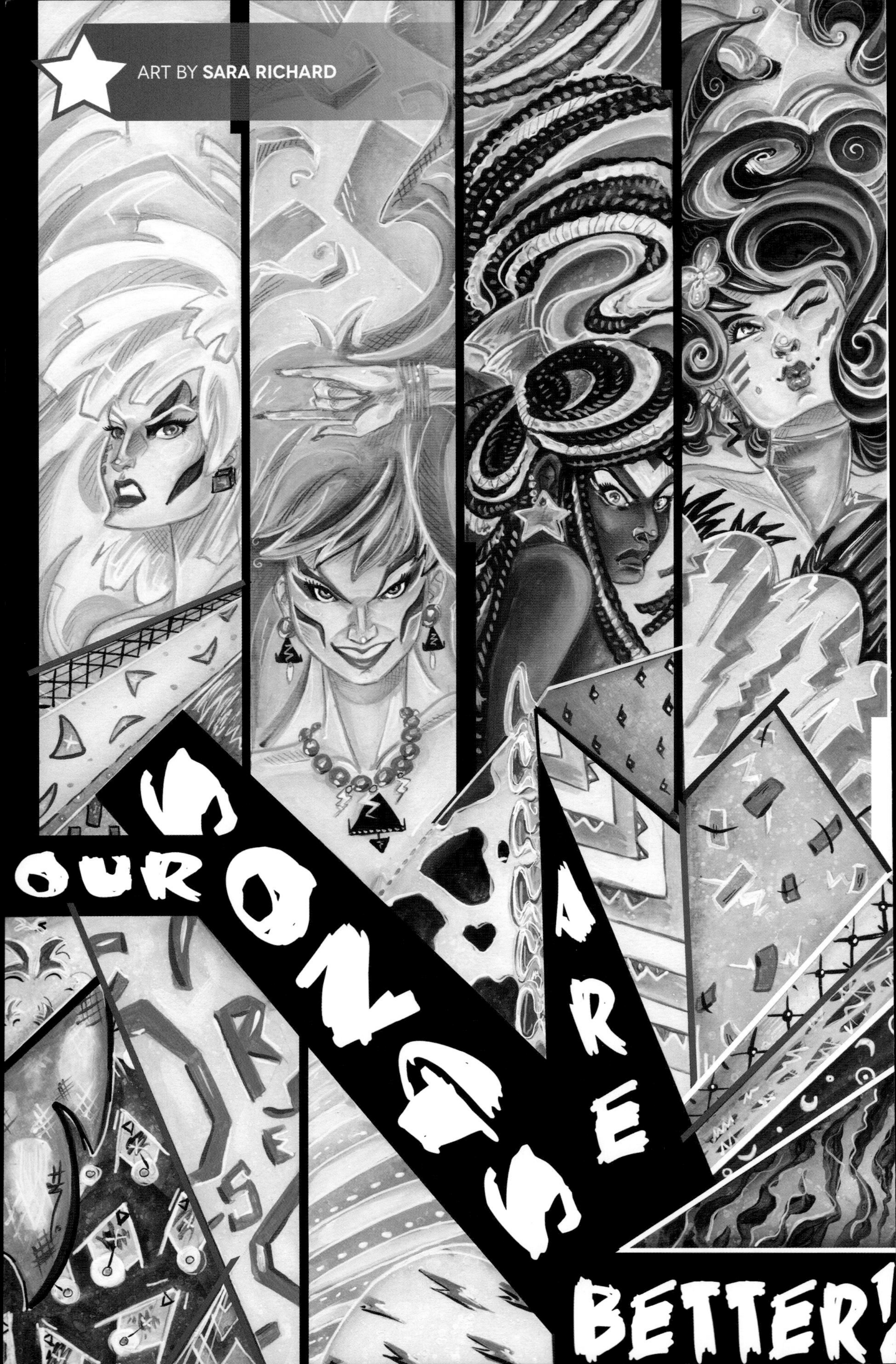
OUR SONGS ARE BETTER!

ART BY **SARA RICHARD**

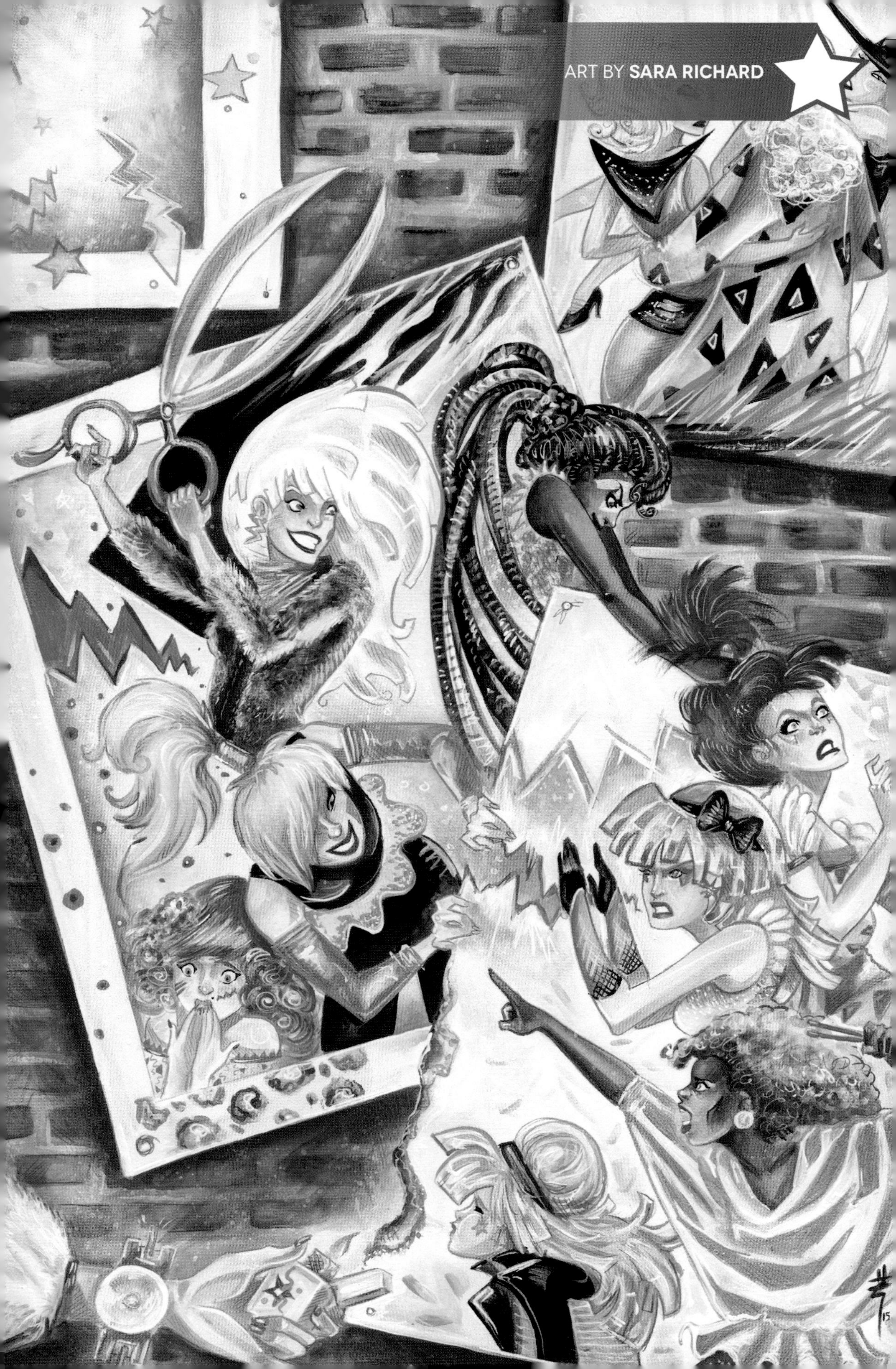

ART BY **SARA RICHARD**

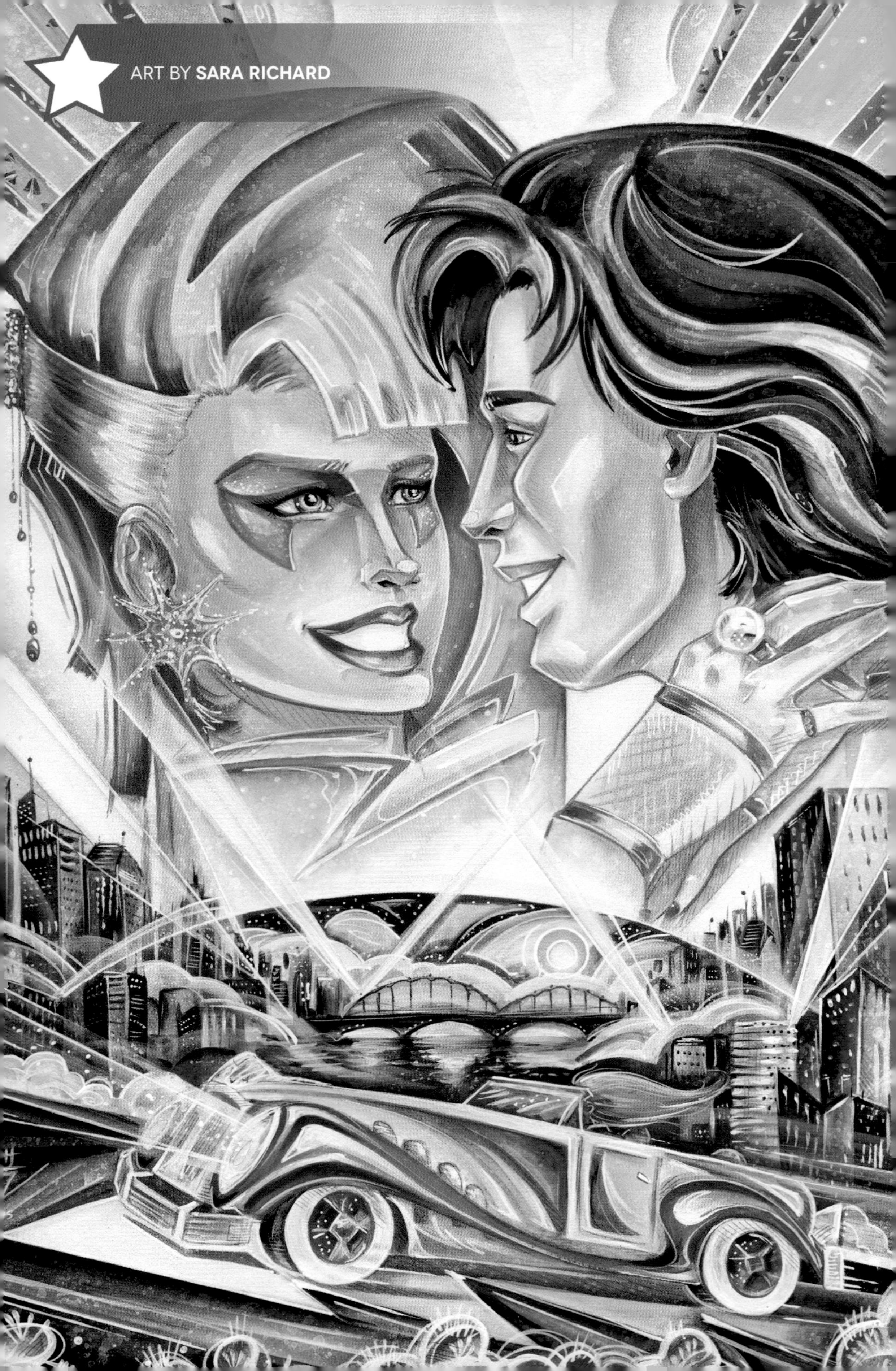

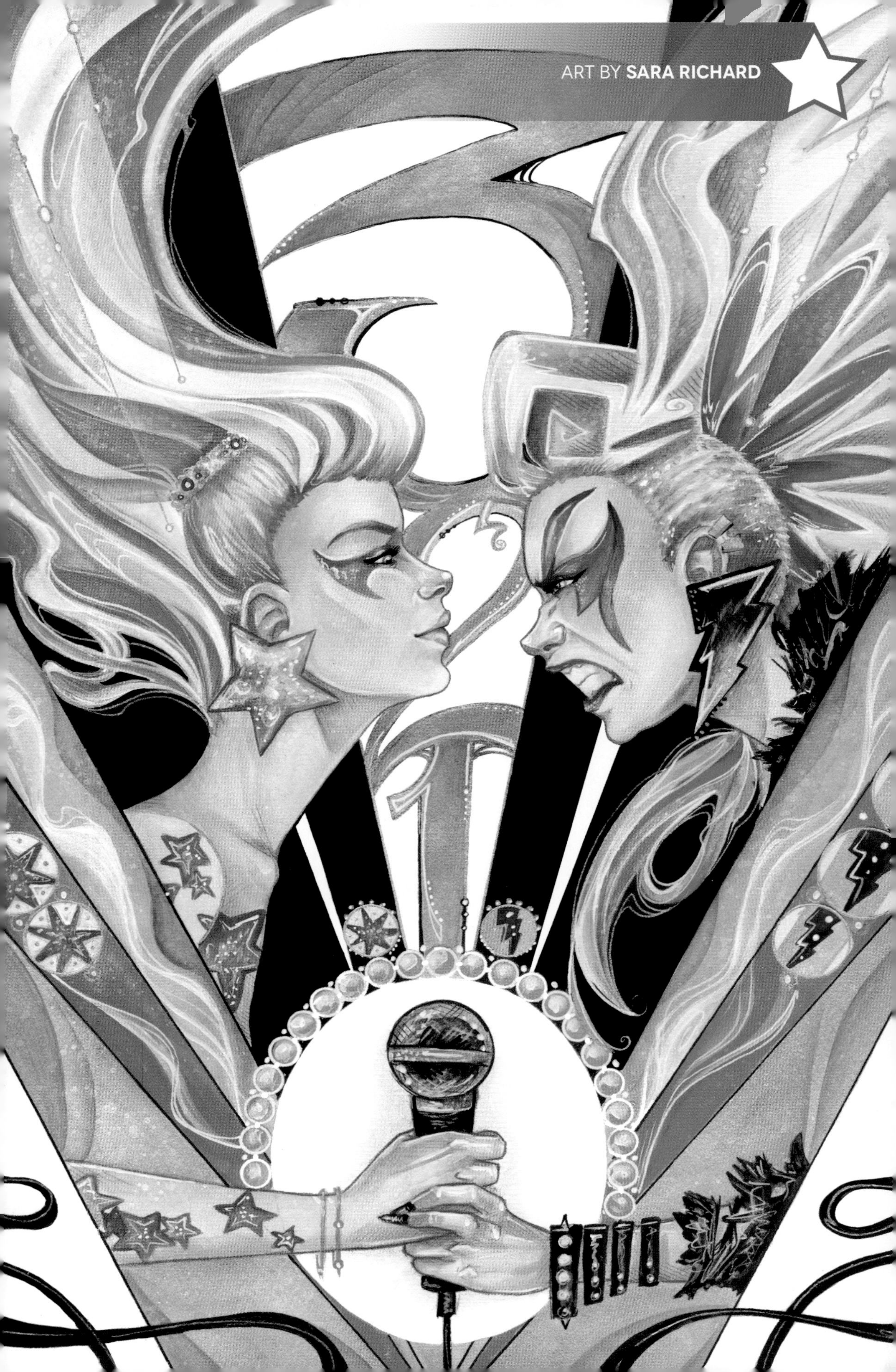
ART BY **SARA RICHARD**

ART BY **AGNES GARBOWSKA**

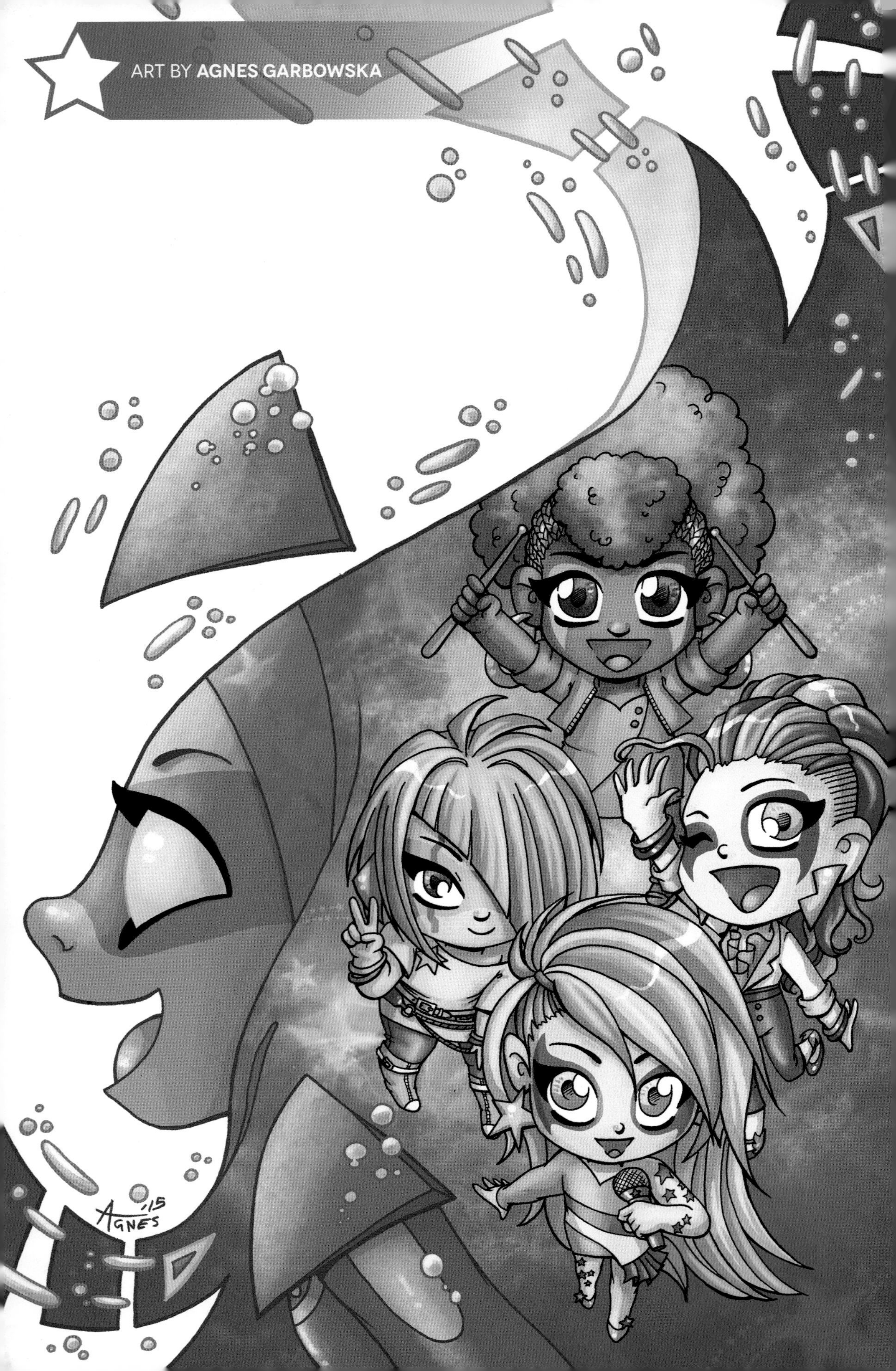
AGNES '15

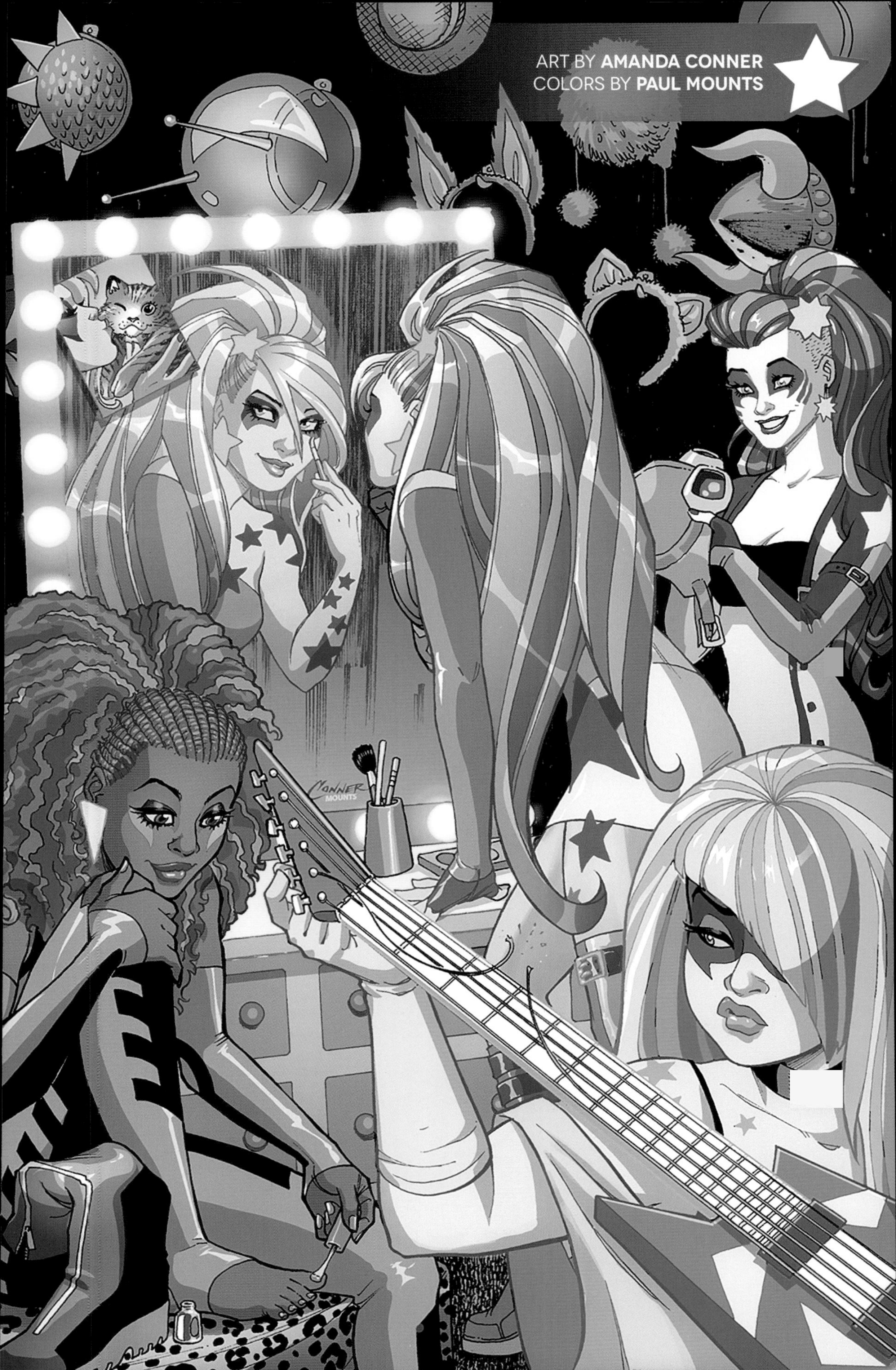
ART BY AMANDA CONNER
COLORS BY PAUL MOUNTS
CONNER
MOUNTS

ART BY **DAVID LAFUENTE**
COLORS BY **JOHN RAUCH**

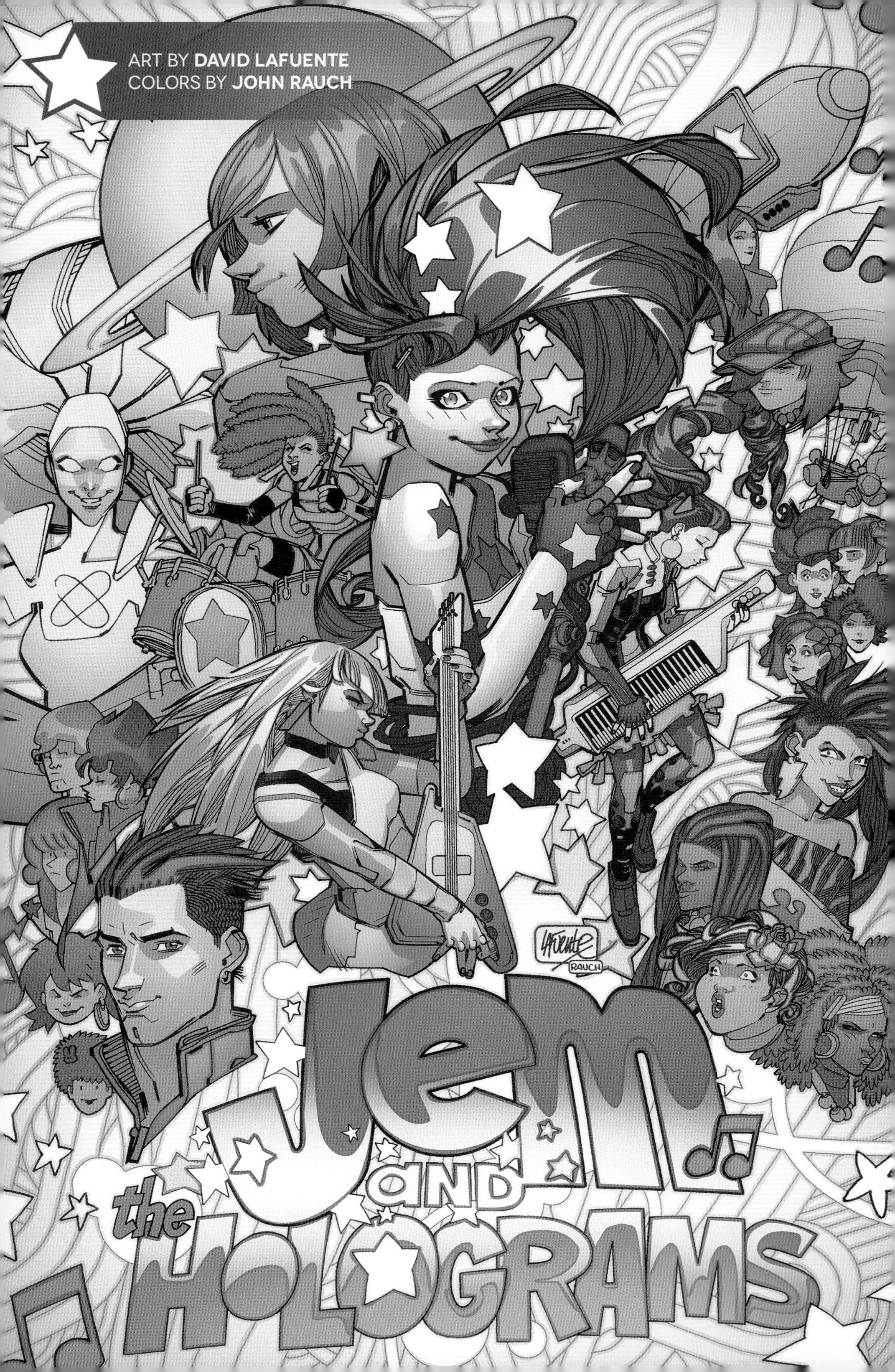
LAFUENTE
RAUCH
JEM AND THE HOLOGRAMS

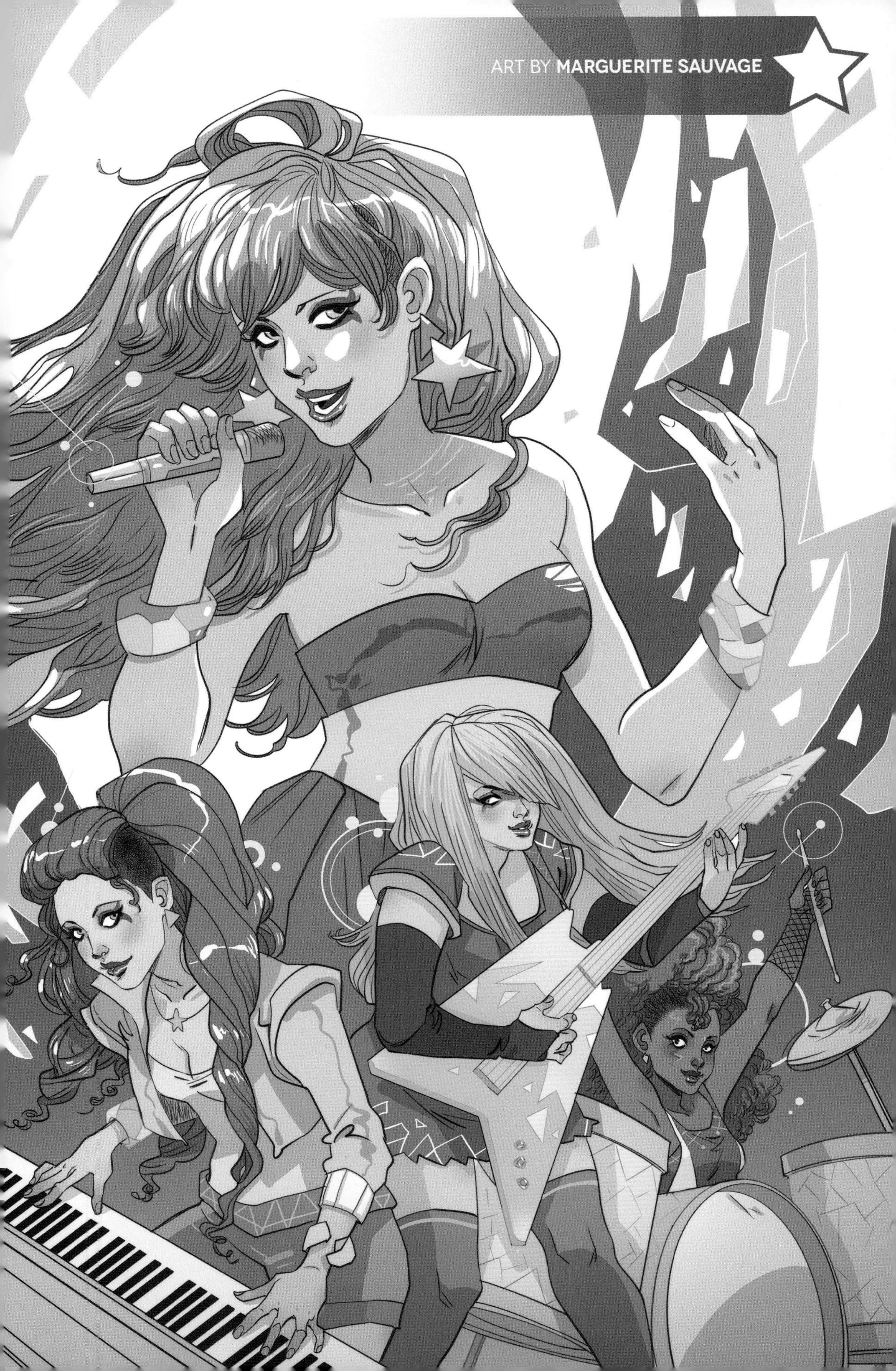
ART BY MARGUERITE SAUVAGE

ART BY **TOMMY LEE EDWARDS**

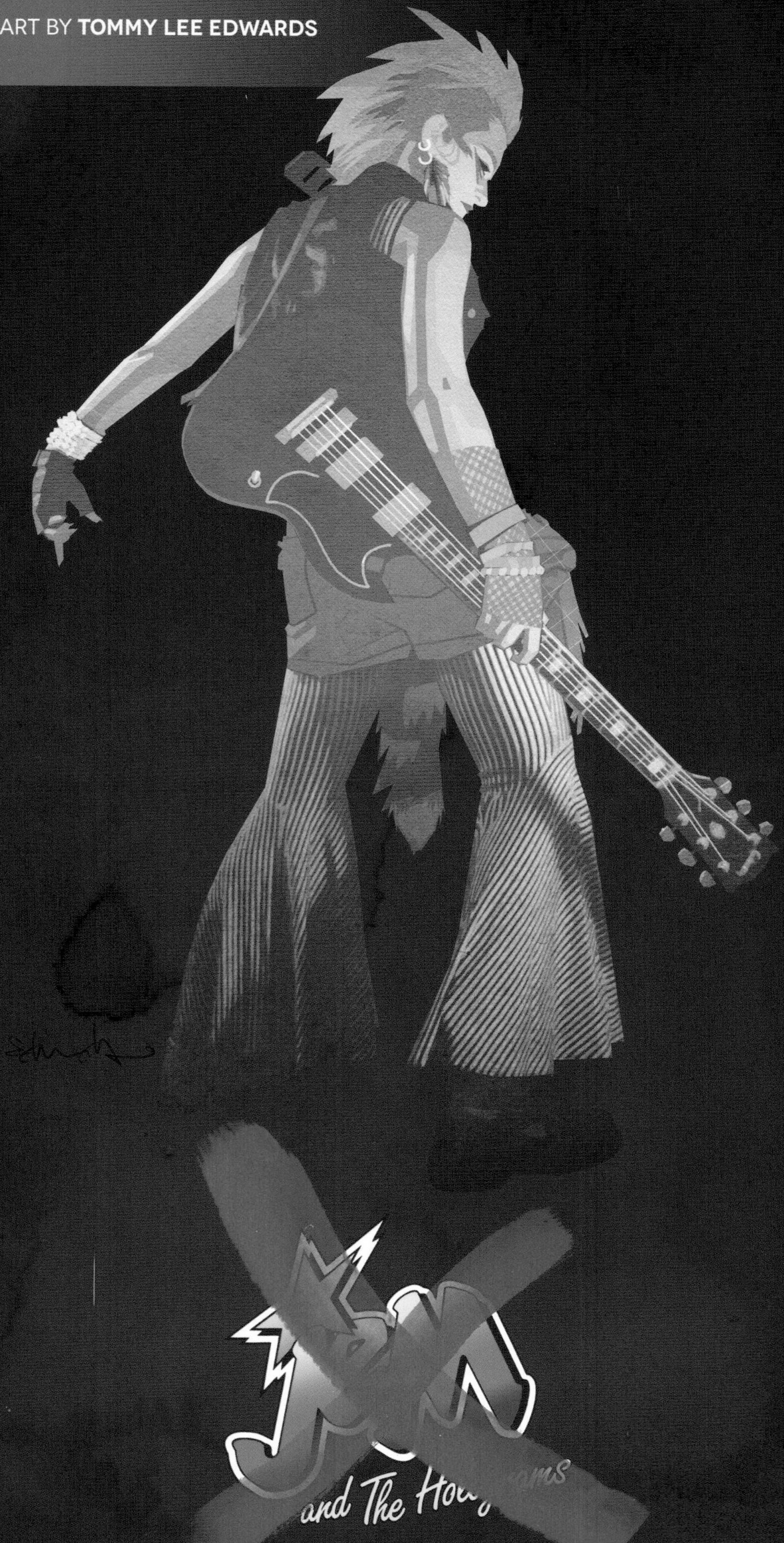

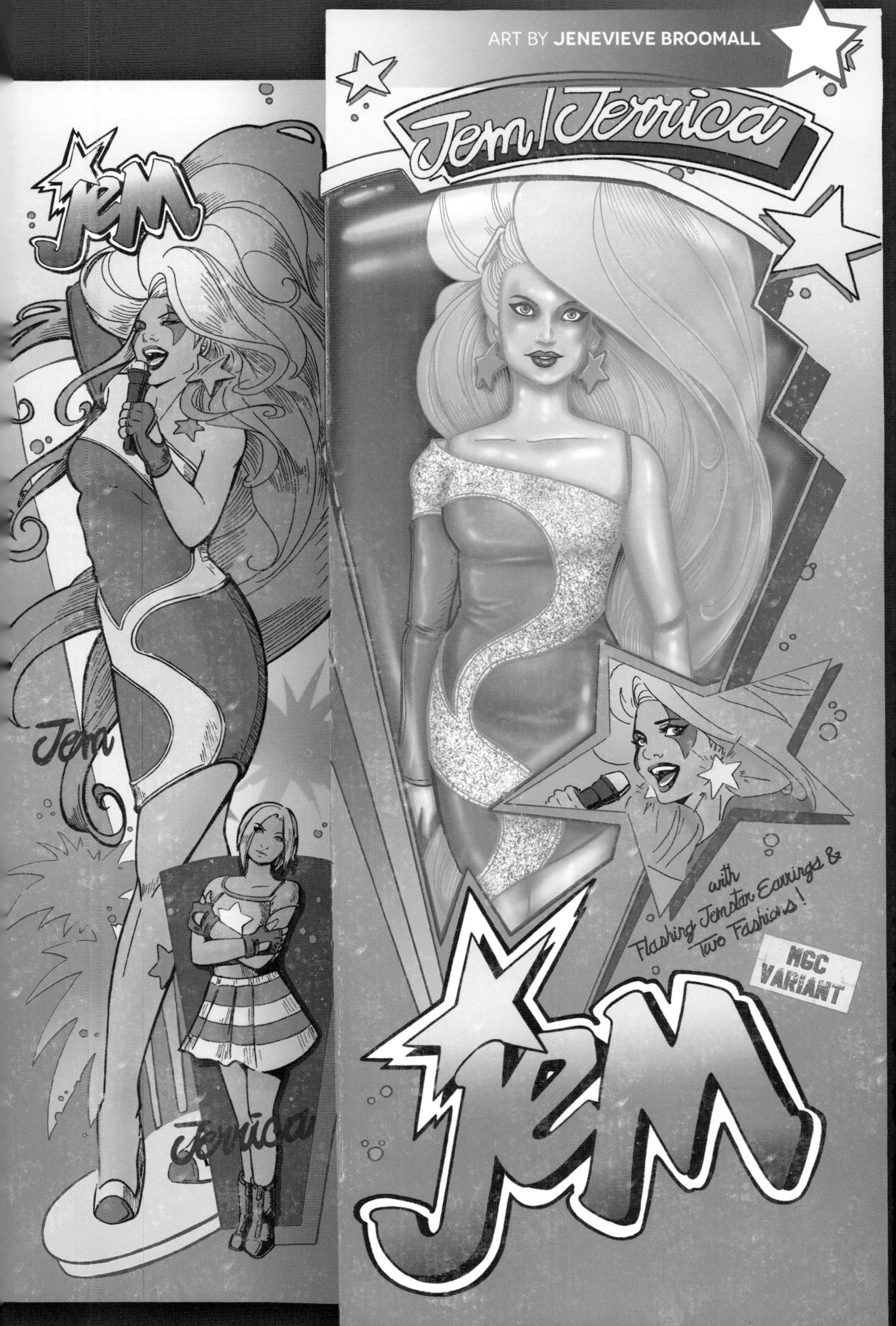
ART BY JENEVIEVE BROOMALL
Jem
Jem
Jerrica
Jem/Jerrica
with Flashing Jemstar Earrings & Two Fashions!
MGC VARIANT
Jem

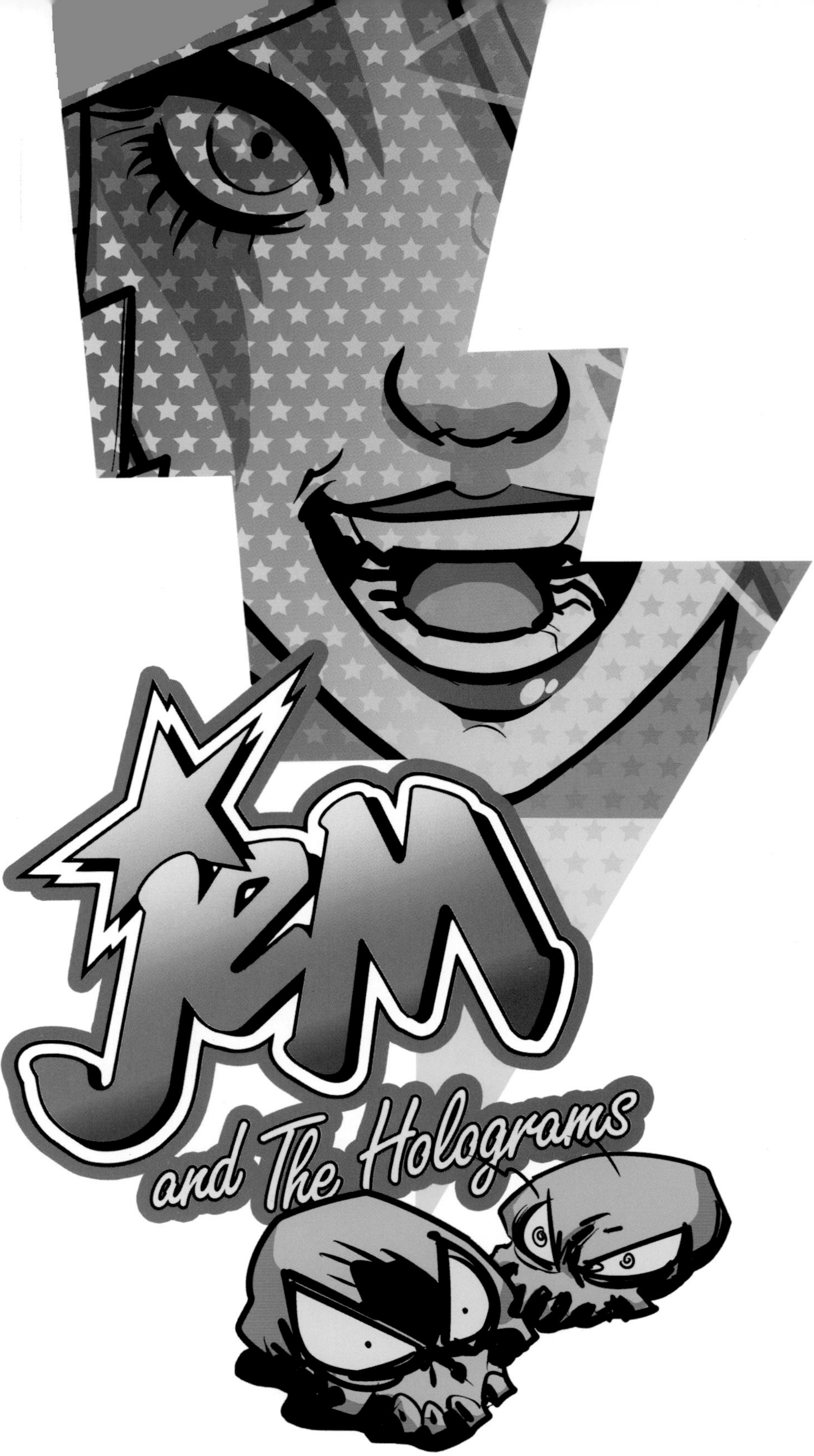
JEM
and The Holograms